I0189615

According to Me

Pike 23lb, March 1970

If you tell the truth, you don't have to remember anything.

MARK TWAIN

According to Me

John Ralphs Craddock

THE CLOISTER HOUSE PRESS

Copyright © 2022 John Ralphs Craddock

All rights reserved. No part of this publication may be reproduced or transmitted in any form or by any means, electronic or mechanical including photocopying, recording or any information storage or retrieval system, without prior permission in writing from the publishers.

The right of John Ralphs Craddock to be identified as the author of this work has been asserted by him in accordance with the Copyright, Designs and Patents Act 1988

First published in the United Kingdom in 2022 by
The Cloister House Press

ISBN 978-1-913460-42-6

Contents

Acknowledgements

O bviously I'd like to thank Me, and thought I'd get it in first in case I forget.

Without a shadow of doubt I couldn't have done this without the unstinting support of my wife Ailsa, who had the unenviable task of reading through the drafts, occasionally wide eyed at some of the things I thought I'd told her but maybe hadn't.

I wish I could turn the clock back and thank my mum Joan and my dad Jack, but too little and too late now. Thanks also to the people at Choir Press, and notably Meg Humphries, with whom they put me in touch, and who somehow managed to professionally edit this ramble through my life. She was blessed with infinite patience, and needed every bit of it.

Finally, I'd like to dedicate this to ALL my family, extended and otherwise. They all know who they are.

Preface

In September 2018 I turned seventy. I couldn't believe it. That was my grandad's age. That wasn't me surely? But it was. I was in new territory. I didn't feel seventy, mentally or physically, but suddenly I was seventy. AND there was still so much to do.

My mum always told me I had a sunny disposition, an optimistic outlook, a positive attitude, a 'can do' approach as a child. So where did that go? Where and how and why have I ended up angry, argumentative, anti-social, controversial, and irritated beyond words by people?

I have absolutely no idea whatsoever.

I never once thought of myself as a sour and cynical individual, perhaps I just hid it better, and now at this age, with nothing to prove and nothing to hide, it's risen to the surface, like scum. These days I voice my feelings, and fuck the consequences. There are no repercussions, neither are there any reference points left to guide me. No parents, teachers, aunts or uncles to explain to me how it got to be like this. Ideally, someone to tell me that this disgruntled state of mind is quite normal at this age and stage. Equally, there is no one to rebuke me.

It's a strange feeling, and I've been wrestling with it for a while. It's not a nice place to be and at times I hate myself for it.

I read somewhere that people who think too much are prone to depression or are depressives by nature. Personally, I think that's bollocks. This relatively recent change in my outlook is born out of despair. A kind of despair for humanity. I don't much like people, but I know deep down it isn't really their fault.

Yes, I think a lot, and the more I think and the more I see, the more I feel this despair. I'm out of sorts with events. Out of sync with the world. Apart from the usual aches and pains associated with increasing decrepitude, which I accept and do my damnedest to subdue, I think I've finally arrived at my allotted destination. I've become a grumpy old man.

More than anything I mourn the loss of time. I think I need another go at life. I wasn't quite ready for this one, so can I have another go please? Try things differently maybe? But I know I ain't gonna get one. Perhaps that's a factor in this relatively newish attitude I've acquired. The disappointing realisation that there are more yesterdays behind me, than tomorrows in front of me.

One of my (I have a few others) pet hates is complacency. In some ways I wish I was complacent, apathetic, just jogging along simply accepting the world as it is. The happy moron, ignorance being bliss and all that, but I just can't. I can't shake off this feeling of frustration. Here I am, rich (comparatively), retired (not really), secure, large circle of friends, and so on. All is well in my life, just like I wanted it to be when I was young and ambitious. In short, I've made it. But nothing's happening.

What did I expect? What was it all for? What can I do about this new-found irritability? Not much, it seems. I have to accept my powerlessness, which I find hard. The only solution it seems is for me to become King of the World! I wish. I'd make some bloody changes immediately. With age comes awareness, and it's this which is the cause of so much of my frustration. I'm unable to convey that to the younger generation. Since they're unaware, they don't see what I see.

I look back over time and life, and see the bumps and dips along the way, all cataclysmic at the time, but seeming now almost inconsequential. I've done a lot, which surprised me when I reflected back, but have I any ambition left? Not really. I'd like to think I've done my best to shelter and provide, and done most of the things in my life I wanted to do, so what's left to achieve?

Then I thought, I know! I've never written a diary. I'll do that. But what about? The EU referendum in June 2016 and the appalling reactions to that event in some ways gave me the motivation.

We voted to leave the EU (I was all for getting out), and it was that which gave me the incentive to vent my spleen.

The fallout from this decision to leave caused me to become ever more embittered. There were heroic efforts by 'those who know best' to overturn a perfectly democratic decision, and I became incandescent with rage. This however served to underline even more my feelings of powerlessness. More on all this later.

In order to let off steam, get it off my chest, release the impotent anger from my pressure cooker, I took to writing about it. I called it *The Daily Growl*. You'll find these ravings at the back of this book. (Update: No you won't. I've removed it. It was in excess of 36,000 words of bile, acid and rancour, took up too much room, and was of no relevance whatsoever to this autobiography.)

I realised, with some surprise, that what I really needed to do was to write about me.

Eventually it became the story of my life. It isn't a famous life, or an important life, and no one will ever know I existed. It isn't an ego trip either. Just my little spot in time, just for the record. My life, as far as the cosmos is concerned, is of no consequence. The cosmos doesn't give a shit about me, and neither will it give a shit about my death.

I now realise that most people of my generation probably feel the same. That came as a disappointment really. Here was I thinking it was only I who felt like this. The realisation that I wasn't unique and alone in my thoughts actually caused me a few problems too.

I've been back to the places from my childhood many times where I perceive my happiest moments were. The places haven't really changed; I have. It's the people who sparked those memories who have gone. It simply isn't the same, so why go back? I personally find it a comfort in the past, but the truth is life changes remorselessly. A constant conveyor belt of change. People drop off the end, and one day it'll be my turn.

8 billion people now on this finite planet, almost treble the number when I was born in 1948, all in the space of just 70 years.

All busy demanding and consuming. To save this precious planet we need to speed up the conveyor belt. Maybe the Covid pandemic that engulfed us in 2020 will help.

How to write about a life then? Real authors know how to plan a book, how to frame it from the outset. I hadn't got a fucking clue about any of this. It just kept evolving, but I decided to trigger my early memories using music. That took me straight back in an instant. When I got to something I thought was either funny, relevant or awful, I stuck them in as 'side stories', and of these there must be quite a few, I reckon. I haven't counted them, but all these little side stories have had an influence on me in one way or another. They make a bit of a diversion, but all are spontaneous. They just leapt into my head at the time of writing.

One other thing I ought to mention. I wrote most of this in 2019, then bugger me, out of the blue in June 2019 here came one of those bumps I mentioned. Just as I was sailing along, self-satisfied in my own little canoe, I got some bad news. I was diagnosed with prostate cancer. Once again, along came my familiar big black cloud of anxiety. It always lurks just over the horizon. Following ten months of shitty hormone treatment, in April 2020 I had radiotherapy.

As it turned out, I couldn't have picked a better time for treatment and recovery. Maybe this was the (albeit dubious) silver lining in the black cloud.

In March 2020 the entire UK population were put into lockdown and thus confined to barracks due to the coronavirus pandemic. This however gave me an opportunity to use most of that year, having now finished my gruelling twenty days of radiotherapy, which left me weak and lacking energy, to force myself to edit what I'd written. What a pain in the arse that proved to be.

I was just congratulating myself towards the end of 2019 at having achieved my goal with this diary/biography. Then in 2020 with nowt else to do and time on my hands, I decided to re-read it. I was appalled. It was, quite frankly, self-indulgent, unadulterated shite. I became my own sneering critic. We all think we can write and I, rather arrogantly, believed I was pretty good at it. It took all of 2020 to edit the thing. In the end I began to hate it, and editing proved to be bloody hard work. A most unpleasant and unrewarding experience. I'd sit in my shed for an hour or two each day, fiddling with it to the point where it became a task, a monster. I had to force myself sometimes to traipse across the orchard and face it down. It was just like being made to go to school when you knew you had better things to do. But then I didn't have anything better to do, other than recover from my prostate treatment. You can read about this experience, which I called at the time *The Prostate Cancer Bugle*, and you'll find this at the end of this book. As for this biography of my life, well it is what it is.

I really can't be bothered with it any more, and dedicate it to my wife Ailsa, who has had the infinite patience and resilience to create some kind of order and structure from my chaotic effort.

Feel free to comment. Contact me at: jc@icouldntgiveashit.com.

JRC
January 2021

Everyone is a Moon and has a dark side which they never show to anybody.

MARK TWAIN

Foreword, or How to Deal with Your Parents

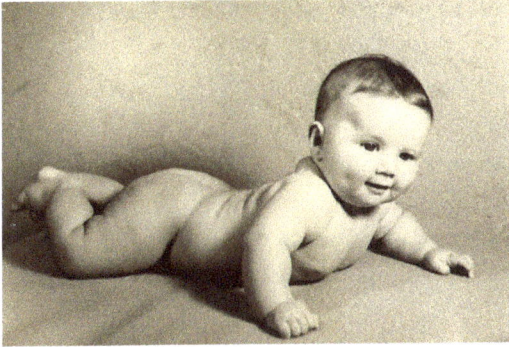

Before they died, I urged both my father and mother years ago to write a perspective of their own lives, especially World War II and all that. I was certain it must have had an influence on them, and in turn on me and their approach to my upbringing, as well as that of my brother Martin, and sister Julia. As the eldest I always reckoned I was the guinea pig on whom they practised their newly discovered parenting skills. Each year I grew, presented them with a new experience. All parents learn as they go along. Doesn't matter if the child is four or forty, each year holds a new and different challenge for the parents. I could never see that at the time, but I can now. For a while you automatically assume and accept that parents are always right. You don't see or notice the influences of their own upbringing, or the effects of war. I got to twenty-eight before I was able to see objectively how their responses, conditioning, and foibles had affected me.

These days some kids may well end up in the therapist's chair, trying to make sense of it all. That seems to be a trend these days, and one I just can't embrace. You are what you are, and usually get what you deserve, including violence. That was my attitude, and I didn't finally shrug off all this parental indoctrination until I punched my father to the floor (of which more later).

Another pet hate of mine is weakness and self-pity. There is absolutely no point whatsoever in blaming parents. They are what they are, and all I know is they do what they think is right, or believe is right, at that time. What I do know for sure is that they loved us unconditionally, and though in the early days before my 'enlightenment', or epiphany (if you want a religious slant) I would lay the blame on them squarely for their lack of understanding of me as an individual, particularly where I was at any given time in my life and the world around me. It was wrong of me to put the blame on them at times, but I now forgive them totally. Although it's taken some time!

Neither Jack nor Joan, my parents, ever did write their story. Theirs was a generation at a particular space in time, and now gone. Which is a shame.

So, since we're dead a long time, it somehow seems important to write about my own fragment of existence. It's something of a self-indulgence I guess, and none of it will be of world-shattering importance, except to me, of course, but I have a strong urge to leave something behind, if only to prove I was once here. This is a particularly recent feeling as I now face medical uncertainty.

Will anyone ever read this? Probably not, but sometimes I feel I have a unique take on things, though a cynical take would perhaps be more appropriate. Anyway, since I'm paying for it to be published please allow me this selfish indulgence. Well, I guess you will whether you like it or not! If it proves to be rubbish, you can always use it to prop up a wonky table, or jam the door shut.

So, where to start, and where to stop?

I was a post-war baby, born in Germany in 1948. I can't remember any of that, and who'd want to anyway? Jack was in the RAF, and Joan was in the army. I guess they were posted there to mop up Hitler's leftover Nazis. As a baby, becoming aware and conscious of your surroundings happens probably at the age of two or three, so I assume I was in a pram in Germany for most of the time, and have no recollection whatsoever of coming back to England. When I did 'wake up' I was in Werrington, in North Staffs.

In the end, well the beginning, I decided to use music as a starting point for this story in an attempt to put some structure into my early days.

The poet Wordsworth used to refer to 'spots of time' in life. He wrote an autobiographical poem, which took years to finish. I know what he meant though. Throughout life, any life, there are segments of time, which suddenly take you on a new path. Sometimes, more importantly, in what appears the opposite direction. With that exact science hindsight, these events in life prove to be pointers, influences, like some directional thing. Even though you may not have realised it at the time they move you, sometimes subtly, other times with a bang and jolt.

I've occasionally thought that there's some grand plan laid out for me. I can fully understand why people believe there is a purpose to all life, but for me no. Life is a random accidental thing, but I admit to thinking now and then there must be a hidden, unknown, guiding hand behind all this. I believe in the spirituality of the human mind, but no way can I ascribe it to a god. It's so easy to think like that. In fact my Dad used to say about religion. 'it's easier believing than thinking'. Or 'religion is the problem, not the answer'. You'll have gathered by now that both Jack and Joan were devout atheists, and wholly out of step at that time with the norm.

I'm sure some people do have revelations, epiphanies, wake up calls, or whatever, and believe there are meanings or think they're being 'called'. By what or whom I've never quite discovered. I sometimes wish it were all true. It's just life on Earth. The world will continue to spin for the next few billion years until the sun runs out of steam, and then ... well ... that's that. My Ma told me years ago that the Earth has only been in a position to support life for about 250 million years (she was an amateur geologist). Not much really when you consider the planet has been around for 4 billion. Just one sixteenth of our planet's existence, and there are no guarantees that this will always continue. The cosmos will see to that. Human perception of time is extraordinarily limited.

I remember when I became ill in 2006 with colon cancer, saying to my surgeon, "why me?? 'Luck of the draw old son' he replied. Not for me it wasn't. I developed a mindset where I searched for a reason, someone or something had to be responsible, I needed to pin the blame somewhere. Occasionally on a starry night I would look up to the cosmos and ask the same question. 'This isn't fair! Why ME? The cosmos never bothered to reply. If it had it would have probably said 'Why not?'

I'm afraid it's just life, and life isn't fair, but continues to trundle onwards remorselessly. John Lennon probably summed it up best, as perhaps only he could: 'Life is what happens while you're busy making other plans'. It was ever thus.

The key, for me anyway, is to quest, discover, learn, strike out boldly in a new direction, maybe take a few chances, not silly risks, get out of your comfort zone periodically, and try to view each new experience with a fresh mind. Both Jack and Joan were a product of their times. Play it safe, know your place, and the regimen of war I think reinforced that. Jack was the epitome of the frustrated angry rebel. He hated conformity. What surprised me most was his inability to see that very same streak in me. Maybe it was jealousness? That I'd never been forced to suffer the same privations he'd endured? I don't know, but one thing I do know is we clashed.

Sometimes a plan doesn't work out, things can and will go wrong. In which case I always try to look for the silver lining in the big black cloud. There usually is one, even if it's not immediately obvious at the time. But no matter how many bad things fate may throw your way, it really doesn't matter. Consider it positively as the price of an education. That's priceless. It's your own ability to deal with adversity which counts.

Chapter 1

*Dear Sir or Madam, will you read my book? It's
taken me bloody ages to write ... will
you take a look?*

Music has been a central part of my existence for most of my
life. I wish I was a talented musician, but I'm not. I have to
work hard at it. I'm quite good to average at a few things, but not
immensely talented in one particular direction. I can swim, dive,
play squash, badminton, sail, fish, cook, play banjo, ukulele and
guitar. I can paint, write (haha), and a few other things besides,
but I'm not outstandingly good at any one thing. In some ways I
wish I was, but I've met a few down the years who had natural
talent, and mostly I found them a bit one-dimensional. Music has
always had a powerful effect on me, as I'm sure it has for most
people, and uniquely transports me back to another time and
place. Music is my kind of wading stick for the past, my own
version of *Desert Island Discs*.

Following my thoughts about time, where it goes, the speed of
it, the future of the human race, assuming it has one, and lofty
thoughts like that, got me round to thinking about my own
memories. I read recently that it is perfectly possible to subconsciously manipulate memory, and change the outcome. Make
yourself the victor, so to speak, of some past misfortune. This train
of thought led me to reflect on some of my own early memories.
Especially my boyhood days. Have they faded and altered? I don't
know, but I'll at least give it a go.

There are some pieces of music which have stuck with me.
Some recall good times, some not so good, and some which were
just bloody awful. However, I'll try not to shrink from the task.

Though I just possibly might. Yep, musical memories might just be the key to kicking off this book.

I was born in Hamelin (where the pied piper got rid of the rats) in Germany in September 1948. The first son of Joan and Jack Craddock, who had ended up there after the war, picking up the pieces Hitler had left behind. My dad was in the RAF. I have no idea about any of that or when I was brought home, but I must have been about eighteen months old.

My very first conscious recollections were Werrington in North Staffs. Most of my mum and dad's family lived in and around Stoke-on-Trent, though my mum was from Leek. Werrington was situated about halfway between the two. These days Werrington is a shitty over-developed mini town, but when I was three or four it was a small village of millstone grit houses. There were the usual obligatory quotas of council houses inserted here and there where common people lived. So my mum said. (We obviously weren't.)

I have no idea how Werrington came to be, what its history was, and what it was actually for. It was possibly five or six miles from the five towns of Stoke-on-Trent, which seemed a long way away. My dad originated from one of these towns, Longton, but my Mum came from the more elitist Leek. Werrington was neither here nor there, and lay at the edge of a stretch of moorland. This for me signalled a freedom to roam. We lived in a draughty cottage, Stone House, in Washerwall Lane. Who named it Washerwall and why? God knows what it means. In winter the house was freezing. Ice would regularly form inside the windows, and Jack Frost made swirling patterns on them. We scratched patterns on these patterns with our fingernails. My brother Martin and I shared this bedroom fridge. We slept on a homemade bunk bed, with a straw mattress, or something like that, and we had identical paisley pattern eiderdowns on each bunk. My brother was two years younger, and I have an early, possibly imagined, recollection of him born on a sunny day in August 1950 in a military hospital somewhere near Shifnal in Shropshire. How or why we were up there I have no idea. My sister Julia wouldn't turn up for another few years, but on the day my brother arrived I'd have been almost two years old.

Anyway, that's my abiding memory of this house. Bloody freezing. It was warmer outside, usually where I spent most of my time. I also developed a burgeoning talent for lighting fires, probably in my desire for warmth. At least it was a useful talent to add to my early list.

The field we had at the back was my playground, which backed on to an old disused quarry with one or two sheer rock faces. Beyond this lay the moorland. I have an intense affinity with heather, mosses, lichens and boggy ground. It was my kind of habitat, frogspawn in the clear marsh water in February, peewits, curlews, skylarks, and meadow pipits in March. These sights and sounds perhaps account more than any for my love of spring. It was an unspoilt, unfarmed wilderness, and to this day I still love and cherish the boggy nature of moorland country. In a way it was a kind of wild home for me. Bluebell Wood lay two fields away on the opposite side of the moor.

Bluebell Wood was a ten-minute scamper across a couple of wildflower meadows, filled with lady smock, cuckoo pint, celandine, and of course masses of bluebells in the wood itself. It had a stream running through it, with steep banks on either side. Using a catapult, we fired a stone attached to twine over a beech branch, attached a rope to the twine, and pulled the rope up and over. We would spend hours swinging high out over the brook, dropping on to the other bank from quite a height. Imaginary parachutists jumping from a burning Lancaster bomber, or more likely bailing out from our favourite plane, the Spitfire, having shot down a couple of ME 109s. We were brought up to hate the Germans. I can't ever remember my wellies being anything other than permanently wet. As were my feet and socks.

I read Richmal Crompton's 'Just William' books, and began to think that she – yes, Richmal, I discovered with some shock, was a she – had modelled William on me and my little gang. We never

3

really had ogres for aunts like he did, but sometimes they did try to hug me, and plant wet sloppy kisses on my face. Girls in general were anathema, and we avoided them at all costs. They just seemed to spoil things.

The garden at the back of our house had blackcurrants, gooseberries, and chickens. My dad loved bantams especially. I think I'd be about three or four when I first became aware of where I was in the world. Then I had to go to school. That was a nuisance. It prevented me from lying on my back in the heather on a sunny day watching the clouds scud by, or in winter jumping into the huge snowdrifts which the wind drifted into heaps behind the exposed drystone walls. We had our own sledges, which my dad made, and on freezing nights would go to a nearby hill and race down it.

I was just about five when I was obliged to go to school. Carol Heywood (I think this might have been Carole, with an e) was my first teacher, and I loved her. Absolutely worshipped her, and bitterly regret not knowing how her life turned out. I think then she must have been about twenty-two, but seemed so much older to me.

Salters Lane County Primary School was half a mile out of Werrington, and that's where I was destined. It was, and still is, a Victorian style of building with high arched windows like a church, and the last time I went there for a trip down memory lane it was still intact, no longer a school, and used these days as a store for Highways England. Mr Chalmers was the head, and his daughter Judith became quite famous as a travel writer and broadcaster on the telly. Sometimes it's not a good idea to go back; it has a habit of shattering memories.

The school was a half-hour slouch for me, down the lane from Werrington. I usually took my time and was frequently late, especially in spring when I'd be preoccupied peering into hawthorn hedgerows searching for birds' nests. I have my first school report somewhere in my little box of personal bits, dated 1954. I'd be about six, so September 1953 is when I had my freedom interrupted by school.

The day I arrived I was incredibly nervous, and my mum, having delivered me there, cleared off home and left me alone in this strange place with people I didn't know. About lunchtime I decided I'd had enough and left. I was halfway home when they came chasing up the lane to take me back. I resisted, was dragged back in tears, and found it hard to believe that I had to go to this place, every day, all day, five days a week. I felt imprisoned. I never really adjusted to school.

Miss Heywood was just about the most inspiring teacher I ever knew, and she loved me a bit too. I could just tell. I grew to like school primarily because of her. My hair was cut short by a butcher of a barber in Hanley. I hated going there for the obligatory short back and sides. I ended up with, to all intents and purposes, what's known as a crew cut. Miss Heywood called me her little Airedale, although I had no idea what she was talking about, but frankly didn't much care. I do know though that she lived in Cheddleton, a few miles up the Leek road, in a small terraced cottage, and may possibly have been engaged. She had long, lustrous black hair, a shining, smiling face, and the nicest of green/brown eyes. Hazel, I recall.

At the age of five I was besotted with her.

One morning I went into the classroom before the others got there. She was playing an upright piano in the corner. The piano was used to finish the day, when we'd all sing 'Jesu's little ones are we, and he loves us you and me', then I'd be first out of the door. This particular morning, I trudged into the classroom, unusually early and on my own. The early-morning winter sun was streaming in through the big windows, and I was suddenly struck dumb. Miss Heywood had her back to me and playing the piano to no one other than herself. I never knew what the tune was until I was much older, but it stopped me in my tracks. I loved it. I didn't know it then, but I know now as 'Jesu, Joy of Man's Desiring', by Bach. It was the most fantastic piece of music I'd ever heard. I'd listened to bits of music at home, usually in snatches as I was in and out of the house. We had the Light Programme, Home

Service and occasionally I'd heard some of Mum's Artie Shaw records, Ella Fitzgerald and Frank Sinatra, but this piano music stunned me. It's been with me ever since. Miss Heywood probably told me what it was called at the time, but I wouldn't have remembered.

My entire early schoolboy memories are wrapped up in that piece of music. She eventually left school to get married. I was heartbroken. Lucky husband-to-be, I reckon. If I'd been old enough to marry her, I would have.

Before I left that school, aged ten, of which more later, I led a gang and got caned a few times for being a 'ringleader'. I didn't think I was, but Mr Martin did. He was in charge of my class by then, and I admit I was a bit disruptive. Mr Martin had wire-rimmed glasses, a fat red face, and was permanently angry. A world away from the soft and gentle Miss Heywood. He was a cruel, hateful, and sadistic bastard. When I left that school, I never looked back once. Even though I've been back since for a trip down memory lane, I can still hear that piano. When that piece by Bach turns up on Classic FM, which it does occasionally, I'm immediately transported back to Miss Heywood, except I'm by now happily married to her of course.

One summer, I can't remember what year but 1958 ish, my dad decided he'd build a swimming pool in the back garden. He dug it out by hand, and concreted it. It wasn't very big, 12 ft long and about 3 ft deep. He was six feet tall and barely did one stroke to get from one end to the other. It was a glorified pond really, but good fun to splash in when it was hot.

I had quite a few pets as I grew up, our dog Gyp and a cat called Pookie, (all our subsequent cats were Pookies) and one or two unusual ones, notably a couple of young magpies and jackdaws, but at this point I had a pet grass snake. It was an adult, about three feet long, and cost me two week's pocket money to get it off the kid up the road who'd caught it originally. It cost me half a crown. A bloody fortune (2s 6d, or 25p today). This snake loved the water and I'd swim it round the pool like a snaky boat. Round and round it went, and I would jump in and catch it as it swam round the edge. It didn't last long though, maybe a week or so, before it slipped out of my grasp as I climbed out. I couldn't recapture the bugger, and it shot through the blackcurrant bushes, disappearing under the chicken shed in a flash. All my money gone in one go.

For some reason I associate this pool entirely with the Everly Brothers. 'Dream' was the one I remember most, though 'Wake Up Little Susie' was a close second, and the one which woke me up to the guitar. I loved the intro to that and still do. During my snake fortnight I would drop into this pool with it singing, 'Dream, dream, dream' ... splash. Somewhere around this time Cliff Richard and the Shadows arrived. Cliff was portrayed at the time as the English version of Elvis. The first record my dad came home with from Stoke was 'Teddy Bear' and 'Jailhouse Rock' (and I loved that one), but it was Cliff's 'Living Doll' which conjured up everything that was good during my early years in North Staffs. These songs lit my musical touchpaper.

I quite liked songs though which were funny, or told a stupid story. Charlie Drake's 'My Boomerang Won't Come Back'. Stuff like that. Lonnie Donegan was another with 'My Old Man's a Dustman'. Musically naff, but I found them interesting. I still quite like daft stories in easy sing-along songs. Chas 'n' Dave are a case in point. My mum dismissed my interest in them, referring to them sneeringly as 'John's novelty numbers'. I didn't care. Even today I still like Allan Sherman's 'Hello Muddah, Hello Fadduh'. I can't remember when this song came along, but the 'Just William' in me could easily identify with the line 'I will even let Aunt Bertha hug and kiss me'.

So, around the age of ten I was musically awoken with a variety of stuff, and Paul Anka's 'Diana' was the one which tore at my heartstrings. You see, I'd fallen in love at school with Beryl Van Houten.

Miss Heywood still lingered in my mind, but had moved on, and Beryl was the eleven-year-old version. I know the name Beryl isn't exactly an alluring name, unlike Monique, or Brigitte. These days Beryl is defunct, like Gladys or Phyllis or Ethel, my Grandma Craddock's name (the other grandma was Nellie), and I suppose they're all indicative of a certain time or generation. But this Beryl was gorgeous. The only Beryl I'd ever encountered up till then was Beryl the Peril in the *Beezer*, or the *Topper*. I can't remember which comic. In my eyes though, Beryl was the one. Strange to think now, but I never thought it odd at the time that a girl with a Dutch name should find herself at a primary school in North Staffordshire. Maybe her father was a Dutch Resistance fighter from World War II, who stayed behind after the war. I never discovered the hows and whys of this, and where she came from and went to I never found out. I never stood a chance because of bloody Alistair.

Beryl was about two classes ahead of me, and this unrequited love was captured perfectly with 'Diana' ('I'm so young and you're so old'). When she held hands with Alistair, it pissed me off. It was like a knife being twisted, and it hurt. I had no idea what I would have done with her should she have held hands with me, but it was the lack of possession which counted. At this point I couldn't wait to get to school for a glimpse of her, before I was mortally knifed in the playground by the bastard who'd stolen her heart.

Then unsurprisingly Cliff Richard made number one with 'Livin' Doll', and that changed everything. I got my own back, hoping to make Beryl jealous, not that it worked. My first girlfriend was Angela Allcock (there's a name to contend with at age ten). Blonde and curly, and the opposite of Beryl, who by now had pissed me off to the stage where I began to hate her. Love and hate aren't that far apart, you know. Angela became my 'Livin' Doll', and best of all she was in my class which meant I could gaze and wink at her all day.

'Livin' Doll' also defines my lifelong obsession with fishing. This swimming pool my dad had made attracted quite a few new friends. One named Stewart was a new arrival in the village. His parents had bought a new house in the rather disappointing housing estate being built on the fields across the way. The wildflower meadow was no more.

Stewart and his brother had fishing rods and showed me how to assemble them, along with the old wooden star-back reel, floats, shot, and hook sizes. He had an old cane rod which he gave to me, along with a few red-topped quill floats. This suddenly became my passion, and most of my pocket money went on fishing tackle. I'd test the floats, pointlessly, in the swimming pool/pond. Fishing, I quickly discovered, became just another way, or avenue, to allow me to explore the countryside in a wholly different way. At the age of eight or nine I could identify all birds by sight and sound. Now there were aquatic birds to discover. Just watching a red quill float sail away under water was a mesmerising experience. I made loads of them using crow or chicken wing feathers, and painted the tops with my mum's nail varnish, which I usually stole from her.

Water, whether still or running, fascinated me and it still does. I just had to know what lay beneath the surface. That was the mystery which drew me. The first fish I ever caught on rod and line was in a canal at Onecote. Stewart's mum had taken us. It was a gudgeon. I was hooked totally.

Cheddleton: Not a big town really, though it might be now. I haven't been back for a while. Anyway, it was bigger than a village, and a few miles from Werrington, on the main route to Leek from Stoke. It lay in a valley. I have no idea if it's famous for anything, but it had an industrial feel to it, due to the disused Caldon Canal, I suppose, with an old derelict mill which lay at the bottom of the hill. This place became the Holy Grail for me. A twenty-minute bus ride away from Werrington. This captivating stretch of water was as clear as crystal, reed-fringed at the edges, and a couple of knackered old locks, with weeds growing out of the rotting timbers. To me it looked like a giant aquarium. I quickly learned to identify fish species, thanks to Mr Crabtree and the *Angling Times*, and read everything I could find on fish and fishing.

Suddenly I was transformed into a hunter. Perch and roach abounded in the canal, and I learned where to find them, sneaking through the vegetation inch by inch, otherwise they'd be gone in a flash. Pike were my ultimate quarry. I can only pinpoint my lifelong obsession with these predatory loners to a family visit to Alton Towers when I was about eight or nine, and long before I got a rod. I watched a guy by the lake put a small live roach on a big hook under a big red float. He cast it out. It bobbed about for a bit, and I watched, fascinated, then the float suddenly plunged beneath the surface. He hooked whatever it was and played it to the landing net. I now recognise it was a pike of about 2–3 lb. It looked mean and fierce. He unhooked it and without warning promptly knocked it on the head. With it still quivering, he curled it up in his fishing basket to take home to eat. I felt really sorry for it.

Discovering fishing was a revelation, but when I discovered pike were living in Cheddleton canal, that was it. They became my focus, and my reason for living. I would creep along the bank, bending the reeds and rosebay willowherb, trying to spot their torpedo shape lying deep down in the weed.

The tuppeny bus ride (my pocket money was twenty-four old pennies a week, two shillings, or 20p today) from Werrington early on a Sunday morning, I'd clamber on a Proctors double-decker bus, complete with my rods, basket, flask, and cheese sandwich or two. In the basket were maggots or worms in a small metal tin, soft bread for roach, and sometimes I'd carry a small bucket of minnows or bullheads, which I'd caught the day before from a small stream. My visits were always on a Sunday, and I was gone for the day. I'd be about ten. Of the two rods, a three-piece one for float fishing and a stiffer two-piece cane rod for pike, I'd then spend hours with tiny pieces of bread trying to catch the roach close to one of the locks. The worms I'd use for perch, which would arch their dorsal fins and attack the worm as it drifted down through the gin-clear water. I absorbed myself all day here, alone and oblivious to strangers, cyclists, and distant traffic noise.

I never spoke to a soul. In fact, my entire hunched body language indicated 'piss off'. It still does today. I did this more or less every Sunday for two years.

If I caught a small roach, which was a better bait than a minnow, I'd use this for live bait. This I hooked on to snap tackle, two treble hooks on a wire trace. My heart would pound when I cast it out, and I'd watch the big cork bung bob around over the weed-bed. Just like I saw at Alton Towers. The tension I felt was intense, and I never once felt sorry for the roach. It was just a means to an end. Sometimes in seconds there would be a flash, and a pike would appear out of nowhere to take it. The excitement I felt was uncontainable, and even sixty years on it's never left me. By almost dark I would gather my gear together and trudge the mile or so back down the towpath to the bus stop, usually humming 'Livin' Doll'. An odd anthem for a solitary pike fisherman.

That song captures everything about that canal, and I really can't explain it. There was a long dark tunnel which went under the road, and I rarely ventured in that direction. But one Autumn evening I did. By now it was late afternoon, and as I headed back to the bridge for the bus, I saw a bronze flash, but only for a second or two. I stopped, hid in the reeds and watched. Down deep in about 5 ft of water I could see about six big roach moving around slowly. They were enormous. Unlike the tiddlers down on the lock. I flicked some small pieces of bread in, followed by my float and a small size-16 hook. I lost sight of the bread, but saw the float twitch a few times. Then no more movement, and when I reeled in, the bread was gone. I knew from my books that big roach were difficult to catch, but I persevered for ten minutes. Every now and then I would see a bronze flank turn. It was incredibly frustrating, by now getting dark, and I was being bitten to hell with mosquitoes which clouded round my head and hands. I could barely see the float by this stage, and then, almost imperceptibly, it began to slide sideways, and with my last gasp chance I struck. There was a solid thump, and I was in. The relief I felt when I slid this beautiful fish over the net and lifted it out was

11

just the most fantastic feeling. It had tugged and fought down below as I prayed my line would hold. Getting it into the landing net was the most triumphant of feelings. Like winning a race or being awarded a prize in front of the whole school. Except there was only me. It must have weighed about a pound and a half. I had no means of weighing it, and in the telling of this little story I wouldn't mind betting it was even bigger, but I let it go, regretting not having a camera. That fish is fixed in my memory forever.

It was dark by the time I made the bus, and my hands and face itched like mad, but I didn't care. I got home about 8 pm, and got the biggest bollocking from Mum and Dad. Homework to do, school in the morning, get your shoes polished, books into your satchel and so on. Then cold Sunday meat, pickles, and bed. My hands throbbed and swellings came up on my face. By morning I was covered in big red lumps and could hardly bend my fingers.

I've since put my relative immunity to insect bites down to this. Nothing which has bitten me since ever produced a reaction like this. The week-long pain and discomfort as the bites subsided were nothing compared to that roach. If anything, they were a reminder, and worth every itch and scratch.

Needless to say, I was back there the following week, same time, same spot, but of those roach, not a sign.

Around this 'Livin' Doll' time, I got my first kiss with Angela Allcock. It happened while I was perched on a radiator in the school hall waiting to have greasepaint applied. I had been cast as Joseph in the school Nativity play and needed a drawn-on beard. Angela was playing my wife Mary. This was a rehearsal in more ways than one. Kissing was what husbands and wives did, so I used that as an excuse. It was quite a moment. I'd be about ten. No virgin birth was to follow.

'Wake Up Little Susie' by the Everly Brothers I mentioned earlier. This song, perhaps more than any other, made me realise I needed a guitar. Skiffle had also arrived, and I'd seen Lonnie Donegan on our old black-and-white telly around this time, performing 'Cumberland Gap', 'Ballad of New Orleans' and 'My

Old Man's a Dustman'. The guitar seemed so simple to play, and it occurred to me that playing the guitar would also be a useful way of attracting attention. Especially the attention of girls.

Nowadays when I think back to my time growing up in North Staffs in the 1950s, I perceive the whole thing with childlike delight. I loved the moorland, and the woodlands, and, long before I had a rod and reel, would find trout in the tiny stream which tinkled through Bluebell Wood. I learned to tickle them, finding them tucked tight under large stones. Sometimes I might catch two or three with my hands, kill them, and take them home to my mum, who would pan-fry them in butter and we'd pick at them together.

Werrington had its usual quota of council houses, inserted in between the older properties, and as I said earlier the common people lived there. My mum wouldn't let me have anything to do with them and I was discouraged from playing with those kids, since they didn't talk 'proper'. They swore a lot and used Staffordshire slang. As if I didn't. And even though I could swear, I had no idea what 'fuck' actually meant. The bigger boys told me that you put your cock into a girl. Really? How? I understood snogging, but this made no sense to me. Where do you put it and how does this floppy little thing fit?

Mrs Mifflin had a shop right at the far end of Washerwall Lane, in a terrace of cottages. It was primarily a sweet shop, and Mrs Mifflin was incredibly old and stooped with white hair. We bought, and occasionally stole, liquorice root and Spanish juice sticks with our pocket money. By comparison, Mr Hill's General Store on the corner of the lane was impressively modern, and smelled of soap. It was full of soil-encrusted vegetables, tinned stuff, and household goods, and smelt of bread and soap powder. This was the main shop in the village, and where I went to run errands for my mum. A sliced loaf and ten Woodbines would be the usual order. When I learned to smoke, around the age of ten, I used to come up with some trick or ruse to get Mr Hill to go out the back to look for something not on the shelves. I had a couple of mates who would help to distract him at this point. I'd then nip under the flap in the counter and steal twenty Senior Service. I usually hid these in the quarry, in a hole which I covered with a large stone. My brother Martin gave them a try, then usually turned green. Learning to smoke was not easily mastered. What a stupid and ridiculous thing to do. Nevertheless, I persevered with it.

I had a deadly enemy in Werrington: John Fowler, a bigger boy, younger than me and obviously common, since he lived in one of the council houses. We were forever fighting. My best mate was Philip Twigg. He had a brilliant sense of humour and would frequently make up poems or daft new words to old songs or adverts. 'Embrey's bread is as hard as lead, if you eat any more you'll drop down dead.' He was a funny kid, very wordy, and acquired a mangy black and white mongrel dog he called Star, frequently attached to a rope. My Dad reversed this and referred to it as 'Rats'. Dad was wordy too. I was good at language and reading, especially *Biggles* and *Just William*, and developed a lifelong interest in twisting words to create new meanings. I still do it today.

Apart from learning to fish, learning to swim at Hanley baths every Friday night with Mart and Dad, I also liked to light fires. I was really good at it too. One evening in late August I set fire to some of the moorland. It was easy to spread around the heather using a bunch of dry grass I'd lit first. On this occasion it went beyond my control in minutes, and I stood there as it unexpectedly whooshed off in another direction on the wind, the sparks lighting another patch of tinder-dry heather a few yards away. I watched in awe as it spread in every direction, smoke billowing and blowing into the distance. I did the only thing I could do. I ran off.

I don't know how many acres of moorland I eventually ignited, but it was a lot. Days later I would still see wisps of smoke curling up into the sky, and at night patches of red fire. All through the village the air hung heavy with it. I went to school reeking of smoke, and every day I thought, fuck me, I'm responsible for all this. The fire burned and smouldered on and off for weeks. Sometimes it would die down after a rainstorm and I'd think, that's it. Then days later it would suddenly flare up on the wind. I didn't know this at the time, but heather roots evidently keep burning forever, as does the peat they grow in.

I curbed my pyromaniacal tendencies after this, primarily because I was terrified of being caught, especially when the fire brigade and police arrived to advise when it got closer to some of the houses. The possibility of burning down the whole village never occurred to me. Off they went, up over the moor with their big red fire engines, and put it out permanently, after first putting out the fire on the railway embankment a mile or two away. That was probably down to me as well, but I would never have admitted to that. We had steam engines in those days, so it could have been sparks from those, but the rail ran along the edge of the moorland, and I think the moorland fire probably crossed over. Either way, I'd inadvertently set fire to about three miles of embankment. It all took some putting out and burned, on and off, for ages, maybe two months. That's a long time to smell like a kipper, and all done with one match. Blimey!

Somehow, whilst growing up in North Staffs the seasons, to me at any rate, seemed more defined. I've never worked out if this was imagined or real, but we got a lot of snow in winter, hot summers, fresh, vibrant springs, and colourful red, yellow and gold autumns. Those usually signalled a depressing resumption of school, and shorter days. I still hate the clock going back today, but on the upside we gathered conkers, pickled them, dried them, fixed them on string and bashed the hell out of them. Not allowed today. Health and safety and all that. Tops, whips, and yo-yos had their seasonal outings as well. No doubt H&S wouldn't approve that either. Times change. Risk and adventure seem to have been squeezed out.

Doris Day was singing 'Que Sera Sera', and as I said earlier, Jack Frost was a regular visitor to the inside of our bedroom. I think our house was heated entirely by one coal fire. Getting out of bed in the morning to go to school was bloody awful, but we made ice slides in the playground, and snowball fights where we split into two groups and hurled these icy balls at each other. In the seemingly long, hot summers we played cowboys and Indians.

The field at the back of our house was our prairie. This was Roy Rogers and *Wagon Train* country. Davy Crockett, Hawkeye and *The Last of the Mohicans*, (Chingachgook was a good Indian). Lone Ranger and Tonto (another good Indian, but good Indians were few and far between). Cheyenne Bodie was on the box, as was *Rawhide*, with Rowdy Yates (played by 25-year-old Clint Eastwood). All these cowboy series were required watching and gripped our imagination. We had cap guns, holsters, hats, and neck scarves, were all keen on acting these programmes out. Apart from the two good Indians, the rest were all bad guys. No one ever wanted to be an Indian. Our dog, a corgi called Tiggy, stood in, as did Star. These dogs were reluctant Indians and never hung around long. The cap guns we fired at them soon pissed them off. It never occurred to us then that the concept of cowboys wiping out the Indians was ethnic cleansing on a monumental scale. Now, of course, all conveniently consigned to history, which is presumably why it isn't on the telly anymore.

Doris Day's song 'The Deadwood Stage' epitomised this era, although I always referred to it as 'Whip-Crackaway'. I rode an imaginary horse out on the prairie, since I was a scout for the wagon train making its way west. I was never one for riding in a covered wagon along with the women and children. I was out there, scouting for Injuns. Apache, Comanche, Cherokee, Navajo, they were all the same. Red faces bad, pale faces good. My name was Flint McCullough, the scout in *Wagon Train*. I chose to be him over all the others. He was taciturn and super cool. Flint (played by Robert Horton on the telly) could easily outrun and out-shoot those pesky Injuns. And he always roamed around ahead, sort of out of the way. I was a bit like that.

Eventually I graduated from being a scout to being a cub, and at the age of nine or ten I joined Red Six, part of the local Wolf Cub pack. It was a novel experience and fitted well with my love of outdoors. We had Akela, the wolf in *The Jungle Book*, who as a bespectacled retired teacher was totally un-wolflike, and Baloo (the bear), his sidekick, an amiable fat-faced chap who looked a bit like Pooh. Bagheera was the panther. I think this might have been the teacher's wife. All nicely woggled up in their uniforms. It was a bit like school, with something of a *Dad's Army* twist, held once a week in a scout hut at the edge of the village. I was quite proud of my uniform, but the green jumper I recall hating. It was made of wool, but it might as well have been buffalo hair, and it made me itch. As I progressed, I got badges sewn on to it for all kinds of things, first aid, knots, and so on. I gritted my teeth with the jumper and wore them proudly as I did my cap. The best badge I got was for cooking on an open fire. They were amazed at my fire-lighting skills. You won't be surprised to hear I wasn't.

Cooking, though, was a skill I perfected from roasting jacket potatoes and toasting bread, especially on Bonfire Night, and I learned to fry bacon on a sharpened stick, which I speared the rasher with, twisting it on, and then turning repeatedly over the embers. You needed a green stick by the way, otherwise there was a danger it caught fire, along with the bacon. The hot, fried, roasted rasher, blackened by the heat, I'd then shove between two slices of bread.

I was told it was also possible to cook hedgehogs by rolling them up in a big ball of clay. Gypsies do that, I'd heard. Evidently the spines come away when you crack the clay ball. I would never have done that. I'd caught many hedgehogs for pets over the years, and they were loveable. I wouldn't do it to a magpie, jackdaw or snake either. I'd had a few of those as pets too. A squirrel I perhaps might have done, except that I never caught one, though I'd aimed my catapult at a few.

We'd sing songs, and play games of tag on summer evenings. It gave me an opportunity to own a knife too. Suddenly my ambition was to get a sheath knife with a bone handle and wear it on my belt like Davy Crockett. A bowie knife was the ultimate. I lusted for one of those. Out of reach to my pocket, but then it's not as if there was much locally in the way of antelope or buffalo herds to shoot and skin, and a knife of that size is a bit big for a squirrel.

Eventually I got promoted to Seconder in Red Six, a kind of Corporal, and then eventually a Sixer, a Sergeant type, which made me the boss of Red Six, reporting to a Senior Sixer. He was a kind of Major, I guess, and usually an arse-licker to Baloo and Akela, who played the role of Brigadier and General. The only good thing about this army style of pecking order was you couldn't be court-martialled or thrown in the slammer for insubordination. A severe ticking-off was about the worst. Nevertheless, I readily embraced my new-found power over Red Six, wanting us to be the best at everything. I suppose I became something of a bully, including developing a fixation with my team having clean shoes. I still love to polish shoes. Even the leather soles still get a dose of polish where they join the heel. Keeps it bendy, see? Some things like this just stay with you for life.

Here you go, here's another one for life. Campfire song. Ready? All together now, and to the tune of 'Roaming in the Gloaming'. One, two, a ... one two three four ... 'Yawning, in the morning, when the Sixer gives a roar, we've only had one hour of sleep and we would like some more. If we had gone to bed when the sun was getting red, then we wouldn't be yawning in the moooooorning ...'

Chapter 2

My mum and dad realised that the local village school was a waste of time. No one ever passed the eleven-plus and went from there to the grammar school. Thus, they hatched a plot to move my brother and I to a town school, and we left Caverswall Primary, to take the thirty-minute bus ride from Werrington to East Street School in Leek. This for me was a wrench, as I gave up cubs and headed towards my eleventh birthday. Mum and Dad knew there was an inherent unfairness in the education system, and in the way places were gained for the grammar school. The eleven-plus was a very important exam which I had to pass to allow me to get there. East Street Primary in Leek had a consistently high pass rate. In other words, it was a fiddle, and the headmistress there, as it turned out, knew it. Nevertheless, I was glad to get away from the evil cane-thrashing Gruppenfuhrer Mr Martin, sorry to lose my close friends (gang), and bye bye Angela Allcock. I never knew what became of Beryl. She left a couple of years ahead.

It was a huge shock to move from a simple village school to this new one, and I was lonely at first. I soon made new friends though, and to my surprise discovered I was quite good at cricket, and a half-decent batsman at that. The primary reason for my unexpected prowess with a bat was because I was scared of the ball. I didn't want to get smacked by that thing. Up until then, all the cricket and rounders we'd played in our field at home had always used a tennis ball, or a soft spongy rubber one. Being hit by that generally left no more than a bruise. However, a proper cricket ball, I quickly discovered, is more of a bloody missile. It's a weapon, it's hard, and if that hit you it was more likely to break your jaw. I didn't like the idea of that, which is how I came to be good at swiping the bloody thing away. Quite successfully as it turned out, but wholly unintentionally.

On one occasion, with my heart thumping throughout, I managed to achieve one of the highest scores as a batsman at this school. Eighty-one runs, I think it was. Mercifully, I was caught out before the law of averages, or my imagination, told me that if this carried on I'd end up in hospital with a cracked skull. I walked with relief from the stump, receiving appreciative applause from the teachers and onlookers around the pitch. They actually pitied me for not making a century. Mad bastards. They had no idea that this record score, by primary school standards that is, was achieved through abject fear, and my excellent batting skills were driven by sheer terror.

East Street seemed 'streetwise' by comparison with my old primary school, and I guess I was perceived as a rather naïve country bumpkin. I made some good friends, but can't remember any of them except for a kid called Dawson, who shared my interest in prehistoric animals. Having a mum whose primary interests were geology and prehistory gave me a bit of an edge here. I also got to learn about Greek mythology, Walter de la Mare, and played out a role as Achilles in Troy. Altogether more interesting, I found, than a thrashing from Mr Martin.

I was heading towards eleven. Mrs Bullock the headmistress was a heartless bitch, who recognised the ploy by Mum and Dad to move schools in order to get me through the eleven-plus, and thus to the grammar in Leek. (Both my parents went to Leek Grammar). For no obvious reason she took an immediate dislike to me. Feeling the pressure, I eventually took the exam. I failed it spectacularly. It was the intelligence test which did it; I never did quite get that. I ran out of time, having spent too long trying to find the catch in the answers, instead of stating the bloody obvious. These days they'd probably call it lateral thinking. In those days it was a straight fail because I was deemed 'thick'. I didn't think I was, but this episode confirmed I must be, because they told me so. Worst of all, I'd let my parents down.

To rub salt in my wounds, Mrs Bullock was allowed a discretionary choice of who should go through to the grammar if there was a borderline exam result. Mine most certainly was, as was Dawson's, as it turned out. Mrs Bullock had a veto of sorts, and she sure as hell vetoed me. Of the thirty kids in my class, twenty-nine, including Dawson, went on to Leek Grammar, but not me. Out of this pack of thirty cards I'd drawn the Joker. It's hard for an eleven-year-old to recover from a blow like that. I felt a complete failure. Any self-esteem I'd had just evaporated. I felt stigmatised and, quite frankly, lost. My parents weren't exactly sympathetic either. Basically, I'd fucked it up, and it was all my fault. Que Sera Sera, eh? It was an early lesson in the unfairness of life.

I consoled myself and went fishing. I knew I was good at that.

So, I failed my eleven-plus exam at East Street School, and got on a bus every day to go to Mountside Secondary Modern in Leek. This was something of a naughty boys' school where the no-hopers went. That was obviously me, then. Downgraded and second best.

During my eleven-plus year we'd moved as a family from Washerwall Lane in Werrington to the outskirts of Cheddleton – Woodlands Avenue in fact, a modern type of bungalow. This was just a few months before I took that fateful exam, so early 1960. I don't recall missing Werrington at all, but maybe I was just preoccupied with the forthcoming exam. The upside to our move, for me at least, was being even closer to the canal. I still went every Sunday, but best of all it was bikeable, thus saving on bus fares. My rods were permanently tied to the crossbar, and my fishing basket strapped on in place of a saddlebag. Just like a horse. Ready to go at a moment's notice.

The school bus I caught was empty when I got on. The night before I'd tried on my new school uniform, and just felt sick. By the time I made it to the bus stop I'd felt so ill I fancied trying out dying for a change. There were a couple of people already on it when I climbed aboard, but by the time it got down the hill into

Cheddleton itself it was heaving. Most of the kids who piled on were not the kind I'd ever encountered before. Swearing, boisterous, dirty, noisy, scruffy (unpolished shoes), and disrespectful to the driver and conductor. Council house scumbags, my mum would have called them. They pushed, shoved and jostled for seats and the driver looked thoroughly miserable. All my newly made friends at East Street had gone to the grammar, and here I was. Wrong place, wrong time. How in the hell I was ever expected to adjust to this I had no idea. This lot were rough, aggressive yobs. We passed over the bridge as we headed to Leek, and for a moment I had a glimpse of the canal. Just for that second I felt like smashing a window and diving out of this mobile shithole, to hide in my sanctuary. In reality I just shrank further into the recesses of my seat and tried to make myself invisible.

I'd felt shock when I discovered East Street Primary was a big school, and now I felt abject terror when I got to this place. Mountside was huge, as were the kids who went there. All of them seemed to tower over me. All 500 of them.

Inevitably it wasn't long before I was bullied. Three brothers, who all caught the bus, picked on me early on. The youngest of the three was backed up by his siblings, which intimidated me. This bullying continued for a while, to the point where I dreaded the return journey, but gradually I adjusted to this new situation, surprisingly quickly in fact. I got tired of the tie-pulling and cuffs round the head and eventually lost my temper. Things subsided after that.

The best thing about East Street and Mountside, however, was the opportunity to call in to see my gran – my mum's mum, Nellie Broome – usually in the late afternoons on the way back from school to catch the bus home from Market Square. She and my granddad Jim lived in Ball Haye Green, at 'Audleigh'. I've no idea why the house was called that, but it's still there and still has the sign on it. They'd lived there for years, or at least all of my life. The area has some wonderful little back-to-back streets, one of which is Milk St. I just loved the sound of that. I could easily imagine my mum growing up there and playing 'Queenie O Coco'. Odd name, and no idea why. This back-street game bounced a ball against a wall. The thrower then turns round and has to guess who caught it, points at the supposed catcher and shouts 'Queeniococo'. I'm pleased to tell you it wasn't a bloody cricket ball either.

Grandma Nellie was a legendary baker (or bake-ess?). Her wakes cakes, scones and meat and potato pie were something to behold. My mum, her daughter, never quite inherited this talent. Scratchings with onion was another of her specialities. On the trudge back to the school bus it was the perfect pit stop. My grandparents were just so incredibly kind, softly spoken and understanding. A perfect antidote to the daytime mayhem at Mountside. I adored them both.

As I said earlier, I was never a big fan of Buddy Holly and Elvis, they were just a year or two ahead, but skiffle came along, personified by Lonnie Donegan. I liked that. This was around 1959, when I was ten or eleven, and just before we moved from Werrington to Cheddleton and subsequently the Mountside hellhole. But I had a banjo. It wasn't a real one, but the closest I could get to a guitar, and I could just about get through Lonnie Donegan's 'Ballad of New Orleans'. I took it to school and showed off.

I'd seen some kid in Werrington make a tea chest bass with a broom pole and one string and actually get a playable sound. This was a turning point for me. On a visit to Hanley one Saturday morning I had enough money accumulated (with my mum's help) to buy this thing. It was made of metal, painted red and yellow and in the centre was a grinning 'Negro' face. All the strings were nylon, all the same diameter, and as a playable instrument it was utter crap. Nevertheless, it lit in me some musical spark. I learned to strum it (badly), but in time to Lonnie when he was on the record player, or radiogram. Mostly it was impossible to tune, but I could keep time, and partly as a result of that I made new friends fairly quickly.

Despite Mountside being a bloody rough school, I suddenly found I was in the top class. This did my self-esteem some good, and in the term exams I was nearly always top. But as the saying goes, a one-eyed man is king in a blind man's kingdom. Most of my classmates were, dare I say it, thick. I was surprised by my sudden and new-found status. Interestingly, I learned more recently that the actor Windsor Davies was a teacher there from about 1956 to 1960. He may well have taught me Maths and English, but I don't recall him. He subsequently became a full-time actor and made his name in the 1970s with the comedy series *It Ain't Half Hot, Mum*.

Though I hated school, and despite my elevation as a star pupil, I suddenly and unexpectedly discovered wanking. I quite enjoyed that, and would fantasise over one of the girls on the school bus. The girls' school was next door to ours. On several occasions, usually during assembly, my best mate would ask me to put my hand in his trouser pocket and touch his cock through a hole he had in it. He was invariably fiddling with it, so I obliged. I had no idea what I was doing, but seemingly he'd discovered wanking about the same time as me, and likewise enjoyed it. He'd writhe around a bit and grit his teeth while the headmaster delivered morning prayers to the packed hall. There was never a climax as it were, we were still too young, but this episode proved to be my first and only homosexual experience. The girls' school was adjacent to us, and I knew without doubt where my preferences lay.

The big boys in assembly were always at the back, the first-formers at the front. Mr R C Neal would be on the stage, along with the other teachers. In the event, he turned out to be a brilliant headmaster. He'd arrived the year before I arrived so was relatively new to the school. He was an inspiration, and in my view wasted on this lot. He introduced fencing, boxing (unusual in those days), and cross-country running. Round the Mount we'd go. I was quite good at that. I tried fencing too. I fancied getting my hands on a rapier to skewer one or two of the twats on the bus.

I wasn't bad at boxing either, though I had a tendency to lose my temper if I got hit. Boxing needs a cool head. I wasn't like that. Football was OK though, having had plenty of practice with my dad in the field in Werrington. I usually wore my red-and-white-striped Stoke City shirt, because I was obviously Stanley Matthews. He was my hero. Eventually at some point I was asked by the PE teacher if I'd like to go in the nets for cricket practice. I gave that a miss.

Mountside proved to be a very steep learning curve in my life, and I have no recollection of any particular piece of music which went with it. Maybe I don't wish to remember and have somehow blanked it all out. I was somewhere between fishing and bird's-nesting as an adventurous boy, and yet felt a growing awareness of girls and my own bodily changes. My voice broke about this time. One second I'd sound like a high pitched eunuch, the next like Ray Charles. I grew hair, and although I'd only ever encountered one person on a cub camp in Cannock, who claimed he could 'fetch up', (a very Staffordshire expression) suddenly and to my amazement I found I could.

One winter's afternoon, leaving the school gates and slouching through the drizzle on my way to the bus via my gran's, I passed an alleyway. I glanced sideways and there was one of the big boys, who had a girl up against a wall, with his hand under her skirt and (presumably) in her knickers. I was profoundly disturbed by that.

Mr R C Neal (the reason I put his initials here is because they used to call him 'Arsey'), well, he picked on me now, but this time for the right reasons.

Cane punishment was prevalent in this school, and frequently used throughout to emphasise authority. I'd been caned once or twice, on one occasion for punching a kid who flicked ink all over my neat homework. The teacher never argued with you. It was simply a request to fetch the Punishment Book. I would leave the classroom and trek across the school grounds to the headmaster's office. That walk of shame alone would induce fear. Then the secretary, a haughty old bitch, would give me a look of death over her wire-rimmed specs, hand me the book and the cane, which I'd carry back. If anyone on this return journey spotted you, they sure as hell took the piss. I used to look at this weapon and wonder how many kids' arses it had thwacked over the years. This cane was well used and thick. Six of the best was usually delivered on the arse, two or four on the hands. On this particular occasion I got six. Years before, at Salter's Lane Primary school, with that sadist teacher Mr Martin, I had learned to put the heel of my thumb near my thighs as I bent over, and this would go some way to thwarting the full effects of the blows, even though my thumbs throbbed for hours afterwards.

Despite my occasional wayward behaviour, Mr R C Neal had somehow, out of hundreds of kids in this place, spotted me and singled me out. By this time, I was pretty much top of the class. I got the feeling he believed in me, and I now began to dare to believe in myself.

My dad got a new job. He'd been a sales rep for a catering equipment company in Blythe Bridge, near Stoke, and had a company car. A little Austin A40, (770 LEH) which the five of us (Julia, my sister, was now on the scene) would squeeze into on our holidays to North Wales. Now though he'd applied for a Sales Manager/Director's job at Electroway in Loughborough, in Leicestershire, and was required to move. We were intending to follow, once the school term finished. Another move yet again to another place. It was 1961, significantly a year which if you turn upside down remains the same. Well, I thought it was. I was heading towards my thirteenth birthday in September.

Mr Neal was aware of our move, and at this point became immensely influential in my life. I was bright, sharp as a pair of new scissors (he said), and usually top of the class (something of a novelty). As I alluded to earlier though, the competition wasn't exactly top-drawer, but by this time I had some great friends. Mr Neal suggested I sit the thirteen-plus and aim for a place at a grammar school in Loughborough. To this day I don't know how, but he contacted the Leicestershire Education Board and fixed it. I took the exam, still flummoxed by the intelligence test, but was interviewed by some crusty old men subsequently, and they passed me. I was still considered borderline – that bloody intelligence test had let me down yet again – but I excelled in the interview. I was considered to be bright and 'personable'.

My mum and dad were over the moon, as was I. I'd been a failure for two years, and now I wasn't one. I have Mr R C Neal to thank for both his trust, belief and foresight in engineering this. So up yours, Mrs 'East Street' Bullock.

So over to Loughborough we went in the summer of 1961, leaving Cheddleton, and my beloved canal, behind.

Chapter 3

In my head I believed I was clever, in fact I thought I was a genius. The problem was no one else thought so. I spent much of my time thinking things through carefully and living in a world of my own creation which no one ever really understood.

My mum and dad had coached me for the interview with these stuffy old magistrate types, but I was nervous and couldn't remember half of what they'd told me. There they sat in an oak panelled room, with little me sitting opposite. The chair was so big my feet couldn't touch the floor, and only my head showed above this huge polished table. I felt as if they were deciding the fate of some miscreant, and about to send me to some penal colony in Australia. I answered their questions with confidence though. In fact, I think I quite impressed them.

After half an hour of interrogation, the chief magistrate put down his pen, nodded to the other two, who appeared to be half-asleep, gave me a thin smile and told me he was approving my application. He was 'allowing' me to go to Humphrey Perkins Grammar School, a mixed school for boys – and girls. That was a bonus. The grammar school in Loughborough was by all accounts full, with no vacant space. Humphrey Perkins, however, was an old and well established school in Barrow upon Soar, a few miles outside Loughborough. I joined my smart-arsed brother Martin, who had automatically qualified since he was an eleven-plus success, and caught the school bus for the twenty-minute journey each morning. On such thin knife-edge decisions does life and fate take you. I was now heading in a totally new direction.

The first thing which struck me when I arrived at this school was the Leicestershire accent. The school itself was historically old, it even had a motto – *Honeste Audax*, whatever that meant – and had houses. Not little terraced ones, but four 'houses' which engendered team spirit. Hastings – red, Beaumont – yellow, Latimer – blue, and Grey – which was green. I never quite got that. Each child was allotted to a house when they started. It also helped rivalry and competition. I got Beaumont.

Nevertheless, it was the accents which fascinated me. They thought my North Staffs one was odd, but I thought theirs more so. They don't sound the Y at the end of a word, but finish it off with 'eh'. For example, I would say hurry or sorry as normal, or so I thought, emphasising the Y as sorree, or hurree, but theirs would be sorreh, or hurreh. The village of Sileby they would pronounce as Silebeh. Because the border of Cheshire and Staffs is close, the Cheshire accent is a milder form of the Liverpool one, and in due course I was able to capitalise on the Scouse accent, and you'll find out why later.

Leicestershire doesn't have bread rolls, it has cobs. And scones, as in 'own', rather than scones, as in 'on'. In a million years my classmates would never have understood North Staffordshire slang, something my mum had actively discouraged, usually with a smack round the head. She didn't want us aligned with the common kids who lived down the road. They thought I was odd, and I thought they were.

Decipher this: 'Cost kick a bo agen a wo and bost it?'

Translated into my mum's English, it's 'Can you kick a ball against a wall and burst it?'

The other thing I missed in our move to the East Midlands was Staffordshire oatcakes. Possibly one of the world's best kept secrets. I have no idea why these are especially peculiar to this county. We lived on them as kids, with cheese, bacon, sausage, onions, or Lyle golden syrup. That was our breakfast. These things would keep us going all day. To this day I believe there are only half a dozen oatcake shops in Staffordshire, and the recipes are a closely guarded secret. Why they haven't been universally accepted I have no idea.

Back in the early 1960s the hit parade, as it was known, was dominated by male singers. Bobby Vee, Bobby Darin, Cliff, Elvis, Marty Wilde, Billy Fury, Del Shannon (who was great), Chris Montez and many more. There were dances held in the assembly hall, mostly on Friday lunchtimes, and all the girls danced. I was too shy and incompetent to join in, but watched, because for me the fact there were girls at this school was a bonus. Watching them dance and jive with an occasional glimpse of their knickers, usually navy blue, was my weekend entertainment.

I'd just turned thirteen, and on the first day I caught the bus I was nervous. This lot seemed well ordered by comparison with the Mountside hooligans. I sat on the only available seat, next to someone who would become my lifelong friend. This was Brom. Over time I discovered he loved music as much as I, as well as an unusual take on words, frequently twisting them backwards. The estate agent Gartons in Loughborough became Snotrag. We loved stuff like that. 'Let's Dance' by Chris Montez was our favourite song of the time.

I settled into this school well. Most of the kids in my class were bright but odd. They weren't exactly academic or scientific, in fact I find it difficult to categorise them; wayward probably. It suited me perfectly.

My biggest problem here was second-year French, since I'd missed out on the first year's syllabus. Mountside never had French as an option, so I struggled with it. Masculine/feminine verbs were gobbledegook as far as I was concerned, but that was about it. I settled into the rest of it with ease.

There were, however, girls in my class, and those became a serious distraction for me. I was quickly hit on by one, who was surprisingly well developed around the school blouse area. When the opportunity arose a year or so later to abandon French and join the girls for a newly formed typing and secretarial class, I jumped at the chance. Typewriter keyboard skills, not that I knew it at the time, have stood me in good stead. Qwerty keyboards are here to stay. It was a double bonus. I learned shorthand, typing, got to look up the occasional skirt, and more importantly it got me out of French classes.

When we moved to Loughborough in 1961 we ended up on an uninspiring housing estate of boring new houses off Forest Road. 40 Kirkstone Drive. I'd settled in at school, made some great friends, and was comfortable academically in the C stream, which was effectively the bottom of the grammar school section. The school had more recently become a newly politicised co-educational one, so D, E, and F class were the thickos, who should by rights have been at the secondary modern school, like Mountside in Leek. The smartarses in the A and B class above us were streamed to be brilliant mathematicians or scientists. My lot in C class, as I said earlier, were generally talented yobbos, but creative and imaginative yobbos. Brilliant in some subjects and crap in others. Like me. English, Biology, Geography, and Art I did well. Woodwork, Physics, Chemistry, Metalwork, all a complete mystery. The best thing about this lot was the collective sense of humour. It's lasted with one or two of them for sixty years. If anyone got too up themselves, we took the piss. I was more than well suited for the C stream.

We'd been in Loughborough about two years, I'd just passed my fifteenth birthday, when one evening I walked into the kitchen. The Bush radio was on, and it glowed on the kitchen window sill. It had a big dial in the middle which if twisted would take you all over the world with hissing sounds and faint foreign voices. I'd acquired a crystal set and earphones at some point and listened to Radio Luxembourg in bed at night, where pop music was the mainstay. The radio was difficult to tune, so these songs would echo through the headset, then fade as the weather conditions interfered with the signal.

The BBC Light Programme (dull) or Home Service (even duller) were the mainstays of radio at the time, and they only rarely played pop music. Mantovani or something was playing, as I poured my tea before I went back to my homework. The radio announcer paused, and I suddenly stood there in shock. 'Please

31

Please Me' came on. I've no idea why it shook me like that, but I was stunned. I immediately wanted to hear it again, but the radio presenter returned to Humphrey Lyttleton, Kenny Ball's Jazz Band, or whatever. It was 1963. President Kennedy was shot in the November, but more importantly, the Beatles had arrived. And with them came Beatlemania.

'Please Please Me' was a song unlike anything I had ever heard before. It's now of course well known, sounds so simple, doesn't last long, but is more complicated to play than you might think. Analyse it, and you'll find the vocal harmonies, use of a harmonica, the chord changes, and the small riffs George Harrison played, combined to create a unique and unmistakeable sound. I found out later that The Beatles' members were on average about twenty-one years old. This was unheard of. When I discovered their ages I was truly astonished, even more so when I found out they wrote their own songs. It's almost taken for granted today, but everything changed almost overnight, and it didn't end there. This was the beginning of a seismic shift in the whole pop world, and I loved every minute of it.

Within the space of perhaps a week, the entire school attitude changed. We became Beatle-obsessed. If ever I knew with certainty what it was I wanted to do with my life it was then. I just wanted to be a Beatle. Except that I couldn't. I grew my hair, combed my fringe forward, as did just about everybody else, and ended up looking a bit like Paul McCartney. The girls loved that, but my voice, which was always a bit adenoidal, sounded more like John Lennon. I developed that by accentuating my existing northern accent, and this in turn enabled me to play on my remote Liverpool roots. As far as the girls were concerned, I was the nearest available Beatle. I didn't really have any Liverpool roots, apart from some very distant relatives of my grandmother's, I believe, who lived in Birkenhead. That was close enough as far as I was concerned. I only ever met them once or twice, when we went to Blackpool, and eventually they moved to Fleetwood further up the coast to run a chip shop. Thereafter we all lost touch.

I knew then I needed a guitar, and went into the music shop in Loughborough and got one. A six-string acoustic Selmer 222. It was what I now know to be a parlour guitar. Small-bodied with a wide fretboard. Too wide really to make it easily playable. There wasn't anything special about it. It was just affordable. About £5 I think, or about two weeks' paper round money. I still have it, battered and bruised though it is. My brother Martin bought a Lucky 7, I think around this time, which I recall as an electric acoustic, and he quickly got to grips with something called chords and taught me.

The Beatles went on to release their follow-up to 'Please Please Me', with 'From Me to You', which immediately hit number one, and then along came possibly the most perfect pop song ever written. 'She Loves You'. I have never ever known a musical force quite like it. For that's what it felt like. We were swept up in the whole Beatlemania thing, girls and boys alike. It was highly unusual for both sexes to be equally hooked, but we were. Our mums and dads were bewildered by it all, and looked on in bemusement at the madness which had gripped the teenagers. The Beatles became transformative in every conceivable way, especially possibility. Somehow, they smashed through every imaginable barrier.

All the Beatles became known by their names, and we knew immediately who they were when John, Paul, George and Ringo were introduced. Each one had individual (and very funny) personalities, which somehow combined with their identical suits on stage. Many clever people have tried to describe this effect, but for me the four individuals seemed to become one person. In other words, one individual with four separate and engaging personalities, each with which we could identify. It was most odd. In fact, very odd. Not only were they brilliant musicians and songwriters – well Lennon/MCcartney mostly – but they were funny and warm, somehow grown up and yet not. We devoured their every word and action. It was truly astonishing. We didn't really know then, but do now, that they had spent the previous three years or so playing the Cavern Club in Liverpool, and clubs in Hamburg, Germany. We thought they had just sort of appeared out of nowhere, which of course to us they had, but their skills and musical abilities were honed there. John Lennon once remarked 'I was born in Liverpool, but I grew up in Hamburg'. I got that, but it's an extraordinary statement from a twenty-two-year-old. He was only six or seven years older than me.

Much has been written about the band which changed the face of pop music forever, and even in the next 100 years I believe they will still be underestimated. However, of all these fantastic records, the song which rooted me to the spot more than any other in these early Beatle days wasn't written by them, was never released as a single, but put out on an EP (extended play). Records in those days were vinyl singles with an A and a B side. They cost six shillings and threepence (6/3d). I got all The Beatles' singles as they were released over the years, as well as the LPs (albums), and I still have all their singles on my 1963 jukebox. EPs were more expensive, and though they went round at the same speed as a single, 45 rpm, they usually had four other songs on them. 'Twist and Shout' was the EP. This was, and still is, one of the most visceral songs I've ever heard. The words are rather pointless, but the gut feel of the opening bars still to this day send shivers down my spine.

I learned much later that 'Twist and Shout' was done in one take, when Lennon's voice was ragged and at breaking point. This song proves it. Evidently his vocal cords were soothed by drinking milk just before it was recorded. You'll hardly be surprised to hear that my brother, who was still in the process of teaching me to play the guitar, and I formed a band more or less immediately in 1964. 'Twist and Shout', for me at least, was the song which inspired it.

Thirty years later Martin and I formed another band, the Ratley Snakes, sometime around 1994, when our jobs and careers were established and we had more time on our hands. 'Twist and Shout' was still a mainstay of our set, and stayed in it for twenty-five years. It's a bastard to sing though, and I can fully understand why Lennon had a problem with it. I did the lead vocal, with Mart on backing vocals, so we always left it till last, as a kind of encore. That song never failed to excite and rouse the audience. Interestingly, we played a gig for my niece's eighteenth birthday party in a barn near Stratford-upon-Avon. She'd invited most of her university mates of similar age, and to my utter amazement these kids were leaping up and down to our music, written and produced decades before. Quite honestly, I believed our set of predominantly 60s music would bomb, but no. Beatles music will continue to span the generations for generations.

Stop press: a few days after writing the above I read some reviews of The Beatles' 'Twist and Shout' on YouTube. There was a particularly memorable version of it in 1964, at their concert in Melbourne. Some of the reviews described the song as Lennon's 'rasping voice at his best' and of them creating a 'visceral sound'. There is unquestionably something unique about it. One comment suggested he was shirtless when it was recorded in Feb 1964 at 10.30 pm. It had been an all-day session, with the band recording the album *Please Please Me* (in one day). 'Twist and Shout' was the last one, and done in one take, first time (unheard of these days). As I said earlier, his voice wouldn't have lasted for a second take.

We revisited Loughborough recently. It hasn't changed much, for better or worse. It was a nothing kind of town when we lived there in the early 1960s, and so it remains. There are some things which haven't changed, like buildings, and what used to be the Essoldo cinema still exists but is now Beacon Bingo. There are one or two side streets which have been pedestrianised, but that's it. Boring. More cars of course, but the town's main claim to fame, or identity, is the university.

Our house was in Kirkstone Drive. But Windermere Way and Ullswater Close were fairly typical of the desire to give these bland and rather undistinguished houses some kind of identity. I guess the builders, before embarking on any development, sit down and subsequently come up with some kind of marketing angle, so even back then they were putting a Cumbrian slant on the place. I often wonder who these bright sparks are who come up with these themed names for dull housing estates.

I live near Pershore, we have Plum Tree Walk and Apple Blossom Way, and since Pershore is renowned for growing fruit, I kind of get that. But Cumbrian names in Leicestershire? A county which couldn't be in further contrast to the mountains and lakes of Wordsworth and Beatrix Potter?

Anyway, Loughborough is where we lived, because my dad had moved his job, and Humphrey Perkins was the school I was designated to attend, as you now already know.

The school of course is where I first had proper contact with girls. The population was 50/50, and as far as I can recall they were all boys or girls. There was no choice of gender, though I recall one or two of both sexes were suspect. But then homosexuality was a criminal offence in the 1960s. In 2020 we now have LGBT (lesbian, gay, bisexual and trans) considerations, and this means that some people can decide what gender they want to be. In other words, if they aren't sure, they can be transformed into someone (or something?) else, but more importantly they can be seriously offended if addressed wrongly. Maybe that should be 'dressed wrongly'. I don't get it.

I used to use a scale for judging masculinity/femininity. Subconsciously I still do.

Basically plus ten to minus ten. Extreme maleness would be say + 10, and at the opposite end at –10 would be extreme femaleness. Marilyn Monroe for example I'd place at –10, Sean Connery perhaps a +10. Get my drift? Venture into minus territory as a man and you'll be gay, and by the same token lesbianism or degrees thereof would be in the plus area. As far as I'm concerned it works as a guide. I guess the 'don't knows' or 'not sures' of either sex would be around zero.

I'd like to think I was a +11. Appropriate, given my useless exam result.

I can't quite decide whether I should put my numerous and varied encounters with women down in one go or write the events as they unfolded. I'll just carry on as is and see where it leads, but it was Humphrey Perkins School in Barrow upon Soar where my womanising encounters began.

When I moved there in 1961 I knew I liked girls, but never realised in a million years that they found me attractive. Having been to an all-boys school prior to my move to Barrow, all the girls I'd ever met when I was perhaps nine or ten were playmates. I was far more interested in bird's nesting, football, and fishing, than any desire to get in their knickers. Puberty and Mountside Secondary in Leek changed all that.

I suppose the same can be said for girls too. They also develop equally, but to me they seemed to develop faster than the boys. It was catch-up time for me.

I mentioned Angela Allcock earlier at my primary school in Werrington. We were both about eight or nine and that first kiss, which in hindsight I believe her attraction to me was due more to my fame in the starring role as Joseph than any inherent desire to be my girlfriend. She was an early groupie. In fact, I turned out to be an actor of such mesmerising brilliance they gave me a starring role as a tree the following year. No one wants to kiss a tree, except maybe a squirrel?

Susan Walker also featured at Salters Lane Primary school. Even now I often think about what happened to her. My best mate was Stanley Leese. (Leese is a good old Staffordshire name.) But Stanley as a baby's name these days? It seems to be of a long-ago era. Both Stanley and I were smitten with Susan. She was truly gorgeous, and a natural bubbly blonde, in a Marilyn Monroe way (without the tits obviously) with bouncy hair. Stan and I decided to toss a penny to decide which half of her we would have. I won. I chose the top half. I hadn't realised at that age what I was potentially missing. Believe it or not, Stan was disappointed with the bottom half he got. So we shared her. Susan, needless to say, knew nothing of us carving her up. We just gazed at her in class with lovelorn emotion. Tricky are these feelings when you're only nine.

Beryl Van Houten, who has already featured, was out of reach (cue gnashing of teeth). Interestingly, she had black hair and dark eyes similar to my teacher, whereas Susan was the complete blonde opposite. Snow White and Rose Red. I fancied them both but had no idea why.

I never could work out, and still can't, my woman preference. However, small blonde women I find I'm naturally attracted to. I'm convinced Susan Walker was (and still is) responsible for that.

My arrival at Humphrey Perkins was another steep learning curve. This was when things really started, and my first serious girlfriend was Sandra, the complete opposite of blond and small. Dark hair, brown eyes, and, for her age, impossibly big tits. She was thirteen and an early developer. I was maybe by this time fifteen. I fall in love easily. Once I'm in, I'm in, as it were, and I went down with this one hook, line and sinker. That's the problem when your hormones take over.

I'd had a few early flirtations with one or two other girls. In fact, in my very first week at this new school I had a note handed down from desk to desk from a quite attractive girl in class who wanted 'to go out with me'. Then there was another, who said the same thing, but who wrote the entire words out to The Beatles' 'She Loves You' in her letter. I had a snog and a fling with both of them (not at the same time). I'd then be about fourteen, but had become aware of something. I'm not sure what it was, just something.

Sandra however was my target, and lusted over by half the boys in my year, so maybe there was an element of competition. She was in the year below me. I honestly can't recall how it all happened, but it did, and we became an 'item' for a good eighteen months. It was an affair of such intensity I was convinced we'd get married. We wrote notes of love to each other constantly when we weren't together, and had an unbearable ache when apart. We were hopelessly in love. And we were only kids.

Losing your mind like this, and becoming fixated on one thing, caused me to lose all interest in any kind of schoolwork. I became indolent and half-arsed about everything. Every song about love or heartstrings had been written only for us. Dusty Springfield's 'I

Only Want to Be with You'. Sandie Shaw's 'Always Something There to Remind Me'. Exclusively mine and Sandra's. We were totally locked into each other to the exclusion of the whole world. How on earth does this fixation happen?

Looking back now though, this obsession I had with her reminds me of an old Cherokee maxim, counselled by an old squaw to a young bride-to-be: 'Remember this: The harder his cock gets the softer his brain becomes'. I hate to admit it but I'm afraid that's what happened to me. The rather more scary aspect of this, when you think about it rationally, is that, subconsciously and perhaps unknowingly, all women know this.

A little side story

It's worth a paragraph or two about Sandra. She lived in Barrow upon Soar and had a twin sister, who actually looked nothing like her. Nice family, her dad was a banker, or in some other upright and secure sort of job. Also, a brother whose name I've forgotten, Colin I think, but he was older by about three or four years, and both the sisters waited on him hand and foot. I found this puzzling. It was part of the 1950s mentality that women were only made to serve men, and this was presumably reinforced by her father on the two younger girls. This family of five regularly went to Cromer for their hols. It was either there or Skegness. Skeggy, as we called it. Cromer is quite famous for crab, and Sandra, to my astonishment, knew how to dress crabs. It was a talent I never suspected from this curvy, modern 60s girlie. I love all kinds of seafood, my dad persuading me to try whelks in Rhyl on our own holidays, with salt, vinegar and pepper, so crab was a positive luxury. Sandra made the most fantastic crab sandwiches. I was impressed. Most girls I knew were usually scared of stuff like this. It tended to be a man thing, ripping off claws and legs.

Sandra's brother was an arse who ruled the roost. I didn't like him at all, and I'm pretty sure he disliked me, since I had taken the attention away by dating his servile sister. Nevertheless, I let him off a bit because he loved The Searchers. 'Sweets for my Sweet' and 'Needles and Pins' were riding high at this time. 'When You Walk in the Room' is still a favourite of mine. It's on my old jukebox. Whenever I hear The Searchers, those memories come flooding back.

Sandra had a bad case of BO. All my family commented. It lingered horribly, with a cloying smell, which remained for quite some time after she'd been to my house. Oddly, I never noticed it. Well, I sort of did, but was too busy concentrating on other things. I was so highly charged, I just couldn't wait to find an isolated place and get her clothes off.

We'd duck into alleyways so I could get my hand up her skirt. Well hidden in the long grass alongside the River Soar at Cotes, I would pull her knickers off. Bus shelters, even on her kitchen floor at 4 pm before her parents got home, cinema seats in the back row, and so on. I was obsessed, and so, I think, was she. The BO thing was of no consequence. I was completely oblivious to it. The Cherokee maxim had taken a hold of me like no other, but at least there was a mutuality in our joint molestation. It has to be admitted that she wasn't terribly skilled in her handling of me, and frankly my techniques were crude to put it mildly, but we were learning. And why not at that age? Besides, hold-ups and tights hadn't been invented, which meant stockings and suspenders were common. It was a huge turn-on for a boy of my age.

This was 1963/4 but in the late 1950s we'd contented ourselves with black-and-white nude photos of women. Most of the ones we found were in tattered old 1950s magazines. Where we got these mags I can't recall, but one of the gang at Werrington would occasionally turn up with one. They were usually soaked, having been flung in some ditch, so we dried out the pages. This could sometimes take time, and we had trouble containing our impatience, but nevertheless it was a big event when one of us showed up with a 'dirty old man' mag. Separating the pages wasn't easy, and we took great care to avoid tearing the pictures. The very furtiveness created an excitement of its own, and we'd usually sneak off somewhere to a shed, or disused outhouse, to smirk, dream and giggle. All these photos of nude models invariably had the pubic area blanked out, but we all crowded together to fantasise. Marilyn Monroe was the epitome of the perfect woman in the 1950s and early 60s, as was Jayne Mansfield, and the object of every schoolboy's desire. To actually see a woman showing off her tits was enough to make an eleven-year-old boy go mad. By the time I was fifteen I was able to put all these fantasies to the test by having a real-live version in the grass. What more could a testosterone-fuelled kid want?

We were an exclusive 'item' in school for well over a year. I was by this time about 16+. She would have been 15+.

At some point she took off with her year group on a school trip for a week to Aberglaslyn, near Betws y Coed, on a coach with a group of about twenty-five others. It was an outward-bound adventure place, canoeing, hiking and so on. I missed her terribly. She would ring me from a call box for sixpence, and I would call her back at my parents' expense, but I noticed as the week progressed that her tone on the phone altered. It was almost imperceptible, but I'm nuanced and sensitive to stuff like this and felt some kind of unease.

She was coming back on the Friday, and I arranged to meet her off the coach in Loughborough. I got there, and when the bus came in there was no sign of her. Two girls I knew well, one of whom seemed to fancy me, told me she got off in Barrow upon Soar, where she lived, two stops back, and then delighted in telling me she had spent virtually the whole journey on the back seat snogging some guy I didn't know.

I was shocked and shattered. When I got home I was shaking with disbelief. My mum put her arms round me and I cried my eyes out (the first and last time I have ever done this). I tried to call her several times at her house but no answer. In the end I got the bus over to there. My mum begged me not to lose my temper before I went. After knocking the door, she eventually opened it, and looked pale. She said she was tired and she planned to call me

41

in the morning, but she didn't know what I knew. I asked her to go for a walk with me and in a quiet spot I absolutely exploded with rage. She burst into tears, and it was over. I realised I had placed all my faith and loyalty in her and I felt exposed, hurt, and above all humiliated. I couldn't face school on the Monday. I felt she'd made a laughing stock of me. My pride was severely damaged. I caught the bus home, turning these events over in my mind. My instinct was to kill this guy, but I still had no idea who he was. But then equally she was as much to blame, surely? I had effectively lost control and I was adrift with anger.

Retribution, retaliation, revenge were uppermost, but then quite suddenly I calmed down and thought it through. The Beatles film *Help!* (which I'd seen already) was showing at the Essoldo that very week, and I saw the poster through the bus window on the twenty-minute journey back. My brother and I knew all the songs by heart. I can still remember all The Beatles' albums in song sequence, and without warning round and round in my head I started singing, 'For I have got another girl'. I hadn't, but it wasn't long before I did. Maybe I just had a moment of realisation, and it was now time to move on. So I did.

Emotions like this are hard to deal with at sixteen / seventeen, and it took some time for me to come to terms with it all. My cocky, arrogant self had been given a dose of comeuppance, but it also forced me to examine my feelings, which were, frankly, all over the place. In short, I grew up. There and then, in the space of a few days. Pride, assertion, confidence, love, loyalty, betrayal, trust; all of these swirled around in my head jostling for supremacy and gave me many sleepless nights. I couldn't handle it; there was no one to turn to, and my pride simply wouldn't allow it. I actually thought I was going to die. Surely no one had ever felt like this before, had they? I wallowed in self-pity for days, and I'd like to think I have never indulged in this humiliating state of mind since. I despise it in others. Someone once said it's not the size of the dog in the fight, but the size of the fight in the dog. I suppose that's another version of 'when the going gets tough, the tough get going'.

In the end I did come to terms with it, but it took a week or so, and unquestionably was a turning point for me emotionally. Not just then, but for life. I guess some people who find it hard to cope under circumstances like this go down. When you think of all the love songs ever written, it becomes clear that a cosmic emotional upset such as this (as I saw it), which for me was so cataclysmic, had been felt by millions. It wasn't just me, then? Surprise, surprise, I thought it was. That's pretty much how I dealt with it. I realised these feelings weren't unique to me. By then I was determined not to go down in a heap. There was only one solution as far as I was concerned. Revenge.

There was a girl at school named Marion. She was gorgeous, seemingly unattainable, the envy of many of the girls, and all the boys fancied her, including me, but none I knew had succeeded. I targeted her. She had long auburn hair and the greenest of eyes (a combination I still find alluring), and in a matter of days I cracked it. Or should I say her. I took her out several times, and behaved like a gentleman. I never did get into her knickers, despite trying hard. She also proved to be incredibly boring, and not a bit like the smouldering sex goddess which was Sandra. Virtually the opposite, in fact, without the BO. Word got round the school of course, and it wasn't long, maybe two or three weeks, before I got a note via the school postal service from Sandra telling me she'd made a huge mistake and could we rekindle the romance. I let her stew for a while, and then took her out. I was surprised, in fact amazed, that when we did meet, astonishingly, I just didn't fancy her any more. Was it damaged goods? Mistrust? Maybe I was unable to get past the betrayal I felt.

The rose-tinted blinkers were truly off, and I realised I had been infatuated from the outset. Such events have moulded me, and it was a steep learning curve. You could say it was the price of an education, but not one I'd ever want to repeat. I don't know now, and guess I'll never know, how my feelings were able to change so quickly. Interestingly, the handsome, good-looking muscle-bound guy I had conjured up in my head, and who'd stolen my girl, looked anything but when he was finally pointed out to me. Fairly nondescript to look at, and in fact a bit of a weed. My imagination got in the way of reality.

If I felt anything at all, it was disappointment with her choice. The result of all this, the silver lining if you like from this big black cloud, produced a swagger in me, some might say conceit. I hope not, but it's likely. I knew now without a shadow of a doubt that I could attract women. I'd never really considered it before, but suddenly I knew, and I regained an immense confidence in myself.

Marion didn't last long, and then there were others. I've slept with a lot of women during my life; I have the approximate total in my head, and there it will probably stay, but one thing I learned above all else was to never ever allow my emotions and feelings to be quite so exposed. I thought I was dying at the time with all the hurt, so I built a hard shell around my heart, locked it up, and never allowed that to happen again. And I haven't. It's a control thing, I think, but also self-preservation.

Only my wife Ailsa has unlocked it. She's the only one who has, and it took me until I was fifty to allow the key into it.

By 1965 the Sandra thing was pretty much dead and buried, and I was onto my third or fourth girlfriend. It almost became a quest, a game in some ways, and I had only one intention uppermost in my mind. That was to get a ten out of ten with each girl I took out.

My brother Martin and I had formed a band earlier; it was inevitable for us to follow the Beatles (the last name we had for it was Finnegan's Wake), and at that time we had Glyn, a friend of ours who lived locally but went to the grammar school. He played bass on a homemade one he'd made in woodwork class. The bass was crap, as was Glyn. Brom, my best ever friend from school bus days, replaced him, and a guy he knew, Mick, who came in on drums. Suddenly it came together, and very well. Brom and Mick had played in a school band The Villains, the band had broken up, as they do when members leave or take up with some girl, so priorities change. Brom and Mick came on board with us. I did lead vocals and rhythm guitar (I still have the guitar), and Mart did lead. We were keen on The Kinks, and in my case, Small Faces. The Beatles, as history shows, were untouchable. The moment a single or album came out it was a must-have. I still have all the original vinyls and singles from that time. Bob Dylan was a force to be reckoned with too, and 'Subterranean Homesick Blues' was and still is one of my all-time favourites, just brilliant, but not the masterpiece 'Like a Rolling Stone' was. Brom was a huge Bob Dylan fan and he influenced me in the rock/folk scene. Bob Dylan's *Bringing it All Back Home* for me is possibly one of the best albums on the planet. *Blonde on Blonde* took over as my favourite, but that was still a couple of years away.

And this is the main problem with this period in the mid-60s. There were some incredible songs released. We were truly spoiled. It was a great time to be alive, and be in a band. The Who, The Kinks, especially 'Waterloo Sunset', which holds a huge number of memories of my time after I left school. Small Faces, Them, The Pretty Things, The Searchers, Hollies, the songs and the bands just seemed to keep on coming. The Beatles were well above them all and each album was better and different to the previous one. They were constantly changing and pushing boundaries. I say we were truly spoiled, but I think we knew it. It was like lifting the lid of a volcano. Then there were the Rolling Stones.

It was on a trip to Penarth in South Wales in and around late 1964 that my brother and I went with Dad on one of his business trips, in his company car, a Morris Minor Traveller. We must have been on a school holiday or something, and it was the first time, and last, that we accompanied him on a sales business trip.

I recall Penarth as grim, dark and dirty. Dad stayed in a B&B, and, as always with him, wouldn't put Mart and I down as a company expense, so we slept in sleeping bags and blankets in the back of his Morris Minor overnight with a torch for company. Penarth is also notable to me for one very important thing. It was the first time I ever heard the Rolling Stones.

In a way it was another 'Please Please Me' moment. The Light

Programme (Radio 1 was still a few years away) was on, and this old car had one of those radios with valves, which glowed on the dashboard. We listened to it as we snuggled down in the back of the car he'd parked round the back of this cheap hotel.

Suddenly, as Mart and I were talking in our makeshift bed, 'All Over Now' came on. I loved it immediately, wanted to hear it again, but as usual it went back to some bland and anonymous music. I hunted this record down and bought it as soon as we were home. I still have it, and it's still on my old 1960s jukebox. This song stayed in our band set for years and years. I used to sing the line 'playing her high-class games' even though it never quite seemed right to me. Only recently, fifty years on, for God's sake, I discovered by listening to it carefully, that Jagger sang 'playing her half-assed games'. A much better line!

I was always vaguely aware of the Stones, for whom The Beatles had donated 'I Wanna Be Your Man' as their first single, but that wasn't a song which 'grabbed' me much. 'All Over Now' was the one that catapulted them to stardom.

It was the second one they released, and which they'd written themselves which really sealed my fate as a lifelong Stones fan. 'The Last Time'. It took me years to find and play the riff which Brian Jones, on his Vox Teardrop guitar, opened the song with. It also has an echoey, snarling feel to it. Even now when I play it on my jukebox it never ceases to make the hair on the back of my neck stand up.

It was around this point that I bought the first Stones album. On there were a number of songs which weren't written by them, 'Down the Road Apiece', 'Everybody Needs Somebody To Love', with a brilliant sliding bass into it. 'Mercy Mercy', 'Down Home Girl'. I think my brother probably got it right when he said the later Stones albums lost some feel, and that they are best known for the singles. I think this is true. Actually there aren't that many, compared to The Beatles, but 'Jumping Jack Flash', 'Honky Tonk Women', and 'Brown Sugar' are probably the most notable ones. I lost touch with the Stones around *Exile on Main Street. Sticky*

Fingers was probably the last Stones album I bought, but having seen them four or five times live, they are unquestionably, if not *the* best, one of the best rock bands in the world. Though I think AC/DC are a close second!

If I ever thought I could reduce my song choices to eight discs for a desert island, I was profoundly mistaken. I keep reiterating this, but music is surely the most important means to recreating the past, and jogging memory.

So far, it's been mostly music and women that more or less defined my life. My school days were a blur, with no real thought about academia whatsoever. We did have one political interlude in 1962/3 with the Cuban Missile Crisis, and the world was about to end tomorrow, but it was a sideshow for me compared to music and girls. I do recall the death of Kennedy, on Nov 22nd 1963, and of course the Great Train Robbery, an audacious heist to relieve a mail train of £3m or something of that order, but although I read the news, or at least the headlines on my paper round, none of it seemed very important or relevant. I strongly suspect this biography will continue in that vein. The music, as did my various relationships, seemed at that time to take over my world.

Isn't it just wrong to expect fifteen-year-old kids to have to knuckle down, go to school, study for exams, and actually be interested in news and politics, when all their heads are full of short skirts, tit sizes, testosterone, and appearance. These were just so much more interesting.

In order to keep up with some attempt to look like a Beatle, I had my Cuban-heeled winkle-picker Beatle boots, which I hid in the saddlebag of my bike. My dad wouldn't approve. This autocratic generation imposed their standards on us, and it was a struggle. His generation favoured 'sensible' shoes. In my case I'd cycle off to town on some date, then change down the road out of sight and swap shoes, changing back before I got home. Cuban-heeled boots, as worn by The Beatles, actually did me a favour. I was and still am a short arse at 5 ft 7 in, but adding another inch to my height made me feel so much better. I couldn't have given a shit about the shenanigans of Mr Krushchev and President Kennedy.

I left school in Dec 1965. I didn't so much leave as was shown the door. I was just seventeen. I didn't feel expelled, but that was what it amounted to. I'd completed my O levels, but badly, in June 1965, and got three out of the four I needed to enable me to go into the 5th form and study for A levels. I was compelled to retake another to qualify, which was English. Mr Fletcher, my English teacher, didn't like me, and I didn't like him either. He'd given up on me, but my mum hadn't. She insisted I retake it. I was left in no man's land for a couple of months, neither, as the saying goes, fishing nor mending nets, until I retook the English exam.

Sometimes I'm inclined to blame Sandra for my lackadaisical attitude to schoolwork, but if I'm honest with myself, it wasn't that, I was just lazy. I was reasonably good at sport, and the houses we were allotted when I first got to school years before were red, blue, yellow and green. As I said earlier, I was put in Beaumont, the yellow house. It proved to be the weakest house at just about everything. For a while I was Beaumont's swimming captain. This house lost most of the time at virtually all the sports we played against the other houses. I've always had an affinity with water, and thank my dad for teaching us to swim at an early age. I won the 100m freestyle for Beaumont. I was famous for ten minutes. That was probably my only school triumph, but at least it gave Beaumont some momentary fame. I sometimes wonder if this clubby inter-school competitiveness was responsible for my general dislike of all clubs and associations.

Rugby, tennis, football, cricket (no, I didn't apply to be in the team), athletics, Humphrey Perkins provided an opportunity for all of them, more so than Mountside in Leek. I liked field sports, and gymnasium training, until I broke my left wrist in 1964 coming off a trampoline and landing on the floor head first with my left arm trying to break the fall. It was never reset properly at the hospital, and I put my inability to play the guitar properly down to this disability in my wrist my, since I couldn't bar chords up the neck. I reckon it's because of this injury that I never became the legendary rock guitarist I always intended, and why I was demoted to the lead singer with the band. My guitar techniques were, frankly, crap.

I was good at Art, and the same with Geography and Biology, and not bad at English, but it was always the grammar which stumped me. I was also crap at Chemistry, Physics, and especially Woodwork and Metalwork. I once made a poker, took it home, and by the time it had poked the fire a couple of times it fell to bits. Same with dovetail joints in woodwork. Mine never quite fitted unless I used a hammer to thump them into place.

I was sixteen when my Art teacher, and to my shame I can't recall his name, thought I had talent. He suggested I apply to go to Leicester Art College. He put the application in for me, together with some of my paintings, and they offered an interview. When the letter turned up at home my father stared at it, rolled it up, then threw it in the bin. 'Graphic fucking artist? Wankers! That's no job. Graphic fucking artists? Ten a fucking penny.' I wouldn't be going to art college, then.

His attitude was the same with music. Any guitar practice Mart and I did had to be behind his back. He hated us 'twanging those fucking things'. Looking back, I find it sad. There was no artistic or creative encouragement whatsoever. And yet he proved in later life to be a good writer, and later I discovered he'd written quite a bit of poetry during the war. Regrettably, I don't have any of those poems; my sister has them, I think, though they may be lost.

As a careers adviser my father proved useless.

Anyway, I retook my English O level, but way too late. Ma had given me some coaching for the precis bit of the exam, and I nailed it. I passed. I wanted to shove the certificate up Fletcher's arse, the bastard who said I was useless. Regrettably he'd left the school, no doubt to fuck up other pupils' chances elsewhere.

I'm not sure how the head had been keeping tabs on me. Mr R Dunn had small weasly handwriting. I judge people on that. Large and expansive script means kind and generous; small, tight and cramped means the opposite. He was that all right. The tightly signed-off letter to my parents in essence implied I was disruptive, rebellious and didn't fit in. He was right, I probably was, but I didn't see it like that. I always was questioning in class, and petty rules needed explanation. I naively thought the teachers would have perhaps appreciated that. Not so. I was out. Disappointed, rejected, and summarily ejected. It was expulsion plain and simple, but in diplomatic language. I can see how difficult I would have been to manage, but on balance the school wanted a quiet life. Deep down though I was ready for the off. Several of my close friends had left to pursue different, what are known laughingly as, career paths, and the place just didn't feel the same. Mr Dunn made the right decision.

As far as careers advice went, there wasn't any. Well apart from my mad, and hated, English master Fletcher, who had been appointed to this sideline task at school, and he had no time for me. Looking back, I get the impression that some teacher or other draws the short straw when taking on the position as a career adviser. Almost an afterthought, a lucky dip. I could imagine them drawing names blindfold out of a bucket in the staff room. Poor old Fletcher. Guess what? He's got to do it this year.

The school curriculum was wide and covered everything from Latin to modelling lumps of clay, but nowhere was there anything which prepared kids for the outside world. Commerce, finance, credit cards, budgeting, interest rates, all the kind of stuff you encounter when you leave. That's the minefield. The career advice I got was dreadful. Uninspiring. No attempt whatsoever to explore a talent, any talent which might lead thought processes to a purpose, a direction. When I sat down with Fletcher, he had a pile of brochures and application forms on his desk. He could hardly contain his boredom as he leafed through them. Mostly trainee courses for banks, building societies, local council admin or some other unutterably dull job.

All in all it was hardly aspirational stuff.

Chapter 4

I wish I'd had a calling. Some people do, doctor, pilot, scientist, but not me. I was a dreamer, highly ambitious but in a vague and unplanned way. I vaguely thought I might be an actor, or a hairdresser. My dad soon quashed that airy-fairy, arty-farty idea. This is how I ended up with five jobs in less than two years. My dad was probably the opposite of Fletcher. He knew best. And because he was a domineering dad, I went along with his suggestions. He said I liked the countryside, which was true, therefore a life herding cows would suit me down to the ground. Farm management was the thing, out in the fields and woods, driving a tractor, I'd love that. Well, I didn't.

The job I got was six days a week on Mr Barker's farm 9 miles from Loughborough near Seagrave. I became a farm labourer. An ignominious start. A nothing job. A gofer. I cycled the 18-miles-a-day round trip, which at least got me fit, but I had to be there at 6 am, which meant leaving at 5.30 latest. I was usually knackered when I got there. This was January 1966, and the weather was typically shite. I'd arrive in the yard, still pitch dark, in my yellow oilskin cape, usually soaked, and then go and help milk the cows, with toothless old Ned, and John the farm manager, who knew about cows and jazz. He introduced me to Stan Getz in fact. *Desafinado*. I bought the vinyl album, but it wasn't really my thing.

I did however learn to drive a tractor, which later helped me pass my driving test, and got to know the names of most of the milking cows. Generally, though, I wasted time in between, looking for skylark or peewit nests when I was sent to bring in the cows. There were loads of rats too, and to waste a bit more time I would try to stab one or two in the feed barn with a pitchfork. That is until Barker's collie dog was electrocuted while chasing one. The grain bin had become live as it swayed in the wind, the corrugated iron sides cut through an electric cable. The dog slid on the spilled grain, hit the side, leapt up into the air and came down stone dead and twitching on the concrete. I think touching the bin with its wet nose didn't help. I'm just bloody glad it was the dog and not me.

You won't be surprised to hear I didn't last long with this lot. I was sacked after a few months with one week's notice. Besides I felt I needed some 'status' in my career, not cow shit and mud. I had plans. What they were I've no idea, but this wasn't for me. Nevertheless, I felt aggrieved. It was another Fletcher and eleven-plus moment. In retribution for my sacking I 'accidentally' sprayed the Barkers' rose bushes with weed-killer on my last Saturday morning. I got on my bike after that and buggered off with my final wage packet, which I blew down the pub later. I meant to go back to the crime scene but never did. This had been my first proper paid job, and this so-called career earned me £5 17 shillings for a six-day week, nine-hour days, plus travelling. I considered it slave labour. My uphill paper round was easier.

I didn't so much decide, more of an idle thought really, that an office job might be a better proposition. At least I was out of the wind and rain, and the hours were more agreeable, not that the pay was much better. I went after an invoice clerk's job with Bass Mitchell & Butlers, a brewery depot in Loughborough. Despite failing Maths O level, I could at least add up. I was offered that, and accepted.

Unquestionably this was a man's world, full of burly, hairy-chested, hairy-arsed draymen. They drove dray lorries, and delivered beer. Hogsheads, barrels, kils and firkins. 54, 36, 18 and 9 gallons in that order. They slung these around with ease. Why these vehicles were called drays I have no idea – from the days of dray horses perhaps. All of them looked like Desperate Dan, and thought nothing of drinking ten pints on their rounds during the day, arriving back in the afternoon, semi-pissed in charge of these 10 ton trucks. It reminded me a bit of a pirate ship. I was Jim

Hawkins, completely out of my depth with the banter. It was a ribald environment all right, where all I did was learn to smoke and drink.

The office was occupied by three or four of us, and permanently filled with smoke, jokes, and drink. The walls were yellow ochre with nicotine stain. The red-faced depot supervisor would sit at his desk muttering 'Auntie Mary had a canary up the leg of her drawers' or lapse into 'Semi-detached Suburban Mr James'. A two-bottle-a-day beer allowance was the norm, and there'd be a big crate of Allbright Ale in the office on permanent standby. Such was the culture, I could drink this stuff all day every day. As the day progressed my invoice figures wouldn't add up. By four in the afternoon, I was so pissed I struggled to see the comptometer print out. I put on weight, began to swear like the real men, then wobble home on my bike at 5 pm. However, I was taking driving lessons by now, and the tractor practice on the farm stood me in good stead. Within a few months and only a few lessons I passed first time. I was after a car now, and got my hands on a Standard Eight. Once I got that I was then able to drive home pissed, just like the real men.

I can't recall which girlfriend I had at the time, but I'm fairly sure she was a sixth-former from Rawlins school. She aspired to be an actress, but one thing I did discover was how useful the back seat of my old car was for a few performances.

The job and the actress didn't last six months. I was bored rigid stamping delivery sheets, but now keeping up with the drinking and filthy banter. I just wished I'd known at this time what I wanted to do, but I didn't. My dad had become increasingly exasperated with my indolence, and I can see why. Two jobs in the space of less than twelve months, and I was useless at both.

I was still seventeen, just about to turn eighteen, and I to this day don't know how I found the application. More likely it was my dad, he really wanted me gone, out of the house. My mum always had a tendency to be overly protective towards me. I'm no psychologist, but I think he saw her forgiveness of my behaviour as some form of disloyalty to him. They were never united in their approach to their kids. In many ways Martin and I had it worse, since Dad tended to turn a blind eye to sister Julia's tantrums. There was an inequality of sorts. Even-handed it most certainly wasn't, and I bore the brunt of this semi-dysfunctional unit. Arguments were frequently settled by fists. For my mum's sake I tried hard not to retaliate, but this rebellious aggressive streak I seem to have was honed here.

My third attempt at a career was something altogether different. I went for an interview in Birmingham for a trainee surveyor's job with the Ordnance Survey. I passed the interview and was offered a place. This time based in Southampton.

Chapter 5

It's a big city. It was daunting, and my dad, with some relief I'm sure, put me on a train in Derby one Sunday afternoon, together with my suitcase, wished me good luck, and strode off down the platform. It was more like good riddance.

The Ordnance Survey is a branch of the civil service, tasked with mapping. Apparently, it originated in the army, presumably to map troop movements or arms dumps. I never did find out. What I'd embarked on was a nine-month trainee surveyor course, split into three-monthly sections. I had to pass each stage to move on to the next. In other words, one at a time. Aged about eighteen, I clambered on to this filthy train with my old suitcase, and wondered what next. My destination was a guest house off the Bassett Road. I was very apprehensive. My first time away from home, and I was, literally, having to find my own way. This was a difficult time for me, and my self-esteem was at odds with my self-belief.

Like the headmaster at school, who'd effectively asked me to leave, my father also seemed to see me as a disruptive and argumentative individual. I know it's accepted as normal in most families that the eldest child tends to be on the receiving end, and generally bears the brunt of change, but my father and I were forever locking horns, just like stags do. I suppose I was a real pain in the arse to him, but he was hardly a pushover. He had an antipathy toward any kind of authority, under no circumstances would he be dictated to, took on all kinds of argument, whether with religious belief, local council, neighbours, work colleagues, or us kids, you name it. He was one of the most aggressive and contentious individuals I've ever known. Surprisingly, he couldn't see the same streak in me, and let's face it, he started it all.

I forgive him now. We are always learning as parents. His upbringing in Stoke, RAF service, losing his elder sister Jocie at twenty-two to kidney failure. All this I think affected him as a child, and society today would probably recommend therapy. The very suggestion of that would have sent him into a rage. I still to this day however can't see how he lacked the wisdom and foresight to see how his own behaviour had been shaped, and thus learn to deflect, utilise or harness the natural spirit or talents in his own children, such as they were. Maybe it's just a generational thing. I really don't know.

I like to think I recognise that same fault structure in myself, and have tried to be careful not to repeat this same behavioural pattern in the treatment of my own children. Discipline is one thing. Severe beatings quite another.

Dragging my old suitcase from the station on a wet Sunday night, I eventually arrived at my digs, a huge old Victorian house. I met up with the other trainees, was allocated my room, and discovered I was sharing with a couple of them. It was more of a dormitory, and there and then I developed an immediate dislike for sharing my bedroom. I couldn't fart, snore, or wank at will. I have the same problem with public toilets. If someone is in the next cubicle, I'm instantly constipated. This attitude, almost misanthropy, has stuck with me throughout my life.

Most of the guys in the digs were a bit older than I and some of them quite worldly. Oddballs most of them, and like my C stream classmates at school, I felt quite at home.

I signed on at the Ordnance Survey training camp in Bassett on the Monday morning. A dull grey block of offices up in Bassett. I knew I'd hate the job the minute I had to sign the Official Secrets Act. I signed in triplicate for the tools of the trade, and took possession of a set square, dividers, two rubbers and a few pencils, as well as a mobile technical drawing board. I couldn't for the life of me think of any Official Secret I was ever likely to discover. The assignment of these tools of the trade was hardly James Bond territory. Not exactly Lugers and Walther PPKs. Or Aston Martins.

It was routine. Par for the course. Admin. Whatever. I was now formally in the civil service. Home had been a prison camp of sorts, dominated by an overbearing, bullying father. This place felt like another.

The other guys on the course, about twelve to fifteen of them, were all about the same age as I, and generally good fun. The best thing I discovered, however, was the Ordnance Survey's Under Twenty-one Club, just down the road by the map printing office. I'd be down there most nights. It was no more than a glorified student common room. Bar, music, and above all women trainees, who were studying the art of drawing and printing maps. I made a beeline for them, and admit I had a whale of a time. Of them all, and some were seriously good-looking, one of the most interesting was a dark-haired, black-eyed, very attractive girl whose mother, I found out, was a trainee medium at the spiritualist church somewhere in Southampton. I hit it off with her, and she persuaded me to go to a couple of spiritualist meetings when her mum would be hosting the event. I learned a bit about the business of séances, and advice coming in from the cosmos. Most of it I thought was bollocks, but the throng there believed every word. It was some kind of hypnotism. At least I thought so.

My grandma, Nellie Broome, her of the scratchings and baking skills when I was a kid in Leek, died suddenly from a heart attack in 1967. It was the first time I'd been to a funeral, and I was dreadfully sad about that. I thought the world of her.

One particular night during one of these meetings some guest spiritualist guy attended, and proceeded to hold the audience in thrall. He was busy giving and dispensing advice to the believers when he suddenly broke off and stared at me. I was lounging near the back idly, wondering if I would ever get my hands on this girl's tits. He pointed at me, and said, 'You've recently lost a loved one?' (true). I froze and everyone stared. I nodded. He said she had a message for me. 'Patience in everything you do'. (false). He then went back to ministering to his adoring flock.

More questions flew through my mind, but I have to say as an atheist I was shocked. How he picked on me without warning I'll never know. This girl and I split up shortly afterwards, but I was seriously unnerved by this weird encounter. I never did get my hands on her tits, but by now I was on to my next encounter. This one was more worldly and less spiritual.

I got to know a guy, a few years older than me, who stayed in the guest house regularly, but worked elsewhere. He knew his way around, and had a souped-up Mini Cooper with a straight-through exhaust. Drove it mercilessly like a fucking go-kart. Great car.

One Sunday morning we went off with two girls from the YWCA. Both were American, and both were gorgeous, and on this occasion we took them to Stonehenge. That was a hell of an afternoon, hot and lazy. We lit a fire, and when we weren't rolling around in the grass, learned how to roast marshmallows in the embers. It's an American thing apparently. Returning them both to the YWCA later in the evening, and since men were not allowed in after 10 pm, I left about midnight via the fire escape stairs. I got to the bottom of the stairwell, which was dark, and suddenly out of the gloom I was 'attacked' by one of the other girl's rivals, who evidently fancied me, though I didn't know it. She gripped me, and went forcibly for my zip, and then literally ripped my shirt off, got me on the floor (I didn't resist), lifted up her skirt and sat on my face. She was a black American called Roz (pronounced Raaz in her best New York drawl). You'll be pleased to know I survived the experience. In fact, I quite enjoyed it.

These American girls were, it seems, just passing through. I never saw any of them again.

I'd been at the OS only a matter of weeks when we decided to have a beach party at Hengistbury Head. This place was between Bournemouth and Southampton. We walked forever across this heathland, and lit a big fire on the beach. I got so drunk on cider and gin I didn't know where I was, and gripping my guitar I tried to get back to the car a mile or two away, but fell into the waves. I was found half in and out of the sea apparently, and my mates dragged me out, and hauled me all the way back to the car. I have no recollection of this whatsoever. All I knew, when I woke up the following afternoon back in my digs, was my guitar made it, but was full of wet sand. I still have that guitar, the one I paid about a fiver for, and which even now rattles with bits of sand from that beach. I have never ever been as drunk since, and it took some time before I fully realised I could quite easily have drowned. It's a control thing, and I was out of it. Never again. Drowning isn't on my preferred list of ways to go.

In nearby Bournemouth, there was the Calypso Club. I'm not really a clubby type, but it was a good magnet for pickups. I learned to dance. Well sort of, more of a shuffle and a wriggle. Eddie Floyd's 'Knock on Wood' was the song of the moment. Hearing that takes me straight back. Great song to dance to.

As far as the trainee surveyors' course was concerned I did diddly squat. It consisted mostly of going round areas of Southampton, and measuring stuff with theodolites. I didn't understand them then, and still don't. Nevertheless, I was learning about things I would never have encountered in Loughborough, and even managing to have a good time on the £30-a-month salary. For me it was an opportunity to indulge. As far as the career path was concerned, I never once took it seriously.

One of my steeper learning curves took place at the Cowherds pub (still there, I'm told) on the Bassett Road, our regular Friday-night drinking haunt. It was there I first encountered shirt-lifters, as we called them in those days, but you'd know them better as gays. I had never ever met one of these 'queers', as they were also known, until then. One of the barmen, Graham, was that way inclined, but I was way too naïve to recognise his intentions towards me. I just thought he was extra friendly. Eventually one of my mates warned me. Graham wanted to know me so badly that he asked me if I would like to move out of the digs and come to live with him in his flat. I almost accepted. My taste for tomato juice and vodka had evidently been a sign that I was that way inclined too. Clearly, he'd misjudged me as much as I'd misjudged him, but he'd often gaze into my eyes and sigh a lot. Once I knew about these 'types' I was wary and on the lookout for the telltale signs. Hands on hips, camp pose, pouts, and so on.

I don't know these days if there is still a bigger proportion of gays in Southampton than any other town, but was told it was largely due to the number of ships and sailors that docked there. The problem for me with all this is that I have no difficulty accepting homosexuality, but I do have a problem with aggressively promiscuous homosexuals, and especially ones who try to hit on me.

I had hitchhiked home for a rare weekend in Loughborough. The journey took forever, via Basingstoke, London, M1, and eventually at 11 pm on a Friday night my dad picked me up from Leicester Forest East services where I'd been dropped by some lorry driver. I'd sloped off from the office early afternoon and it had taken me until then to make it. I went back on the train on the Sunday, more costly but less hassle. It was late when I got into Southampton, and as I lugged my suitcase up the Bassett Road back to my digs I noticed a furtive-looking guy following me. He eventually caught up, and offered to help carry my case. I declined his invitation but he became persistent, and in tiredness and anger I finally flipped, and punched him in the face. He went sprawling backwards over a little wire fence and landed in a flower bed. Appropriately enough I noticed it was a bed of pansies.

I doubt I could do that today without a knife being involved. I didn't hang around to look at my handiwork, and legged it back to the digs as fast as I could. I have Mr R C Neal, Headmaster at Mountside School in Leek, to thank for this. His introduction to boxing lessons when I was twelve came in handy.

You won't be surprised to hear I failed the first three months of the Ordnance Survey training course. I'll give the civil service its due, they didn't want to give up on me. It took me some time to realise that I'd given up on them. They made me do the three months again.

Now I'd kind of bonded with the original bunch of guys, and

developed a camaraderie of sorts, but they now moved onwards and upwards to part two of the course, whereas I went backwards and started from scratch, but this time with a new batch of recruits. I lost touch with the original lot, and in the process lost motivation, assuming there had been any to start with. Something I very much doubt.

Three weeks into the new course, and I'd been with some girl the night before, had a riotous time, and was thoroughly debauched. I recall the bed linen being soaked when I climbed out of it at 4 am to go back to my own place. Her room-mate had evidently slept through it all on the far side of her room, but a towel had come in handy to stifle the moans and groans.

I was knackered when I checked into the office at 8.30 that morning, but my assigned task was to survey some old WWII bomb site in the city. My supervisor cleared off to check on some other trainee, but it was such a nice day I fell asleep in the sunshine among the rosebay willowherb. And that's where they found me, snoozing against a pile of rubble. They more or less sacked me on the spot.

I've never had a distinction in any exam whatsoever, not even a gold star, although I did win an Osmiroid pen in a writing competition once when I was about ten. It was a surprise to learn that the first real distinction I ever gained in my life was to be the first trainee surveyor ever to be sacked from this course. I didn't blame them, I held no grudge, but they made me return every rubber and pencil I'd been given, and those I'd lost or broken I had to pay for, deducting the agreed few shillings from my final salary. This episode for me summarised the entire ethos of the civil service. Whitehall civil servants included. How bloody useless do you have to be to get the push? If I were a civil-service mandarin I'd take an axe to the lot of them, including me, who was possibly the most incompetent civil servant ever. And I definitely won't be applying to be James Bond any time soon.

If I held any grudge at all it was towards my father. Even today I still can't understand why he lacked the foresight to be more imaginative in his career advice, or even begin to attempt to provide some guidance or help, to channel whatever talent I had, or more importantly lacked, in some better direction. He simply didn't look beyond me getting a job, any job, whether it was the right job or a job which would lead somewhere useful. All I had ever wanted was to be an artist or a rock star. That was the kind of job I fancied. I just wish I'd had the courage to drop out, but then in a way I had. Except I was kicked out.

The overwhelming feeling I had at the time, and still feel now, is he just wanted rid of me. Out of the house and as far as career advice was concerned, well, there wasn't any. I can see how difficult it was for him at the time when he had an idle rebellious dreamer on his hands. I think he perhaps thought any job would do, especially one away from home. Some years before all this I'd applied to Findus Frozen Foods (they of the fish finger fame) to work on a trawler. I quite liked the idea of that, but didn't get far with it. I just thought it'd be fun to piss about on the sea. That was how empty-headed I was.

I left Southampton, and returned home, with Procul Harem's 'A Whiter Shade of Pale' at number one and 'Waterloo Sunset' in my head. Waterloo was the station I arrived at before changing for Leicester, and back eventually to Loughborough. Both those songs evoke memories of that time, but mostly bad ones.

I arrived back with my tail between my legs. I had lost an unloseable job. My dad subjected me to sarcastic derision at every opportunity, and I was ridiculed constantly. He then laid down even more rules. I felt a total and complete failure. And things were about to get even worse.

Chapter 6

I returned home after the sack from the Ordnance Survey. Having collected my final salary (in cash), minus the deductions for my lost pencils and rubbers, I walked out of the place on Friday lunchtime. It was June 1967. I never caught up with my original mates to say goodbye. 1967 is now known as the Summer of Love, and with total irresponsibility I decided to make my way down to an area of Southampton which was a haunt for prostitutes. My tail might have been between my legs, but my libido was very much intact, and in my head I thought I'd dare to see what opportunities lay in this seedy area. I have no idea why I did this, but thought I'd kill some time before catching the train back home to Loughborough, and waste some of the cash in my wallet.

A woman crossed the street and accosted me. She was blonde, wore sunglasses, and dressed in an orange two-piece suit. Brazenly I faced her. She lowered her sunglasses slightly, stared at me directly, and said, 'Five pounds if you're up for it, sonny.' My confidence evaporated. I legged it to the station. I just wished she hadn't said 'sonny'. She was about thirty-five, and me, just eighteen. Besides, I didn't like her orange suit.

So back I went to jolly old Loughborough, and once again to search for some kind of career direction.

Southampton had been very successful from a woman scoring aspect, but an unmitigated disaster as a career. I'd certainly tasted hedonism, but frankly the civil service should have known better than to employ me. I should have known better too.

With 'Waterloo Sunset' ringing in my ears, and Dad's sarcastic rants about my failure to hold down a job, I felt completely at odds with my world. I simply had no clue whatsoever about what I wanted to do. I truly envy people who have absolute certainty about a career path. Doctor, pilot, scientist, all seem to me to be callings. I had none. Apart from girls.

I was given a new set of rules to follow back home. Get a job pronto, be in by 10.30, make my own bed, and most importantly a contribution to the household budget immediately.

It's hard to believe now that my Ordnance Survey salary was about £35 a month net, and I had no savings. I was broke. £400+ a year, which wasn't much more than my farm labourer's wage packet. It all went on rent, food and piss-ups.

So the Ordnance Survey was the third job I'd had in the space of eighteen months, and I now needed another.

I had passed my driving test first time in December 1966, and driving a tractor was a big help in achieving that. That's about the only good thing which came out of my six-month career in farming. I had acquired my first car, a Standard Eight, and was now able to get about. I had some memorable times in that thing, as I alluded to earlier.

I got a job quite quickly as an invoice clerk with a Whitbread brewery depot, a distribution centre somewhere off the Derby Road in Loughborough and about a mile away from the other brewery depot, where I'd learned to swear and smoke like the real men, so I had previous, as it were. This was around mid-1967. I quite liked the place, and met some interesting people. It proved to be the longest job I'd ever held down so far and I almost felt I was a success at last. I'm afraid it didn't last that long though, about a year, which was a life sentence as far as I was concerned.

Once again I found I couldn't add up the invoices properly and got bollocked for it. The primary reason, just like the other place, was the two-bottle allowance each day. History began to repeat itself. I sometimes took my two-bottle allowance home, but occasionally the office staff would open the bottles in the morning, especially if it was someone's birthday. My preferred beer of choice was Flowers Brewmaster. Bloody strong stuff. In the event of such an occasion I was, once again, usually pissed by 11 am.

Faced with this temptation my ability to exercise some self-discipline was zero.

I wish I could say that I left Whitbread for health reasons, or from choice, but I can't remember exactly how we parted company. Mutual dislike probably, but the only thing which really stands out for me was a weedy little guy in despatch called Johnny, who was a few cards short of a full deck. At lunchtimes we would take the piss occasionally, and ask him to show us his cock. For a little guy he had the biggest one I've ever seen. He'd unzip his overall and lay it, and I do mean lay it, on a bench. He once lined up half a dozen old halfpennies alongside it to prove a point. Whether it ever got proper use though I very much doubt.

As I said earlier, 1967 is often referred to as the Summer of Love, and it was. The music at that time was incredible, and *Sgt. Pepper's Lonely Hearts Club Band* arrived. Many things have been written about that album, which was unlike any other the Beatles had produced. There are other albums which I prefer. *Revolver, Beatles for Sale, Hard Day's Night, Rubber Soul*, but this latest one took some getting used to. It isn't one of my favourites (though I do love 'Being for the Benefit of Mr Kite!'). Just before *Sgt. Pepper* was released the Beatles released 'Strawberry Fields'/'Penny Lane' to a mixture of reactions. Songs which I initially didn't much like, but which have grown on me down the years. However, a few months later they made a film, *Magical Mystery Tour*, and here was one song, perhaps my very favourite Beatles song of all. 'I Am the Walrus'.

I had settled into Whitbread OK and by the end of 1967 was having a whale of a time. Having been used to doing my own thing in Southampton I found it hard to adjust to the discipline of being home once more, my father locking me out of the house one night because I had failed to call to say I'd be late in. It's not cool to have to slope off to a phone box when you're with a bunch of mates down at the Barley Mow on a Saturday night, so I didn't call him to ask his permission to stay out.

This was the second time I'd done this, and he wreaked his

revenge and locked me out good and proper when I got back about midnight. On the first occasion when I failed to ask his permission to stay out longer than 10.30 pm I'd climbed on to the parapet beneath my bedroom window and tapped on it to wake my brother. He opened it to let me in. In the morning when he found out what had happened my dad was livid with both of us for defying him.

On this occasion, despite throwing stones at the window, my brother wouldn't dare open it. Dad had also bolted the doors to the house from the inside just to make sure my key didn't work. I was left with no choice but to break into the garage. To make matters worse it was snowing. I found an old carpet inside, and rolled myself into it. By 7 am on the Sunday morning I was blue with cold. My dad opened the door about 8 am. I was frozen, and my mum was in tears. He never uttered a word.

I then knew with certainty that I had overstayed my time here. This was now February 1968 and I really did need to get myself in gear and make some plans.

The Beatles film *Magical Mystery Tour* was released at the same time as the single 'Hello, Goodbye'. Appropriate given my unwelcome return to the family fold. The film itself hasn't really stood the test of time. It was mostly self-indulgent rubbish. Nevertheless, the songs were brilliant.

'I am the Walrus' is the one song though which has never left me alone. There was something about it I found intriguing. I didn't understand it and still don't, but have played it regularly for fifty-odd years. It's weird, surreal, meaningless, and magnificent – and I've never tired of listening to it.

I have no woman memories associated with it, or traumatic events, apart from this constant friction in the home, and stand-offs with my father. The only thing I do know is Lennon had heard that his English teacher back at his old Liverpool school was analysing some of his earlier songs as poems. Lennon was evidently scornful of this. 'I am the Walrus' was written randomly, writing one pointless line a day with the first thing that came into his head. The very aspect of this I really liked. When the song was finished and recorded, he evidently said, 'Let the fucker work that one out.'

The opening notes on the piano were inspired by the siren of a passing police car. Recorded radio-twiddling had never ever before been put on a song, and the 'yellow matter custard dripping from a dead dog's eye' was something I could easily identify with growing up in North Staffs. This was skipping rhyme from my time in the playground at Salter's Lane Primary School. 'Yellow matter custard, green snot pie, all mixed together in a dead dog's eye, mix it thin or mix it thick, and wash it down with a cup of cold sick.'

You won't be surprised to hear that the girls at that primary school taught me to skip. I only learned so I could get a glimpse of their knickers when their skirts flicked up and down.

By the time we got to mid-1968 I had been an invoice clerk at the Whitbread depot for eight or nine months. I knew it was dead-end and I was going nowhere. My wages were sufficient to make a domestic contribution, but tensions continued to rise at home. Dad again.

My brother Martin was in the final year of his A levels, and heading for college, seemingly already shaping his future. Mine was haphazard, uncertain, and my father bore down on me in every respect, finding fault with just about everything and anything I did (though he never locked me out again). Being the eldest of three siblings is hard work. It seemed to me almost as if I was the guinea pig my parents used to practise their parenting skills on. I accept though, that for my parents at least, I must have been a bloody handful, and an especially difficult guinea pig.

I've often wondered if my dad was born completely at odds with the world, and out of time with events. 'Stuck in a time warp' is a bit of a hackneyed old phrase, but his general resentment and pessimism against everything and seemingly everybody was in sharp contrast to my mother, who was always the optimist, unrealistically so at times, but didn't have a care. She sang at the kitchen sink, and was always full of enthusiasm. The Beatles and Rolling Stones she loved. Dad wasn't the least bit interested. I was now nineteen and my only ambition was to get a better car and junk the Standard Eight. I did in the end, selling it to my best mate. I bought a Ford 100E, with chequered go-faster tape down the side, and space enough on the back seat for whichever girl I was involved with.

We also continued with a band of sorts, first it was called the T Set in the early days, then I changed it to Finnegan's Wake. I took the name from a book I found lying around somewhere. I've never read it.

My brother, as I've said before, taught me to play the guitar when I was about fourteen. Martin was, and still is, by far and away the most musically gifted one, and he and I between us decided on the songs our band would practise. We played a few gigs, mostly Kinks and Stones stuff down at the local youth club. I was usually dressed in a salmon-pink polo neck and flared hipsters, and cut quite a dash as the lead singer. Well, I thought so. I was more amazed by the attention I got from some of the girls at the youth club, and needless to say made the most of it.

In many ways I wish I'd been allowed to go to Leicester Art College. My father, as I said, had quashed the very idea of it. I had an instinct, almost a calling, to do it and who knows what path that might have led me down. For me it just underlines a parental mindset prevalent in the 1960s. You will do this my way, and get a proper job. Whether you have a talent for it or not. I sometimes wish that both our parents had encouraged us to be musically more creative.

Nevertheless I was ambitious in a wholly unplanned way, but couldn't see much of a future. I was just idling my way through this job at Whitbread, which with hindsight I can now see. Now I'm older can understand more of my father's anger and frustration with his truculent air-headed son, but I never quite understood why he didn't harness this spirit, this creative streak such as it was. He just suppressed it. I resolved years later that I would never bully and squash any spirit or talent shown with my own children and I hope I haven't.

Around this time there were physical fights and extreme bouts of temper from my father, for both Mart and I. Beatings were common, especially when we were younger. I was asked by my mother to not respond and punch him, for her sake mostly. She would be in tears and weep for some time after altercations like this. She also got the brunt of his violence too, leading on one occasion to him punching her in the face. Her nose bled so badly they had to call an ambulance, and took her away. This was 1 am in the morning. We only found out when she came home later. We could hear the shouts and screams from the (relative) safety of our bedroom. Whether from this hair-trigger domestic environment or not, I found I was becoming ever more aggressive. It was a point in my life which could easily have led to my ending up in police custody. I can see it all now, but back then I couldn't.

I needed to make some changes quickly, more than anything to get out of this pressure cooker. I applied for assisted passage to Australia. I thought fuck it, if I'm going to make changes, they'll be big ones! The assisted passage cost £10, so around May 1968 I applied to Australia House for the forms, which I filled in, sent to Australia House, and after much to-ing and fro-ing with paperwork I was (eventually) accepted.

Almost at that very same time, mid-1968, my father threw me a newspaper ad for a Business Studies course at Redditch College, starting in September. It was grant-aided, and I needed four O levels, which I had, but no A level, which was required. It was a fateful turning point. To this day I don't know how I scraped on to this course. The college probably needed the grant money, and nudged me through. I think I had to promise to sit an A level, which I did eventually. Law and Economics. Passed the former, failed the latter. This was despite cheating through the exam with crib notes (rolled up my sleeve). I never did get the hang of Economics.

Australia went out of the window. Another crossroads in life which I missed. Who knows what might have been? And here's the thing. These signposts of life shape the rest of it. It's just an ability to recognise them as such when they appear out of the blue. Luck, chance, and opportunity. Decisions are much easier to make when you're young, simply because if you screw up and things don't work out you can at least have another go. As we age choices become more limited, especially if you have a mortgage and kids, and the opportunity to rectify mistakes disappears.

I spent a large amount of the summer of 1968 in a tent up in Criccieth. By this time I was working my notice with Whitbread, and I think it was probably the only job I ever had from which I wasn't sacked. Criccieth is a kind of spiritual home for my family, and for me particularly. We had been going there for holidays since I was seven, usually by train from Stoke, changing at Crewe. Then Ruabon, Conway, and down the coast to Pwllheli, eventually puffing and steaming into this beautiful little seaside town. I recall our dad lugging our suitcases from the station. Hard work, especially with no wheels on them either. We raced across the football field in excitement, while he toiled behind, to find ourselves back in Queen St at number 7, Miss Elias' B&B. In fine weather Criccieth was, and still is, unrivalled, and luckily we always seemed to get the weather right. In later years we went by car, and the only thing I remember carrying was a two-piece fishing rod and swimming trunks. I would fish all day between the tides from the far side of Castle rock for dabs. I'd gut them and Miss Elias would dip them in breadcrumb and fry them for us. This hunter-gatherer thing has never ever left me.

The campsite, Mynydd Ddu, was out of the town and up the hill beyond. Occasionally we had a coterie of girls who joined us, some from school, some local. I helped with mackerel fishing trips which were run from the beach. Excess mackerel I sold round the caravan sites for sixpence each. Useful beer money. Brom and Mart camped there, had taken guitars, and wrote songs. Some of those they wrote between them were really good too. The summer of 1968 was exceptionally hot. When the weather is hot and sunny in North Wales you can keep the South of France. It's truly unbeatable. The sparkling crystal-clear sea glints below. It may not have the bar Tabacs, restaurants and wine choices, but so what? It has pubs. I loved it and still do. Criccieth for me became almost a spiritual second home.

Then I smashed my car up. My favourite girl-puller. There were six of us in my Ford 100E coming out of Porthmadog one Friday night heading for Black Rock Sands. I was pissed, missed a bend, and hit a wall, which took the passenger side of the car off. This was weeks before the breathalyser and drink-driving laws came in. I was lucky, so were we all. There were too many of us in it. The car was unmanageable with the weight, and I was anything but sober. The car was just about driveable. Fortunately, the police weren't involved, but I was more upset that my pride and joy was a mess. I never considered the fact that we could all have easily been killed.

Friday nights in Porthmadog were a regular occurrence, and I had quite a few mates who were local, Welsh, and about the same age, and on one occasion I met a girl early in the evening, Nerys Roberts. We disappeared up an alleyway for a while. She went home early, and off we went once more to continue the party on Black Rock Sands, where surprisingly I met another Nerys Roberts, and ended up with her in the dunes about 2 am. The first and only time I've ever had it away with two different girls, both with the same name. I just thought it worth a mention!

Chapter 7

Here I was, heading in a completely new direction. My dad drove, and I felt shades of deja vu back to the time he'd taken me to the station in Derby, and then releasing me to the tender mercies of the Ordnance Survey. He was tight-lipped on the drive down. Here we go again. I knew what he was thinking. We arrived in Redditch on a cold, wet and windy night. I was now about to embark on yet another career project. A two-year Business Studies HND course. I had just turned twenty a week or two before, which he sarcastically said was 'a bit old for a student'. He was probably right.

My digs, or lodgings, were in Jubilee Avenue. It was a smart semi, not that I could make out much in the driving rain, but the family who provided the lodgings proved to be a kindly lot, giving me freedom of the house and urging me to help myself to whatever was on the go in their fridge. Quite a change from home. We always had to ask for the smallest thing, whether a biscuit or to borrow a hammer. That's an attitude I've inherited from him. I'm happy to lend if I'm asked first. However, if anyone takes without asking ...

I had grant aid for my HND course from the government, topped up by my dad, who I suspect was glad to pay it just to get me out of the house and out of his sight. Nevertheless, I was immensely grateful for his 'investment'. On this rain-soaked night he'd delivered me to my lodgings, cursorily wished me luck, and, just like he had in Derby, didn't look back.

Arriving at college the following day was a revelation. The college building in Arthur Street wasn't anything special. A concrete technical college, primarily set up to teach engineering skills to apprentices, with an HND Business Studies course sort of tacked on, for aspiring managerial wannabes. I immediately found a number of like-minded people. My self-esteem had taken a battering over the previous two years or so, but not my self-confidence, and though that may sound contradictory, deep down I was not at all pleased with myself. I'd had something like five jobs in less than three years, and been sacked from most of them.

It was a surprise for me though to find a number of the newly enrolled students had been through a similar process as I. I really do envy people who know what they want to do. Even at twenty I was clueless. To illustrate the point I had grade 1 O level Biology (science) and grade 1 O level in Art. Two almost diametrically opposed subjects. Someone once said to me I'd end up with a job painting frogs. The gap between those two subjects was enormous, and as I've said before I needed something to focus on, but still I had no idea what it was. This course was yet another throw of the dice.

I tended to hit it off with the second-year students who were nearer to my age, and in their final year. The new arrivals, like myself, were mostly just out of school sixth form, but one or two of them were of my age, and like me had tried their hand at various jobs before they started the course. Up until then I thought it was just me who was a no-hoper. It was gratifying to find there were quite a few other no-hopers. My father had spent the last two years or so drilling into me my uselessness, and I believed him. This was an age where we accepted what we were told. We were brought up to believe parents know best. So, as I said, it was something of a surprise to find others who had encountered a similar upbringing. I thought it was just me in a poisonous father/son relationship.

I quickly discovered that the culture in the college common room revolved around music, guitars, smoking, drinking and playing cards. It was right up my street. I could do all of those things easily. My previous experience was now paying off.

The girls there tended to fall in to two categories: the 'Touch Me

Not's and the 'Come and Get Me's. The former tended to be bookish and serious, the latter seemed pleased to be off their parents' leash. That suited me fine.

The course itself was primarily developed to cover all aspects of business. The primary subjects were Accounting, Commerce, Economics, Statistics, Law, and Marketing. I was intrigued. It was different. Needless to say, I was crap at the mathematically biased subjects, but I immediately took to Marketing, which itself was broken down into Sales, Brand Management, and Advertising. I liked the psychology of sales, liked the psychology behind advertising, and branding too. Subliminal sales. This sought to persuade the 'consumers' they needed something they didn't know they needed. Clever stuff. People were now known as consumers. It was new to me. Whatever happened to customers? Consumers of course drive consumption, and that's how we ended up in a 'consumer society'. I actually disliked that term, and still do. I always think of consumers as termites. Which is probably about right. I consider it impersonal, describing units and groups of people who couldn't think for themselves. Like sheep. Which is also probably about right. One thing which irks me even today is hearing some pompous, sanctimonious politician refer to people as the 'general public' or 'consumers'. I'm sure, like most bad habits, it originated in America in the 50s and 60s. Not for me. I don't want to be grouped like that, I'm not one of them and never will be. I find it disparaging, even if I am considered a consumer.

For some strange reason I also took to Law. I liked the balancing of justice, and in fact it's the only A level I got. Accounting and Economics bored me rigid, and as I said earlier, I failed A level Economics despite cheating in the exam. I also cheated through my exams in the HND Business Course finals. Businessmen are known cheats, so I didn't see a problem with it.

I settled into this new environment quickly. Then I fell in love. All within a matter of weeks. I met Janet through her brother Geoff, a second-year student and guitar player. She was funny, carefree, uncomplicated, and happy-go-lucky, and I was welcomed into a loving home by her family, who lived in Wythall, just south of Birmingham. They were a cosy, close-knit family – something quite alien to me. Lovely people, and it was Janet who eventually became wife number 1. In some ways looking back I made a mistake, becoming involved as I did so early, and denying myself many other opportunities with some of the other girls, but the harmony and relative stability of her home life, compared to the tempestuous environment I'd endured, more than compensated, and was something I perhaps needed. I had fierce arguments with her father, but in those days I was still a radical, rebellious, left-wing Labour-voting idealist. He was a pillar of the Establishment, and revelled in his status as Senior Tea Taster at Typhoo Tea in Birmingham. They had family Sunday lunches, preceded by a glass of sherry. This was another world to me.

I also rediscovered fishing. Something I hadn't done for a few years. I encountered a fellow rebellious personality, Andrew Zollman, aka Zolly, and we became lifelong friends. He was a highly intelligent, opinionated cynic, who practised (as he put it) the art of consumption. Mostly in the pub. Despite his quick wit and sharp mind he was a lazy bastard, who did the bare minimum to scrape by. Wholly out of condition physically, he nevertheless had no qualms about settling scores with his fists. He was aware of my quick temper, so we never actually crossed swords. He invented the term 'Craddocked', usually after I'd been in a heated argument, or settled it with my fists. I told you. Those boxing lessons came in handy.

Side story

It was Zolly who helped land my first ever 20 lb+ pike. A freezing cold day on the last day of the coarse fishing season, March 14th 1970. The pike took a spinner with virtually my last cast of the day. Neither of us could contain our amazement at the sheer size of it on the bank. Despite catching many pike over the years we'd never seen anything like it. In a split-second decision I wrapped it in a wet coat, put it in the back of Zolly's minivan, and legged it the twenty minutes back to my hovel. I desperately needed a photo, and got it. This black-and-white photo taken in the (filthy) bathroom of my digs holding this fish means a lot. I tried to keep it alive in the bath overnight, fully intending to put it back the following morning. It was a naïve and stupid thing to do. The fish ran out of oxygen, was probably stressed anyway, and died. The prized photo still sits on the sideboard in my dining room. At the time I was upset, but a day or two later found a brilliant taxidermist in Leicester and delivered the corpse to him. Mr J Shelbourne, on the Harborough Road. He was eighty-odd then, and now long gone no doubt (unless his wife had him stuffed?). Months later he rang me to say it was finished.

The fish itself sits in a glass case underneath my sideboard, along with the photo and still remains there fifty years later. The entire episode I remember like it was yesterday. My dad had a brass plate engraved for me. Surprising actually, since he wasn't the least bit interested in fishing, but I was grateful. The fish weighed 23 lb, and the rod I caught it on is there too.

This little two-piece fibreglass rod has history too. A couple of years later, in 1972, I was using it when Zolly and I were arrested by the police. We'd discovered a trout lake near Barnt Green, a mile or two from my flat at the time in Hopwood. We'd crawled through the hedge and indulged ourselves in a bit of poaching. This was about the third or fourth time we'd been there, and we'd evidently left tracks which the eagle-eyed bailiff had spotted. These illegal excursions would follow a Friday night in the pub, then back to my place. We would usually stay up all night, have a fry up about 3 am, and plan our day's fishing with an early start. Dropping into this pool was something of a warm-up exercise. The cops nailed us at four in the morning. They'd been hiding in the trees, given us ten to fifteen minutes to catch the evidence, and using worms for bait, and trout do like worms, we soon had several in the bag. Just as we were about to leave, while Zolly was reeling in his last trout, they pounced on us out of the mist, along with one very irate bailiff who'd come puffing and panting from the far side of the lake. It was what you might call a fair cop.

The police confiscated our rods, and very nearly impounded the minivan, which we thought was well hidden up a nearby farm track. It was deemed our getaway vehicle. We were then escorted to Bromsgrove police station, several miles away. The trout we caught were also confiscated. These were presented a couple of months later (frozen) in Bromsgrove magistrates' court. Laughable really, especially when Zolly asked if they could prove they were actually the same trout we'd caught. We were each subsequently fined £5 for fishing without a licence, and £5 under the Theft Act. We pleaded guilty. Even for my fertile imagination, I couldn't find an excuse to explain the half a dozen 2 lb trout we'd clobbered with worms. Having accepted our sentence, we then asked if we could buy back our rods. The magistrates agreed, and we paid a few quid to retrieve them. What happened to the money I've no idea, but the case made the front page of the *Birmingham Post*. 'Two anglers fined but allowed to buy back their rods after police keep a 4 am vigil'. I still have the cutting. This infamous rod is now redundant and sits alongside the pike case. I've never used it since.

When I arrived in Redditch in 1968 I didn't stay long in the lodgings in Jubilee Avenue. The landlord and landlady's own son was away at university by the time I arrived. It was his room I occupied, and in a strange way they began to adopt me, and to some extent treat me as if I were him. Bit by bit they began to introduce more and more petty rules and regulations. Milk in the fridge, tea bag in the bin, top on the jar, tidy your room. That kind of thing.

Things came to a head one Saturday night. They were out and I was with Janet on the sofa in their front room, in complete darkness. I had my hand up her skirt at the time, when suddenly the door opened, all the lights came on, and I was effectively caught with my pants down, and her knickers on the floor. We'd been so busy with each other we never heard their car in the drive, or the front door open. The landlady was furious, and I recall her asking me 'what the hell' I thought I was doing. I think I said I thought it was 'bloody obvious'.

That was it. No more of this. Unexpectedly there was a room spare at 'The Farm'. A few of my newly found musically-inclined mates lived there. I was out of Jubilee Avenue in a matter of days. It would have been hours, but I'd paid to the end of that week.

Marlfield Farm on the Beoley Road was a crumbling, rambling old place. Now demolished, the rolling farmland that sloped gently down to the town is these days covered in houses, the land 'seized' in pursuit of someone's grand plan for a 'satellite' town scheme. This was now Redditch New Town. If ever there was an uninspiring destruction of a fine old market town, this was it. Droitwich went the same way, as did Telford.

As I implied, several of my more wayward student friends lived there. It also had a legendary reputation for wild parties. My name was on that room. I moved in. All five of us shared the cooking, the housework (not that I recall much of that), a mangy cat we named Teapot, and we all played guitar. The Beatles had released the *White Album*, and that album became the soundtrack to my student days, and in some ways defined my relationship with Janet.

The Farm, as it was universally referred to, was a magnet for more or less the entire population of the college. I've no idea why, but it had some sort of indefinable charisma. It was owned by a local farmer, John Bomford, who farmed the land but lived in a bigger farm up the road. He was just the kind of landlord we liked. Never came near us, didn't care too much how we treated the place, as long as we paid our rent. £2 10s a week (£2.50). I know this fifty-odd years later only because I rewrote a song to the tune of 'Paddy McGinty's Goat'. There was a TV favourite at the time that more or less made it his signature tune. Val Doonican. By the way, one shilling was known as a bob, and there were twenty shillings (bobs) in a £1.

So with the Paddy McGinty tune firmly in mind, herewith: 'John Bomford's a farmer but don't live at Marlfield Farm, he rents it to students who don't do any harm, we all like the place and it's fifty bob a week, the trouble is the bog's blocked when you go for a leak' ... and there's more but I won't bore you with it. John Bomford died in a head-on collision on his way back from some horse racing event. He was probably in his mid-forties, though he seemed much older than that to us. We all went to his funeral.

As I keep referring to throughout all I've written so far, it's the music which provides the power of recall, and no, 'Paddy McGinty's Goat' isn't the one which summed up my time here at Redditch its 'Revolution'. And that's the power of The Beatles.

'Revolution' was a double-A-sided single on the flip side of 'Hey Jude'. If ever a song encapsulated the rebelliousness within me, and the times we were living in, that was it. The guitar intro still makes the hairs on the back of my neck stand up. The *White Album* was released more or less at the same time.

Usually on a warm Saturday morning we would sit around outside in the farmyard on rusting machinery, and old hay bales, and practise forever 'Blackbird', 'Julia', 'Ob-La-Di, Ob-La-Da', and Dear Prudence, amongst many of the other brilliant tracks. On one occasion Mart came up for the weekend from Chelmsford, where he was studying, and showed all of us the chords to 'Rocky Raccoon'. We still play it today.

Side story

There were five of us students at The Farm. As I alluded to earlier, we all played guitars, and were all at various stages of finishing the Business Studies degree. There was one guy however who was older than us all. Richard Whitehouse. He was tall and balding, and aged about thirty-one or thirty-two. He lodged there, uncomfortably I guess, and occupied a room downstairs. The rest of us were upstairs. He was some kind of farm manager or consultant, and tended to view us as dissolute and irresponsible.

He was probably right. He did however have a gorgeous girlfriend who would visit this hovel, much to her evident disgust, at the weekends.

Now the parties we held there were legendary, and although I like to get up these days early in the morning, sometimes we'd be so pissed from the night before it was usually sometime in the afternoon when I'd surface from my pit. Around this time in 1969 I found a sex book. I can't remember what it was called I'm sorry to say, but this little bedside book provided an insight into female anatomy. There's an old joke about what the difference is between a clitoris and a golf ball. Answer: Men will spend ten minutes looking for a golf ball.

I'd been reading this book and learned quite a lot. I began experimenting as it were.

One Saturday morning we were all in the farmyard as usual, sitting in the sun on bits of rusty machinery, strumming guitars, and planning a wild party that evening, when Richard strolled out of the house clutching a mug of coffee, and came over to us, blinking into the sunlight. He looked dishevelled, and had evidently had a hard week. He sat on a straw bale and listened to us practising. I can't recall how the conversation came about, but he told us his girlfriend was coming over later and staying the night. The subject inevitably turned to women. With my newly discovered authority, I then mentioned the clitoris. No one, and I mean no one, had even heard of it, including Richard. That surprised me a bit. Everyone paid attention, so I continued to explain, with my air of expertise, exactly where it was, and how little attention men paid to it. I used my guitar to demonstrate. It was, in some ways, female shaped, if you see what I mean?

The following day, we were back on the machinery, recovering from an alcohol-fuelled night. There was no sign of Richard, who hadn't joined the party. He'd bolted himself in his room to get away from the noise. When he finally appeared in the yard, he looked utterly shagged out. We stopped playing and stared at him. I assumed his girlfriend was still in bed. His shirt was unbuttoned, he was wearing boxer shorts, and flip flops on his feet. His thinning hair was unkempt, and his face seemed hollowed out. Normally he dressed in immaculate farm suits, tweedy stuff, with a waistcoat, tie and checked shirt, but this was Sunday morning, and he looked trashed. He did however wear a beaming smile, and came over to me, by now the acknowledged sex expert. He thanked me over and over again. His girlfriend was worn out, by all accounts. He'd obviously found it.

So 1969 came and went at The Farm, and I made it into the second year of the HND course, having (somehow) passed the first year. To my astonishment I also achieved an A Level in Law, but failed Economics, as I said earlier.

There were three cataclysmic events which shaped my life at this time. The first was an emergency appendectomy.

I was in my bed at The Farm, and found one morning I simply couldn't get out of it. I had stomach ache, and was surprised to find that it seemed to seize the muscles down my right side. I stayed in bed. By pure chance Spike, one of my fellow farm inmates, came back at 11 am to pick up some books he'd forgotten, didn't like the colour of my face, and called an ambulance. I protested, but he insisted. Good for him. I was taken to hospital in Bromsgrove with bell (in those days) clanging, and blue lights flashing. It was snowing too. When I got there they didn't piss about, and after a brief examination of my abdomen, put me straight into the theatre. I came out minus my appendix. It had apparently swollen to such a size that it was on the point of bursting, and peritonitis means curtains. Mum and Dad came down the following day and the surgeon told them I was within minutes of them losing a son. Evidently a grain of uncooked rice was the culprit. Vesta curries were a 'boil in the bag' fast food in those days. I'd eaten it the night before. The rice grain had lodged in the neck of the appendix and irritated it to the point where it turned nasty. Apparently tomato seeds can have a similar effect. Be warned.

The second event concerned Janet. She was pregnant. I was shocked, half pleased that I wasn't infertile, and terrified as to what I'd done, for both myself and her. I was a second-year student, halfway through this course, with no money. She had by this time left college, started a secretarial job with an estate agency in south Birmingham. She also had no money. We had nowhere to live, and no means whatsoever. It was a total and unmitigated disaster.

I don't know whether fortunate is the right word, but the Abortion Act came in around 1968/9. We kept the whole thing quiet, borrowed £100 from a friend at college, and went down to London to the Brook Street clinic, and there the deed was done. I have never forgotten that day. I met up with my brother in Leicester Square while Janet was in there, and he was incredibly supportive. To this day I have never been able to reconcile my feelings over this. Joy on the one hand, and absolute guilt on the other.

Janet herself was immensely brave, and I was proud of her, if only for her decisiveness alone. We realised it was disastrous for us both, but it bound us together, and in some ways forever, for there is more on this subject, but later. That child would be fifty now, and it continues to haunt me to this day.

The third event, as we headed towards 1970, was that The Beatles broke up. Change is constant, and at times seems sometimes imperceptible. Each day of routine seems very much the same as the day before, then along comes something dramatic and sudden. When this happens it's a shock and takes time to adjust. The Beatles weren't just a band, they were a way of life. They were always going to be there. Underestimated by some at the time, they'll still be underestimated in years to come. The disintegration of the Fab Four was one of the saddest and most poignant events in my life. *Abbey Road* was the last album, except that it wasn't. *Let It Be* was subsequently released and somehow it followed Abbey Road, despite much of it having been recorded at an earlier time. As usual my brother Mart unpicked 'Here Comes the Sun', and showed us the guitar rundown, which is the riff which makes the song so distinctive. George Harrison's best song ever.

I don't think I've ever truly got over this loss. Sure, there were new bands coming through like Cream, Led Zeppelin, Black Sabbath and so on, but nothing, absolutely nothing to touch The Beatles. I didn't relish a new decade without them.

The lesson I have learned from events like these is that change is inevitable and constant throughout life. Nothing is guaranteed. It's dealing with that change which is important.

Whilst writing the above, I've been singing in my head 'Que Sera Sera', which I mentioned long ago when I was ten. Doris Day from about 1959, a decade earlier. It's not exactly a life changing song, and yet in some ways it is. The words seem simple enough, but it carries a message. What will be, will be.

I left college, and Redditch, in 1970, complete with my diploma, and set off to find a job. I felt more motivated and focused than I had ever done. I had decided a career in sales was for me, primarily because I could get a company car, big tick there, and not be office-bound. Another big tick. Been there, done that. I also got engaged to Janet. Shamefully I did it in a phone call to her dad. It was a crass and ignorant thing to do, but at twenty-one it never crossed my mind. He gave the OK nevertheless.

Whilst applying for various sales jobs, back to Loughborough I went, and this time my dad seemed pleased with me. I had something to show for myself I suppose, and found I was developing a new sense of purpose and direction. I had a piece of paper with a qualification. I was actually worth something. At least somebody else thought I was.

Almost immediately I got a part-time job, to raise cash while I was searching for a 'proper job'. I became a ward orderly in a geriatric hospital, complete with my own dazzlingly white coat. Storer House, as it was known, in Loughborough. As it turned out that provided another set of life lessons, and in so many diverse ways.

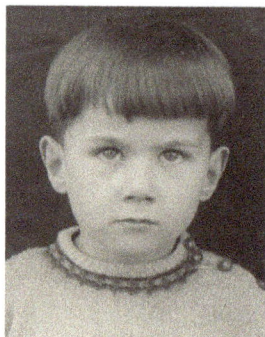

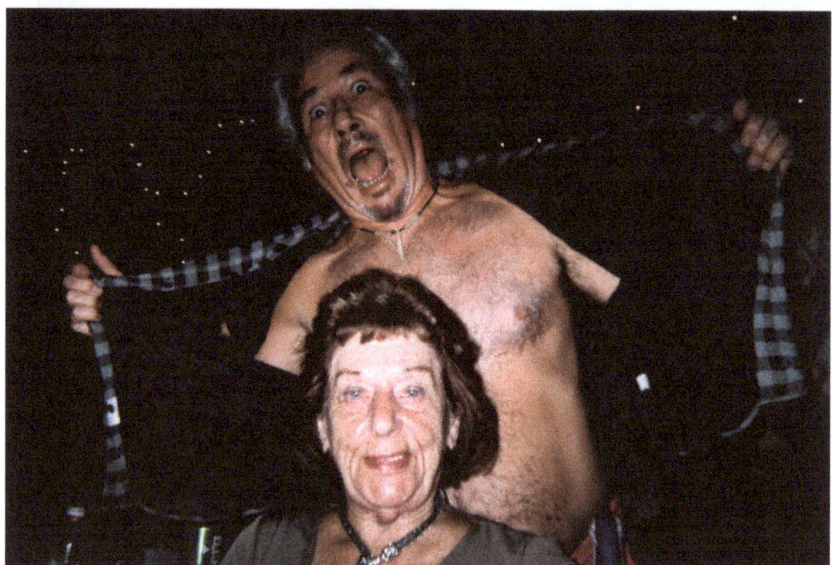

CAVERSWALL, HULME & WERRINGTON COUNTY PRIMARY SCHOOL
REPORT FOR TERM ENDING ...July, 1956........

John Craddock ...Class ...III......No. in Class ,.28..Position ...17..
in Class

Total marks gained...704......Marks possible ,.1600......

...ct	% marks gained	Class Position.	Remarks.
...re	80	2	Good has worked well .
...g	90	2	V. Good for his age .
...ng	40	5	Fair could do better .
...ition	93	2	Good, vivid imagination .
...r	Absent .		V. good but rather slow .
...iting	45	12	Poor exam, can write quite well .
...etic:	70	4	Good .
...etic: Mech	35	9	Disappointing exam .
	100	1	V. Good .
...e	60	5	Fair .
...al ...ion	90	2	V. Good. very interested in this subject
	86	5	Good shows imagination .
...rk or work	72	11	Fairly good .
...y			
...phy			
...ur.	100	1	Excellent shows keen interest.

Attendance	Conduct	Next term
y. 20th.. 96/126..	Very good this term .	begins .September 4th... ends ..December 20th..

TEACHER'S REPORT

...is position would have ...higher if he had ...missed the English exam ...orks hard & is a pleasure ...ch .

B. E. Leek.

HEAD TEACHER'S REPORT

John has made excellent progress during the year.

.....A. E. Venn.....

Chapter 8

A ll the people in the hospital were in some form of terminal decline. They would never leave, except in a box. It was a cruel place to be, and at my age something of a shock. Somehow I thought this would never ever happen to me. I'd made up my mind. I fully intended to live forever.

I cycled back home after my first day at the hospital. It was a summer's evening. Storer House could be compared, I suppose, to a hospice nowadays, and as I left the smell of medicine, disinfectant, urine, and shit behind, I knew these patients would never again experience this kind of simple cycling pleasure. I had no car now. The old Austin of England A35 I'd had in my last year at college, which I paid all of £15 for, was rusting away in a scrapyard somewhere. I'd had a rear-end shunt in Lincoln in the pouring rain, after I'd been playing banjo at some folk gig. The insurance company wrote the car off. The repair (£20) was more than the car was worth. It was some experience being back on a bike, but an even bigger experience working with and tending to dribbling old people.

I learned to light a pipe for one old man, who was allowed to set fire to his St Bruno once a day. Hard to imagine smoking in a hospital ward now, but it was his one simple pleasure of the day. I learned to play imaginary bridge with another, who'd lost both his legs in the trenches during WWI. He sat at the end of the bed each day all day, supported by a metal frame, just gazing into space. Many times I wondered where his thoughts and memories might take him. I would walk past with a trolley and he'd always catch my eye, his face would light up and he'd perhaps bid one diamond. I'd pause, look at him and bid one heart, and walk on to the end of the ward. On my way back he'd up the bid to two clubs and I'd reply two spades and so on. This imaginary game with a pack of imaginary cards went on for perhaps half an hour, backwards and forwards, until we ran out of bidding.

The founder of the well-known high-street cobbler chain, Mr Timpson, was incarcerated also. He was a particularly difficult patient, who always liked his own way, (surprise surprise for an entrepreneur!) and at ninety plus didn't take kindly to a jumped-up twenty-one-year-old kid telling him what to do. I used to take him by hand to the toilet, and lock the door on him with a screwdriver from the outside of the cubicle. This was common practice, and the patients would be forced to sit there until they'd been. He would shout from the inside of the cubicle and declare that he'd 'been'. Most often he hadn't, and after twenty minutes of stand-off I would take him back to his bed, in which he'd promptly shit, with a wry smirk on his face. It wasn't uncommon for him to hobble down the ward holding his cock out straight from the gap in his pyjamas and sing 'Onward Christian Soldiers'. His body was failing him, but his mind certainly wasn't.

Barbara, a kindly nurse, probably in her mid-thirties, who mentored me in the ways of some of these patients, summed it up perfectly: 'Life is a circle, dear: you're born bald and wrinkly, and you die bald and wrinkly'.

Dementia patients were common too, very much like the guy who played imaginary bridge. Barbara explained to me that we only vocalise a fraction, maybe 10%, of what we're thinking at any given time. These hidden and invisible thoughts are of little relevance to general conversation, but dementia patients verbalise these thoughts, so whilst it may sound like unconnected gobble-degook to the casual listener, it was relevant to the speaker. They understand what they mean; it's the recipient, the listener, who doesn't. An obvious truth perhaps?

It's only now that I can fully appreciate the sheer indignity and humiliation these terminally ill people must have felt, to be pushed and ordered about by a twenty-one-year-old 'wet behind the ears' kid in a white coat. It gave me some kind of an authority

I hadn't earned. These people had lived a life. I was only just starting out.

The most important lesson I learned from my days at Storer House was dealing with the death of my grandfather, Jim Broome, in 1970. My mum had moved him down from Leek in North Staffs to live with us. He had reached the point where he was unable to look after himself, just like the patients in my care and, as mentioned before, his wife, my grandma Nellie Broome (her of the baking fame when I was a boy) had died suddenly and unexpectedly of a heart attack a few years earlier in 1967 (while I was with the Ordnance Survey), whilst sitting in a chair knitting.

Grandfather Jim occupied the spare room in Kirkstone Drive. My brother Martin was still away at college. I'm fairly sure now my granddad had prostate problems, and would visit the toilet what seemed like every five minutes, day and night. Over a relatively short period of time he deteriorated and became bedridden. I don't remember how old he was, seventy-eight I think, and he was the last surviving grandparent I had. It's strange now to think that he was diagnosed with a weak heart in the 1930s and avoided the war, and yet of all four grandparents he survived the longest. He died rambling and incoherent, seeing imaginary candles burning, and wild animals and monsters sneaking around his room. He knew they were there by the shadows they left on the wall in the imaginary candlelight. He died in my arms with a horrifying death rattle. I remember calling for Mum, who was busy downstairs in the kitchen cooking cauliflower cheese. The smell of that is forever associated with his death. Amazingly, she seemed to take it in her stride in a very matter-of-fact way. Her father had gone.

I knew how to prepare the body prior to the undertaker's arrival. I tied his arms to his side, his big toes together, and closed his mouth and eyes, and then used a bandage of sorts to wrap around his jaw and tie over the top of his head in a bow. It was pitiful. This was a kindly man, who had played both the squeezebox and harmonica, and grew the most amazing strawberries. Time was up, and another human being had fallen off the conveyor belt and disappeared back to the cosmos.

'Subterranean Homesick Blues', released in or around 1965 by Bob Dylan, was probably the first song he'd released where he'd moved away to an electric sound. I loved it. Up until then it was mostly 'Blowin' in the Wind', 'The Times They Are a-Changin'', 'Don't Think Twice, It's All Right', mostly played simply on an acoustic guitar, and aimed predominantly at the counterculture of folk music, with a stab at the disenchantment of politics, war, injustice and so on. 'Subterranean Homesick Blues' was different. I loved the line 'don't need a weatherman to notice where the wind blows'. More than appropriate for the weather patterns we've inflicted on ourselves worldwide and the increasing lack of common sense and self-awareness. I also love the song as both an almost meaningless monologue and the fact it's written, more or less, around one chord. Took me awhile to work out 'Johnny's in the basement mixing up the medicine' but taking drugs was something which had never entered my life. Apart from the occasional spliff of course.

Besides, my musical influences had been mostly Beatles so far (what's wrong with that??). Dylan was such a huge influence on me growing up in the 60s, and I have my mate Brom to thank for that. He was the first to introduce me to *Bringing it All Back Home* and *Highway 61 Revisited*, two of my all-time favourite albums.

The 1970s proved to be a decade quite unlike the 60s and for me, as you'll see, proved to be an emotional rollercoaster. I was depressed with the fact The Beatles had split, and musically it was almost as though a curtain had been brought down on a main meal of wonderful inspirational vibrant music. As we went into the 70s with glam rock, T. Rex, the persona non grata Gary Glitter, and the likes of Roxy Music (better), it seemed to me to provide a fairly mediocre, rather bland and unappetising dessert.

It's hard to know where to begin with the 1970s, so probably with my new job.

In 1970, after my stint with the geriatrics at Storer House, and the death of my granddad, my torrent of applications for sales jobs finally resulted in an offer. I got a trainee sales position with a communications company, Telephone Rentals Ltd, based in Cornwall Street, Birmingham. They sold intercom, staff location (tannoy), and time control (clocking in and out) systems. The entire sales aim was to improve communication and thus cut costs for the business.

By now I was engaged to Janet, and back to Redditch I went, bunking down with an old mate from college for a while. Didn't stay there too long, at the flat I mean. It was an untidy shithole. I moved to my own flat in Hopwood, with an old mate Tim Rogers. That too was a shithole, but it was my shithole. Unsurprisingly this place was demolished a few years later. This was the base from which I fished, and despite my betrothal to Janet, had a number of one-night stands. It was also just up the road from Barnt Green trout lakes. The very place where Zolly and I were done for poaching in 1972.

My sales training with Telephone Rentals involved a six-month intensive sales training course in London, and it was this I think which triggered my antipathy, and ultimately downright dislike and hatred of that city. I loathe it even more today. Grey pasty-faced people, jostling and pushing, eye contact non-existent. Filthy litter-strewn streets, tube stations, traffic ... repeat after me ...

Hasn't changed a bit. If anything it's worse. Well maybe some areas have improved, but the sheer weight of the place. Jeeezzzz.

Part of the sales training was interesting, but mostly involved a tube journey from Finchley, then spending the whole day plodding round the East End, or the city, prospecting for potential sales targets, and nine times out of ten having the door shut in my face or someone telling me (nicely) to just fuck off. It's called 'cold-calling' and not only cold, but humiliating. We would then bring any leads back to the office, and practise telephone sales techniques to make follow-up appointments with a Senior Representative to guide us, for a full-on sales visit. I learned a lot, missed Janet, hated London, met a few nice guys of my own ilk, but more than any of these things I missed the countryside. I couldn't wait to get a train out of this prison.

There was at least a decent social side to this six-month programme, and I did at least have some riotous times with this bunch of trainees. Since I was engaged, I had the urge to chat other women up when we were out in the pubs and clubs, but I felt an intense loyalty to Janet. We'd been through quite a bit together. Not least an abortion. I resisted the urge to take any social intercourse further, much to the astonishment of my fellow inmates. There was an element of been there, done that. And I was only twenty-three.

I could go on about this course, which was more of a regime, a bit like the Ordnance Survey. They made me cut my hair immediately to short back and sides, where before I'd been a long-haired Paul McCartneyesque student. I had to wear a suit, and felt it was more a uniform. But I conformed, partly because I felt up until then I needed to 'knuckle down', as my dad would have said. Instinctively I was uncomfortable with it all. At this point in my life I was well and truly on the horns of a dilemma. A huge part of me wished I'd gone to art college.

I finished the course, six months of it, which on reflection stood me in good stead for later, and I enjoyed the psychology of sales. It was clever, and helped me to think on my feet. Eventually I moved back to the Birmingham office, something of an expert in selling telephone intercom, time control, and staff location systems. But God, it was boring.

Telephone Rentals then decided to move me to Shrewsbury, promoting me to Assistant Area Rep, at £750 pa. I didn't get a say in this move, it was expected. TR was a very disciplined operation, and regional directors or senior sales managers were looked on in awe. Like gods. I didn't get it really.

Anyway, my new job sounded good, but in reality this was another name for a cold-calling salesman, and I did the drudgery for the area rep, prospecting as they called it, on his patch in

Shropshire for leads. But I got a car! A Diamond Blue J-reg Ford Escort 1.3. At least I wasn't stuck in an office. I was finally going somewhere. I wasn't altogether sure where, but I could at least be out and about and hide from vigilant managers. There were no mobile phones, hard to believe nowadays, but I loved the Shropshire countryside and it was easy to sit up on the Long Mynd around Craven Arms and soak it all in, hidden and unseen. I learned to blag some of the calls I didn't make.

I kept the Hopwood hovel on, at least it was next to the canal, but found a one-bed basement flat in Shrewsbury, with a bit of garden out the back which opened on to the banks of the River Severn. This was my home for five days a week, before going back to Hopwood and Janet at weekends. The landlord lived with his wife upstairs. They had a daughter. Long dark hair, brown eyes. You can guess the rest.

At night she would play James Taylor continuously. 'You've Got a Friend' takes me straight back there. As much as I love James Taylor, hearing it from above played incessantly nearly drove me nuts whilst I was writing up my call reports down in the basement.

I almost broke off my engagement to Janet, but the fact I can't even recall her name is probably why I didn't. She was about nineteen, an only child and a bit mixed up. I can't recall why she was, but she also was one of the best-looking girls I'd ever met.

Her parents were wary of this relationship she'd developed with the 'tenant'. I ought to go back one day and see if I can find the location of this place but I doubt I could. Significantly though I'd been unfaithful to Janet. I felt guilty. This was the first time I'd properly cheated, despite the London opportunities, where I did in fact end up with some girl I'd met in a nightclub in Bayswater. I didn't know at the time, it was dark in this club, that she was bisexual. This was a new one on me. She ended up in my hotel room one morning black and blue from the beating she'd received from her girlfriend, who found out she'd been with me the night before. As for the girl in Shrewsbury, well this was different. It became a second relationship Monday to Friday, so I suddenly found I could justify it to myself. I was lonely wasn't I? I needed company didn't I? And besides, I was helping this girl with her difficulties. Wasn't I? This ability to justify my wayward behaviour marked the start of a very slippery slope.

Though I spent Monday to Friday in this little bedsit, during the day I'd be out cold-calling (prospecting) for sales leads on behalf of my boss, the senior area rep for Shropshire. It was hard work, in fact depressing and soul destroying at times, but in the end I wasn't long in Shrewsbury. A matter of months maybe. This was on-the-job training of sorts, and Telephone Rentals had plans to move me around to different areas of the West Midlands. Nevertheless I got to know this beautiful county well, and half the time would veer off down some back road in the middle of nowhere to check out a pool, or small river, with a view to sneaking a bit of fishing in on the side. This for me was what a sales job was all about. Company car and freedom to roam. Friday afternoons I'd leg it back to my hovel in Hopwood and spend the weekend there, to plan a fishing trip (this was the time of the infamous poaching episode), or catch up with college friends in some boozer in Redditch, as well as spend time with Janet.

Another little side story

One particular Friday night I went out drinking in Redditch with my flatmate Tim, Zolly, my fishing buddy, and another mate from student days. We all crammed into his now notorious mini-van, yes the very same one the police almost confiscated. The four of us left the pub, and as I was literally walking out the door, two girls, of maybe eighteen, who were on their own in the bar, engaged me in conversation. Within minutes the pair of them were in the back of the minivan. How we squeezed six of us in I don't know, but we did, and took them back to Hopwood. Our intention had been to play cards and carry on drinking, but that didn't last long. Tim hit it off with the blonde one, I with the other. She was dark-haired with green eyes. Not dissimilar in fact to the girl in Shrewsbury. We began to play cards but in no time at all, maybe twenty minutes, Tim took the blonde by the hand, stood up and bid us goodnight. I followed his lead and off upstairs I went with mine. Our two mates carried on drinking downstairs. I've no idea what time they left. All this happened so quickly, in fact within an hour of meeting these two good-looking girls, that I can't recall the slightest feeling of guilt about my infidelity. I got her up to my bedroom, which was a bit of an unkempt tip, and turned a bedside light on to sort of give it a seductive feel. Wasn't terribly successful, so I found a candle and lit it. It was marginally better. She immediately clasped me and squirmed around as I fondled her on the bed. It's almost comical to recall, but as I stripped her down to her bra and knickers, I noticed the bra was red, and her knickers green. A shiny satiny green. Janet always wore a matching set, so it was a bit of a surprise, and for a moment I thought I was looking at a set of traffic lights (my mind is funny like that). When I was at school I developed a technique for undoing bras one-handed, while my other hand was elsewhere, and employed that expertise here. She seemed impressed. I won't bore you with the rest, but it was frantic, and by 2 am I was knackered. Although I took a break at times and smoked a fag through the open window, she just urged me to go back for more, so I obliged. She eventually lay in my arms stroking my face, and by now I desperately needed to sleep. The guys downstairs had gone by now, and just as I was drifting off there was a soft tap on my door, and in came the blonde. She was 'lonely' and thought she might join us. In the event it transpired that Tim had fallen asleep before he even got going, and she'd lain there listening to her mate and I in the bedroom below. I went downstairs and made coffee for the three of us, went back upstairs and both were in my bed. By now it was 3 am, the main road outside was silent, I could hear Tim snoring away in the bedroom above, and I can honestly say I have no idea where I got the energy from, but I started all over again with the two of them. Intriguingly they seemed equally familiar with each others' bodies, stroking, cuddling, gasping, and sighing, with their hands and fingers exploring each other. I guess today they'd be described as bisexual, not that I cared, but it was a hell of an experience dealing with two, and not as easy as it might sound. This is the one and only time in my life I've ever had a threesome. It takes discipline and stamina, believe me.

If anyone ever tells you they are 'fucking tired', let me tell you with certainty. They don't know the meaning of the phrase.

I hardly slept at all, but somehow managed to get the dishevelled pair out of the door by 7.30 am and onto the early morning bus back to Redditch. I never saw either of them again. I did promise to call, but never did. I went back to my wreck of a room, and crashed out. Janet showed up at 10 am. We had prearranged to go shopping. Later that day we too ended up back in my room, and I hoped she wouldn't find any shred of evidence from the previous night. She didn't, but since it was a Saturday night, which seems to be the usual night for sex, I had to put the Friday experience firmly out of my mind. She was, after all, my fiancée.

I think I must have slept all day Sunday. I can't recall ever being so tired, but I needed to rest didn't I? I mean, I was heading back to Shrewsbury the following morning, and no doubt would be seeing the landlord's daughter Monday night. A heroic performance all round perhaps? Or is it the action of a devious, debauched, lying bastard? Both I think. I was however surprised at how easy I was able to lie. Here it was again, that continuing ability to self justify. I don't analyse this stuff too much, but my general feeling or attitude is one where I make a decision solely based on the fact that the opportunity may never happen again. Therefore why not take it? Since I'm not religious, the morality of what I do or have done never enters my head. Nevertheless this was the beginning of my own self-doubt about an ability to maintain fidelity within a marriage.

Chapter 9

Janet and I married on 15th April 1972, at Wythall Church, nowadays sadly in total disrepair. 15th April also happened to the anniversary of the Titanic disaster I discovered later. I was twenty-three, she was twenty.

An hour or two before the event I was in a pub with brother Mart, my best man, both of us dressed in our best suits. I was brooding over a pint and I confided in him, expressing my concerns about the wisdom of this marriage. He airily dismissed them and put it down to nerves. I didn't. I put it down to doubts about true love. My evident ability to engage in extraneous relationships without any trace of conscience had thrown me. It led me to think of two things. Either I was sowing wild oats at a frenetic speed before I was cast into the straightjacketed prison of married life, or the marriage wasn't right. I loved Janet, but deep down I knew with certainty that all that stuff about 'one man and one woman being true to each other' was simply bollocks. This was a vow I was about to make, and in all honesty I would go in and say it glibly but I knew it would be a lie. The bottom line is that quite simply I hadn't got the guts to call it off. The sheer excitement and anticipation that everyone became infused with, the cars, photographers, bridesmaids, friends, catering and so on her excellent parents had arranged, as well as my new fellow guitar-plucking brother-in-law Geoff, a lovely man, made it all the more impossible for me to back out. I just wish my own parents had taken me to one side and guided me, but they too were caught up in the excitement of the day. I just couldn't bring myself to let everyone down.

I really was torn in two. My gut instinct told me it was a mistake, but my guilt over her abortion, and the wonderful family

I'd joined who'd taken me under their wing when I was a penniless student, won out. As it turned out it was a lovely wedding day, and both my mum and dad, and her parents got on well, and as a party it was a good one.

Perhaps I saw this as the beginning of a new life, and the end of a dissolute one. I'd obviously had affairs and one-night stands during the two years we'd been engaged, not many, but enough to sow seeds of doubt about matrimony. Nevertheless to this day I can't recall any qualms whatsoever about my disloyalty. I have no idea how I rationalised or justified this philandering spirit, but somehow I did. What I didn't realise was this. This would continue. It was just the start.

I think the lesson is this. If there's a doubt, there is no doubt. And if there's a desire to play away from the beginning, then it's the beginning of the end. Love should be easy. If it isn't easy, it's not right.

Looking back we shouldn't have married, but these mixed feelings of guilt caused me to chicken out and go ahead. I did the right thing by everyone except myself. Even driving later that day to our honeymoon hotel at the Bron Eifion in Criccieth wasn't without incident. I took my company car to a car wash, to get rid of the good luck lipstick scrawled all over it. As I reversed out I hit an upright pillar and dented the wing. I suddenly lost my temper. Janet sat there terrified. It was an inauspicious start.

1972, married, with a 95% mortgage, and living in a linked detached new house on a housing estate in Stourport-on-Severn. Our parents jointly put up the £500 deposit between them as some kind of marriage gift, and we were very grateful. We had little if any disposable income. The house cost £4,995. Mortgage was £4,500 and a heavy burden. Seems like peanuts today. We had no furniture to speak of apart from a telly, record player, and double bed. We shared this with our little dog Dylan. A mongrel crossed border/cairn terrier. Janet was a secretary at the Health Authority in Kidderminster, and I continued my job as an Assistant Area Rep, but now based in the West Midlands with a different Senior

Rep. Then suddenly and without warning, and right out of the blue, I was asked by my boss to move. I was to be promoted and take up a Senior Rep's job. But based in bloody Hertfordshire! They knew I'd only been married a few months and only just bought this house. I thought they'd done it on purpose. The timing was lousy. It was decision time, and frankly I'd had enough of the nit-picking discipline of this company. I turned it down and left. I don't think they were too surprised. Maybe it was their way to get rid of me. I'd been with them barely fifteen to eighteen months, but the sales training I'd received from them stood me in good stead for the rest of my life.

My father had been involved with the catering equipment industry since we moved from Staffordshire, and knew a lot of people within it. He introduced me to an urbane, kindly and educated man, Noel de Mille. He lived locally in fact, just outside my old stomping ground Redditch. This guy had invented the infra-red grill, a gamechanger in fact for the pub trade, which spawned the beginning of a new trend. Food in pubs. This was new, and provided a continuing and alternative to source income as the drink-drive laws kicked in and hammered beer sales. They gave me a big territory. West Midlands and South Wales. Freedom for me to roam even further. I went out on the road selling grills, cold-calling on pubs, and selling these things mostly by demonstrating toasted sandwiches. Bear in mind, this was premier league stuff, compared to the usual fodder served in pubs. Up until then most pubs thought jars of cockles, crisps, pickled eggs, pork pies, and warmed up pasties was the pinnacle. The pub trade was about to be revolutionised, and is nowadays an accepted eatery of choice. Food was the only way to make money as beer and alcohol sales slipped.

They gave me a Vauxhall Viva, which I perceived as a move up from my Escort, a boot load of grills, and off I went. It was pub door-knocking sales stuff, but I had been toughened by my sales training in London, and I successfully sold these things all over the place.

I worked on a small salary plus commission, and with the first three months commission I managed to save that money and bought the car I had wanted ever since I was a kid in the 1950s. I had one as a dinky toy. A 1957 MGA coupe. Red, it had fibreglass wings, a noisy worn gearbox and leaked oil. But I loved it. I found it in Redditch of all places and paid £250. To me it symbolised my arrival as an independent salesman, and was a constant reminder of my relative sales success. When I was nine years old I always promised myself I'd buy a grown up version one day. Now I'd achieved that boyhood dream. I kept that car for twenty-five years.

With this new job there was no control over me whatsoever, a world apart from the confines and double-checking I'd endured with TR. Aside from a weekly sales sheet I had to complete, I hardly, if ever, had a boss breathing down my neck. I was free it seemed to do what I wanted, set my own rules almost, plan my own week, with virtually no supervision. Right up my street. I was virtually my own boss and I revelled in this lack of control. And that's the reason as to how things in 1973 went so very badly wrong.

Janet and I had settled down well in our house in Stourport, and probably been there for about twelve months. She had her routine as a secretary, while I wandered off at will.

One day I sold a grill to a guy in Worcester. He ran a fast food/takeaway business. Peter and I hit it off socially so one evening, at his invitation, I went for a drink with him in Worcester. He introduced me to his friend Meg. It wasn't his wife, she'd just come along to get out, and they knew each other through mutual friends. I quickly learned she'd recently split from her husband. She was thirty-three, I was twenty-four. She had auburn hair which shone, and the most intense and beautiful green eyes. I fell hopelessly in love with her in the space of ten minutes. I felt sorry for Peter. We more or less ignored him entirely. It was like a key fitting a lock perfectly. I wish I understood it, but I don't. It all immediately felt just ... right.

Easy to look back now with the science of hindsight, but I really don't think I'd ever been in love before, and even though I'm aware of this weakness within me to fall in love easily, I honestly didn't know what hit me.

We began an affair almost immediately, and given the freedom I had it wasn't difficult for me. It got to the stage where I just wanted to be with her all the time, and hated leaving. It would be trivial to say I was some kind of toy boy, but I guess I was. Meg had two children, a boy aged about six and a girl of eight, and they all lived together in a tied cottage near Malvern. Every aspect of her, and I mean every aspect, both physically and mentally, was a revelation. She loved folk music and arts. Poetry she showered on me, and introduced me to authors I'd never heard of. Her luxuriant auburn hair, eyes, and body oozed charisma and excitement. She loved the countryside, knowing all the things I did, but more, introducing butterfly identification and beekeeping as well. We were out of sync in age, but in total harmony in every other respect. Physically it was perhaps one of the most intense relationships I'd ever embarked on. It very nearly destroyed me, in the most ardent and mystifying of ways.

The soundtrack to this love affair in the Spring of 1974 was Clifford T Ward. He wrote the most wonderful songs, and coincidentally lived in nearby Kidderminster. Every song on the album *Home Thoughts from Abroad* defines my involvement with Meg. There isn't a single song which doesn't trigger memories from that time. If I were to pick one I'd have difficulty. 'Wherewithal' probably, but 'Jigsaw Girl' would be a logical choice. After many, many close encounters with quite a number of women, I'd found my piece of jigsaw at last. Or so I believed.

I heard recently that professional writers never use exclamation marks. In fact I've actually tried to avoid the use of them throughout, simply because it implies that I'm shouting, or speaking forcefully, but my relationship with Meg developed to the point where she consumed my mind (and body) almost constantly. If I were to catalogue every detail of what happened there would be exclamation marks after every sentence. I had never known such an intensity of emotion in my life. I can't describe the feeling adequately. It was a tidal wave which engulfed me. Once again, whilst I felt guilt and sadness that my marriage to Janet was in tatters, and this all happening within twelve months of marrying her, I simply didn't have the guts to tell her. Whether she knew or suspected secretly I never knew. If she did she was in denial, or simply not picking up on my lies and deceit. What stopped me telling her? I don't know. I should have let go of the marriage, and come clean. And yet I didn't. Somewhere, and somehow, my head was ruling my heart.

The big problem I began to realise were Meg's children. Nice kids, but I wasn't ready to take on a girl of eight and a boy of six. That was the crux of my dilemma.

How I did this for three years I do not know, but that's how long it was. 1973 to 1976. Well very nearly four years actually, as you'll see. In that period of time I'd changed jobs, as well as becoming a complete expert in ducking and diving, and lying through my teeth of course. I left the grill company, W M Still & Co, and joined Jackson Boilers, part of a big engineering group, Tube Investments (TI) and was now their West Midlands Sales Manager. A step up in title and salary. Great company actually, whose head office and factory was in Elland Road, in Leeds. Their soon to be new Managing Director proved to be a pivotal figure in my life. I now sold water boilers and coffee machines. The big old chrome things in cafes, which hissed and gurgled on the counter. Probably collector's items now.

The factory was right next door to Leeds United FC and their training ground, where Don Revie managed the likes of Billy Bremner, Peter Lorimer, and Norman 'Bites Yer Legs' Hunter. On the occasions I was there I'd watch them practising. A Hillman Avenger was my transport. Never have I ever seen a car less suited to vengefulness. How the hell they come up with these ridiculous names like Viva and Escort is beyond me. What for fuck's sake is a Toyota Yaris??

It would take more time and space than I care to elaborate on here to describe how I managed the job, the marriage, and the affair for all of this time. The fact that I got away with it and wasn't apprehended is still a source of amazement to me. But I worked it all out carefully. My primary ruse, or perfect alibi, was night-fishing. No one had a clue where I was, or more importantly, what time I'd be back.

My primary locations for this were two pools on the Westwood Estate near Droitwich. The pools were full of wild carp. I found these pools by accident whilst having lunch in my car, in between sales appointments, and had parked up on the estate road. I chatted for a while to a local, who mentioned them. Permission was only granted to fish by the gamekeeper, John Spurling. The pools turned out to be secluded, weeded, and overgrown, and the second I saw them it took me straight back to my childhood, fishing the gin-clear water of Cheddleton canal in the Staffordshire countryside. A haven for wildlife, and originally designed as stew ponds for the monks at the Westwood monastery centuries ago, before Henry VIII came along and wrecked them. The carp were somehow imported from Eastern Europe, a baffling trip, and grown by the monks for food. Quite unlike common and mirror carp, these fish lacked their deep bodies, and were more torpedo-shaped. Once hooked, they took off like missiles.

On this particular day of discovery, I drove up the rutted track to the gamekeeper's cottage, and knocked nervously. The gamekeeper, I learned, had something of a fearsome reputation. The door flew open angrily, and I almost shrank back, and there stood John Spurling, a gruff, red-faced, no-nonsense individual. He was in a hurry, but nevertheless gave me permission to fish. I was cock-a-hoop. Over time he became a lifelong friend of mine, as well as all of his family, and had a huge influence on my life. He became a father figure to me in some ways, and was a wonderful and knowledgeable countryman. He subsequently introduced me to game shooting. I thought the world of him. John ended his own life in 2009 at the end of a twelve-bore. A fit of continuous depression was responsible, which we could all see, but he simply couldn't shake it off. I performed the eulogy at his funeral.

Night-fishing was the perfect excuse to go out at 7 pm, usually on a Friday, fully kitted with fishing gear, fish for a couple of hours, and then spend the rest of the night with Meg, leaving at 6 am to get back to Janet. It involved several changes of clothes en route there, and en route back. I hid my smart clothes in the boot of the car, just as I'd hidden my Beatles boots in my saddlebag all those years before. These days I'm appalled by my deceit. Then however it was more of a game. A high-risk game for sure, but infidelity is like that. The rush of adrenaline at the sheer risk of being caught, never mind the testosterone-fuelled sex.

Another little side story

I think I had probably been in this affair for about three or four months, and Meg meanwhile was working on a formal divorce from her husband, a guy I didn't know. What I did come to realise is that separation, especially where young children are involved, creates huge emotional stress. Meg's son, who was about six, was particularly affected, and see-sawed between his mum and his dad at weekends. Her husband was also upset at this sudden loss of his family, but I never had a true appreciation of it all. They had split before we met, and since I wasn't in any way the cause, shrugged it off, and carried on dodging between the two women.

On one Friday night in July things came to a head. Meg had asked me to take her son fishing, since he'd always wanted to go, and her husband had never taken him. She told me he had accepted the situation with her new life and was now resigned (allegedly) to the impending divorce. So she asked me if I could please take him fishing, drop him off at his father's house in a village near Worcester, and then make my way over to her place in Malvern for the usual Friday night assignation. I agreed.

I picked her son up about 6 pm. He was excited and had been

looking forward to it all week. I wasn't sure I was, but nevertheless took him to the pools at Westwood. I showed him floats, reels, rods, and maggots. Real Mr Crabtree stuff, but this time I was Mr C, and he the junior learner. One thing I've learned when taking kids fishing is they need to catch something quickly, so I set up to fish for small rudd. The carp were wily and required stealth, time, and patience, and time was one thing I certainly didn't have. We caught a few rudd very easily on maggots, and he soon got the hang of it. He was delighted. We left the pool about 8 pm, having spent an hour or so hooking these obliging little fish, and he directed me to his dad's house. His dad was pleasant, civilised, and shepherded his son into his cottage. This was the first time we'd met, and I began to wonder why Meg had had so much difficulty with him over the divorce, signing papers, arranging maintenance payments, and so on. I didn't understand any of it. All in all he seemed like a nice guy. As arranged, I went on to Meg's place. She was dressed up to kill (for me that is) in a short skirt, skimpy top, and looked gorgeous, and out we went for a drink. We ended up in bed about 11 pm, just as it began to rain. And it sure did rain. In torrents. It crossed my mind at that point if Janet, who was presumably at home in Stourport, would ever buy my night-fishing alibi given this appalling July weather. Any sensible angler would have gone home, and so should I. Except that I didn't.

I was sure my fishing alibi would never, forgive the pun, hold water, and for the first time I began to have doubts about the wisdom of staying here with Meg all night. It was by now 1 am and for the past two hours we'd been engaged in an extensive and passionate lovemaking exercise, quite oblivious to the rain outside, which continued to lash down.

I was just thinking of making my excuses and leaving, when suddenly and out of the blue there was a furious banging on the front door downstairs. At first I half thought the rain had caused part of the roof to fall off, or something like that. Meg peeked out from behind the bedroom curtains in the candlelit bedroom, and there on the pavement outside stood her husband. The rain poured off him, his hair straggled across his face, and he was absolutely soaked. More ominously for me he had parked his car across her drive and blocked mine in.

This for me was one serious dilemma. Through the noise of the storm I could hear him crying and moaning and saying he loved her. All he wanted, he said, was my name and address to use in his divorce case to prove adultery. I didn't like the sound of that one bit. I stayed upstairs and thought hard about how in the hell I could get out of this. Meg eventually rang the police, and in due course a squad car showed up. The police evidently dismissed it as a domestic incident, and I watched this scenario down below from the spare bedroom. After five minutes they got in their car and disappeared. Her husband meanwhile continued howling and wailing. Christ knows what I'd got myself into here, but an emotional volcano for sure. A matter of minutes after the police had gone another bloody car appeared. Meg identified the driver as one of his friends from the rugby club, who had presumably come to support his mate. Rugby club? Jeeezzz ... things were getting even worse. I began to think my time was up, and I'd be beaten to a pulp by some twenty-stone full back. Both of them sat there in the car and waited. By now it was nearly 3 am. I went down to the kitchen to put the kettle on, and was trying to think fast. Then suddenly he appeared at the kitchen window. Presumably he'd seen the light shining across the drive. He stood there, hair and face plastered, clothes wringing wet, pleading with me through the window for my identification. It was pitiful, and in that instant I realised there and then with utter clarity how deep emotions run when two people, with children they love, go their separate ways. Through chattering teeth, he continued to repeat his request for my name and address. I think had it been me out there I would have battered the kitchen door down in anger. The police had clearly warned him not to cause trouble, and he didn't. Naturally I declined his request. In fact I told him through the glass that he was tired and emotional, and the best thing for him was to go home. I also noticed at this point that he was more than 6 ft tall.

I switched off the kitchen light and went back upstairs with my mug of tea. I was thinking very carefully. Meg watched through the curtains as her ex went back to sit in his car, only this time alongside his rugby-playing mate. I knew I needed to break this deadlock, or stand-off more like, with some decisive action. There was a phone box in the village (it's still there in Madresfield), and I decided to get to it somehow and phone my mate Peter. Yes, the same Peter who'd introduced me to Meg. I wouldn't say it was his fault exactly that I was in this predicament, (though I could make a case for it?) but I was sure he would help me out and do as I asked, since he lived not far away in Worcester. The next stage of my plan was for Meg to keep this bedraggled ex-husband engaged, by talking to him through the rain from the bedroom window. I didn't care what she said as long as he stayed at the front of the house.

The rain never let up for a minute and continued to sheet down as I opened the bathroom window upstairs. I looked down. It seemed a long way, and I've never been one for heights, but needs must. I climbed on to the rim of the bath, and out through the window I went, shinning down the slippery drainpipe. It wasn't easy, but I eventually dropped on to the patio, completely out of sight from the front of the cottage. Through the back garden I ran in the pitch dark. They say the darkest hour is just before dawn, and I agree. It was now 4 am. Climbing over the back fence, I made my way across a field of wet waist-high barley. I was soaked by the time I got to the road, having crawled through the hawthorn hedge bordering the field, which scratched and impaled me with its thorns. I stood on the pavement for a second and took stock. I could hardly believe this was happening, but it definitely was. I made it to the phone box, heaved the heavy door open and flung myself inside.

The rain meanwhile came down harder and clattered on the roof. With some relief I fished out some coins and rang my mate.

His wife answered after many rings, and was astonished to hear me. She put him on, and he was equally astonished, but agreed to come and get me. Meanwhile I sheltered in this phone box. It was now 4.30 am, and just beginning to get light. Still the rain hammered down. I cannot ever recall such a storm in July. This was supposed to be summer surely? Maybe it was punishment for my nefarious exploits, and striking me down from on high. That's how it felt. I almost began to believe in God. Or maybe the Devil?

After about ten minutes or so, I saw some headlights coming down the lane, and felt immense relief. It was Peter, or so I thought, except that it wasn't. It was Meg's husband's car. I simply couldn't understand how he knew I'd escaped, but he didn't know. It turned out subsequently that he hadn't a clue. Evidently he just wanted to use the phone to call his mother, who was looking after the house and children. He sat outside the box for fifteen minutes. I had my back to him and, receiver in hand, pretended to be on the phone. My heart was thumping.

Eventually I saw his car door open. He got out of the car and approached the box. At this point I knew I'd have to use my fists. If you have to fight a tall guy, and I'm only 5 ft 7 in, you have to go in fast and low under the arms to do some damage. I was coiled and ready to turn to hit him as he opened the door. As I spun round quickly and looked up to face him, it was his turn to be astonished. He simply couldn't believe it was me. I was fully expecting a serious fight, but suddenly he appeared to crumple up, his shoulders sagged, and became abjectly apologetic. This was the last thing I was expecting. He said since I wasn't in the house he now couldn't use that as an adulterous fact in his impending divorce. I stood there terse, soaked, and very angry, but a bit of me felt really sorry for him.

In the 1970s there had to be good reasons for filing for divorce, it's relatively simple these days, but adultery was a major factor for the courts to grant a divorce, and that included the name and address of the adulterer. In other words me. He asked me to step into his car out of the rain, which I politely declined to do, and at this point Peter turned up outside the phone box, in his pride and joy, a purple Cortina GT. He knew Meg's husband, pre their split, and they began to exchange pleasantries. I wasn't in the mood, and told him brusquely to get in the car and take me to Worcester. The last I saw of the soon to be ex-husband was him standing dejectedly in the phone box.

When we got to Peter's house I did my damnedest to dry off, his incredulous wife providing me with towels. It was now light, and about 5 am Meg rang to say the coast was clear. The ex and his rugby-playing mate had left. She then brought my car over to me, and after coffee and a hug or two Peter gave her a lift back to Malvern.

I arrived back home about 7 am, having changed back into my fishing gear en route. My wet clothes I dumped in the boot. I stood before a wife who I just knew didn't believe a word about my night-fishing exploits. Surely this couldn't continue, could it? But it did.

This emotional see-saw occupied me totally, continuing from 1974 to 1976. Christmases and birthday occasions were the worst. New Year's Eve especially, Meg's kids' birthdays, who now saw me very much as a father figure, but absent much of the time (I worked away of course). Meg's family gatherings, Janet's family gatherings, two social lives, neither of which had a clue about the other. I had two sets of friends. It was almost as if I changed into a different suit with a different persona. I went up to Yorkshire, met Meg's family up there, and on what pretext I made to Janet I have no recollection whatsoever. It was dreadful, all self-inflicted, and proving impossible to split myself in two. How I ever thought I could was simply stupid. The lies and deceit continued, and I naively believed I could deal with all this without any effect on me. I was wrong on that. Sooner or later I would fuck up and get caught.

It's impossible to describe the stress a double life creates. I wanted to be there, but I was here, and I wanted to be here when I was there. Somehow I managed to make a success of my job, in between all of this shit, despite the see-saw consuming me most of the time.

It became a nightmare. One lesson I've learned more than any other is that a relationship has to move. Forwards or backwards. It cannot stand still. Like water, it eventually stagnates. This affair of three to four years came to an abrupt halt in 1976.

What follows now is more of a book within a book, for that's what this has become. Prepare yourself for a complete diversion to the events so far.

Chapter 10

———————

By the beginning of 1976 Meg had trained to become a teacher in Rural Sciences, my sales job was routine, Janet continued to work at the Health Authority in Kidderminster, Stourport was boring, and the steam was somehow going out of this affair. It became more mundane, almost normal in some ways, but Meg still captivated me. By this time she had landed a job as a Rural Science teacher at a school in Cleobury Mortimer, and I helped her with the purchase of a house in Rock, a village near Clows Top. The delusion continued and I now had a social life with her teacher friends, and was known at the local pub, then back to Stourport I would go to take up my social life there. Somehow I squeezed a fortnight into a week. Nevertheless, things were moving on, and I knew I couldn't keep the lid on this for much longer.

I needed something by way of escape. I instinctively knew I had to break this cycle, but didn't know how.

1976 was an exceptional year, if not only for being one of the hottest years on record. By mid-March an area of high pressure settled over the country, and there it stayed. Day after day for weeks, hot days and cloudless skies. Streams and rivers dried, and water shortage emergencies were declared, each day seemingly hotter than the day before. By midday the heat was stifling.

On afternoon sometime in April I drove out of Birmingham along the Hagley Road in a shimmering heat haze of traffic, having finished my sales calls for the day. On impulse I pulled up and went into a news agency to buy a drink. Whilst there I picked up a copy of the *Birmingham Post*, a paper I never normally read, but there must have been something in the headline to have caught my eye, and back to the car I went. No air con either in those days so it was an oven on wheels.

I can't recall why I even bothered to turn to read the classified adverts. That I will never know, but in bold type I saw the words 'Activity Holiday: join us on an adventure to Kathmandu'. I was intrigued and called the number that evening from home. No mobile phones in those days of course. I spoke with Mike, and he explained that the idea was to take an old bus across the Asian Highway to Nepal. They were having a meeting that weekend and I was welcome to go. So I went.

I arrived on the Saturday afternoon at a nondescript semi-detached house somewhere in Halesowen. The plan, I discovered, was to take this old coach across the Channel to Europe, and camp along the way. Stopping very little on the first leg since Europe was expensive. Vienna was to be the first base camp. Then onwards to Venice. Yugoslavia next (as it was then). Down the Dalmation coast, into Greece, and so on, right across until we got to Nepal. The places described were just names to me in an atlas. The thought of actually going to them was another world to me. It was something of a breathtaking adventure and not without risk. I'd never been abroad, unless you count Anglesey. I'd talked about it countless times at college with my student mates, but it never came to anything. We all just followed the same path, got engaged, married, and mortgaged. Mike, the leader of this trip, had done it once before with his wife and a mate, and simply wanted to do it again. For me it was an opportunity to simply get the hell out of it. And best of all I had company to learn the ropes.

There were perhaps fifteen of us at the meeting, all of varying ages. Most were early twenties, a few girls, a couple of women in their fifties, divorced most likely, and then me aged twenty-seven, hiding a double life. Some were still in hippy mode, ex-students probably, excited by lure of the Asian Highway, and the appeal of unlimited supplies of dope to be found along the way. Some it turned out were just mixed up (as if I wasn't). I hit it off immediately with Karl, a Brummie, a bit older than me, recently divorced, whose sole aim was to pursue the purest Afghan gold. It was he who subsequently introduced me to Pink Floyd's *Dark Side of the Moon.* A complicated band, whose music I'd never really appreciated. This was the premium album to get stoned by, as I was reliably informed by those in the know. It seemed to me the whole trip was designed as a hippy trip to Heaven. One or two were of an age where they just wanted some adventure, presumably a last fling to take memories from in later life. Then me, who just saw it as a means of escape. I liked all of them instinctively, they were an odd, dislocated bunch. I signed up there and then.

My resignation from Jackson Boilers a week later came as a shock to most in the company. With the economy in decline, a three-day week for some factories, and union activism in the ascendancy, thus interrupting electricity supplies, it was probably the worst possible time to throw in the job. As my work colleagues, and my dad especially saw it, they thought I was completely mad, and were probably right. My motivation was different though. I needed to get out of this pressure cooker before insanity took over. For me it was a lifeline.

It was now May, and the trip was scheduled to leave in June/July time. We had another meeting and Mike provided us with sheets of copied notes with tips and hints of all we needed, medical requirements, maps, currency, and all the places we intended to visit. He then showed us the bus we were to take, which was parked along the road from his house. It reminded me of the one in *Magical Mystery Tour* without the psychedelic swirly patterns. He'd removed some of the seats to create more space. The bus looked a bit old and knackered, but evidently serviceable. I paid the £50 deposit. The total cost was expected to be around £350. I was now well and truly committed. I had my 'get out of jail free' card.

I sat Janet down when I got back. She didn't seem the least surprised when I told her I was leaving. I packed up some of my stuff, including my trusty old guitar, and moved it all to Meg's place near Clows Top. Meg was clearly upset that I was leaving, but Janet still didn't know I'd dumped my meagre possessions there. I now had a plan and a course of action. During this time I arranged to take my MGA to a guy who had a factory in Coleshill where I could park it up. Dylan, my little terrier dog, was a problem. He was the only one who knew about my complicated life. I'd confided in him many times. That dog was probably my best (and only) friend and I loved him dearly. Janet, oddly, appeared unconcerned about him, so there was no custody battle. Besides he was my dog really, and carried many of my secrets. Just a year or so before, he'd had an accident with a van when he ran across the road. It broke his thigh, a horrifying injury, and cost me a small fortune at the vets to get it pinned. I knew I'd miss him more than anything else, so my sister Julia, up in Boroughbridge in Yorkshire, agreed to look after him. She already knew some of my complex lifestyle, so she could at least talk to Dylan in confidence.

Janet and I planned to put the house on the market. She knew instinctively it was over between us, and anyway was looking to find herself a place in Kidderminster, so the dog and my car weren't top of the list of her priorities.

I then borrowed money from Barclays (£1,000) based on my share of the equity in the house at Stourport, which had risen in value and doubled to £10,000. A profit of £5,000 in four years, split 50/50 between myself and Janet. Inflation had rocketed the value, and with it taken the economy of the country into a downward spiral. Despite the continued glorious weather, all around was doom and gloom. I couldn't wait to get the hell out of it.

While I was busy tidying my affairs, working out my notice, buying camping equipment, organising traveller's cheques (in dollars), I also needed some jabs. On the notes Mike had provided were certain requirements which were deemed essential, some needing certificates for different countries. Yellow fever, cholera, blackwater fever, hepatitis, and other hideous sounding diseases. I have a pathological hatred towards hypodermic needles, but I braced myself, and organised appointments at the local medical centre in Stourport. I had to have these jabs in stages, and now I

115

know why. The typhoid one was nothing. A tiny little jab. I wondered suddenly what all the fuss was about. Two days later I was poleaxed. I felt bloody awful for days afterwards. Then there was the jab for hepatitis C. Mysteriously this needed to be administered by a doctor, and had to be timed for maximum effectiveness. Two weeks before I left I discovered that the injection took eight weeks to develop this protection, so I needed to gauge when I would be most at risk.

I went along one evening with Meg for this most important of injections. It was called gamma globulin, at least that's what it said on the notes. Into the surgery I went. Nothing I thought could be worse than the typhoid one. How wrong I was. I was told to drop my trousers, lie on the couch and turn on my side. The doc approached with a needle the size of a small thermos flask, filled with purple liquid. I was terrified. She then stuck it in the cheek of my arse, and it went in deep. I could feel the tears welling, but gritted my teeth. After what seemed like half an hour I eventually heard the click of the syringe and she pulled it out. I tried to sit up, but she ordered me back down, and to turn over. I asked why. She told me it was only half a dose. She was to administer an equal dose to the other half of my arse. I almost wept. It was truly the worst injection imaginable. I recall hobbling out of that place like a disabled sailor. My arse felt like it had been beaten with a baseball bat, and when I got to the car I could barely get in it. Meg opened the back door for me and I lay down on the back seat gasping in pain. I was totally incapable of driving so she took us back to her place. Never have I experienced anything like it, and I hope I never will again. It took me a week to get over the bruising.

Whilst serving out my notice at TI Catering Equipment in May/June, and the sweltering heat of this extraordinary year continuing, drying up rivers and turning the grass brown, I got a call from the Managing Director, Mr Crathorne. He was a bit of a god-like man, feared by most of the staff, and yet a relatively young man to be in charge of a Tube Investment company. He was about forty, and had been put by the TI Group board into TI

Catering Equipment Ltd, my employer, to kick arses. Which he did. Formerly Jackson Boilers, it had been bought out by the TI Group, who amalgamated the manufacturing of their commercial arm Creda Electric, and New World, the gas division. Crathorne was a formidable operator, and most were intimidated by him. Me included.

I went up to Leeds at his request, to arrange the handover of my car, and files too. He summoned me to his office. I knocked and nervously entered. He sat behind an enormous desk, in a huge mahogany-panelled office, and brusquely waved me to a seat. He then asked me what on earth I thought I was doing giving up a well-paid job. I never mentioned my current self-created domestic mess, which was of course the primary reason. I told him I needed to travel. Something I had always wanted to do, but marriage and mortgage had got in the way. I fully expected him to call the nearest hospital and get me admitted for taking leave of my senses. The UK economy was on the floor. A job was worth having, and more importantly keeping. I'd had this reaction from just about everyone else, my father especially. But not from this guy. They all thought I was mad, but not Crathorne. He surprised and astonished me by being fully supportive. There and then he asked me not to leave the company, refused to accept my resignation, and then, out of the blue, offered to grant me six months leave of absence from the company. Would I be OK with that? Of course I bloody would! No salary, but pension and National Insurance contributions would be paid. It took awhile for the enormity of all this to sink in, but I was delighted. During this rather nerve-wracking meeting I plucked up the courage to ask him how he had developed such a stellar career. He then gave me a piece of advice which I have never forgotten.

Look forward to people ten years older than you, and if you see yourself in their position and following in their path, a path which you'd rather not follow, pause, and begin to make a ten year plan. Then implement incremental or major changes to it every three years, but to nevertheless stick to the ten-year plan. Once there, reassess, and make another ten-year plan. As far as I was concerned, I had no plan whatsoever, apart from get out of this situation. His words caused me to stop and think where I was going and what I wanted to be. I still didn't quite know then, but it caused me to concentrate. I was twenty-seven and needed to put a stop to this aimless lifestyle. In other words I needed to grow up. The way I saw it, this forthcoming overland trip would provide an opportunity to reassess what was and was not important. Above all it would give me the freedom to think.

Crathorne himself had started out in TI twenty years before with a BSc (Honours) degree in metallurgy, didn't like the trajectory he was on and went to night school to qualify for a master's degree in General Management, which he felt was more in tune with his talents. He was now firmly on a route of his choice, and running all aspects of this business. Interestingly he also asked me if I ever got to Australia (which was my ambition) if I would do a little job for him. He wanted me to carry out a survey of the catering equipment market in Australia, and that I should contact a mate of his at GEC Sydney, where a letter would be waiting for me. This group of companies had their own export division but Crathorne deemed it to be 'fucking useless'. I was still a bit numb from his refusal to accept my resignation, but I accepted his offer, and with his blessing, and still reeling a bit, caught the train back home from Leeds to Meg, having been embraced with good wishes from all the office staff. Now I had a focus. A project. Assuming I made it to Australia of course.

My goal had always been Australia. I'd discovered via my fellow traveller mate Karl, who had become my new best friend and rang me regularly and excitedly about our impending voyage, that Trailfinders in London did 'bucket shop' flights. I didn't quite know what these were, but soon discovered that two students, one from Australia, and one from England, had met somewhere in India, and decided between them to start what was effectively a student travel business. They bought up unoccupied space in airlines around the world very cheaply, and operated on a

118

shoestring from a tiny little basement office in Earls Court. I'd been to see them armed with my trip notes. The office was staffed with a few young, long-haired kids whose only qualification, it seemed, was that they'd travelled. My trip goal was Nepal, and I intended to leave the group there, but then what? I didn't intend to fly home. These guys pointed me in the direction of Burma, Malaysia, Thailand, Singapore and Australia, and fixed the flights I'd need to take with a degree of flexibility on the times and dates I needed. The only proviso for Australia was that I had by law to have a flight booked out of that country, as well as a travel visa, which they organised. I dug into my little pot of capital and paid up, not even certain I would ever make the Holy Grail, which for me was Sydney. I wanted to repay Crathorne for his faith in me, but more importantly saw this as a chance to rebuke my dad, who had sneered at me years before saying 'Send me a card when you get there' at the time I was putting in my application for the assisted passage to Australia in 1968. As you know, it didn't happen, and I ended up in Redditch.

Trailfinders proved to be a huge boost for my confidence. They gave me yet more photostatted handwritten notes. Places to go, what to eat, what to avoid, and a general awareness of what to expect in some of these exotic places I'd only ever read about. Nowadays Trailfinders is a hugely successful worldwide business. From little acorns and ideas such big oak trees grow, eh? If ever you fancy remote travel, Trailfinders are the go-to people.

Chapter 11

This is a big side story. It gets a whole chapter.
And a long one at that!

I joined the bus in Halesowen on a Saturday morning in early July. I can't remember the date exactly, but I didn't care for dates and times. In my head I was already gone.

Meg came to see me off, with a couple of my friends, and after tearful hugs and 'take care's I climbed on with one rucksack (Karrimor) filled with essential clothing, and my sleeping bag and tent tied to it. I can't remember how I felt. Nervously excited, I suppose. The weather had continued with these cloudless blue skies, and heat. As I said earlier some seats had been removed to accommodate luggage, as well as space for the fifteen or so of us to move about. The driver Mike had a co-driver to share the driving, and he'd also asked us to bring tapes of music we liked. Yes, cassette tapes. No CDs, iPods, iPads, mobile phones, music streaming. None of this was invented. He had a stack of these tapes, and would pick one at random.

The rest of the group I'd hit it off with, having already met them, so I settled down in my seat, a seat which I commandeered for the entire trip. Karl sat opposite. I can't remember the names of all of them, and to be honest it doesn't much matter. I was entirely concerned with myself. This would prove to be the proverbial trip of a lifetime, and my thoughts turned to all those years ago in the common room, when we students sat around planning major overseas adventures, all of them to have fallen away and disappeared as we went our separate ways. It may well have been eight years earlier, but better late than never, eh? This time I really was doing it.

The first tape Mike played on the way down to Dover was mine. And the first track on the tape was 'I'm Alive' by The Hollies. More than appropriate. For the very first time in my life I was actually going abroad. I was alive and kicking at long last, and all the people over all those years who spent years talking and never doing something like this, I'd trumped. The expression 'Those who can, do, and those who think, talk about it' is more than apt. My first discovery as I embarked on this trip is that the world is divided into doers and thinkers. You won't find the doers at home talking about things. They've gone. They're doing it.

In some strange way I felt as though I'd shut the door on a past life. I didn't feel the urge to ring home when we got to Dover with 'missing you already' tears. None of that. I was looking forward in another different dimension to a new life.

I sat on this bus and scribbled furiously in a school exercise book. Every sight, every impression, every new thought. I'd decided to do that from the very start, to help reinforce my thoughts and memories of all these new experiences. Even though I have these books still, I'm writing this from memory. Writing commits things to memory and this is the proof. It works forty-four years on.

On the way down to Dover I sat there and reflected on the past few weeks. I considered myself lucky. Very lucky. I'd retained my job, extricated myself from the stress of a dual relationship, had a few quid in my pocket, a wedge of traveller's cheques, and was off and running just as I'd dreamed. Above all I learned quickly the need to budget for the foreseeable, the next three months. A very useful cash flow lesson for the future.

I don't propose to detail all the events of those three or four months on this bus, it would take another book, and one day I may write it, in which case I may have to refer to my exercise books, but I'll precis the journey, and a few of the more notable occurrences in due course.

The bus arrived in Dover late afternoon, some four hours after we'd left Birmingham, and an hour or two before we sailed.

Oddly I can't recall now where the ferry from there was going. I think it might have been Zeebrugge, but I don't think it was Calais. Bruges? Possibly, but not that it matters much. I just remember standing on the deck watching the cliffs of Dover recede in the twilight as the ferry got underway. I was in quite a wistful mood, and in something of a turmoil inside my head. Eventually the coastline disappeared into the gloom and I wondered when I would see England again. I wondered at this point how the soldiers of World War I must have felt. In many cases they never ever saw England again.

As I've said before, this was the very first time I was actually going into what for me was the unknown, and was grateful for the company of the others, a few of whom had done this before. The plan was to race through Belgium, and aim to get to a campsite near Vienna by morning, so we drove through the night. I only got occasional glimpses of the countryside, which was flat, with lines of poplar trees along the roads, and square fields. That was it. Belgium, I concluded, was boring.

To do full justice to the trip I was embarking on would need another section or book reserved exclusively for it. I have the aforementioned diaries and exercise books describing events along the way in far greater detail, but was determined wherever possible to put my thoughts down on paper. As it's uncertain whether I will write that book, I will now devote the rest of this chapter or mini book within a book, to what happened and where I went. I suppose it will inevitably be the more memorable events I'll recall. Those which had most impact on me for all kinds of reasons.

Austria

We arrived in Vienna late morning, having stopped at times for coffee and snacks through the night, and found the camp site somewhere on the outskirts of the city. I had slept a bit during the journey but was tired. My tent was a Vango Force Ten. I loved that tent. It was orange, made of some heavy-duty cotton with a flysheet and sewn-in groundsheet. Didn't take me long to put up. I rolled out my sleeping bag, adjusted my watch to the new time in Europe, and along with most of the others caught up on sleep. My first impression of Austria was mountains. Dozens of them. Huge, snow-capped and glowering, and all looking down on little me. The Alps. Most impressive, and it made my familiar Snowdonia look a bit toytownish. We went later into Vienna, a beautiful city with wonderful architecture, and if you've never been, well you should, or Google it.

It was cloudy, rainy, the campsite was soggy, and it felt unseasonably cool, but after the heatwave, by all accounts continuing in England, it made a welcome change. I can't remember if we cooked as a group, or we ate out. Money was tight for us all, so I doubt it was the latter. That was the essential purpose of legging it quickly through Europe. What I do recall is mooching around Vienna, posting a card back home and having a beer or two with my new mate Karl, the skinny thirty-five-year-old ageing hippy, his thick Brummie accent seeming oddly out of place in Vienna.

Back to my tent, and I quite simply crashed out, and slept like the proverbial log. We took off again first thing in the morning after a hasty breakfast, heading for Venice. The scenery along the way was in total contrast to Belgium, with narrow steep mountain passes, and wooden chalets dotted along the slopes and valleys. Trees, fir woods and lakes. I was mesmerised. I also found it strange that within twenty-four hours or so of leaving my dog Dylan, estranged wife Janet, girlfriend Meg, and her two kids, they had become almost an irrelevance. That was a surprise. How quickly memories can fade. It really seemed a lifetime ago that I was rushing round like a maniac, emotional, tearful, uncertain of the wisdom of all this, and merely forty-eight hours had elapsed and I was in another world. This sudden transformation astounded me.

Italy

I can't quite remember how long the trip took from Vienna to Venice, but I do recall the campsite, which was near water and misty and warm when we arrived. I could see the lights of Venice across the bay, or river, or whatever it was. As we pitched our tents that evening the mosquitoes arrived in clouds. I had some repellent, part of the kit I needed, and I'd never had cause to use it before. Basically it didn't work. If anything they seemed to thrive on the stuff. They were almost as immune to it as I became to their bites eventually. It was something I became used to, particularly over the coming weeks.

I was asked by the sister of one of the guys on the bus if I would accompany her into Venice. Her name was Leslie. About twenty, small, petite, a pretty girl with unusually shortly cropped hair. This I learned was deliberate. She'd had it cut for convenience in the event she couldn't find a suitable hairdresser along the way. My hair was the opposite. Now I out of suits and ties, it was inching over my ears, and heading in the direction of my hippy days at college. I tried to imagine Leslie with long dark hair, but failed.

Neither of us had ever been to Venice before, but she had an ambition to waltz in St Mark's Square. She certainly knew more about Venice than I did. I knew nothing whatsoever about St Mark's Square, and even less about dancing. I obliged, and managed an awkward waltz with her to a violin quartet who were playing outside one of the restaurants. I recall this spacious square having the most incredible acoustic atmosphere. Leslie was funny, and knowledgeable. She knew her history, and enlightened me on Venice and its history. The city isn't sinking. The sea level is rising, as it has been for thousands of years. Astonishingly, 40,000 years ago it was hundreds of miles from the sea. Climate change is continuous and ruled by the cosmos.

The square was a piazza, with what I remember as smooth marble slabs. Gorgeous architecture lined it, and tourists with cameras clicked away. Most of Venice was ancient and exquisite, crammed with small shops and restaurants. The gondolas fascinated me, and paddled up and down the narrow litter-strewn canals, I held hands with Leslie, and was beguiled by the place. We visited coffee shops and various bars, and by the time I got back to the campsite around 11 pm, I was unbelievably pissed.

I fell into my tent, and she followed. By then it was probably midnight. I don't know how quickly all this happened, but one moment we were lying there giggling, and the next she was out of her jeans and all over me. I didn't think of England at all, just went for the moment. And nothing happened. Some people call it brewer's droop, but try as I might I went nowhere. Here I was with this semi-pissed woman I hardly knew, panting breathlessly, under me, and I was helpless and hopeless.

Mentally I tried to figure it out. I put it down to the booze, but maybe somehow, somewhere in the back of my mind was guilt? I don't know. Perhaps it was the short hair, which gave her a boyish appearance? Was it that? I looked for excuses but I can tell you this: It caused me more than a little consternation. Never, ever, with any woman I'd known intimately had this happened before. Leslie made some kind and sympathetic comments which frankly didn't help. She pulled on her clothes and staggered off back to her tent. It bothered me for days afterwards, but neither of us ever mentioned it again on the entire trip. Leslie and I remained friendly but I didn't try to make it up. This was the first time I'd ever experienced some form of erectile dysfunction.

It didn't take me long to forget about it though. The reason was simple. I'd already set my sights on another girl I'd noticed from the outset. She, coincidentally, was also travelling with her brother. About thirty, long-haired and voluptuous. More my type.

Yugoslavia

A merging of three countries – Croatia, Serbia, and Bosnia – which were all ruled by President Tito. A ruler and dictator, who in turn was under the Communist control of the Soviet Union. Yugoslavia was a satellite outpost of the USSR, and they backed Tito with armed force.

The weather was exceptionally bright, warm and sunny, and we arrived in Split with the Aegean Sea sparkling along the coast. Split was a shock. It contrasted with the weather insofar as it was the drabbest, most depressing place I'd ever encountered. High-rise, ugly, dilapidated apartments. God knows what it must have been like on a wet, drizzly, overcast day. I think to live there would drive anyone to suicide. This was socialism in action. As far as I was concerned it wasn't working.

We stopped overnight here. I have no recollection of the campsite, but couldn't wait to throw myself in the sea, and having pitched my tent was first in. Crystal-clear, and the most amazing blue. When I clambered out up the pebbly beach, tingling with the joy of water, Mike (the leader) pointed out the sea urchins. I'd never seen them before, and never noticed them. These black spiny creatures were all over the rocks. I prised one off with a stick and saw the spines were needle sharp. Had I trodden on one it was a hospital job. The spines are brittle, enter the flesh and break off, which makes them probably about the most poisonous thorn in the foot ever. I was lucky I missed them. I'd now learned another lesson. The other of course was not to get pissed when you have a woman in your sleeping bag.

Our destination was Dubrovnik. This is an ancient city, and has a castle surrounded by a high battlement. What I noticed most were the bullet holes in the stone. In fact some fierce fighting had taken place here, no doubt during WW2, but there may well have been a revolution of some sort when Tito took over. History isn't my strong point, but Dubrovnik was a lovely city, at least in the centre, and in the suburbs I could see the ubiquitous high-rise apartments, as with Split, all in disrepair. Communism wasn't working for them either.

By now Sandra was with me. This was the one I'd had my eye on, who as I said was also travelling with her brother. This wasn't the Sandra from my school in Leicestershire either. That Sandra, you know the one, who occupied me in so many ways when I was sixteen. By pure coincidence this new Sandra also happened to be from Leicestershire.

Slim, long dark hair, and recently out of a broken relationship, (weren't we all?), she was travelling on the bus with her brother Phil, and like me, had sought escape from the mess she'd left behind. I'd noticed her early on, as I said. With my lamentable Venice performance with Leslie now firmly behind me, and still managing to remain on friendly terms, I felt that Sandra, cheesy I know, was more 'my type'. We spent the afternoon roaming round Dubrovnik and found the whole experience of the place, and the sheer adventure of what we were doing, exciting. The day culminated in a rather languorous kiss, sitting together on a large rock under the castle walls, and gazing out to sea as the sun went down over the Aegean. It was very romantic. I loved it.

We became a couple from this point on, though she was very attached to her brother and tended to follow him as if he were some kind of guardian. Nevertheless, it was for me an enhancement to the trip. I often think the importance of any relationship is founded on shared experiences. I really needed someone with me to share those experiences, and unfortunately I seem to fall in love very easily. I knew in my head time was limited for us both, but I enjoyed all of it while it lasted.

Greece

From Yugoslavia we touched on Albania, and all I recall of that was forest-clad mountains. Over the border we went and after cursory glances at our passports, the border police waved us through and we and arrived in northern Greece. The landscape changed almost instantly from high towering peaks to a flat plain. It was hot. It had been hot at home, and then cool across Belgium and Vienna, humid in Venice, almost spring-like in Yugoslavia, but Greece was seriously hot. Getting off the bus the heat hit me in the face, and almost immediately I was drenched in sweat. By now I was travelling in shorts and cotton tee shirt.

I'd drunk Pernod once or twice at home, my Mum quite liked that stuff, but here was Ouzo, a Greek version, which turned cloudy when mixed with water. There were expansive beaches, olive groves, dust, and tavernas. We stopped at one for lunch. Olives, feta, tomato and onion salad, kleftiko, meatballs and beer. I delighted in this new-found experience. We take this stuff for granted in delicatessens and supermarkets. It was all totally new to me, and I loved it all.

We continued south to Athens. I could see the haze of pollution way off, and by God it was a hot huge city, and chaotic. I've never been back, never had the opportunity, or more to the point desire, but that was my impression. I like driving, I really do, but I'm glad I wasn't driving this bus. It seemed everyone was in a tearing hurry. Exhaust and car horns. That was Athens. Filthy and full of traffic, and then suddenly and out of all context was the Parthenon. I never expected it. It was a shock. This ancient monument sits in the centre of this heaving city on a volcanic rocky hill. All the photos I'd ever seen of it had given me the impression it was out in the middle of nowhere. A bit like estate agents who always take the most considered photos of a property for their particulars, which lure you to view it, and you then find its next door to a railway yard. That was the Parthenon, sitting right in the middle of this mayhem. To my inexperienced traveller's eye it was all wrong and out of character.

Over the next day or two we travelled across northern Greece via Thessaloniki. At some point we stopped at a ruined Roman amphitheatre. A deserted place seemingly in the middle of nowhere, and vegetation growing out of the old stone structures. This place had been buried for several thousand years, until discovered by some archaeologists who were still in the process of revealing the extent of the place. Under the ruined buildings were catacombs. Evidently this was the place where they kept the wild animals for the gladiators to fight. I found it fascinating as well as gruesome. There were stone pigeonholes, and a guide explained that this was where cloths were soaked in the blood of various menstruating animals. They would then be draped over some unfortunate woman, which enticed the male of whichever species to rape them whilst they were strapped down. Donkeys were commonly used apparently. This was, how can I put it, crowd entertainment on another scale. I vaguely wondered if lions and tigers had been persuaded to perform and what might be left of the woman when they'd finished. Maybe they ate her instead.

Turkey

Onwards to Turkey. Istanbul was the first taste I actually had of the East and it all seem to change instantly. The crossing point from West to East. Mosques and Arabs, burkhas, turbans and Ali Baba sprang to mind. I'm no anthropologist, but as my journey progressed I could see the change in people, their dress and their facial characteristics particularly became more noticeable. The smiling olive-skinned Greeks gradually became bronzed, scowling, hook-nosed Arabs.

Two nights in Istanbul (Constantinople as it was originally known), and I met many other travellers from various countries in Europe, and one or two surprisingly from the United States, and there were always backpackers from Australia. The campsite was situated in the suburbs, and all these travellers were doing the same or similar to us. Some heading east, some west. Istanbul was a real crossroads. As I've said before, these people were the doers. I was impressed.

There is the Pudding Shop in Istanbul, it was very famous then, though whether it still exists today I don't know. It serves, as the name suggests, nothing but puddings. Big sticky sweet things. This place was THE Mecca for travellers and hippies from all over Asia, a meeting point, where notes and cards were pinned to the walls notifying the whereabouts of individuals and promising to meet on such and such a date.

Apart from a visit to the famous Blue Mosque, I walked to a huge busy bazaar and bought an onyx pipe. I was warned and advised to be prepared to barter, not accept the first price and be quite prepared to walk away, which I did. The price as I recall started out at about a fiver, and I ended up with this thing for about £1. I smoked a pipe in those days, and had taken with me from the start about 2 lb in weight of Condor ready rubbed tobacco, my nicotine drug of choice. Besides I was unsure of what if any pipe tobacco might be available on a six-month trek. I rationed myself accordingly. I did find some pipe tobacco on one occasion. It looked like it smelt. Camel shit.

On the way back to camp, admiring the pipe I'd virtually stolen, I went through a series of alleyways and became aware of being followed. Two men behind, one loitering in front, and despite giving them the slip, found they continued to trail me. I had a catapult in my pocket which I'd brought from England, along with a bag of marbles. It was my idea of protection. I was always good with a catapult as a kid, and used to knock cans off the wall with my home made one. This was a proper one, which I'd concealed in my gear. It wasn't that I was paranoid, just cautious. I was glad I had it now in the top pocket of my Levi's shirt, with a couple of marbles in my jeans. The guy in front of me slowed to a stop and turned. My hands were shaking, but I loaded this thing, fired it straight at his head about four or five feet away, and couldn't miss. He clutched his hands to his head and yelled. I legged it. The two guys behind ran to him. I'd been right in my instincts. In fact, I was quite proud of myself, and then suddenly began to wonder if I'd damaged his eyesight. My sympathy didn't last long, but before I knew it I was back to the relative safety of camp. I kept that catapult with me all the time after that, but never had occasion to use it again. And it was dead easy to hide from any customs scrutiny. Knives and guns were the usual target.

When I was a kid, I played the part of Achilles in a school play. I had no idea who Achilles was apart from a warrior who fought with Hector, to rescue Helen of Troy, who in turn had been abducted from Greece to Troy, and damn me, Troy I discovered, at the age of twenty-seven, was in Turkey. I thought at the age of ten or eleven it was a made-up place, but no it wasn't. We left Instabul and over to Troy we went. It took more or less all day to get there across desert and scrub and farmland. There was the usual visitor centre, and there in the middle stood a big wooden horse. I remembered the horse from school, and how the Greek soldiers had hidden in it before they came out at night, opened the big doors to let their army in who in turn promptly wrecked the place, abducting Helen in the process and shipping this tearful, distraught woman back to her homeland. Women, eh? The cause of so much war and grief.

I always felt a bit sorry for Hector. Achilles slaughtered him, before he himself was shot in the foot with an arrow, and that finished him off. That's the Achilles heel of course, and I remember hobbling off the school stage to die a hideous death shortly after I'd skewered Hector with a plastic sword. I didn't like the kid anyway, but the real Hector was a nice guy. His only crime was falling in love, and Helen has much to answer for, I reckon.

I'm not one for museums and history, and apart from my school play connection, found it all mildly interesting. Then off we went the following day down the coast for a bit and over some mountainous terrain lining the coast. The mountains were steep-sided and forested below. Up and up we went, and despite the cloudless skies it grew colder. The roads were narrow and very twisty and at times the bus had difficulty negotiating the extreme bends. Then suddenly and without warning a lorry loaded with tree trunks came roaring up behind us, diesel fumes belching, decided to overtake us on this insanely narrow road. As it did it pulled in sharply, to handle the next bend and avoid sliding over the 500 ft precipice. Despite Mike braking sharply, the lorry made it past us, but the tree trunks sticking out the back didn't. They smashed into the front of the bus, bringing us to a standstill, the windscreen glass sprayed all over the road, and the radiator hissing steam. These overhanging logs had literally ripped off the front of the bus. It was a miracle Mike wasn't killed. The lorry disappeared off round the next bend never to be seen again. Mike was badly shaken but furious.

We were now well and truly stranded up in these mountains, with not a sign of anyone. We simply didn't know what to do. Then an old Skoda came rattling down the road. Somehow, we managed to explain to the driver what had happened, and asked him to get help. Half an hour went by, as we mooched around wondering what would happen next. Then out of nowhere two army trucks arrived, loaded with young soldiers carrying machine guns, who promptly arrested us. They examined our passports, then climbed on the bus and checked our gear. Eventually they fixed up a rope of some sort to the bus, and towed the stricken vehicle, with all of us on board, down the mountains. Our brakes virtually burned themselves out.

Eventually we arrived at the small town of Silifke, to be towed into a military police compound, where we pitched our tents for two nights whilst we negotiated with the police chief, since we were all in custody. Why I'll never know, I felt it was something of an event to them, to while away a bit of time. The chief, or garrison commander, had apparently ordered his troops to find the lorry. They had no chance, but scurried off nevertheless in their jeep-like trucks looking for a truckload of logs which could be anywhere by now. So there we were for two days, pitching our tents in this dusty compound while they scampered around futilely. Needless to say, they failed totally to locate the culprit, but by now were running out of paperwork to fill in. Mike, in exchange for a couple of bottles of scotch, secured our release. The radiator we fixed whilst we were stuck there, but the rest of it was a mess, and we limped out of the place with no windscreen, and drove down the coast for a bit to a campsite of sorts on a remote beach. Here we stayed for two weeks while arrangements were made to get replacement parts sent over from the UK. The bus was towed to a local garage to await the spares. It was a long wait.

This remote coastal area near Silifke is now a resort area for package holidaymakers known as Olu Denis. I went there some years ago to do a diving course, staying in a fancy hotel. In fact I also did a paraglide jump up in the mountains. All 6,000 ft of them above the beaches, and managed to land on the beach right next to my wife and two children. It's astonishing how much had changed, but that's progress I suppose, or not. Turkey was in those days ruled by a military government, and now is part of a thriving tourist economy. One morning, I went exploring and after some time trying to get my bearings, eventually found the little campsite we stayed at all those years before. It still had the same broken fence around it and the same little olive trees. They hadn't changed.

Being stuck on a beach in my tent for a couple of weeks became boring, though I had one hell of a suntan. I met many locals, and learned how to snorkel properly by equalising my ears under water, courtesy of a US pilot who was stationed nearby. We became regular swimming mates. He also taught me both how to catch and cook octopus (simmered in seawater for a couple of hours with whole lemons, then chopped up and fried in garlic and olive oil).

When I did the dive course years later, I recognised some of the reefs I'd snorkelled, but of the octopus there was no sign. Evidently the bays had been dynamited by the locals. Not exactly sustainable fishing. The reefs have been degraded and ruined.

Eventually the main parts we needed to get the bus operational arrived from England. Not the windscreen though, which did eventually turn up much later, though where and how I can't recall, and finally, and at long last, we left. All of us were pleased and delighted to be back on the road. My relationship with Sandra had developed, although she seemed overly concerned with her brother and what he felt about this sex-fuelled romance. She always returned to her tent, whatever the hour, to be with him. It was odd in a way but she must have felt an obligation to him. It didn't bother me though. I loved my own space, I still do, and dozing off with my book in my Vango Force Ten was bliss. Besides, sharing a sleeping bag isn't easy, and neither was privacy, although I always pitched my tent right at the edge of the site, virtually on the beach, and as far away from the group as I could decently be.

The entire group of us had gelled together well though, and each night was food and booze, and conversation. It was however probably around this point in time I felt I was socially distancing myself. I don't quite know why. It was possibly the two- to three-week delay stuck in Turkey. I was frustrated by that. I hadn't got a timetable to speak of, but I'd given myself four to six months to be away, and had an itinerary of sorts in my head. This enforced delay had taken time out of my hands, and I was impatient to be moving on. I knew these friendships I'd developed wouldn't last, and there was no way I intended to come back with any of them. I was already way ahead and eagerly looking forward to being free of them and travelling alone. In the matter of a few weeks since I'd left England, I was suddenly an experienced traveller. I'd learned a hell of a lot in quite a short space of time.

Despite the missing windscreen, we finally got going. Over to the hot sulphur springs of Pammakale first, a stark sparkling white blob of a mountain slope, in total contrast to the sand and brown of the scrubby desert. Hot springs to laze in. Quite an amazing and unexpected treat. We then climbed into a mountain range and with the windscreen gone it became appreciably colder. Mike drove relatively slowly. The air pressure inside the bus flexed and vibrated the rear windscreen with the build-up of air, which required us to open the side windows at the back to release it. When it was cold it was very cold, and slowly we made our way across Turkey's hinterland, towards Iran. It seemed to take forever to get across Turkey, at least three or four days, and I suddenly noticed it had turned particularly cold at night in the tent, though Sandra did her best to warm me up. Searing heat during the day in desert country, unlike water, is released quickly at night. Turkey is also a big country, much of it desert and rock. I realised the country was much bigger than I'd thought.

Eventually we arrived in Ararat, close to the Iranian border. Just like Troy I always thought Ararat was a made-up name. A bit like Gotham City in the Batman series. Or Toytown, or whatever. I was wrong. Ararat exists, and the Bible is correct, because Mount Ararat was the actual place where Noah's Ark came to rest, after the forty days and forty nights of rain which God had instigated with the sole intention of wiping out the scum of humanity. I have to tell you, he didn't succeed. Mount Ararat was a snow-capped peak not far away from the town of the same name. Of the Ark there was no sign that I could see. Or the animals which had gone in two by two. They'd long scarpered.

I tried to visualise the Ark sitting on top of this mountain as the water subsided. In fact I half expected to see it sitting up there like one of those wrecked Spanish galleons. The locals hadn't made a replica either, like they'd done with the wooden horse in Troy.

It was also hard to imagine the whole planet being soaked too, especially in this dry and arid landscape. Besides, in those days the planet was flat, which meant that the water would have run off the edge. As the story goes Noah had been busy building this big ship in anticipation of the flood, and then crammed two of every living creature into it. I never got that as a kid. Surely the flies would have been eaten by the spiders, which in turn would have been eaten by the birds, which would've been eaten by the cats, and so on (which reminds me of the song about 'there was an old woman who swallowed a fly'). It was a great story when I was ten years old, and still is a great story, in the same way Santa Claus is a great story. It was probably about then that I realised what stupidity it all was.

Noah's story however was delivered by my teacher in complete solemnity. I would have been about five. Back then I believed it. Then as I got older disbelieved it, for the reasons above. But now finding the actual, real Ararat on the border of Turkey and Iran was altogether a big surprise. While I stood there looking at this mountain in the distance, for a split second or two I questioned my dismissal of the Noah story, and suddenly wondered if it might have been true after all. But no, because there was no sign of that wrecked Ark up there on the hill. I finally concluded it was definitely a lie.

It's only nowadays I realise how close we were to Azerbaijan, and Georgia. I never knew those places existed. At that time it formed part of the USSR. The border of Iran was one of the most hostile of places. I hadn't really thought much about Turkey, insofar as it was a pretty laid-back place, and despite the predominant religion of Islam, was something of a hippy heaven. Iran was another world. The border guards were officious and took forever to check our paperwork. Just prior to this forensic examination, just outside Ararat, Mike had pulled over to a nearby café and then asked us to examine the underside of the old bus. We crawled around in the dust under the thing looking for suspicious packages. We weren't looking for bombs, we were looking for dope. Evidently drug dealers use unsuspecting travellers to carry through their stash, often strapped to a back axle or the shock absorbers. If the traveller gets caught, it's jail. Assuming they get through the border without arrest, the dealer will then follow the target vehicle until it eventually comes to a stop somewhere. While the vehicle is unattended they then quickly and surreptitiously retrieve the package. Here for me was another steep lesson learned.

The Iranian border office itself was staffed by humourless, uniformed, armed police. We queued for ages while they relentlessly examined our passports and scrutinised bits of paper. Inside though was a museum of sorts, with an array of examples showing the lengths creative drug smugglers go to. Hollowed-out shoes, aluminium tubes in rucksacks, bike handlebars, the back axle of a truck. All kinds of inventive ways to get dope into Iran, and presumably out, since Afghanistan lay ahead. Suffice to say after an hour of intense scrutiny we were allowed through.

Iran

The less said about Iran the better. I have absolutely no desire to ever go back. There was a general air of hostility from the outset, from the moment we crossed the border to the time we left, which we did a couple of days later. Whether it was a collective paranoia which affected us all on the bus or not I don't know. All I knew of Iran was that the Shah was in power, and ruled with ruthless authority. He apparently had secret police everywhere. You could almost feel it.

Tehran was awful. Busy and dangerous. I have never ever been to any place where the driving was so bad either. They had no concept of brakes or speed. Just went flat out everywhere. I have no memorable or pleasurable recollections of this city whatsoever, and after an overnight stop in a campsite outside of Tehran, we left. I was glad to get out, and felt gripped by an ultra-sensitivity to the menace of the place. I felt the population was somehow cowed. They had a beaten look about them.

A matter of six or seven years later the all-powerful Shah was overthrown in an Islamic Revolution by the return from exile of the infamous Ayatollah Khomeini. He had been living in France for some years. His triumphal return to Iran took place in the early 1980s, still a few years away, but why France accommodated him for so long in the first place is beyond me. I often wonder why despots and dictators are given refuge like this, without any reference to the population. Who knew he was in hiding there? He was no doubt busy during that time gathering momentum and support for his eventual takeover of the country. The very best I can do to sum up Iran was a kind of Western consumerism meeting a medieval mindset. Anyway, the Ayatollah subsequently returned, took the Western bit out and sent them back to the dark ages. Forty years on they're still there, still ruled by a religious elite of Mullahs, who also happen to be embracing the very latest technology to build nuclear weapons. They're also a dab hand at fostering hatred between other Middle East countries, notably

Iraq, Syria and the Gaza Strip especially. A malign influence throughout the region.

Footnote: The Shah fled to America, presumably with all his loot intact in a Swiss bank. He died of cancer a few years later.

Afghanistan

Next came Afghanistan, and once again we endured rigorous border checks leaving Iran. Death penalty notices were also prominent for drug dealers. I was glad to see the back of that country. Never been back, nor would I want to.

Afghanistan was a wild, mountainous, rock-strewn, dry desert of a place. It felt wild. Similar geography to Iran, but just … er … wild, and untamed. The road and its smooth tarmac was out of context in many ways with the scenery. The road followed the valleys and occasionally big lorries could be seen in a cloud of dust coming toward us. Very few if any cars. This road was a supply road, and the main artery for the Asian Highway.

Suddenly and out of nowhere we hit a dust storm which tore down the valley. We had no windscreen of course, and very little time to prepare ourselves. The sand rained in through the front with incredible force, into our clothes, hair and eyes. It filled the interior, and the pressure of it blew out the rear windscreen, which popped and shattered into the road behind us. It was like sitting in a wind tunnel with stinging shrapnel hurtling through it. I ducked behind a seat, found a burkha type of scarf, wrapped it round my head and eyes, and put on my sunglasses. This stuff was a sharp grit-like substance, and we had no choice but to stop while this thing lashed the bus. In ten minutes, and just as suddenly as it arrived, it was gone. I've heard of dust devils, but this was fearsome. We then proceeded to sweep out as much as we could inside. It had formed piles of grit in corners, just like miniature snowdrifts. Then we climbed back into our mobile tunnel. With all of us suitably protected in the event of another one, we made our way, very slowly, to Herat, an hour or so away, freezing our nuts off in the process. Despite the clear cloudless blue sky, it was bloody cold.

There was a dry gulch of a rain gulley running alongside the road, and at one point I noticed a pale blue Volkswagen Beetle, apparently abandoned, with the windows smashed in. It looked vaguely familiar as we passed it. I learned later in Herat that the two occupants, a newly-wed husband and wife from Germany, both of whom I'd briefly met at the campsite in Istanbul weeks before, had been murdered, and their bodies were now lying in a morgue in Herat awaiting repatriation. Evidently their passports, watches, and money had been taken, as had their lives. She had also apparently been raped in the process. Afghanistan was a wild place all right.

Herat was green and comparatively lush by comparison with the countryside. Small narrow streets, donkeys, mud-walled buildings, starving skinny dogs. Only much later did I learn that Ghengis Khan had laid siege to this place, and subsequently slaughtered 160,000 men, women and children. He spared no one, for fear of weakening his ruthless reputation. His soldiers took four days to finish them all off with their swords, and by all accounts were exhausted from their exertions.

The market in the centre of Herat sold hash. A hippy paradise, and the cloying scent of marijuana pervaded the entire square. It was just like any provincial market square, but as well as the vegetable, fruit, and meat stalls, instead of seeing the expected blocks of cheese on display, they sold big blocks of hash. This was Karl's Holy Grail. I don't remember how much he bought, but it was a lot, and he did tell me if he could get it back to England unscathed then he could, and possibly would, retire on the proceeds.

Sandra, who wandered round this place with me, had a good figure and firm tits, and would often walk about bra-less in a skimpy vest and tight jeans. Iran had been a lesson in covering up, but in Afghanistan it was a mortal sin to go around with bare shoulders, never mind with her nipples sticking out, and stick out they did. They didn't need my tongue to encourage them, the cold did that. Despite covering up her head and shoulders with a big white cotton sheet, she still drew the lascivious attention of these robed, turban-clad, toothless, black-eyed Arabs. The Arab women were fully covered with black robes, just their eyes showing. As far as the men were concerned, Sandra might just as well have been naked. She was unnerved by all this and pleased to get back to the 'normality' of the campsite.

We stayed overnight here with our hollowed-out bus, before leaving, once again slowly, the following morning.

Along this dusty twisted highway we made our way to Kabul, virtually in the centre of Afghanistan. The mountains towered each side away into the distance, and suddenly ahead a small dust cloud appeared some way across this desert plain to the right. It was a group of kids, probably fifteen of them in ragged robes, racing down the slopes towards the highway to intersect the bus. Mike asked us all to fish around in our packs for sweets or biscuits, and as we drew near he threw them out into the road. The kids scrabbled around in the dirt, fighting amongst themselves as we passed. Since traffic was virtually non-existent on this road, the kids could spot from the hills any truck coming down it. Sometimes the lorry drivers threw out empty packets of fags or sweets to keep them away from the wheels, and the next lorry which came along usually got stoned in anger for this trick. It was a kind of mobile mugging, I suppose. Mike didn't take any chances, and anyway we only had the side windows to smash, since we were still without windscreens. I assume the rocks would have come straight through into us, but we didn't trick them and I assume they were grateful for these meagre presents.

Kabul came next, a bigger city than Herat, much busier, with mopeds, bikes and cars, though as it turned out I didn't see too much of the place. There was no campsite, it was deemed too dangerous for Westerners, so this was the only part of the trip where we stayed in a hotel. I don't really remember too much about this either, apart from it being concrete with guards on the door. Under the circumstances I'm pleased we did.

For no evident reason I became ill with a sore throat, and this turned into raging tonsillitis in no time at all. I stayed in bed for the three days we were in Kabul and didn't see any of it, in fact at one point thought I may have to go home. Mike even decided to make enquiries for flights for me back to England, but I really was determined to continue. I almost prayed to get better. I was definitely too ill to travel, but thanks to one of the girls, I was provided with some of her penicillin rations. After three days of being bedridden I recovered, thanks entirely to the selflessness and kindness of this girl. One thing which struck me on this trip, and one I'd become increasingly aware of, is how the slightest scratch or insect bite seemed to turn nasty and virulent in this part of the world. Not for the first time I reflected on the antiseptic life we lead in the West. Seems we have well and truly undermined our immune systems with drugs and antibiotics.

On the day we left I'd recovered from this bad throat, but hadn't eaten a thing for two days and was now starving, so I went with Karl down to the open market that morning, where I gorged myself on stewed goat and brown rice. What a huge mistake that turned out to be. Weakened but now back on the bus, within what seemed like minutes my guts suddenly turned to water. At the very first stop I found the very basic toilet, and suffered the worst bout of diarrhoea imaginable. My guts remained like this for days, and eventually weeks. Whatever I ate subsequently seemed to go straight through me. We had left Kabul early in the afternoon, onwards to Kandahar, but I was weak and lacked energy, and any opportunity to stop for a break was a welcome relief. All I concentrated on was finding the bog.

After several hours on the road we took a break at a roadside shack, seemingly in the middle of nowhere, and it was getting dark. I still felt weak and was urged to steer clear of solid food, and drink only bottled water or tea. I ordered black tea (chai) and once again my guts signalled urgency, and I rushed to the toilet, situated outside in a dilapidated shed. In the gloom of this filthy toilet I saw a hole in the ground with some kind of seat arrangement. There was a huge pile of shit glinting at the bottom 4 ft below, which crawled with flies and what I assume were giant maggots. Irrespective of this nauseating sight I relieved myself over this shit hole, literally a shit hole, got out of there as quickly as possible and rejoined the others.

Back on the bus and ten minutes down the road I felt something was missing. I then realised that in my haste to get out of that dump I'd left my bag behind in that disgusting shed. This was something that had never left me on the entire trip. It was part of me, almost akin to losing an arm or leg. This bag contained absolutely everything I possessed. Money, traveller's cheques, credit cards, and of all things, my worst nightmare, my passport. I panicked. It's bad enough losing your wallet or car keys in normal times, and these were if anything extremely abnormal times. I was filled with absolute dread and horror, and yelled to Mike to turn the bus round and head back. Eventually the shack came into sight and we pulled up in a cloud of dust. Now almost dark, I leapt off the bus and sprinted across to the bog and kicked the knackered door open. To my immense relief the bag was on the floor behind the door, where I'd left it in my haste to get my trousers down. Stolen passports fetch huge sums in Afghanistan. The Germans were murdered for theirs.

We camped outside Kandahar and I have no real recollections of that place. We left early morning for the Khyber Pass. This place was a wild boulder-strewn valley with mountainous terrain. It was also extremely dangerous. In fact one of the most deadly places on Earth, where everyone was armed, and every weapon under the sun could be acquired. From Kalashnikovs to rocket launchers. The Khyber Pass is close to the border with Pakistan. Having been ill in Kabul, and now with this stomach bug, not only had I lost track of time, dates, and news, I also lost a stone in weight in the space of a week. Food didn't stay in my stomach for long and went through me in what seemed like minutes. Despite being ultra-careful with everything I ate, and drinking only cold boiled water, it sure took its toll on my reserves. My jeans and shirts sagged off me.

Pakistan

Over the border we went, with no hassle whatsoever, despite an armed militia just up the road in the Khyber Pass, and into Pakistan. I immediately liked it. The glowering Arabic profile disappeared almost at once to give way to light-brown-skinned, round, smiling faces. All the lorries and buses were painted and garlanded with flowers and religious trinkets, and it felt green and lush after the harsh desert lands of Afghanistan.

I didn't understand, as I do now, about the tensions between the Muslim and Hindu faiths, any more than I understood the Muslim and Christian conflict, but what I do recall of Pakistan was that it felt green and friendly. Apart from our women on the bus continuing to cover their shoulders, as a mark of respect to the Islamic faith, which was something Mike had asked them to do from the moment we arrived in Turkey (Sandra included), there were no restrictions placed on us whatsoever. I met some interesting and fascinating people here.

There is also, I noticed immediately, a huge gulf between the haves and the have-nots. The rich and poor divide is emphatic. In Peshawar I met a guy who owned a printing factory. He evidently lived in a palatial home he shared with his mother, father, brothers, sisters, and their respective spouses, as well as all their children too. He didn't see the point of having many houses for individuals, when they could all share one big one and live together. According to him it was all very harmonious. It wouldn't work with the Craddock clan, that's for sure. And this shared accommodation attitude perhaps explains why Pakistani immigrants have no problem sharing a small house in Birmingham with all their family. It's a cultural thing I suppose.

Whilst I was in this park area chatting to the well-heeled impeccably dressed print factory owner, I noticed some young kids crawling around on a nearby rubbish dump, scavenging for food scraps. I asked him if they ever got ill. He said they wouldn't live long lives and would perhaps die of cholera, typhoid, malaria or some other hideous illness, but that their digestive systems were attuned to unhygienic food. I gave a wry smile at this, given my own intestinal problems. It was then that he referred to us in the West, as I described earlier, who live 'antiseptic' lives. Our obsession with cleanliness, he maintained, has undermined centuries of evolved immunity.

Writing this some forty-four years later, and with a better understanding of our Western dependence on drugs and antibiotics, often prescribed for the most minor of ailments, it's made me realise the truth of this prophecy. Even the medical people now agree that we need to withdraw from this dependency on drugs, and endeavour to build up our immunity once more.

I can't recall how long we were in Pakistan, maybe a few days, possibly a week. I really had lost track of time, and dates particularly. Anyway, whenever it was, and I think it might have been Lahore, I got a letter from my dad, courtesy of the Poste Restante service. This was an International Post Office of sorts, and we were given a list of these at the outset of the trip, so family and friends could write in advance of our arrival to whichever destination it was. I was slightly surprised to hear from him. My mother tended to do most of the writing, and here he was putting pen to paper. It seems an oddity, in this day and age of Instachatwhatssnapgram and all those other mobile phone related ways of communication, that this Poste Restante was about the equivalent of the Pony Express, or Pigeon Post. If anything this was slower, so the news I got from home was usually about two weeks old. That's time enough to die, be buried and not know!

My dad had spent the latter part of his RAF service during World War II in Karachi. I've no idea what business the RAF had in India. I thought it was Germany who was the main target. Karachi is now in Pakistan, having been partitioned from India after the war was over in 1948. It was a great letter, and very supportive of both me and the trip. Originally, before I left, he dismissed it as a timewasting 'jolly'. The most memorable line in his letter read: 'Life is a long time in some ways, but now mostly yesterdays'. He would have been at that time in his mid-fifties. But it's an essential truth all right. I didn't fully understand it then at twenty-seven, but I most certainly do now. In fact the more I write this, the more the realisation dawns that I've lived quite a long life, even though sometimes it doesn't seem so.

Typing this up now on a laptop, in a digital photography age, with text and email messaging at my fingertips, underlines just how archaic that postal service now seems, and bear in mind this trip was a mere forty-odd years ago. It didn't matter that the news contained in them was old news, any news was a highlight. To receive a letter from family and friends (and lovers) was something I treasured, and I would refer to constantly, reading and re-reading each line as if they were gold. I still have most of them. There's something about words on paper which has a more tangible feel. In the last fifteen years or so I've only just come to terms with text messaging. Sometimes I imagine trying to explain this to people in medieval or Stone Age times. How can little buttons on a phone fling random letters out into thin air, only for them to be reassembled in perfect order on someone else's phone on the other side of the planet? It's witch doctor stuff.

And speaking of gold in those letters I received and kept, we eventually arrived at the Golden Temple in Amritsar. This is the HQ of the Sikh religion. I recall a lake, surrounded by a high wall. It was night when we got there. In the centre of the lake stood a gold temple, illuminated by spotlights. This temple sat at the end of a wooden walkway, like a pier. The temple itself was no more than about the size of an average semi-detached house, or so it seemed to me. Astonishingly it was entirely covered in gold leaf, and all around the pathways and entrances, the petals from orange flowers, somewhat similar to marigolds I'd imagine, were strewn. The whole place glowed. My lasting memory is one of an orange and gold experience. The most surprising thing about this place was the evident wealth. Outside the walls of this place was abject poverty. It was underlined by every shack and crumbling building outside these walls. In the dark and filthy streets beyond, beggars, dead dogs, and even the occasional dead donkey lay in the dirt. Never have I witnessed in more dramatic fashion the divide between rich and poor. The 'haves' had it, and the 'have nots' most certainly didn't. This was capitalism for real.

India

Onward to Delhi we went. A city divided into two. The relatively modern New Delhi, built and designed by the British rather along the lines of Cheltenham and Bath, the Old Delhi, a mishmash of poverty, shacks, street vendors and general traffic chaos. Old Delhi was dominated by the magnificent Red Fort. The great capitalist divide was even more evident here.

I see I'm now up to 50,000 words with this. Whether it was a good idea to include the six months of travelling I'm not sure, but it proved to be such a formative experience in later years that I feel I have to. I have also decided that I want to finish the thing in December, and although it began as a ramble and rant, this whole thing has begun to take a form, a life, as it were, of its own.

So here I was, more or less halfway. 1976 in Delhi, and still suffering from my dietary encounter in Afghanistan with an almost complete inability to hold any food in my system for more than a matter of hours. Whatever I'd picked up in there was still with me, and wasn't going away in a hurry. I consumed huge quantities of sterilised water, in the hope it would wash out whatever this tenacious little bastard of a bug was, but more importantly in an attempt to keep myself hydrated. This thing had persisted and weakened me to the point of exhaustion. I lacked energy, lost weight, and was now down to about 10.5 stone from the relatively chubby 12+ stone when I started on this trek. I was bearded, long-haired, and looked ragged. In fact I began to take on the appearance of the locals. I still continue to this day to dress as informally as I can. I feel awkward in natty attire. In fact I've always been a scruff, right back to the *Just William* days, but in India I took this look to the extreme. I blended in with the scene perfectly.

Because of the accident we'd had in Turkey, and the three-week delay that caused, I made a decision to leave the group. By now I felt secure in my travel experience, and was more than alert for rip-offs and scams. I was now a seasoned hobo. The others were sorry to see me leave when I announced it, especially Sandra, but I'd made my mind up. I was in a hurry, and had had enough of following a set programme. It was time to fly this cosy nest.

We camped in Delhi, and as always I pitched my tent as close to the toilets as I could. Stomach cramps in the night were my signal to crawl to the bog. My stools, as the medical profession so delicately call shit, were non-existent. It was more like green slime.

We'd been in Delhi a matter of days. On a bright Saturday morning I made my way (once I was certain I wouldn't get caught out with my unpredictable bowels) through the Delhi throng to an Indian Airlines travel agent. I was impatient to get a ticket to fly to Kathmandu, missing out the bus leg. The crowds heaved and jostled, so I pushed and shoved my way through them, getting more and more angry by the minute. Beggars and pushy salesmen. trying to offload all kinds of meaningless trinkets. Betel leaf chewers sat on the pavement behind mats loaded with fruit and veg, and would repeatedly spit red juice into the gutter. A scruffy little man, bearded in filthy garb, suddenly and without any warning, jumped out of a doorway and accosted me. He wanted to tell my fortune. I dismissed him with a glare, almost threatening him with my fist to leave me alone. He said quite brightly and with a smile that he'd see me later, remarking as he left that he could tell I was preoccupied. I forgot about him.

I found the agency, after taking many wrong turns, and after the usual form-filling and cross-checks, passport, visa and so on, which took at least an hour or so, I triumphantly booked myself a flight from Patna to Kathmandu. Relieved that I now had a plan, I relaxed, and began to make my way the half an hour walk back to the campsite. Despite the Saturday mayhem, I never once felt threatened, as I had in Turkey, Iran and Afghanistan.

Out of this heaving throng, the strange little man jumped me once more. I still wasn't in the mood to talk to anyone, but he pulled at my sleeve and asked me with some urgency to talk to him. He asked, as I expected, for some 'silver'. What the hell, I was armed with a ticket, and a plan, so I humoured him. We ducked into a shop doorway where a flight of concrete steps led to the floor above. He again asked for silver, but I was skint, and had no small-change rupees on me. I had a cheap silver ring on my finger which cost nothing, so gave it to him, and in return he pressed a small folded piece of paper into my hand and asked me to clasp it tightly in my palm. He then sat me down on the steps, and proceeded to ask me many personal questions.

It was odd, but what happened next astonished me, and something I've never ever been able to explain. I felt I was transported back in time to the events in Southampton with the girl I was seeing, whose mother was a medium in the spiritualist church there. Regrettably I can't remember all of this, but here goes. He first asked me my favourite flower. He'd given me a pad and stubby little pencil to write down my answers, which he couldn't see. It was the kind of little pad a waitress takes your order with in a restaurant. I wrote Bluebell. He then asked for my mum's first name. I wrote Joan. He asked me the age of my girlfriend back home. Meg, aged thirty-seven. And so on. He mentioned my Grandma Broome, not by name, but that she was watching over me in some curious way. He said I'd be rich, but not by winning the 'lottery', and by that I assumed he meant luck. This of course was way before the National Lottery, scratch cards, Euromillions, Lucky Dips and stuff like that.

Basically he made it clear that I'd have to work hard, from the bottom rung of the ladder, as he put it. And on and on these revelations went. After ten minutes of this I was unnerved, my hands were sweating, and although I'd tried to be cool and nonchalant the little piece of paper he'd given me when we first met was soaked in my palm. When he'd finished asking me all this personal stuff he asked me for the paper I'd been writing my answers on. I tore it off the pad and he scrutinised it, his little brown eyes screwed up. He ummed and aahed for a second or two and scratched his beard.

He then asked me to unfurl the little piece of paper he'd originally handed me, which was by now wringing wet. I spread it out on the step. In his funny little scrawl everything I'd written down on my piece of paper matched his. I was dumbstruck. I mean, are there bluebells in India? How could he have got Meg's age right? My mother's first name? There it all was though, word for word. He stood up, having sat cross-legged in front of me, shook my hand, wished me luck, and with that he was gone, disappearing instantly into the crowd. Before he left he solemnly told me that I was being watched over by some Indian guide who would endeavour to protect me.

I am still dumbfounded by this all these years later, and never been able to explain it. I bet Derren Brown could, or some TV hypnotist, but I'm damned if I can.

I got back to the site still shaking a bit, but thankfully made the toilets and relieved myself, and didn't venture out of my tent much for the next day or so, despite the others urging me to come sightseeing. I was still not right, but gradually my stomach and guts had begun to settle.

We left Delhi after about three or four days, and headed to Agra, and this was where I'd depart. I remember the kite hawks wheeling about over the city as we left, and mentioned these scavengers in a letter to my dad back home. Very similar looking to red kites. He said he recalled them. In the RAF they referred to them as shite hawks.

If you've never seen the Taj Mahal, it's worth going. What struck me most, apart from the fact it's much smaller than you think from pictures, is once again the contrast between rich and poor. This pure white marble mausoleum was built from some of the best marble ever found anywhere in the world. Tons of it was junked to end up with the finished result, which in itself took twenty-odd years to build. It can never be recreated. The quality of that marble is unique, geologically it doesn't exist, and neither do any of the 22,000 people who worked on it. I can't remember which king or maharajah had it built, or the name of the dead wife (shame on me), but it was done in her honour. The cost would bankrupt an average country today. He evidently cut the hands off the architects and designers so they could never reproduce it. Thankfully he was carted off to some Indian sanatorium somewhere before he embarked on his next project. To build an identical one, but this time in black marble.

Inside the Taj Mahal is what appears to be a wrought iron fence, but in solid gold. It surrounds the tomb of the Queen. This is a replica. A little notice on this fence tells you that the original resides in the British Museum. I don't know if it's still there or ever been returned to its rightful place. I'll leave you to decide on the morality of this larceny.

Beyond a marble wall, which surrounds this marble marvel, is an absolute trash dump, wholly at odds with the extraordinary splendour of the Taj. A small filthy river runs through it, and I gazed at two dead and bloated donkeys, semi-submerged, and festering away in the heat of this foetid water. The ubiquitous flies were swarming on them. Another stark reminder of the haves and have-nots.

I didn't camp that night, but booked a hotel locally in Agra, and said an emotional farewell to my fellow travellers. My train for Patna (where the rice comes from) was leaving at 10 am the following day, and I didn't dare run the risk of missing it. My relationship with Sandra had developed quite nicely in the intervening weeks, so I booked a double room. She was still under her brother Phil's 'protection'. He really was a nice guy, but she continued to feel an obligation to go to the campsite first, before joining me at the hotel later.

When I asked for a room, the old guy on the reception asked me if I wanted a quiet room. Puzzled, I asked him why.

'Is your woman with you?' he asked.

I told him she would be there later.

'Is she noisy?'

I asked him what he meant.

'Does she make a lot of noise when you fuck her?'

Lost for words is a wholly inadequate phrase. Even gobsmacked isn't right. Stunned is perhaps more appropriate. I got the quiet room at the end of a dark corridor. She did, and she was.

Sandra came, and went. We were both worn out, and I was grateful in a way when she slipped out of the bed at 3 am. After searching for a while in the dimly lit room she eventually found her knickers and wriggled into them, pulled on her jeans and tee shirt and, with tears in her eyes and one last lingering kiss, went back to the campsite not far away. Back to her brother and her tent.

Oddly I was so focused on getting that train I didn't feel much in the way of regret. Not that I remember anyway. We both knew this parting of the ways was coming. and now it had, in more ways than one. This fling of six to eight weeks had served its purpose, for her as well as I.

Although we subsequently wrote to one another on my eventual return, I never saw her again.

After Sandra left I dozed, but didn't sleep. I was too keyed up. I left the hotel at 6.30 and was in the station ten minutes later. The station in Agra was big. Paddington-sized, and even at that time of day was busy, with people shouting and yelling at one another. I was now travellin' light (Cliff Richard, circa 1962). I'd left my tent with the group on the bus hoping and trusting that they'd eventually repatriate it for me when they got back to the UK (which they did). I'd grown attached to that tent. It had history. All I carried was my rucksack with sleeping bag tied on.

The train to Patna was due to leave mid-morning, but I wasn't taking any chances. I arrived early, impatient to be moving on. When I left the hotel I was still tired and sleepy, primarily because I'd been busy with Sandra until the early hours. The old guy was still on duty, and gave me a knowing wink as I paid the bill. I got a taxi to the station not far away. I can't recall the exact time the train was due to leave, but it was already on the platform loading up with cargo well in advance of its disembarkation. It took me awhile to find the right platform through the heaving confused masses. It was an estimated seventeen-hour journey across Northern India to Patna, with an arrival time of 6 am the following day. The heat of the day was just starting to build, compounded by the heat from the various steam locomotives on different platforms. I hadn't seen steam trains for years. They were wonderful. My platform, when I found it, was taken up with a coal-stained, but nevertheless gleaming, shiny green, brass-polished, steam-hissing locomotive, which gave the occasional toot and made me jump. People were milling everywhere, carrying all manner of luggage, bags, suitcases, and searching for their pre-booked seats.

I'd booked a first-class compartment but couldn't find it. Wandering up and down the platform I found an inspector, who kindly directed me to the back area of the train. I guess there were twenty coaches on this thing and it seemed to stretch for miles out of the station. It was a long walk. I found my coach eventually and discovered my compartment, with the bed tucked and folded into the wall of the varnished wood cupboard. I don't know what the trains are like in India today, but the whole experience was like stepping back to Crewe station in the 1950s, clutching my few belongings as my holidaying family changed there for Ruabon, then Conway, then finally landing us all in Criccieth for our summer two-week holiday. I was immensely excited then, and was excited now. The hiss of steam, the coal, the hooting whistle, the shouting, and above all the smell. There is something quite unique about the smell of a steam train. I was transported immediately back to my childhood, eight years old, and, in my mind at least, the experience was identical. Green and cream carriages with gold edging, some maroon, cream and gold, but they were exactly as I remembered.

I have a picture I drew in crayon of the Flying Scotsman (I think) drawn when I was about this age. It's framed and resides in my kitchen at home. The locomotive I drew was blue and gold.

The other famous train in the 1950s was the Mallard, which I recall as maroon, so I reckon this one is definitely the Flying Scotsman. This station in Agra served as a wonderful memory trip. Evidently many of the steam locomotives when decommissioned in England in the late 50s early 60s were shipped over to India, and here they all were, right before my eyes. Truly a step back in time, and all lovingly looked after.

When I eventually located the right coach number and found my compartment, I discovered I had it to myself. Not for long though. Despite the first-class designation it was scruffy and the seats threadbare, but only later when I took a peek at other areas of the train did I realise how relatively luxurious it was. The rest of it was shabby and crowded. Eventually I was joined by two Bengali guys, who were of a similar age to me, and their English was excellent. They were interesting and companionable. I still have the diary somewhere where they'd tried to explain to me the Bengali alphabet. Bengal is now of course Bangladesh.

As I said earlier, apart from the briefest of thoughts, I suddenly found didn't I miss Sandra (despite the hectic night we'd had) or in fact any of my fellow travellers, with whom I'd spent so many weeks, one bit. Nor did I even think of Meg, or family back home. Somehow in some curious way I had drawn a line under all of it. I was now firmly embarked on stage two, except that I was now an experienced traveller, free to go wherever I wanted and at whatever speed I chose. It was a liberating feeling. I almost felt as if the bus trip had been an O level course in travelling. I was now, finally, on my own, eager to embrace stage two. This was the A level course. I was totally unaccountable to anyone. And that's the way I liked it.

The train took off on the dot at 10 am and the journey was by and large uneventful. My two compartment companions were delightful company, questioning me constantly about life in England. Not for the first time did I hear them refer to the 'mother' country. The British Empire had ruled over this vast continent, and our laws and way of life were ingrained. To emigrate to

England was the main goal for most I met in Pakistan and India. We trundled past village after village, stopping at many of them to load more people on. The countryside rolled by with hills and jungle in the distance. India is truly immense. A few hours in, we stopped mid-afternoon at some station in the middle of nowhere to load more coal.

A man stood on the platform amidst the steam and smoke. On his shoulders was a wooden yoke and suspended from each end were buckets on chains. In front of him was a stack of dried banana leaves. My Bengali friends got off and urged me to follow. I was quite hungry, having eaten little earlier. In one bucket was a dark, malevolent-looking gravy, the other was filled with hot hard boiled eggs. I bought four eggs and put them in my pocket, and he took a dried banana leaf, which were all shaped into bowls, and filled it with some of the gravy. I also bought a clay pot of sweet milky chai (tea), took a sip, found it revolting, and immediately threw it away. It put me off milk in tea for life.

Back in our compartment the Bengali guys then peeled the eggs and dipped them into the gravy. I followed their lead and did the same. I bit into the gravy-covered egg and it nearly blew my head off. I couldn't even begin to compare it to an Indian restaurant menu. I knew my way around madras, vindaloo, and phall curries, but this was in a league all of its own. This liquid was capable of taking varnish off the table. Nevertheless, I ate the lot. As for my continuing battle with my digestive ailments, well it was kill or cure I reckoned. Probably kill.

My bed was folded up inside one of the wood-panelled walls, the crisp white cotton sheets neatly tucked into it. I pulled it down, and climbed up onto it. It was rather like climbing into an envelope, and as the light faded over the Indian countryside as we continued to rattle through it, I was glad to get the opportunity to sleep. I have to say I was knackered, unsurprising really given the previous night. My Bengali friends respected my need for an early night, and lay down on their own bunks. About midnight I was awoken by a commotion in the corridor. The Bengalis were up, had switched on the light, and were trying valiantly to keep our door shut, yelling at the people outside to piss off. I got a glimpse of the throng in the corridor who were all pushing and shouting. With the door firmly locked, and despite the racket going on outside, I quickly nodded off once more.

At 5.45 am the train stopped abruptly. The huge sun had risen over the jungle plains. I was up and already dressed, saying my goodbyes to my fellow travellers, and ready for Patna at 6 am. The train remained motionless. Then dead on the dot of 6 am it rolled into Patna station. I learned later that the railway prides itself on timekeeping, so we'd hung around up the line for fifteen minutes just to prove a point. Their impeccable timekeeping was a continual surprise to me, and no doubt a source of pride to them, I guess. Or should I say to be more precise.

When I managed to get off, after a push through the crowd in the corridor, I climbed down to the platform, and waved a final goodbye to my Bengali friends. Then I looked up. I was stunned to see the roofs of all these coaches festooned with people and their possessions. Clinging on with whatever handhold they could find. I guess if mine was first class, theirs was probably fifth class. No Health and safety mandates in place here. There must have been thousands crammed onto this train.

Patna station was relatively quiet by Agra standards, and I found the gents' first, and then the buffet. I was hungry once more. All the signs for the platforms and toilets were painted green and gold, reinforcing my 1950s feeling that time had stood still, and the buffet restaurant, as I stepped inside, was spotlessly clean. There was no one in the place, apart from a European-looking woman of twenty-five or so sitting at a corner table. The tables were clothed in white linen, matching the napkins, and the cutlery was shiny and clean. It was lovely. An English oasis almost, in the middle of India.

I heaved off my rucksack, sat down and picked up the menu. The waiter was neatly dressed in a waistcoat, with a white cotton napkin draped over one arm. I was attended to immediately, looked down the very English breakfast menu and ordered Welsh 'rabbit'. That was how it was spelt. The woman in the corner had just been served scrambled eggs, and was moaning loudly about the toast, or tost, as it was spelt. Evidently it was 'overdone, mate', in what I assumed was an Aussie accent. I shouted good morning to her, and smiled, and we introduced ourselves across the room. I discovered she was a Kiwi (New Zealander) and heading for Kathmandu, as was I. She brought over her scrambled eggs and joined me, and we shared a pot of tea. This was Kate. We then decided to team up and travel together, and no, I didn't fancy her in that way, but it turned out she was a good laugh, had travelled most of India on her own, occasionally with a few Aussie mates she'd encountered along the way, and planned to catch up with them in Kathmandu.

Nepal

We took a rickshaw to the airport, the front of the station was a sea of them, and all of them clamoured for our business, to cycle this thing three or four miles to the airport. Patna International Airport wasn't. It turned out to be no more than a dusty strip with a few sheds dotted here and there, and after the usual laborious paperwork and passport checks, which seemed to take forever, we climbed aboard a small twin-engined Cessna, the only plane I could see on the entire airfield. I think we were the only passengers too, and before I knew it we were up in the air. The pilot was chatty and friendly and I sat up front with him. I love the take-off and landing in small planes. The flight was probably forty-five minutes, but what a breathtaking flight it was. The flat terrain of India gradually gave way to hilly country, which turned eventually into the most spectacular mountain range imaginable. I guess we might have been flying at 15,000 feet, and some of the snow-capped mountains towered up into a sky of dark blue thousands of feet above the plane. If you think the Alps are impressive, go take a look at this lot. These were the Himalayas.

I didn't hang around with this 'sheila' Kate for too long. She had one of those sandpaper voices which grated on me, but she did introduce me to a few of her mates, who were all blokey Aussies, and she slotted in immediately. There was nothing girlie about her. This lot lived for their beer, morning, noon and night. There's something about Australians abroad. It's almost as if they intend to personify their country's reputation as beer-swilling Crocodile Dundees, by acting it out for real wherever they are in the world. The nicest Aussies I ever met were in Australia. These guys, however, were anything but humble. One even put beer on his cornflakes to underline his ultra-masculine attitude. Maybe they're deeply insecure in some unfathomable psychiatric way. All I can say is 'Go stick yer head up a dead bear's bum, mate.'

Kathmandu was a shithole. Insofar as the streets were muddy and rutted, with most of the buildings dilapidated and in dire need of repair. I found a room in a traveller's hostel, and lived in it for a couple of weeks. The shower was a bucket, punctured with holes, and suspended on a rope. All you had to do was tip water into it. Showers had to be quick.

I hired a bicycle and rode round the place, visiting monkey-strewn Buddhist temples, and various other areas of this city. I quite like Buddhism. If I had a religious belief it would be this one. It was explained to me by an orange-robed, shaven-headed monk that their philosophy is to get through life as peaceably and agreeably as possible. A-Z, he said, without setting out to harm anyone. I get that. I didn't much fancy one of their initiation tasks though, which apparently was to sit outside at night, in winter, under a soaking wet blanket in the Himalayan foothills. The idea was to dry the thing out through body heat. In my view that's taking mind over matter a bit too seriously. My sleeping bag did me just fine, given the single sheet and blanket I had in my threadbare room.

I don't recall Kathmandu having much in the way of traffic, mostly bikes and mopeds, but when I wasn't living on papaya, which I bought from street vendors, or fresh mangoes and lychees,

I spent most of my time in bars with the Aussies. One minute I'd be a fruit bat, the next an experienced beer connoisseur. At some point I met Wolfgang through this little gang I'd joined. Wolfgang was German, blond, podgy, and aged about thirty. He declared, 'I vant to see Everest.' So did I.

We became good mates. He knew how to drink beer too, so had quite a bit in common with the Aussies. A couple of days later we took a bus, which was more of a transit van with seats and windows, and generally falling apart. After an hour or so in this heap of rust and dents, we found ourselves fifteen miles out in the Himalayan foothills. We disembarked with our packs, and began an all-day trudge up a narrow rocky path. Wolfgang had a map of sorts, so I followed. It was hot, humid, and by 11 am truly stifling, but onward 've vent'. Wolfgang sweated a lot, but the new lighter me had no difficulty. At some stage we passed a grove of ugli fruits and I climbed over a wall and picked one. They're like grapefruit, only football-sized. I was in fruit bat mode now and found it thirst-quenching. We then encountered a Nepalese kid of about ten or twelve. He was sitting on the wall around this orchard, and in good English offered to carry Wolfgang's pack, and mine too, but I declined. I was travelling light with just a few bits and my sleeping bag. The sweat-stained German swung his gear onto this kid's back, and on the three of us went, higher and higher. Apart from becoming cooler as we ascended, I simply can't describe the scenery. Spectacular is inadequate. These snow-covered mountains towered into a sky of cosmic blue.

At around 5 pm we arrived at a goatherd's hut, some 7,000 ft up this hill. I call it a hill because the mountains around dwarfed it. The roof was of straw and grass thatch, with two mats on the floor inside, and a creaky wooden door. This would be our home for forty-eight hours. A farmer turned up and we gave him some rupees. The boy, who had toiled for several hours with Wolfgang's stuff, asked for a small fee. Wolfgang told him to fuck off. He said to me the boy had offered to carry his gear, hadn't mentioned a price, and too bad but he wasn't paying. The boy left, and with tears in his eyes, trudged back down the track in the gloom.

Despite the following day dawning bright and clear, Everest wasn't. The valleys below were covered in mist and fog, and although we knew where Everest was, it was covered in cloud. We ate goat's meat and brown rice, and generally mooched about for the rest of the day with no sign of the cloud base lifting. Another night on the mat in my sleeping bag with Wolfgang's snores for company. I got up at first light, to find Everest in the distance sparkling in the sun. It had what seemed to be a plume of smoke drifting away from the summit, but there it was at last. This legendary rock, all 29,000 feet of it. I shook Wolfgang out of his Germanic slumber, and we both stared at it for an age. He was mesmerised. So was I. It really was mesmerising. Even though it seemed in touching distance, I learned it was seventy miles away and a full two-week trek just to get to base camp. Perspective is an odd thing. The Malvern Hills are just seven miles away from me, and yet Everest seemed about the same.

I left this grumpy German that morning, since it was still early, and despite still not feeling too well knew I had a long hike back down the track, which of course was much easier in the cool. Irrespective of this guy's attitude, he was extremely funny (for a German). I have often regretted not staying in touch with him. He had decided he 'vanted' to stay and gaze at Everest all day. I shook hands, slung my rucksack over my shoulder and left. Maybe he was so taken with the view he never came back down and could still be up there for all I know. Either way I never saw him again.

I picked my way back down the track for what seemed hours, stumbling and swearing as the heat began to make its presence felt. I passed the ugli fruit grove lower down, with no sign of the kid sitting on the wall, and by mid-morning made it to the collection of shacks in a village, where the 'bus' would take me back to Kathmandu.

I found the bus stop, in the centre of a dusty square, and assembled with some of the Nepalese villagers to wait. They were mostly women, who seemed excited to go to the big city, even appearing to have dressed for the occasion. I recall their big-hooped gold earrings fitted through holes in their ears. It made me think they'd been operated on with one of those paper punches, and I tried to imagine how an ear can be flattened sufficiently to punch a hole through it. Their ears jangled every time they turned their heads, but the women largely ignored me, so busy were they with their noisy chatter.

The bus duly showed up, clanking its way through the dust and into the village. Once again it appeared to be the same type of transit van with seats. I got on and settled down at the back. The women followed, and then came the goats and chickens. All of them had their legs tied and were stowed in the overhead luggage rack. The noise in that truck was an unimaginable racket, and I remember being aware of the sunshine filtering through the ears of these chattering women sitting in front of me, their gold earrings flashing in the morning sunlight. I was tired after that three-hour trek and tried to doze off, but it wasn't possible. Two or three of the men from the village sat up front with the driver. About five miles or so out of the village we approached a very steep hill. I had the feeling this vehicle would never make it, and I was right. It coughed, spluttered, and died. The men got off and peered under the bonnet. I could see steam and smoke, and scratching of heads.

In the end I left my seat, clambered out and tried as best I could to explain in my best Nepalese to try a push start. My best Nepalese consisted mainly of hand signals. They finally got the message, so we then began to push the thing to the brow of the hill. I had already walked the 200 yards to the top of the hill and seen the long gentle slope down the other side, and felt we may be able to bump-start the thing. As we pushed from the back I suddenly realised the women were still on board. I climbed back inside and ordered them off. I didn't need any Nepali for that. The chickens and goats stayed on the luggage rack. They dutifully got off, never ceasing their conversation, and still nattering away trudged along behind us as we triumphantly made it to the top.

There was back-slapping and handshakes all round. I then tried to explain to the doleful looking driver what I wanted him to do. Eventually he got the message. I checked the ignition was on, got him to put it in second gear with his foot firmly down on the clutch, and we heaved it over the hill. Down it went, slowly at first but gathering speed. Several times it jerked, banged, and blew out white smoke, but eventually ended up in a cloud of dust at the bottom. It was dead. The animals weren't though. I could still hear them bleating and clucking as we made our way down.

When we made it to the bottom I noticed the bus had come to rest amid what appeared to be a ruined temple of some sort, with large stone pillars half buried in the long grass. The women once again climbed into the dead bus, and removed some provisions. They soon got a fire going. I was impressed. They positioned some of the broken stones round the fire, and then found a large flat stone and balanced that on top to make a hob. I was even more impressed. Remember, I was a seasoned arsonist at the age of ten. Then mixing up some kind of flour, they proceeded to cook flatbread chapati-like things on it, picking each one up with their fingers and turning it over on the hot stone, while the fire roared away underneath. All this in the space of twenty minutes. I was now more than impressed. It reminded me of my cub days cooking on an open fire, and the prized badge I got for it. This however was in another league. I at least had a frying pan. They just used whatever was to hand.

I thought for a second or two that they might slaughter a chicken or something, but they didn't. They summoned me over, and folding one of these things, filled it with some kind of meat and vegetable mix, and handed it to me. A Nepalese version of a (spicy) wrap. Their generosity was humbling. And there we all sat, amid this ruined rubble with our impromptu lunch while we waited for another bus to show up. They assured me that one would be on its way, but how they knew that, and how they made contact, I had no idea. No internet or mobile connectivity out here. It hadn't been invented.

After about an hour of sitting around, I saw a dust trail in the distance, and stood up. Coming towards us was a gleaming air-conditioned coach with blue-tinted windows. This was more like a proper bus. It pulled up and with a hiss of its doors disgorged about thirty Japanese tourists, all dressed immaculately with their Nikons and Pentax cameras dangling from their necks. They then proceeded to photograph the ruins, us too, me included. Somewhere in Tokyo I bet there's an old, faded photograph of me, long-haired and in filthy jeans sitting astride a stone pillar. My instinct was to barge on to their bus to claim Western privilege. After all, I was used to a degree of luxury. Surely I belonged, didn't I? In a matter of minutes they were all back on board, and away it went, leaving me standing forlornly in the dust.

I have often thought about this event. It was almost a Titanic moment, that curious feeling of pulling rank. I wanted to get on that lifeboat. But I'm glad I didn't. I know now that I was right to stay with my Nepalese companions. Goats and chickens included. I like to think I did the honourable thing, rather than abandon them to their fate. Notwithstanding the fact that I was never given the choice. Had they offered a lift what would I have done? That would have made my dilemma worse. Fortunately that never arose.

Eventually another 'bus' trundled over the horizon. Everything was taken off the abandoned one and transferred. It was now early evening, and as dark settled we made it back to Kathmandu. All in all it was quite a day. As far as I know, the dead bus is probably still there amid those ruins.

I was planning to leave Kathmandu a few days after my Everest expedition, on a pre-booked flight to Bangkok. A couple of interesting things occurred before I left. The first of which was Delhi-related. You'll recall the little Indian man who jumped me on that fateful Saturday morning while I was preoccupied with sorting my flight to Kathmandu and who subsequently begged to tell my fortune? He had also referred to me as 'Mr John', even though I'd never given my name. It never occurred to me at the time, only much later when I thought about it. How he knew this was another mystery.

Two weeks later and 1,800 miles from Delhi, I was pushing my rental bike late one morning through the streets of Kathmandu to deliver it back to the hire shop. Across the street I heard someone shout 'Mr John! Mr John!' I looked across, and astonishingly, there he was, still in the same dirty, ragged robes. I stood and stared in utter disbelief. He waved, shouted greetings to me then promptly disappeared back into the crowd. Never to be seen again.

There is something mystical, spiritual, and mysterious about the Indian subcontinent. What it is or how it came to be I have no idea. I've never been back. Maybe I should. Who knows, I may just bump into him again.

By the time I was due to leave Kathmandu I calculated that I was running out of money. My book of $100 traveller's cheques was getting a bit thin. I can't recall how much I had left, but it wasn't sufficient to cover a flight to Australia from Kuala Lumpur, which my Aussie mates suggested was the best option. I'd already paid for my pre-booked flights thus far, including one out of Australia, but that was months ago, back in London. I deliberately hadn't booked an inward flight to Australia because of the uncertainty of my timetable, and now I knew I couldn't afford it.

And here's the second interesting event which occurred. The answer to my shortage of funds lay in getting my hands on an Australian Student Union card. This would reduce the price of the flight by about 70%. My Australian friends in Kathmandu had suggested obtaining a forged card in Bangkok for about $50, but the travel agent in Kathmandu advised me that Qantas was well aware of this scam, and constantly on the lookout for forgeries. I needed a properly authenticated one, and the travel agent came up with a plan.

This was his idea. He suggested I go ahead and book a flight on the basis that he had seen my card and verified that I had one. He then told me to take the booking form to the Australian Student HQ in Bangkok, say I'd lost my card along the way, or perhaps (and quite likely) it might have been stolen, but much would depend on my acting ability. If I could play Joseph in the Nativity play, surely I could act the distraught student whose card had been nicked? My Aussie friends said it would never work. It was entirely down to my ability to act out this lie. Nevertheless I took the risk, went ahead with a small deposit and booked my flight to Australia from Kaula Lumpur. All I had to do was act out a scene in Bangkok, and find some way of getting to Malaysia.

Thailand

Two days later I flew out of Kathmandu on a night flight, for the two hours or so to Bangkok. Kate was with me, and a couple of the Aussie guys. On arrival we descended from the plane and the smell of fume-laden air hit me immediately. The air was thick with it. We took a taxi and made for the Grace Hotel, the epicentre, so I was told, for backpacking travellers.

My first impression of Bangkok took some getting used to. Neon lights, cars, tuk-tuks buzzing like bees, with the filthy exhausts belching smoke, bars, women for sale, live sex shows, restaurants. It was in short a complete shock. I felt like a monk leaving a monastery and walking into a disco full of naked women. I knew it wouldn't take me long to adjust though.

The Grace Hotel was huge, and milling with people. The Aussie guys had pre-booked. I hadn't. There were no rooms available. I wasn't sure what to do, and thought I'd have to find somewhere else, which was a pity, I'd grown used to the company of these Aussie guys, and we got on well.

I was about to find a plan B, when by chance two American girls nearby at the desk overheard my conversation and offered me a place on the floor of their room. They told me they were leaving the following day, and if it was OK with the hotel I could take over their room. The hotel receptionist agreed. So up to the third floor with these two women I went, unloaded my gear, and laid out my sleeping bag on the rug in the corner.

Both the girls were fat, in that oblivious-to-other people, loud American way, and evidently shared a double bed. They winked at me knowingly, told me Bangkok was Heaven for a single guy like me, gave me one of their keys, and down I went to the bar to meet up with my Aussie friends. They'd teamed up with another one of their travelling mates in the meantime, who'd rendezvoused with them here. A new face to me. This was Pete Gilbert, the son of a mine owner from Perth. We hit it off immediately. Why is that? I've often wondered. What hidden wavelength or instinct is at work to know instantly that someone you've never met before would soon become a really good mate? I've no idea, but a shared sense of humour is a key I think, and oddly we looked a bit like each other. I felt I'd known him for ages, just never met. A bit like dear old Wolfgang, probably still stuck up there in the Himalayan foothills absorbed by Everest. I soon learned that Pete really knew his way round Bangkok, having backpacked round Thailand, Laos, and Cambodia for a few months. Just the kind of mate I needed.

I reckon I hadn't been in the bar more than a few minutes before I was surrounded by girls. Despite being dressed in jeans, boots, denim shirt, and an old Levi's jacket, complete with beard and long hair, I was suddenly a film star. The entire bar was filled with women. All of them wore short skirts, high heels, had the most lustrous hair, and were beautifully made up. It was like a giant party, where the women outnumbered the men five to one. The parties I was used to were the opposite. Suddenly I was the Brad Pitt or George Clooney of Bangkok. Believe me, I got a lot of attention. Despite my Joe Cool looks though, I kept firmly in mind what this was all about. They were really after the thing I was most short of. Money.

By the time I made it to the bar for a beer, I had three girls clinging to me. This was the 1970s and I don't think ladyboys had put in an appearance yet, so I'm fairly sure they were what they were. These girls were about twenty, and utterly gorgeous. I eventually peeled them off. I found the suddenness of this situation difficult to adjust to, but it didn't take me long. Besides I was tired after the travelling, so made arrangements to meet with Pete the following day, swallowed the remains of my beer, and disappeared off to my shared room. It was late by now, and little did I know that another shock awaited me.

I slipped into my room as quietly as I could, undressed and slid into my sleeping bag. The two girls were asleep, or so I thought. I was just drifting off to sleep when I heard some sighing, then some moaning and then an occasional squeak and groan. The two fat Americans began humping one another under the covers as I pretended to sleep. Lesbian sex wasn't quite how I imagined it.

I said my goodbyes to these two the following morning as if nothing whatsoever had taken place, thanked them for their hospitality, and went down the lift for breakfast, to meet up with my new-found mate.

I can't really remember how long I was in Bangkok. Possibly ten days, maybe more, and most of it was a blur, but this marked the start of one of the most riotous and sexually debauched episodes I could ever have imagined. One song, which haunts me to this day, was played in just about every bar, dive and disco I entered: 'Get up and Boogie'. And while I was in Bangkok I most certainly did.

I could enlighten you, bore you, or even excite you, depending on your disposition, with the finer details, of the women I met, all intimately, the drinking and late nights, but if I did it would fill another book. On one particular occasion, and I'm almost embarrassed to reveal this, I slept with four different women in the same day. This is an entire episode in itself. I went to live sex shows in downtown Bangkok, one act showing could be done with half a dozen ping pong balls, and was amazed, astounded even, to see fat Chinese women sitting in the front row right alongside the stage watching these performances. Most had their hands up their skirts, presumably relieving themselves with the excitement of sitting a few feet away watching live sex. I doubt they had any other option to be honest. I couldn't imagine any man wanting to hump any of them.

On the flip side of this sleaze, I met some incredibly kind and generous lovers, who showed me the sights of this heaving polluted city, as well as their bodies. One particular girl stayed overnight and volunteered to show me round the following morning. The floating vegetable market, the temples, she even bought a couple of silk shirts for me out of her hard-earned savings. Maybe I was worth it?

Nearly all the girls I met lived in hostels when they weren't out to catch the eye of rich Westerners (me of course not included). They were overseen by what they described as a mama sahn. I don't think it's spelt like that, but that's what it sounded like. They paid a rent of sorts to this mysterious overseer when they came 'home', having left their bed or bunk unoccupied the night before. I suppose she was some kind of maternal pimp. Most of the girls had come to Bangkok from the countryside for money, having been encouraged, by their fathers usually, to go to earn a living in the usual way among the bright lights and bars of the big city. This entire culture was spawned by the Vietnam War, when US troops were sent to Thailand for R&R. Not, I guess, that they ever got much rest, or very much in the way of recuperation either. It all came to a halt in 1974, when the war ended. This was a couple of years before I got there. There were no troops around when I arrived, but there sure were a lot of women left behind looking for the main chance.

On one memorable occasion Pete took me downtown to a Turkish baths. There was an entrance for men, and around a warm shallow swimming pool inside were perhaps fifteen to twenty girls sitting around the edge, all giggling, with their feet dangling in the pool. All of them wore tiny bikinis. There were numbers pinned to their bra straps and Pete led the way. All you had to do was pick one, then into the hot spa first for an underwater massage. You finished the encounter in a discreet cubicle. We spent most of the afternoon in there.

When we left, I was surprised to find that on the other side of the building there was an identical entrance for women. Those I saw going in were the blue-rinsed American types. Presumably their husbands were otherwise engaged in high-powered business meetings somewhere in the city, so their wives had the opportunity to indulge themselves for the afternoon. I often wonder what type of men awaited them on the other side, and whether they'd be able to perform to order with some of these chubby, hot, sweaty Westerners. I don't think I could have managed, judging by the brief glimpse I had of them. But still, why not a facility for women? Casual sex isn't just the preserve of the male. Even though we think it is.

The street food in Bangkok was cheap, nutritious and spicy, and I developed a lifelong love of Thai food as a result. I also found a cart which parked every evening in the grounds of the hotel, which had a deep fat fryer on board, and I'd eat hot fried chicken and fresh pineapple. I loved the place, and Pete, who had been my experienced guide around Bangkok, suggested we go to Singapore. So we did.

Before doing so though I went by bus (which took all afternoon) to the Australian Student Union HQ in the suburbs of this sprawling city. It was a long shot, and I almost didn't give it a try, but unbelievably, I got away with it. I obtained my authentic Australian Student Union card, having produced my reservation kindly put together for me by the agent in Kathmandu. I then acted and lied through my teeth about the loss of the original card, and put on an Oscar-winning performance worthy of Sir Lawrence Olivier. The sceptical Aussies, those who remained at the hotel, couldn't believe it when I told them what I'd done. How I got away with it Buddha only knows. If I say so myself, it was some result. I now had a $100 flight to Sydney. A fifth of the normal fare.

Pete already had a flight booked for Singapore, so he left a day or two before me. I had a pre-booked flight down to Kuala Lumpur and said I'd come down from there to catch up with him, but how I wasn't sure. He left, and I had one more night on my own in Bangkok.

My last night in Bangkok was interesting. The Thai government were on the brink of war with Cambodia (Pol Pot's lot, I presume) so they imposed a midnight to 4 am curfew in Bangkok.

That night I was in a bar with a girl named Lec. I only remember this because there were refrigerators back home with the same name. She was anything but frigid. This girl introduced me to a few things too. Tiger Balm for instance. I'd never heard of this stuff. It was a magic ointment. She rubbed it on her temples to clear a headache, and called it her 'Buddha'. It could fix anything, she said, from insect bites to bullet wounds. I was so engrossed in conversation with her that, Cinderella-like, we missed the midnight deadline, and had to stick it out in the bar till 4 am. We took a taxi at four back to my hotel room, and she proceeded to teach me the finer points of her body. Then sat me on the bed, knelt down in front of me, held my hands … and sang. It was extraordinary, and lovely. Then, following her instructions, we tumbled into the sheets. My abiding memory of this woman is her reference to Western men. She declared them to be 'too hasty'. I learned a lot from her. In that short space of time, I got to know every inch of her body. The hows, and more importantly the wheres.

Malaysia/Singapore

I checked out of the Grace Hotel late morning for the airport, and left Lec there with the few dollars I was able to stump up. I had a reputation with most of the women I'd met as a 'cheap Charlie' (I still am), and though the women needed paying, it was only ever discussed afterwards and never beforehand. Unlike prostitutes, they simply wouldn't go anywhere with you if they didn't like you. There was a moral compass of some sort there.

I stayed one day and night in Kuala Lumpur, and wandered round the markets, where I bumped into two Malaysian guys who were driving down to Singapore the following evening. They were delivering durians. I had no idea what these were at the time, apart from some kind of fruit, but I soon found out when I joined them later in the evening for the taxi ride. They had an old Merc, the boot of which was filled with these things. They stank. I slung my rucksack and trusty old sleeping bag on to the back seat, and climbed in. My two cohorts seemed oblivious to the smell. Durians are large spiky fruits, about the size of a melon, and I once heard them memorably described as the equivalent of eating raspberry blancmange in a gents' urinal.

We travelled down to Singapore later that night in this stinking car, but I couldn't wait to get out. After travelling all night, with an occasional stop, they kindly dropped me at the address Pete had given to me about 8 am the following morning. It was a huge relief. I handed them a few dollars for fuel and waved them farewell. I had tried to get an impression of this city, or mini country, as we entered but was more than preoccupied with escaping this mobile toilet I'd been imprisoned in for hours. Like Kuala Lumpur, Singapore seemed to have two distinct sides to it. Gleaming, towering skyscrapers and office buildings, and, like most other cities I guess, poor downtrodden districts. Pete was ensconced in the low-cost budget area.

It was a guest house of sorts. I rang the bell and he eventually got up and opened the door. I followed him inside, found the room he'd reserved for me, threw my stuff inside, and out we went into the street to a small stall. We breakfasted with hot coffee, sweetened with condensed milk, boiled eggs, toast and jam. All very civilised after that memorable journey. We sat in the sunshine and caught up on events since we'd last seen each other. It seemed ages ago, even though it was only a few days. The talk was mostly, and inevitably, about women. One of them though had apparently left him with an unexpected present. He told me he had to go to hospital later for a check-up, since he was finding it excruciatingly painful to piss. Sure enough he was diagnosed with gonorrhoea and given penicillin doses for the rest of the week. Suddenly I was concerned about my own exploits, and worried that my romping in Bangkok may have had consequences. It turned out I'd had a lucky escape. Oddly the possibility of contracting an STD never crossed my mind, and this of course was way before the AIDS virus. I made a decision to curb my philandering activities after this, because, quite frankly (and literally), I was shagged out.

We stayed in Singapore for a few days before I had to leave for Kuala Lumpur and onward for my flight (courtesy of the Australian Student Union) to Sydney. Singapore was an antiseptic place compared to the mayhem, traffic and chaos of Bangkok, and judging by the shiny concrete and glass offices was vastly more prosperous. I learned there was no unemployment benefit available anywhere to anybody. Everyone was required to work. The tube stations were clean and spotless, and we went everywhere on them. There were signs for No Smoking, signs for not dropping chewing gum, and signs which read No Durians. I was more than happy to endorse that.

We met up with one of Pete's Aussie mates whilst there, and he introduced me to a place which served something called a 'steamboat'. Platefuls of slivers of raw fish, chicken, liver, and prawns were served together with a big bowl of steamed rice. A gas burner was placed in the middle of our table, on which sat a pot of boiling stock. We cooked by picking up the raw food on our chopsticks, and dipping it into the stock, and then into a bowl of chilli oil. The stock became a soup, which we then ladled into the rice. It was quite fantastic, a kind of raw-food fondue.

Like so many things in life, most situations are temporary. As the Buddhist monk said to me in Kathmandu, we must accept change, the trick being to adopt and adapt to that change. In other words, embrace and accept it. Sometimes I find that extremely hard to do. Although I like the permanence of a relationship, say, or find a friendship worth cultivating, or a place which I want to hold on to forever, inevitably it crumbles, moves, changes. Sometimes it's health, sometimes it's geography and distance, sometimes things just go stale, but the speed with which I made friends and lost them on this trip was astonishing. Pete Gilbert was a natural mate. He just was.

I think true friendship boils down to a shared sense of humour.

That to me seems to be the secret of its longevity, as well as an effort on both sides to stay in touch. Email/Facebook and all that social media stuff makes contact so much easier today. It was unavailable to me then.

Pete stayed on a few more days in Singapore before he headed back to Perth. I left him there in the digs to recover with his penicillin pills, and took the bus to Kuala Lumpur. We vowed to each other to stay in touch, had bonded in the space of a fortnight or so by our joint exploits, even though it seemed much longer than that, and after a kind of manly, gruff, emotional farewell, off I went. I never saw him again. We wrote to each other on my return, but in due course lost touch completely. Life has a habit of getting in the way it seems.

Having the benefit of a $400 saving with my cheap flight, I indulged a bit and bought a Pentax camera and a small tape/radio whilst in Singapore. I then recorded a tape of my thoughts and some of my experiences of the trip so far to send to Meg. Needless to say I left out the more salacious stuff. As I spoke into this machine, with the roar of planes taking off behind, me I found my conversation stilted and awkward. It didn't feel genuine. I said I loved her and missed her, but I didn't. Not really. I'd changed. That realisation was a shock. I was now facing the future, the past firmly behind me, and ready for what was for me the Holy Grail of the trip. I posted the tape to Meg. It was like posting a duty. I grabbed my faithful rucksack, delivered it to check-in, and off I went to board the overnight plane for Sydney.

Australia

The DC-10, or whatever these wide-bodied jets are called, was damn near empty. I slept across four seats for the night flight, and got my first glimpse of Australia when I peered through the window at 3,000 ft as we came in to land. I was incredibly excited. Here I was on the other side of the world. It was 8 am in Sydney on a Saturday morning. I emerged from the plane blinking, felt the warm air and bright sunshine on my skin, and not a cloud to be seen. This was November, it was supposed to be winter. Except that it wasn't. I was heading into Australia's summer. Everything was upside down. The sun was moving slowly to the North. It took me a while to adjust to this opposite view of the world.

I had absolutely no idea where I was going. The day in front of me was a complete mystery. I had no contacts and knew no one. Outside of the airport I thought of the telegram I'd sent from Bangkok to relatives of a workmate of mine at the office in Leeds. He had assured me they would be more than happy to put me up, and I just hoped he'd forewarned them of my travels, but having sent the telegram, I had no way of knowing if they'd got it. Fingers crossed they had. I knew Mike and Helen lived in Queenscliff, on the north side of Sydney somewhere near Manly, but other than that I hadn't any plan B. I clutched a city street guide, caught a taxi to the Manly ferry, and thirty minutes later found myself in this bustling place, with small ferries, boats and yachts ploughing backwards and forwards across this huge harbour of sparkling clear blue water, and gazed for the first time at Sydney Harbour Bridge spanning it all.

I climbed on to the neat little ferryboat, lugging all my gear on to a spare seat alongside me on the deck. Sitting opposite was a neat-looking guy in a light cotton jacket and shorts. The ferry trip took about half an hour, and we struck up a conversation. I quickly discovered the Aussies will engage in talk with anyone. Perhaps the rucksack and sleeping bag naturally attracted attention, and he was really keen to hear where I'd been and what I'd done. So in the half-hour journey across Sydney Harbour I gave him a brief synopsis of everything. He seemed envious.

The Aussies are an adventurous lot, and this guy was no exception. Turned out he was a doctor in Sydney and had just finished his early-morning shift. For my part I told him I was flying a bit blind, well completely blind in fact, but had this address in Queenscliff, for people who may or may not be expecting me. His car was parked in Manly and he generously offered me a lift. Queenscliff, as the name implies, was up a very steep hill some three or four miles outside of Manly. I accepted gratefully and threw my gear into the boot. By this time the sun had begun to burn, and his air con was a relief. He found the address after a ten-minute drive, which was a small house tucked down a side road on a pleasing estate of smart houses right at the very top of the hill. He waved me goodbye, wished me luck, and away he went. I stood there for a few seconds, picked up my gear, trudged down the path and knocked on the door. This was crunch time. If they hadn't got my telegram, then I hadn't a clue what to do or where to go. All I knew was I was on the other side of the world with no one's support. I began to plan my next move if I drew a blank here. It was likely to be the YMCA most probably. There was no reply, and no sound of anyone at home. With increasing dismay I stood there for a few minutes wondering what best to do, then heaved the rucksack on to my back. Just as I did so and was turning to leave I noticed a sliver of paper wedged close to the Yale lock. It was tiny, no bigger than a postage stamp. I pulled it out and unfurled it.

It read: 'Sorry not in. Back soon. Key under mat. Welcome to Australia John.'

I'd arrived!! At last!! This was November 1976.

One of the first things I did in Australia was get my hands on Marmite, or Vegemite as they call it, Heinz tomato ketchup, and Cadbury's chocolate. I'd missed them terribly. But most importantly I wanted a post card. You may recall my father, ten years earlier after I told him I was going to Australia, sneering, 'Send me a card when you get there.' So I did. I absolutely loved writing that card to him.

Mike and Helen were Yorkshire bred, in their forties, and had come out to Oz in the 1960s on the £10 assisted package. This was the one I'd intended to take in 1967, before I opted for college and Business Studies. Such are the twists and turns of fate. They had two kids Edwina (eleven) and Chris (nine) and the lot of them made me feel welcome and special.

For the first week or so I relaxed, and recorded various tapes which I sent home. The weather, the outdoor mentality, and the unspoilt nature of Australia I loved. The skies were a cloudless deep blue, and the days got hotter. The night sky was clear of pollutants and the starscape was unrivalled. The constellations were quite different to the ones I knew back home, no Orion's belt, Pole star, or Great Bear, but for the first time ever I saw the Southern Cross, which sparkled gloriously.

I learned about the poisonous stuff too, especially the redback and funnel-web spiders, both deadly back then, but antidotes to the poisonous bites are now available. I didn't realise when I arrived that the shiny black spider crawling slowly across my bedroom carpet proved to be a funnel-web. When in my ignorance I approached it, instead of running, as most spiders will, it turned on its hind legs like a crab to face me. It wasn't a bit afraid, which I found disconcerting. It was such an aggressive-looking little bastard I took off my shoe and flattened it, something I wouldn't normally do with a spider back home. This bugger just looked malevolent. I showed it to Mike and he confirmed its identity.

The red-backed spider was another venomous one, though not quite as deadly as the funnel-web. I decided I wanted to catch one, and went under the stilts of the house to search among bits of rubble. I eventually found one under a slab and used a plant pot to trap it, then shook it into a bowl of methylated spirit, pickling it alive. I eventually brought this redback home in a tablet bottle. Everyone thought I was mad, and I probably was, but I kept that bottled spider for years as a trophy and memento. It eventually disintegrated into a meth-and-spider soup.

The Pacific Ocean crashed on to a beautiful white sand beach at the bottom of the cliff, and Mike taught me to bodysurf on the big waves which rolled in, and they sure were big. I would frequently disappear under them and be carried underwater to be deposited gasping on the beach. There were Prawn Nights. These were special, and didn't look remotely like the prawns I was used to back home. They were immense, like a mini lobster without claws, and served cold on a big silver tray, with mayonnaise dressing, during the cabaret interval in the nearby Diggers Club. I love all kinds of seafood, and I gorged myself on the things.

The Diggers Club, just down the road, was a big five- or six-storey building where Mike worked. Although he was a self-employed electrical contractor, he served as their resident electrician. The Diggers was a kind of giant working men's club, spanning several floors. The top floor was cabaret/dancing, the next floor down a restaurant, and then three or four floors of fruit machines. This was how the place was funded. On a Friday especially it heaved noisily as hard-earned wages disappeared into these ravenous slots. They whirred, tinkled and flashed, and occasionally a lucky winner would get four cherries in a row. The cash would cascade out of the thing on to the floor, accompanied by whoops and cheers as they gathered up their prize. I'd seen these things in pubs, but never anything like this.

Australia was different in so many respects. I listened to the radio a lot. The presenters were more irreverent than those at home, but the song which sticks in my mind more than any other and takes me back there instantly is Boston's 'More than a Feeling'. Like the previous songs elsewhere in this tome, the lead break sends shivers down my spine. There was a hilarious Sydney radio programme. Norman Gunston was the presenter, a sometime TV comedian, and possibly the most outrageous DJ I'd ever heard. In fact he was bloody rude in a Kenny Everett kind of way. It was so refreshing. I loved his programme and taped it. I still have it somewhere, and likewise that too can transport me back.

After a time of twiddling my thumbs, running on the beach, swimming each day, and soaking up the sheer delight of being here, I decided to contact GEC in Sydney, as requested by John Crathorne, my MD in Leeds. My sales job seemed like years ago, but in fact it was only a matter of months. So much had happened I'd lost track of time, and I had to think hard to jolt myself back to reality. I was on leave of absence and at some point I would have to go back.

I'd sent occasional cards back to my office in Leeds, and felt a sort of obligation to reconnect with the real world, so I rang GEC and spoke to Tim Smallwood, the General Manager at GEC. He'd been expecting my call, so off I went into Sydney to meet him at his office. Small, dapper, about forty, wearing a short-sleeved shirt and a tie, but no long trousers, just neat shorts (I loved the informality of it), he handed me the promised letter from Crathorne. I opened it there and then and read the first line. 'Welcome in from the bush, John.' I suddenly felt proud of myself. I'd made it. The letter contained an offer. For a fee of one month's salary, about £250, he asked me to do some research of the catering equipment market in Australia. Although I needed the money, I felt curiously ambivalent. I realised I'd collected a treasure trove of experience, and done it all on a shoestring. I couldn't begin to put a price on any of this. What was the need for the great god money? I concluded that the best things in life really are free.

Following this request from the big boss, I spent a few days making calls and visiting one or two catering equipment dealers in the city. The object of the exercise was to find out and establish the reasons why my company, Jackson Boilers back in Leeds, were unable to successfully export their water boilers and coffee machines into Australia. I made copious notes, and learned a lot. Despite my ragged, shaggy, hippy appearance, Smallwood said to me there and then that if I ever decided to emigrate to Australia he'd offer me a job. I was flattered, in fact so smitten was I with the idea of a life in Australia, I nearly accepted there and then.

But I still had a complicated domestic situation to sort out back home. In just those few months of travelling like a hobo, I'd managed to put it all out of my mind, though I knew I'd have to deal with it at some point in what was now the rapidly approaching future. Those problems all seemed so far away, even though they lurked in the recesses of my head. The very thought of the mess I'd left behind there, which really, being honest with myself, I'd just delayed dealing with, was all still there. (The reality of it all was that I'd done what any man in my situation would have done. I ran off!) I had to face it all sooner or later and I knew that, but I was consoled by the fact that Smallwood must have thought I was worth it. For a fleeting moment, and despite the daunting prospect of having to face sorting out my affairs, this job offer provided me with some reassurance. It was a kind of back up escape route, if everything back home went tits.

I spent a few days writing up my report on Manly Beach, then decided to take a look at the wider Australia. I took an Ansett Pioneer bus, and headed for Adelaide, where Meg's relatives, cousins of hers, lived. The journey took all day, via Broken Hill, where jacaranda blossom grew on the houses, and an old disused opal mine gave me an opportunity to ferret about in the heaps of spoil. I actually found a piece of opal, not worth much, but I kept it for my mum.

The outback was awe-inspiring and immense. Hot red desert for mile upon mile in every direction, with occasional brush, eucalyptus groves, and groups of kangaroos heading off in clouds of dust. Like Mike and Helen, Meg's relatives were originally from Yorkshire. They too had settled via the £10 assisted package, and they happily accommodated me for a few days. What bit I saw of Adelaide had a more genteel feel. It was greener and less whizz-bang than Sydney. That was my impression anyway, but I've never been back. Another Ansett Pioneer bus took me back to Sydney, this time via Canberra, but it was one long bus journey, as if I hadn't had enough of those, and several days later I arrived back at Mick and Helen's.

I can't quite recall how long I spent in Australia, a few weeks maybe, but I wanted to get home now. It was approaching Christmas, and I felt the urge to go. I was also running out of money.

Hong Kong, Delhi, Home

Mick and Helen took me to the airport. They are friends I've stayed in touch with ever since. After a few emotional hugs and handshakes I flew out of Sydney to Hong Kong. Seven hours or so on this plane, to be deposited into the heaving mass of humanity that is Hong Kong. Noisy and very crowded, and much like Bangkok in many respects. I went on the Star Ferry to Hong Kong Island, took some photos of the Kowloon skyline, and in the evening spent some time mooching round the food markets. I was aghast at what I found, and horrified to find that the Chinese have no sentimentality towards animals whatsoever. Live partridges crushed in cages were hauled out and plucked alive, giant frogs had their back legs cut off and the quivering bodies thrown carelessly into the bin. I discovered the Tiger Balm gardens. This amazing stuff even had a small park dedicated to it, and needless to add, having been introduced to it by Lec, I took a couple of jars home. It's now freely available in Boots and other pharmacies, health shops and the like, but back then no one had heard of it. Scratches, bites, itches, rashes, headaches. It seems to be a cure-all for everything, except Chinese consideration and respect for other living creatures. I instinctively disliked this race, and I still do. It's only a matter of time before they take over complete economic dominance, and with what environmental consequences God only knows.

Apart from my quick trip by ferry to Hong Kong Island, not realising when I arrived that there are two distinct sections to this city (the other being the New Territories), I took an Air France flight out of Hong Kong.

I'd arrived a few days before at night, but we took off in daylight, and although I'd noticed as the plane came in that there were many high-rise apartments above us as we came in to land, hadn't fully appreciated just what a tiny runway this was for a Boeing 747. Taking off with a full load is evidently trickier, and this time I could see that. As we took off amongst the high-rise flats and buildings I could glimpse families serving food, or watching the telly. I'm not sure who was the more disconcerted. Me probably. These people were obviously used to Boeing 747s flying in and out of their kitchens. Since those times Hong Kong's runway has been extended. I've subsequently spoken to pilots who claim that Hong Kong is probably the most difficult airport in the world for landing and taking off. I'm glad I found out that fact much later.

My flight was bound for Paris, touching down in Bangkok to collect more people, then Delhi, where I'd disembark, then onward to Paris. It was odd transiting through Bangkok, where I'd been only weeks before, but even more odd when I arrived in Delhi at 11 pm at night.

Delhi airport is about 15 miles from the city, and the place felt deserted. Well actually it was, and I waited and waited and waited for my rucksack to arrive at baggage reclaim, but it never did. All I had was what I stood up in, my hand luggage, and sleeping bag.

Once I'd known the date I'd intended to leave Australia, I sent a telegram from Sydney to make a hotel reservation in Delhi. I fancied a couple more days in this city, since I'd been so ill I hadn't seen as much of it as I'd have liked. Since Thailand and Australia, my digestive upsets seemed to have more or less disappeared. I had intended to spend two days in Delhi before making the flight to Baghdad, and then onwards to Heathrow. I stood there in this semi-deserted airport and with an increasing sense of rage realised my rucksack was still on the plane. By now well on its way to Paris.

The enormity of this loss sunk in. I was livid, upset, emotional and very angry. I'd had six months of backpacking travel to find that my trinkets, keepsakes, maps, letters, clothes were lost, but most importantly all my notes and exercise books which I'd used to faithfully record my thoughts and experiences.

Forlornly I assessed my position. I had money, passport, and the bare essentials in my hand luggage, and for some unknown reason my faithful sleeping bag. To this day I can't account as to why (mercifully) I hadn't attached it to my rucksack as usual, but thank Buddha I hadn't. That was it. All my treasured possessions were heading to France. By now it was 1 am and freezing cold. December is very cold in Northern India especially at night. Disillusioned, and more than a little disgruntled, I made my way out of the place. I found a half-asleep taxi driver and took the thirty-minute ride to my hotel in Delhi.

Eventually he dropped me off at the cheap hotel I'd booked, and rattled off in his beaten-up Humber Snipe lookalike. Then the next shock awaited. The hotel was locked and in complete darkness. I hammered on the door, and my already fragile mental state turned to real anger. I'd been travelling for twelve hours, all my possessions were gone, it was now 2 am, I was bone-cold, and to say I was tired and emotional was an understatement.

After what seemed like an age, I looked through the metal barrier on the door and peered into the darkened reception. There I saw a coal brazier glowing in the corner, still dimly alight. In this semi-gloom I made out a figure wrapped in blankets, fast asleep on the reception desk. I continued hammering on the door and the figure stirred, climbed off the desk, came to the door and, rubbing his eyes, let me in. This presumably was the night manager. His English wasn't too good, and mustering as much calmness as I could, I explained I had a reservation. Looking through a big book he told me he couldn't find it. I was shivering, very tired, and felt my temper begin to rise. There was no reservation. He examined the book ten times but it definitely wasn't there. I unrolled my sleeping bag, and told him I was going nowhere until the morning. He went back to his blankets on the desk, and left me to it. I got as close to the brazier as I could and slept on the floor next to it with my hand luggage for a pillow.

In the daylight things don't always seem so bad. It turned out there had been a fire at the telephone exchange in Delhi, so my telegram from Sydney never made it. They found me a room that morning, and I used the phone to try to get through to the airport, but it was useless. The phone lines had also been damaged by the fire.

I was in Delhi for no more than forty-eight hours, so made the best of it, and went off to one or two of the familiar places I'd known months before, and since this was now about one week before Christmas, bought some presents. Rings and silver bracelets mostly, to replace those which I'd collected over the previous months that were now in France.

I was resigned to their loss, and left Delhi two days later in a shared taxi to the airport with a girl I'd met in a café the day after my arrival. I can't recall her name, but like me, and of a similar age, she'd been travelling around India and was now heading home for Christmas too. She reminded me very much of Kate, the travelling companion I'd picked up in Patna and travelled to Kathmandu with. I'll call her Kate 2. She was lovely, but not in a fanciable way, and sympathetic over my lost luggage.

We got to the departure lounge at the airport with no more than a couple of hours to spare before the flight to Baghdad, and checked in. On instinct I told Kate 2 I was going to try one last time to try to find my luggage, just on the off-chance it had been sent back, so dashed over to the arrivals section. I eventually found the lost luggage department, and gave my flight details to a bored-looking uniformed jobsworth. Indolently he showed me the lost luggage rooms. There were three of them, divided into one week's lost luggage, one month, and one longer-term one. As I looked inside the first one, it was full to the ceiling with suitcases and bags. If my gear was here, this was the room it should be in, but it wasn't, and a bright orange rucksack would stick out like the proverbial sore thumb. It wasn't, so just in case it had been put into the one-month room by mistake, he opened that door. Again it was filled with bags and suitcases. Even if it had been there I doubt I would have seen it buried amongst this stuff. Floor to ceiling was filled with luggage. My jobsworth told me smilingly that there was no point looking into the long-term lost luggage section, since my rucksack had disappeared only three days before, but I insisted we look. He opened the door to that room with evident irritation, and there, on the top of this pile of dusty abandoned luggage it sat. I couldn't believe my eyes. My jobsworth seemed more concerned that his system of aged lost luggage wasn't working properly.

He dragged it off the top of the pile, but in true civil service fashion wouldn't let me near it without the appropriate paperwork. I just wanted to grab it and run. In the event it turned out Air France had sent it back to Delhi within twenty-four hours, but with the phones down I had no way of knowing that. I had no choice but to get a signed piece of paper from the Air France office up on the second floor. It was an untidy mess, but amongst this mess I found someone who double-checked its return in a book, and I got the chit with the all-important return number. He gave me a returns document which I duly signed, and ten minutes later was back to find my jobsworth, who was now smiling condescendingly with another group of upset lost-luggagers.

I was panicking. Time was of the essence, but eventually I nailed him and handed him the document he required. He courteously handed over the rucksack to this sweaty, unkempt, stressed-out individual standing before him. Heaving the familiar old thing gratefully on to my back, I raced back across to the departures terminal with minutes to spare, and finally checked it in. I was the last one on and recall the plane more or less revving up as I scrambled up the steps. Kate2 had reserved my seat and taken care of my hand luggage, and was waiting anxiously for me on the plane. She shared my absolute delight and immense relief that I'd recovered my long-lost travelling companion.

A brilliant but nerve-wracking end to more or less six months of dirt and grit, people and experiences. The finale was to find on our arrival at Baghdad that there had been a delay to our flight due to the transit lounge being blown out by a terrorist bomb, a matter of hours before we'd arrived. We were herded into what was left of the transit lounge, and I watched in disbelief as a goat was dragged out on to the tarmac, its throat cut, and sacrificed on the runway, with cups of blood thrown on to the nose cone of this Boeing. A message for Allah, I was told, with the intention that He would ensure the safety of the next plane to take off. I guess this archaic act just about sums up my entire travelling experience. medieval religion and ritual meets twentieth-century technology. Forty years on and not much has changed it seems. ISIS, beheadings, and stoning. So much for progress, eh?

My journey back to Heathrow, Christmas, New Year 1977, Meg, my family, and of course the opportunity to resume my Sales

Manager's job, was uneventful.

And perhaps this deserves a footnote. A kind of PS.

My old fishing mate Zolly picked me up from Heathrow. I remember his incredulity when he saw me. I must have been unrecognisable, with hair was down to my shoulders and my weight down to 10 st 6 lbs. He delivered me to a hotel in Droitwich, where Meg had booked a room, we had a celebratory drink, he left, and Meg and I spent our first night together in months. It was a strange, passionate, but tender night. Almost an exploratory one. I hope you see what I mean.

I eventually drove up to North Yorkshire a couple of days later to Boroughbridge. I was desperate to get my little terrier Dylan, who had been with my sister Julia and her husband. My mum and dad came up to rendezvous with me. My mum was tearful, my dad shook my hand, for the first time ever in a gruff awkward way. This was possibly the closest we ever got to affection. He was proud of me. I just knew it. But not a word did he utter.

As for my dog, Julia told me he was asleep in the greenhouse down the garden. I went down on my own, and there he was. Fast asleep in his basket. I crept up on him, and gave him a poke. He woke, blinked and I picked him up in my arms. He began to shake uncontrollably, and somehow gripped me, licked my hands, my face, he clung to me. He didn't need to talk. He just wouldn't leave me alone. If I'd had pockets big enough he'd have climbed in and through them into my skin. I never left that dog again. I loved him dearly.

The End
Well not quite. Here's another footnote:

I was debating with myself whether or not to take out this trip section, and put it in as a separate thing altogether. It's taken up a great deal of time and space, but it was such an important part of my life, I've decided to leave it in.

At some point, at some ill-defined time in the future, I fully intended to write the thing as a book, with more detail, especially the more salacious bits. The who, when, what, how and where. But then it would have become largely a porn book, and you wouldn't have wanted that, now would you?

The lessons and experiences I gained, even though at the time I was unaware of them, and with the usual given perfection of hindsight, have stood me in good stead since. They've come to my rescue on many an occasion since, and yet at the time I was travelling the impact of them was lost to me.

Of all the experiences, one aspect, perhaps the most important one of all, was that I finally proved to myself my self-reliance. That alone inspired in me a confidence to take chances, to decide my own future and subsequent direction. Not that I had a bloody clue at the time what this was likely to be. Most importantly I'd thrown off the shackles of parental control, which had been considerable in my upbringing. Parents unintentionally plant their own conditioned responses into their children. They may have been relevant in the times they grew up, but as times change some become increasingly irrelevant. The poet Larkin summed it up with 'They fuck you up, your mum and dad, they may not mean to, but they do.' I was twenty-eight when I finally threw the irrelevant ones in the bin. Larkin put it more eloquently, or perhaps more succinctly. Parents spend the early part of your life with guidance to their own standards. It becomes almost a kind of ideology. The difficulty is sorting out which bits to keep and which bits to dispose of.

Delhi 1976

Chapter 12

Janet, as you'll recall, was a love affair from college, which grew into a habit. It was expected (by the parents) that we would follow the same pattern and settle down to mortgage and kids. She went along with it, and so did I for a time. But I believe I would have been forever restless. That was the reality. I was trying to fit into some conventional frame which simply didn't fit. Janet didn't think like me, and I could never really understand that, or why others didn't either. To a large degree I am still restless today, a blessing and a curse, but I doubt I would ever have achieved my goals had I not been, even though I had bugger-all of an idea what those goals were at the time. I'd like to think though that I've now done that. The point is, this trip was entirely responsible for instilling into me a level of determination not only to not let events defeat me, but to surmount obstacles.

But what is a personal goal exactly? It took some time for me to work that out. What was it I actually wanted to do, and even if I did work it out, how would I follow that up with an achievable plan? I thought about this for weeks and months.

In the end I boiled it down to one motivational factor. Unaccountability. Some may say it's driven by selfishness, but that implies that I'm inconsiderate to others, and I sincerely hope I'm not. I'd prefer to say I was focused. Almost to the exclusion of others who often concluded that I was one-dimensional. The bottom line is that I simply don't like being told what to do. I wanted and intended to make my own decisions in the future and stand or fall by them. That way there was no one to blame for failure, but equally I wanted to be appreciated for any successes. How was I ever going to achieve that state? I couldn't see it then, and it took a few years, but ultimately there was no other way. I had to work for myself.

Just to illustrate a point with my newly discovered independence, here is a little . . .

Side story

There was a warmth to my mother, a fireside comfort, she was inherently sympathetic. It was a quality wholly lacking with my father. My relationship with him was always more distant, and if he was violent in nature – and God knows we'd experienced that, especially my brother Martin and I when we were kids – there was always sneering sarcasm and criticism he could fall back on to belittle us. We'd always seemed to be dancing around him, always trying to please. This stopped with me in 1977. I was twenty-eight, and not long back from my overland trip.

He'd been at his cottage for a few days, and I joined him on a Saturday morning. The plan was to walk the Derbyshire hills around Alstonefield the following day. I'd got my old MGA up and running and took that. It had recently had some bodywork done on the boot and had been freshly repainted. Mum joined us that afternoon, and in the evening we had dinner. After a few drinks, at 9 pm he went to bed to read or do his crossword by candlelight as dictated by his usual routine. There was no electricity in this place. It had only just been equipped with running water, such were the luxuries of living in the middle of nowhere.

Mum and I sat talking by the fire, when I realised she'd parked her car across the gateway, which meant I was unable to get mine out. She decided to move it, and went out into the pitch-blackness. Her reversing skills left much to be desired, as did her general driving, and suddenly I heard a crash. I went out to see that she'd accidently hit the accelerator instead of the brake, and reversed into the back of my recently repaired pride and joy. I went mad, lost my temper, swore at her, and lambasted her for her carelessness. I was seething, she was upset, then I heard the sound of thunder coming down the stairs. My father, dressed in only his pyjamas, came at me in a furious temper, put his face two inches from mine, and screamed at me, spittle flecking into my face, screaming that it was only a piece of metal and what was the problem. I didn't reply, I just hit him. And down he went. As he got up, I hit him again, and he lay on the gravel drive for several seconds. Then he got up and went back inside. I was shaking with anger, and admit I was out of order, but drink heightens the senses, and adrenaline was rushing through me. My mum continued to cry, not for my shouting, but for what I'd done. She'd never suspected I had this side to me, and neither did he. She begged me to apologise, which I did with some awkwardness as he lay upstairs back in his candlelit room. I got something of a gruff reply but no more. I also apologised to my mum for my outburst.

That night as I lay in bed I hardly slept. What had I done? What I realised I had done in fact was throw off twenty-eight years of a bullying father in the space of a few seconds. This was a new me. I wasn't intending for him to push me around any more. This was something which shocked me, and no doubt him, at the time.

The walk the following day was a trial for us both. Barely did we speak a word to each other. This fight was never ever mentioned again. I didn't feel a bit triumphal, but the status quo between us had changed for good. In time, although he never said a word, I just knew he had developed a greater respect for me.

It was entirely down to the trip I'd done. I'd changed. I was no longer a jumped-up little shit. I was more of a jumped-up bigger shit. I was my own man at last, and that evening underlined it once and for all.

Chapter 13

―――――

What I'm now going to do is write everything from the time I came home in early 1977 to the beginning of 1980, which effectively concludes my first thirty-odd years on this planet. It so happens that this was also an appropriate time of my life to begin the next phase.

Since I began with this in 1953, I will now go back and read all 60,000 words so far, edit some of it, and commence this next chapter. I'm now going to begin with the next three years, and what a bloody rollercoaster three years they proved to be.

1977

January 1977 found me home and living with Meg in North Worcestershire. She'd changed her name to Craddock, it was easier she said, and to all intents and purposes we lived as man and wife. I still loved her, but began to view this love in a slightly more detached way. I assumed responsibility for her two children aged fourteen and twelve. As mentioned previously, Meg had trained as a Rural Science teacher and landed a job in the small town of Cleobury Mortimer, just over the border in Shropshire. She was always a countrywoman and loved this job. Her kids went there too.

As for Janet, she and I divorced amicably a few months after my return, with a £25 quickie at Worcester Crown Court. We'd sat down at some point and agreed which albums (I got the Lindisfarne album), which furniture, and which possessions we each wanted to keep. I got custody of Dylan the dog. We also knew solicitors do their damnedest to foster acrimony between parties by stirring up shit. We were having none of that.

Mud-slinging, or more accurately shit-slinging, is how they make their living. They thrive on it, whilst cynically upping their costs in the process. Janet could have slung bucketfuls in my direction, but graciously she didn't. The house we'd originally bought was sold and the proceeds, £5,000 we split 50/50. My six-month jaunt had cost in total around £1,000 including flights – doesn't seem much now – and that was for everything. I banked the £1,500 balance, and Janet and I walked away from each other. We resolved to stay in touch, and we did.

Years and years later, in 1997, when I met Janet's father again as a result of the funeral of his only son Geoff, my ex brother-in-law (he died suddenly and unexpectedly of complications with Crohn's disease, aged just 47) he complimented me on the honourable way in which I'd dealt with the divorce from his youngest daughter. I was shocked. This was the guy I'd had many furious rows with years before when I was a lefty radical student, and he a right-wing pillar of the Establishment. We became quite close after that, but not for long. He died a year or so later.

I wrote up the Australian catering equipment report on my old Olivetti typewriter in early January 1977. I hadn't gone back to work yet, even though I was back on the company books again. Bit by bit the euphoria of my triumphal backpacking travels had begun to subside, and as I looked out of the window on a rainy January morning, while typing up my report, I idly wondered where I ought to be right now. Fiji? New Zealand? Samoa? Borneo?. Suddenly out of the blue I realised I was depressed. I didn't want to be here. I seemed to have catapulted myself from feckless traveller with an open road ahead, straight into a domestic prison. I began to realise that back to the drawing board was going to take some serious adjustment. It wasn't a prospect I relished. I wasn't unhappy with my adopted family, it just wasn't the same. Or maybe I wasn't the same.

The report spanned some ten pages, and after some tweaking I sent it to Crathorne, my MD up in Leeds. I was due to be back up there the following week. I got a haircut, put on my pinstriped suit, smart shirt and tie, and felt utterly ridiculous. I looked the part, but didn't feel it. I later caught the train from Birmingham and went up to Leeds to pick up my files and my Hillman Avenger. I was about to resume my job as Sales Manager for the West Midlands.

The train journey was in complete contrast to the train I'd taken across India. No one spoke, just stared out of the window, or concentrated on their crosswords. I was back home all right.

I can tell you honestly I have never felt more out of sorts. I hadn't appreciated how much I'd changed, and underestimated completely the sheer impact this travelling had had on me. I looked like me, but I wasn't the old me. It simply didn't feel right. Ominously my relationship with Meg didn't either. It all seemed wrong.

When I arrived in the office, everyone stopped what they were doing and applauded. Jean, the MD's secretary, had collected all the cards I'd sent from the trip and pinned them to the notice board, where everyone had the opportunity to read them. I felt like some kind of hero, or prodigal son. Repeatedly I was asked where the best place was on the trip, and the answer was: All of them. Each stop or country was unique and different. Whilst I acknowledged the back-slapping and excitement of being back, it only served to underline my profound feelings of disenchantment.

However, I needed to earn a living, so gritted my teeth and went back to work. All my customers in the West Midlands wanted to hear my stories too, so it was a kind of death by a thousand cuts. My Australia report was well received however, and had evidently gone down well with the MD. The next two or three months were a drudge though. Every day I seemed to wrestle with domesticity and sales routine.

Suddenly, and much to my surprise, in April 1977 the MD summoned me to Leeds. So impressed was he with my grasp of the market in Australia that in those ten pages he'd learned more than any of the export reports he regularly received from head office. The bottom line of my report was simple. The water boilers we made were far too expensive to sell there. They had a competitor, Whelan, who produced a commercial water boiler at a third of our prices. In fact when I contacted Whelan, they asked me if I could find an agent for them in the UK. I gave them my father's company, Lincat. Needless to say, I didn't mention that in my report.

Anyway while I was idly wondering what I'd been summoned up here for, the MD unexpectedly offered me a promotion. I was to become Export Marketing Manager. The job, however, was to be based in Leeds. I didn't know how I'd feel about this. It was an escape of sorts, but into a bigger prison.

The UK hadn't long joined then what we knew as the common market, which eventually morphed into the EEC (European Economic Community) and subsequently, as we all know, the EU.

I was all in favour of tariff-free trade between half a dozen countries, so I swapped Birmingham and the West Midlands for Western Europe and Scandinavia. This was my new territory. It was now Amsterdam, Copenhagen, and Oslo, making a welcome change from Wolverhampton, West Bromwich, and Dudley.

I don't know if the MD was clever enough to recognise and attempt to harness my restlessness, or whether that report I did sealed it for me, but I suspect it was more a case of 'Craddock knows about foreigners, we have all this antiquated catering equipment, gathering dust in the warehouse. Let's see if he can flog it to Johnny Foreigner.' This was fairly typical of British industry attitudes at the time. The reality was that this equipment was designed in the 1950s and had had no investment to upgrade and redesign. It's a kind of arrogance, I think, and was endemic in the mindset generally of British manufacturing. What essentially they were asking me to do was to sell a horse and cart to a car dealer.

Marketing is the essence of moving, upgrading, modernising, rethinking, re-designing, and endeavouring to forecast or anticipate what the customer's needs are. Instead of trying to sell this outdated kit, it would have been far better to send it to the scrapyard and start from scratch.

My new job proved to be an impossible task. I was trying to sell to markets which were now way ahead of us. Nevertheless I looked the part, had a fancy title, and got to know a number of countries, Norway, Denmark, Sweden Netherlands and so on, which ordinarily I'd never have done.

It sounded glamorous, and it was, but I was mostly living out of a suitcase, and a hotel in Leeds. I went home at weekends, but slowly and surely Meg and I grew further apart.

I also had a new girlfriend, Esther, a West Indian girl who worked in our accounts office. She was fit and lithe, and supplemented her salary as an occasional 'go-go' dancer at weekends in one of the Leeds clubs. Spending the occasional night with her made me realise just how unfit I was! She cooked for me occasionally at her flat, soaking pork chops in West Indian chilli sauce, and then frying them. After that we'd down a glass or two, and disappear into her bedroom. She had a wonderful body, and her dark skin seemed to glow with health.

Just to complicate matters, as only I can, whilst living Monday to Thursday at the hotel in Roundhay Park, I had a bit of a fling with a girl who worked there, and she'd wake me in the mornings with a tray of tea, and for good measure put her hand under the sheets and give me a little 'massage'. A pleasant way to greet the world, don't you think? She was about twenty-five, smart, funny, intelligent, and was only doing hotel work until she got her big break, which she did. Her name I daren't say. She went on to become quite a famous DJ a year or two later with the BBC. I went out with her several times, and perhaps one of the more memorable evenings was her taking me to the theatre in Leeds to see Equus. A disturbing play involving a character who blinded horses.

You can perhaps imagine how extremely hard I found it to shake off the itinerant lifestyle I'd become accustomed to, and even though today I'm settled, I have never successfully shaken off that occasional feeling of restlessness. It's something within me, I think, but whether the trip was responsible for exacerbating this restlessness or not, I don't know. Perhaps it was something I was born with.

Then, as if life up in Leeds wasn't complicated enough, I took up with Janet once more. Curiously I'd missed her. She was part of my education in many ways, and we had emotional history. Even though I was living with Meg at the weekends, I would often come back down from Leeds or Oslo, Copenhagen, or wherever, a day early, and then go to stay the night with my ex-wife before going back 'home'.

It was insane, and this self-inflicted lifestyle nearly drove me mad. It was guilt, driven by a desire to make amends, and I built lie upon lie upon lie between three women. By the end of 1977 I was a mess. I still looked the part and carried out my job as best I could, but the lies and deceit I'd concocted were inevitably going to get me, and sure enough they did. This ridiculous lifestyle I'd developed all came crashing down in 1978. I have never been so truly mixed up in my life, and I had nobody, absolutely nobody, to blame but myself.

1978

One of the worst things about affairs, and I've probably said this before, is the helpless feeling of being split in two emotionally. I continued this hedonistic lifestyle more or less throughout 1978, but the job and the travel were taking their toll, and as I said before, trying to sell antiquated products abroad was an uphill battle. However many marketing reports I wrote to the board of directors, urging them to redesign and modernise, they fell on deaf ears, and went into the pending tray. I was incredibly frustrated by this. I had the title, but no power.

I bet you've missed a side story for a while, so here's one.

In March 1978 I found myself in Oslo to meet a dealer who wished to distribute on our behalf. This was unusual. For some reason he spotted something about our range of deep fat fryers which suited the Norwegian market, so off I went to meet him.

As I flew into Oslo that night from Heathrow, I could see the sparkling twinkly lights of the city below. The air seemed crystal-clear. When I emerged from the airport the cold hit me like a sledgehammer. The temperature was –40 °C. I'd been there once before and the weather then had been almost tropical in comparison. The cold air caught the back of my throat and I felt the hairs in my nose freeze. Jeez, it was cold all right. But a dry cold, not that wet, seeping cold we get in England. I grabbed a taxi and climbed into air-conditioned warmth, which deposited me at a lovely hotel in the city that my dealer man had booked for me.

He met me for the first time the following morning. A charming guy in his late thirties. I can't remember his name, but we'd spoken many times on the phone, and he knew of my interest in Viking history. He gave me the grand tour, spending the day exploring Norway's Viking heritage at the Viking Museum, and showing me around Oslo, a lovely, clean, crisp city. There was snow in places, but old snow which had been compacted by the cold. The streets were clear, as were the pavements, and I wondered idly where they'd put it. Winter didn't seem to bother any of them. We discussed food over lunch, and he explained how the Norwegians invented gravlax. Wrapping a salmon in dill and burying it below the tideline, marking the site with a stick, and leaving the brine of the sea to do the rest for a few days. I ordered it, and have preferred it to smoked salmon ever since. We also discussed business, and a deal on these fryers was in the offing. He wanted 300 of them. That would just about clear out our warehouse of these things, which had been gathering dust for about a year. It all looked promising.

I was there for three days, and on my last evening he invited me to his house in downtown Oslo for what he called a typical Viking supper. And to meet his wife.

It wasn't a house the taxi took me to, but a large apartment on the third floor of a high-rise block of flats, of which there were several in this suburb. It was still freezing cold, although I'd got a bit used to it by now. I crunched across the frozen snow, made my way up the stairs, and knocked at the door. I was greeted by one of the most stunning women I've ever encountered.

If you conjure a thought about Scandinavian women, your imagination would probably take you to the blonde woman in ABBA, or the actress Britt Ekland. The woman who stood before me was the exact opposite. She had jet-black hair which shone like raven's plumage, About 5 ft tall, a gorgeous figure in a tight-fitting black dress, with flawless skin. It was the eyes though, the so-called window to the soul. She possessed the bluest of blue eyes I'd ever seen. She was probably thirty-one or thirty-two. I simply couldn't take my eyes off her, and I deliberately had to make an effort to avert my gaze from time to time from fear of embarrassment. When I was a kid, my mum used to tell me not to stare at people. I did my best here, but believe me it wasn't easy. To complete the set she was intelligent and spoke perfect English. Her husband meanwhile appeared totally and affably indifferent to what I felt was a visible and obvious mutual chemical reaction. An instant exchange of invisible communication almost. I've been around a bit, have witnessed similar before, never been able to explain it, but on a scale of one to ten, this was eleven.

You often get an impression of someone over the phone, or an impression of what someone's partner is like from meeting their spouse. These two were wholly different. He with a small moustache, bit of a paunch, mousy hair, slightly balding, and then her. He was married to a Nordic goddess. It didn't fit my perceived stereotype at all.

My host sat me down and we proceeded with the Viking meal. Predominantly cheese, pickled salted fish, dry biscuits and aquavit – a kind of Scandinavian schnapps, which he consumed with amazing enthusiasm. As the evening progressed he became more and more pissed, to the point where he threw an occasional empty shot glass into the mock fireplace. His eyes began to roll, and his tie loosened, but I hardly touched a drop of this stuff, not that he noticed. It seemed lethal to me, and I poured a few glasses surreptitiously into the indoor plant pot (I hope the cheeseplant survived), and threw one or two into the fireplace, just to be sociable. In the meantime, as he began to falter, I engaged his wife in conversation. She was fascinated by my travels across Asia and Australia, and as we talked I became ever more infatuated.

When he was more or less out of it, she asked me if I liked music. I nodded, 'Yes, of course I do', so she went to the far end of the now darkened sitting room and flicked through a few vinyl albums. The only one I recognised among the Grieg and obscure Norwegian stuff was an Elvis LP. I gave her the thumbs-up and she put it on the turntable. 'All Shook Up' was the first track. By now her husband was more or less slumped over the table, comatose. She looked across at him snoring away, then abruptly disappeared, reappearing a few moments later from her bedroom off the hallway, dressed in a long black see-through night dress. Looking up at me, she asked if I wanted to dance. How could I ever refuse? Apart from black knickers, she was naked under it. I was in something of a daze and seriously struggling to get my head straight. If anybody was all shook up, it was me. So we danced, and closely. When we got to 'Love Me Tender', my arms were round her, and her head lay on my shoulder. Right then and there I had this incredible revelation. An insane feeling I'd found my true partner. It was instant. It wasn't just physical desire but an extraordinary feeling of rightness. I felt I needed to escape with her immediately. I glanced across to the far side of the room and her husband, the guy I was supposed to be doing business with, was by now fast asleep.

I knew where this was leading, but in my mind wondered fleetingly whether or not this guy was bribing me in some way to get a deal, using his wife as bait. My instincts told me it wasn't a set-up. I think she was just in a bad marriage, as I had been, and still was, given the mess I was currently making with Janet, Meg, and my liaisons in Leeds.

The lights were down and she became ever more clingy and cuddly. I kissed her neck and she made slight moaning sounds. To say I was aroused was an understatement. She fitted in to me perfectly, like a piece of jigsaw, as we swayed to the music together. Suddenly, without any warning, the atmosphere was shattered by a hell of a banging on the door down the hall. The moment evaporated. Aroused by the banging, my host woke from his alcoholic slumber. She dashed into her bedroom to change. He stumbled down the hall, opened the door, and a small blonde woman fell through it. By now all the lights were on and this woman was sobbing hysterically. Both husband and wife, who had now changed back into proper clothes, tried to calm her. I just stood there uselessly, as they spoke to her in Norwegian. Eventually, when this intruder finally got her heaving sobs under control, they sat her down on the big L-shaped sofa. It was then I saw the damage to her face. Badly bruised, lips swollen, as she continued to shake uncontrollably with my hostess's arms around her. I continued to stand idly by, the proverbial spare prick, hapless, not understanding a word of the garbled conversation.

It eventually transpired that the woman had been in a row with her boyfriend. He had beaten her black and blue outside a hotel bar where they'd been drinking. She'd grabbed a taxi and fled to her best mate for consolation and comfort. The atmosphere began to calm down after about ten minutes, even though I hadn't a clue what they were talking about, so I picked up my coat and suggested I leave. As I did so, the door in the hall was hammered in, and I mean hammered, then finally kicked in, as the lock gave way to the splintering of wood. A huge man stood in the doorway of the sitting room, nostrils flaring like a bull. He wasn't tall, in fact he wasn't much taller than I at 5 ft 7, but his chest and shoulders were immense. He was, it seemed to me at the time, as broad as he was tall, and filled the doorway. The blonde screamed and climbed over the sofa to hide. I have seen some big guys in my time, but I tell you, this guy was not only powerfully built, but in a very bad mood. My still-dazed host immediately introduced me. The bull glared at me first with his glittering eyes, then engulfed my hand with a handshake that made me wince. I could almost hear the bones crack, and despite my fixed smile I tried hard to not look intimidated. In reality I was scared shitless. The blonde remained quivering behind the sofa, but eventually they managed somehow to sit the bull down, who seemed to take up the entire sofa. and my host went to the kitchen to make coffee. The tenseness in the atmosphere I felt I could have photographed, but gradually it eased. The blonde came out in due course and sat warily and tearfully on the edge of the sofa opposite the bull. Her yellowed bruises by now turning purple.

Once again I felt I needed to make a move to leave, even more so given this situation, so my host slipped quietly out into the hall to call a taxi to take me back. These Norwegian phones make a dinging sound when the receiver is replaced, and this one was no exception. The bull heard it and immediately the atmosphere turned sour once more. He rose from his seat and stormed into the hall. I heard my host shout as he was thrown bodily down the hall. The bull then ripped out the phone and threw it after him. I watched my host go flying past the sitting room door, followed immediately by the blur of a green and cream phone, which smashed into the wall and bounced back in pieces of plastic, springs, bells and wires around the hallway. When both of them came back in we all sat in terrified silence. I whispered to my host to ask him if he had managed to get through and he nodded. I noticed his nose was bleeding. The stand-off continued and I began to know what a hostage situation felt like. Ten minutes later, and how I sat through that ten minutes I have no idea, there was a knock on what was left of the door. It was my taxi driver. The bull it seems thought my host had been calling the police. I got up nervously to leave, and with a grimace shook hands all round. By now it was midnight, and still freezing outside. As I walked down the hall with as much feigned confidence as I could, the wife dashed ahead of me and into her bedroom. Out of sight of the others she kissed me on the lips, then handed me a beautiful, thick, woollen Icelandic polo necked jumper. She told me she'd knitted it for her husband, but wanted me to have it as a keepsake. All the blue and grey colours of the pattern, she told me, were hand dyed from Icelandic clay. It was lovely, and as I accepted it gave her a look which I hoped she'd interpret as 'If only'. With a mixture of relief and regret I made my way down the steps and out into the freezing air.

When I got into the back of the taxi, I let out a deep breath and muttered something along the lines of 'Fuuuuck meeeee! What a night.' The driver, realising I was English, said, 'Where to, mate?' in a Sarf London accent. I was astonished. He was, it turned out, from Walthamstow, and had married a Norwegian girl. Yet another surprise, as if I hadn't had enough surprises that evening. As he took me back to the hotel, I related the evening's events. He nodded knowingly, as though it were an everyday occurrence, explaining that the Norwegians don't handle drink too well. I'd say he was spot-on with that. It transpired that there is zero tolerance of drink-driving in Norway, and if caught it's prison. Add in a measure of GBH, and it was hardly surprising the bull had reacted the way he did. I reckon he would (and should) have gone down for some time.

I was flying back to Heathrow the following day, and fell into a deep sleep full of Viking dreams. I dreamt my Ice Goddess was with me on my own Viking ship, just her and I sailing to God knows where, her black hair streaming behind in the northerly wind. So certain was I that this was just a dream, that when I awoke I still couldn't quite believe what had happened. The previous evening's events were all part of that dream, I was absolutely convinced of that. Still a bit dazed, I climbed out of bed to begin packing. And there, on a chair in the corner of my bedroom, was the jumper.

I never saw them again. I don't know if they were all murdered, or escaped. No idea. In fact I flew out of Oslo that morning, clutching that jumper with my mind made up. I went back to Leeds and resigned. Not just because of this, but the deal would never have come off. They reckoned it was too much hassle to make a minor alteration to shift these fryers. As far as I'm concerned they may well be still there rusting away in a shed. I concluded finally that my job was a hopeless task. I hated my boss, a jumped-up university type of know-all, and besides I had also been approached with a better job offer for a rival company, based once more in the West Midlands. I saw it as a stop gap, but in reality it provided an opportunity to find my feet back home again, and to sort out my domestic difficulties. As it turned out it did nothing more than intensify the affair with my ex-wife. I knew I really needed to sort out this mess once and for all, and I did, but not in the way I expected.

The End. Well, of that side story at least.

I was now heading for thirty. Meg was almost ten years older than I. My mum put her oar in as only she could. She knew I possessed what she described, rather genteelly, as a 'roving eye'. The pressure was on me since Meg's biological clock was running out and she wanted another baby. As for me, well I was still mentally upside down in some traveller's dreamland, between Kathmandu and Australia. I was finding it extremely difficult to settle. My mother doused me in cold-water reality, telling me that in the longer term, when I was forty and Meg fifty, I would almost certainly be looking back at women ten years younger. She sure knew me well, and didn't mince her words. If I was intending to leave, and deep down I felt I would, I should go now while Meg still had her looks and youth, and the opportunity to find someone else. That hurt, but I couldn't deny it was good advice. My continued affair with Janet, I realised, was largely driven by guilt. I had been see-sawing back and forth for too long, the inevitable happened and Janet became pregnant, once again. The same woman this happened to ten years earlier when we were students.

I was well and truly busted. The whole thing was blown out of the water. I had no choice but to tell Meg, who became completely hysterical and ran off into a rainy night. I found her eventually in a ditch, soaked and sobbing. As for Janet, she took the decision to have an abortion, this for the second time in her life. Meg had been to see her to discuss adoption, but Janet was never going to allow that to happen. She was tough and decisive, as was Meg, and now both these women knew the score. I was utterly untrustworthy. They met and compared my lies, then made my decision for me. I was out.

For some indefinable reason, and just a few months before all this happened, I used the remains of my equity in the Stourport house as a deposit and bought a small terraced cottage near Droitwich. Maybe I'd already had some kind of premonition of the way things were going to go, but it proved to be a smart move. Towards the end of 1978 I moved in.

All I had was my job, a guitar, clothes, fishing tackle, and my old MGA. The only real companion I seemed to have was Dylan the dog. He was the only one, it seemed, who had any faith left in me.

My social life evaporated, along with self-esteem, as well as the trust of the two women I thought I had loved most. I went into self-imposed exile and wallowed in a self-pity I hated. In the blink of an eye I transformed from a frenetic and hectic lifestyle, to one of a total recluse. I was also incredibly lonely, for a while at least.

Welcome then to 1979.

1979

Apart from the loneliness, I was somewhat surprised to find I adjusted quite well to my single lifestyle. This was an unseen and unknown benefit of my trip, which had toughened me mentally.

One of those things you discover which you didn't know at the time but fell back on. I'd dealt with adversity and loneliness before. The only difference was that had been by choice and free will. The situation I now found myself in had been imposed. And that's the difference.

My relatively new job with the new company gave me no restrictions, in fact I was left to my own devices for most of the time. No boss to monitor me constantly. Always a dangerous thing. I'd often slope off to go fishing or play squash in the afternoons. As far as I was concerned it was a means to an end, but the routine became deadly dull. I began to harbour thoughts of starting my own business, but with what, and how? All I knew was I was sick and tired of corporate life. I recognised though that I was still in some kind of transition. I'd simply done too much travelling and experienced too many things to allow myself to slide backwards. That's how I saw it anyway.

When I came back from my travels, I thought about a change of career direction. A sales career gave me much freedom, and the opportunity to earn well, but it didn't satisfy my anarchic leanings. I needed an outlet for my opinions. That's it, I thought. I'll be a journalist. I could travel freely and go to hotspots around the world reporting on war and injustice. And didn't I have an ability to write? Well I thought so, but soon found out I couldn't.

I approached the Berrow's group of newspapers in Worcester. My starry hopes were dashed immediately. At thirty I was deemed too old to either apply for a job or start at journalistic college in Cardiff. They suggested I go freelance, and what did I know about? I thought about this for a bit then suggested I wrote a fortnightly column on matters in the countryside. I could easily fit that round my job. The Editor asked me to submit three 500-word articles, typed up and double-spaced. So I did. Took me a few days to come up with subject matter, and he returned them in the post a few days later, scrawled all over with red pen. Basically he told me they were rubbish, but, and it was a small but, he may be able to do something with the fox article I'd written.

Re-write it please. So I did, and I was delighted to see it in print later that week. All the travelling I did around the West Midlands, or my fishing expeditions, enabled me to find subject matter. A kestrel perhaps on the dual carriageway, or the river in flood. Thus began my freelance journalist's career. For all of a fiver for each one. In the event it served as nothing more than an outlet, an opportunity to rant in public about pollution and destruction, usually by the agricultural vandals otherwise known as farmers. Above all it provided me with an escape from the boredom of the job. At least I knew what I was writing about. When I wasn't stuck in Birmingham I was out shooting, fishing, walking Dylan the dog. In many ways that little dog, that ragged, mangy, disobedient border terrier cross somehow saved my life. I was convinced he understood everything I said. I'd talk to him for hours.

After six months of going to ground in this cottage, and hardly any contact with either Meg or Janet, I began to resurface, and bit by bit gradually rebuilt some kind of social life. It took time, but I was soon up to my old tricks again with a few one-night stands. This time though there were no lies or deceit involved.

Then something extraordinary happened. One of those unexpected out-of-the-blue events. I was promoted to National Sales Manager. I was in fact on the brink of moving to another job, but was compelled to attend a national sales meeting. Since I had the other job in my pocket, I could afford to be outspoken and strident about the lamentable performance of some aspects of the company. The group had recently taken on a youngish, dynamic Sales Director, and he spotted me during one of my more outspoken moments. Most of the sales force sat in sheepish silence so I more or less had the floor to myself. The next thing I knew, he took me to one side during a break and invited me to the London office. I went to the office in Shaftesbury Avenue a few days later and there and then over lunch he offered me a job to run the sales force nationally. A huge boost in salary, and a brand-new Vauxhall Cavalier GT to boot. It was a hell of a promotion and I jumped at it. What I didn't realise, though, was that travelling the UK's motorways, and arriving home late to my dog, a cold house, and cooking for myself, only intensified my sense of loneliness. What meagre social life I'd begun disappeared. Saturday nights were usually the worst of all.

However, I liked this car. It gave me a kind of status. I was important, wasn't I? Following on from my well used Ford Escort, it was luxurious. It was also fast. In fact I was completely unaware of how fast this thing could go. Within a week I was done for speeding on the M6. A motorway cop hauled me over to the hard shoulder just outside Carlisle. He told me sternly he'd had a job catching me. I'd been listening to the Rolling Stones on my tape cassette, a luxury my previous car didn't have. I was tracked at 108 mph. The song playing at the time happened to be Route 66, a great driving song. I never realised my speed was such, and anyway I was in my usual world, far away. It was a severe offence, I was told, and I ended up with six points on my licence and a £100 fine in Carlisle Court. Probably about £500 today. These days it would have been an automatic ban.

I didn't bother going up for the hearing, but wrote a letter of mitigation to the court in which I blamed the Stones for my lapse in concentration. The rep I had been on my way to see lived in Dumfries, and he later sent me a clip from the local *Carlisle Herald* or whatever it was. 'Motorist blames the Rolling Stones for speeding fine'. Take heed. Rock music doesn't go well with sedate driving. I guess Route 66 should go into my musical memories too. Great song, courtesy of Chuck Berry.

As I wore my hair shirt in Wychbold, did my time, or penance as it were, and felt thoroughly ashamed of myself, I tried hard to develop some kind of social life. The fact was I didn't really know anyone, and my social circle, which had revolved around Meg's life and her teacher friends, was no more. When couples split, it's very hard for friends to divide their loyalties. Besides I was thirty-one and most of my old mates were married with small children at this age. They had other priorities, so my feeling of loneliness increased. I like being on my own, but I like to choose solitude, and as I said earlier when solitude is forced on you it isn't easy. I didn't realise it at the time, but emotionally I was vulnerable to falling in love with whatever and whoever came my way. Except that I had no way of meeting anyone. It wasn't as if I went to a busy office every day. I was stuck in a car most of the time, and travelling to all corners of the UK. The car was my office and the only occupant was me.

Today of course online dating agencies proliferate, and even now I'm surprised by how many people find themselves in such a position to need to do this, so my situation back then was not at all unusual. On balance I think they work well. The chances of meeting Mr or Miss Right from a very narrow social group are virtually negligible. The internet has these days widened the pool dramatically. But in 1979 dating agencies existed, and one morning I picked up a letter on my doormat inviting me to join one. It was a handwritten letter from an agency somewhere in the Cotswolds. I binned it. Then I got another invite, and then another. Someone must have put my name forward. Whoever had proposed me I had, and still have, no idea. In the end I rang the woman who sent the invite. She persuaded me to sign up. They were short of single men, she said. So I thought why not? It was a free service. I had nothing to lose, so I put my profile details onto their 'mailing list'. (I recall them describing me as 'mercurial'??) Lo and behold, a week or so later various letters began to arrive. There were more lonely single women out there than I realised, but nearly all of them seemed a bit sad and lost, describing how they had been through the mill of relationship break-up. I could sure identify with that.

Want another little side story?

I had a few liaisons with one or two of these lonely hearts, but found most of them boring, sad and depressing. I wasn't in the mood and really didn't need that. Except for one though, who was a senior manager with a clothing chain. Her shop was based in Stratford-upon-Avon. I wrote a reply to her letter and we eventually met halfway at a pub. She was slim, dark-haired, and had a neat figure. She dressed well, and was probably about thirty-five or thirty-six. I took her back to my hovelette, having made a few hapless gestures as to the state of the place. Dylan seemed to like her though, giving his seal of approval by pissing on the leg of her chair. I apologised, wiped it up and made coffee. As I handed it to her, she told me she had no intention of going upstairs on the first date. I was taken aback. In fact I was taken a lot aback. I had no intention of taking her up there either. Upstairs was an even more of an untidy shithole than downstairs. We parted company, had a peck on the cheek, and she said she'd like to see me again. With that she left.

I was busy travelling, and she had work commitments, but a couple of weeks later we arranged to meet, this time in Stratford. I reappraised her. She wasn't bad-looking at all, but not in a smouldering sex-driven way. I was unfussy. All I was looking for was no more than a shag.

Back to her place we went, where she'd pre-prepared some kind of ratatouille thing. It was a neat two-bedroom apartment in a small block just near the town centre. The apartment was festooned with horse brasses and horsey pictures. If it had been a pub, I'd have guessed the Coach and Horses. Astutely, because I'm quick like that, I guessed she liked horses.

Needless to say, equine stuff became our main topic of conversation as we sat there and ate. I know fuck-all about horses, apart from the fact they kick and bite, but I made an effort to clip-clop along with the conversation. I then got up, took my very large glass of Cotes du Rhone, and plonked myself down on this very big, very posh, soft sofa. Then suddenly she disappeared. For one moment I thought I was back in Norway. When she reappeared she was wearing a black baby doll outfit, tinged and trimmed as I recall with a tangerine-coloured lacy thing. Nice, but not a patch on my Ice Goddess. So we got down to business, and she didn't hang about either, which surprised me a bit given her coy remarks a week or two before.

And I performed well, I have to say, but I'd had a wealth of experience in Thailand, and she groaned and gasped and complimented me. It was only afterwards as I fondled her, and I'm not sure how to put this, that I felt some lumps around her more intimate regions. It seems she suffered with piles. I didn't actually look, I didn't want to, and fortunately for me I only discovered this after we'd finished. I didn't say anything, and nor did she, but that was enough for me to avoid a replay and not fix up another session.

Chapter 14

At some point my mother came down from Leicestershire to visit me one Saturday morning. She went round my cottage with a vacuum cleaner and dustpan, berating me at the same time for living like a slob. I was never going to settle, get married, never give her the grandchildren she wished for, nag, nag, nag. I was the eldest of her three children and a total disappointment to her, and so on and so forth. That conversation wasn't particularly helpful but I took it on board.

In order to break this vicious circle between travelling and lonely weekends, and really there was only so much fishing I could do, I got a job working on Saturday mornings in my local fishing tackle shop. I didn't need the money, just enjoyed the company more than anything. My now lifelong friend, Geoff, who owned the shop, was the key to lifting me out of this weekend gloom. I met many local anglers and got to know most of them socially. Bit by bit my social circle widened and improved. My neighbours were also a godsend, and took care of my washing and generally fed me on occasions.

Then one day my dad rang me to say he was coming to Cheltenham to staff an exhibition of catering equipment. Was I doing anything? If not would I care to come along? I wasn't, so I did.

He and I had already had harsh words about my domestic problems. I think he thought I was an indolent, womanising waster. I'd have probably thought the same. It's just that I seemed unable to shake myself out of this reverie. I wasn't really a Sales Manager, I was a hobo in a suit. What I didn't like though was his interference in my affairs. He had been in touch with Janet without my knowledge, which I only found out about by chance. I was angry with him. I knew he was trying to help, he really liked her, as did I, and wanted somehow to heal the split. He ended up as a result by just muddying the waters of what had been an immensely painful break-up. What he also didn't know, and with the exception of Meg no one else knew, was of her abortion, which had created a whirlpool of emotions in every direction. It was our business.

I went down to Cheltenham, partly to tell him to mind his own business, as well as try to explain, without going into details. Here we both were having a broken conversation as customers came and went, when I became aware of three people standing there. Val was one of them, accompanied by her parents, who, I discovered, owned a hotel in Stroud. She was incredibly good-looking in a long-haired Kate Bush sort of way. I fixed my gaze on her and thought … er … Wow! I guessed she was about twenty-six, and very stylish.

The long and the short of this encounter was that I found an excuse to stay at the hotel, discovered she owned an MG Midget, had recently broken up with a long-term boyfriend, and was single. My own rather dilapidated MGA coupe was the perfect opportunity to invite her to an MG Club meeting. I wasn't bothered about the meeting, but a chance to get to know her better. We were both single and both out of a damaged relationship. We at least had that much in common.

That was it. We became a couple, and though she worked odd hours at the hotel, we nevertheless developed this chance meeting into a relationship. I think we both needed it at the time. I came to dislike her parents, and they in turn disliked me. I perceived them as shallow and snobbish. I discovered they had wrongly assumed me to be the heir to my dad's business. When they discovered the reality, they probably felt cheated. That's my interpretation of it anyway. In essence I don't think they thought I was good enough for their daughter. And I probably wasn't. Having said that, as I got to know them better I saw how they were users of people, their daughter included, and would make promises which they never kept. Her father especially, who was entirely self-seeking, and only cared for one person. Himself. I grew to loathe him over time

So 1979 came and went, and I went into 1980 with Val. The reason I picked up on these specific years, 1976-79, was because they had, with hindsight, the greatest impact on my life. In fact everything which happened to me since has led from those pivotal, influential years. I felt from the moment I set out on my overland trip, to the point where I blew myself out of the water with Meg and Janet, was in some ways another lifetime lived. It was brilliant at times, intense, stressful, and absolute hell.

So it's best if I deal with the next decade as a chapter, and try to pin down some of the momentous things that happened to me. I'll do the same with 1990, 2000, 2010, and take it up to the now, 2020, where I'm currently sitting in my old dressing gown labouring away on this old laptop.

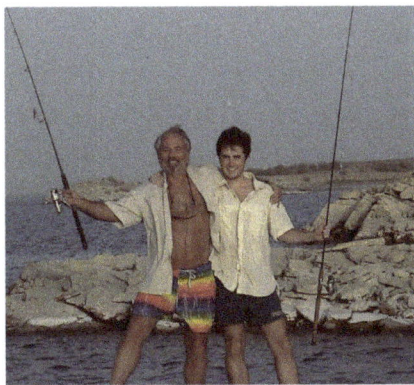

Chapter 15

1980–1990

Val and I made a good couple. We were similarly single, she came from a solid background, despite the antipathy I felt for her parents. She was a natural mum. In other words she looked after me, and God knows I needed looking after. She wasn't quite the soulmate that Meg had been though.

Quick side story

A matter of weeks, if not days, before my fateful meeting with Val, I found one Saturday evening that I really missed Meg. I mean really missed her. This intense feeling just overwhelmed me, rather like some drug, some kind of opiate. It left me with severe withdrawal symptoms. We hadn't been in touch for months and I'd heard from a mutual friend that she was over the hurt and upset I'd caused as a result of my affair with my ex-wife Janet. Ironic isn't it to think that my affair with Meg had lasted for almost four years, and all of that time behind Janet's back. Instant karma maybe. I'd done the same to Meg now in reverse. Nevertheless on this particular Saturday night, while I was in 'grieving over the past' mode, I picked up the phone on impulse and rang her. I was nervous, thought she might be out with some new bloke, and I'd have been insanely jealous had she been, but no, she answered. After skirting round the subject she said let's meet. I said when? She said now.

We met halfway. I had a bottle of wine and a couple of glasses in the car, and we rendezvoused in a pub car park. She didn't want to go in, but suggested we go somewhere quiet. Jumping in alongside me, we took off. We didn't go too far. There was an open gate leading into a stubble field at the top of a hill. I drove this Vauxhall Cavalier across it. Fortunately it was dry and the stubble crackled under the wheels. We sat for a few moments gazing at the view across to the twinkling city of Worcester. Then the full moon rose, casting its white light over the countryside.

I poured out a glass each and there we sat in silence. Then I poured some more and we talked. It was painful, but by the time we were on our third glass we were on the back seat. Fortunately she wore a skirt, no knickers, and kicked off her shoes. It briefly occurred to me in my slightly befuddled state that she'd come prepared, not that it took me more than a few seconds to remove my kit, and for a moment I felt slightly vulnerable. The moon was no doubt shining on my arse. I felt I must have been visible for miles, and for a moment I imagined the whole of Worcester was watching my performance on the hill, like some grotesque stage play. The wine however had gone to my head, and I was soon past caring. We both were in tears, our emotions running all over the place, knowing it would never work, but we just had such an insatiable appetite for one another.

Sitting in the back of the car in the silver light, we quietly finished the wine. Mournfully I drove her back to the car park in silence, alone with our thoughts. We'd been in that field for so long the pub had closed. Still in shreds, she drove away. I drove back to my place more or less pissed. If I'd been caught I would have lost my licence, and my job too. The intensity of emotional upheaval provokes the taking of risks like this.

Whatever happened that night was cathartic for us both. A love that was never meant to be. It would be fifteen years before I ever saw her again at her daughter's wedding. I've never seen or heard from her since.

1980 (cont.)

A couple of months after Val and I met, some time in early 1980 I was summoned to London by my Sales Director one Monday morning to our office in Shaftesbury Avenue. He announced that the General Sales Manager was retiring. This guy was a rather flabby individual who had been given the role as more of a convenience when my company merged with his. In other words he was accommodated in the new group. My position as Field Sales Manager, the hands-on one, was to be made redundant. I was shocked. I was only thirty-one, and faced with this sudden and unexpected change. But then nothing is forever. My Sales Director asked me when I could move to London to take up the new position to be based there.

I hated London. I still do. I know there are lots of interesting and cultural things to do, but it's the sheer weight of people. Fundamentally I'm a creature of the woods and fields and streams. This place was a traffic-filled, fume-laden hellhole as far as I was concerned. I caught the train back. I needed to think, so I did what I do best. I procrastinated.

I told Val when I got back. I'd only been with this company for little over a year, so a redundancy package from them was out of the question. After a week of thought, and some pressure from my boss to make a decision about moving to London, I declined the offer.

My boss wasn't altogether surprised. He remarked that had I been married, heavily mortgaged and had a couple of kids, I would have had no choice but to move. It made me realise just how free I was, and just how shackled I could have been.

The microwave boom had just begun. We take them for granted these days, but back then they were something to be wary of. A mysterious gamma ray machine. It was nothing of the sort. It simply used radio waves to generate molecular heat, and since I'd spent ten years in the catering equipment industry, I knew they were harmless. In fact I knew a great deal more than the ignoramuses in the big stores who hadn't a clue. It was an opportunity. I could use my extensive knowledge of these machines to specialise. I decided to surf this microwave boom and go into business on my own.

I walked away from the job in London with a two-month salary severance, and resolved to go it alone. It was something I'd always thought I'd do, but now I was faced with the reality of it. Val had a steady job, was now living with me having left the slavery of her parents' hotel. Much to their annoyance, by the way. They'd decided to sell it anyway and promised to buy her a modest cottage with some of the proceeds, which, surprise surprise, never materialised. Val was now a manager with a contract catering company, working just down the M5 in Gloucester. I discussed with her about setting up on my own and she backed me. For which I shall be ever grateful. Her income was crucial, knowing that I may earn nothing at all in the first few months.

I banked the two month's salary cheque, cashed in an insurance policy worth all of £1,500, which the bank matched with a £1,500 overdraft facility, and that was that. My working capital, all £3,000 of it. I was on my own. It was a bit scary, but I reasoned that at thirty-one if it all went tits I could always get another job. People don't voluntarily go into business on their own without good reason, and it's usually circumstance rather than design when they go it alone. I guess that's why 95% of people are employees, and 5% employers. Only an R in the word makes that difference. I was now in that minority.

I rented a small lock-up garage in the centre of Cheltenham, hardly an ideal showroom, and advertised locally to drum up enquiries. My desk was a piece of plasterboard balanced on wooden legs. I had a red telephone, a filing cabinet, a spiral notebook, an invoice book, and bugger-all else. That was the beginning of Cheltenham Microwave Centre. With some of the money I bought about half a dozen microwaves, cash up front from the suppliers, who wouldn't trust me with a credit account. That was my stock. I had no fancy car any more, so bought an old

Morris Minor van. It cost me all of £50. I delivered microwaves to customers from that. I was so ashamed of it that I would park it round the corner from the customer's house and carry these things to their door. It sure kept me fit.

In due course, and bit by bit, by about 1981 I was beginning to make a few quid. Nationally we were in recession, but Thatcher as PM began to revolutionise the economy, and the microwave business began to take off. I'd moved from the garage to a basement in an office block within a matter of months, and that served as a basic showroom, but again was hardly ideal. I'd also put myself about with commercial catering equipment and the wine bar culture was also taking off.

The answer lay in getting my own premises. That way I could be landlord and tenant. Rent is a big overhead with any business, so acquiring my own place enabled me to control the rent, just as long as it covered the loan. The company would effectively be buying me an asset. I needed a more central showroom, service facility, and somewhere with convenient car parking for customers. By now I was employing one or two people to demon-strate microwaves. Val, as a knowledgeable catering manager, helped with evening microwave cookery courses to back up the sales effort.

Quite simply, although it didn't seem so at the time, this was the way I did it. I took out a £5,000 home improvement loan, secured on my house, gave the money to Val (she had no capital of her own) and we used this as a deposit to buy a house in Tewkesbury. Her salary got us a residential mortgage. I didn't qualify since I had no salary to speak of. Certainly not one which any bank or building society would consider. I then rented my own house to cover my original mortgage for a short time until I found suitable business premises, and we both moved down to Tewkesbury. In due course I found a property for the business in Cheltenham, sold my own house, and having paid off the mortgage and the loan, used the equity from that sale, all £5,250 of it, as my deposit for the commercial mortgage which Barclays provided after some serious arm-twisting. The business was just two years old. I now had my own personal premises for which the company was paying. The building at 52 St James St in Cheltenham cost just a fraction over £20k, but we now had two assets between us which would increase in value. So I hoped.

In today's money that premises would be valued at around £200k. Ten times what I paid for it in 1982. That's inflation for you.

With these two properties we now had somewhere to live and somewhere to run the business. These were the acorns from which grew a decent-sized oak, forty years on. I reasoned that if I could own properties and rent them out, they would provide a small but steady income in the future as the mortgages were chipped away.

From the outset it was never my intention to run a microwave and catering equipment business forever, and three years in I began to recognise my weaknesses. Up until then I thought I was unstoppable. It was my accountant who told me that yes, I was ambitious, yes I was a good salesman, yes not a bad entrepreneur and opportunist, but as an administrator I was a disaster. I was also an appalling manager of people, and would frequently get angry with my burgeoning group of employees. But hell, it was my money being risked not theirs, so that's how I justified my bad management style. The other thing which took its toll: I was working six days a week. I hardly ever switched off.

I'd never envisaged anything more than ten years of this. I had my ten-year plan, influenced by my boss in Leeds years before. It became a hallmark of my attitude to life. ten years is about enough for anything and anyone. About the life of a passport, before you have to re-do the thing again. With this in mind my thought was to get to the age of forty, sell the business, and retire early on the winnings. It didn't work out like that of course. So much for goals, but I can pinpoint this to be the exact time in my life where the seeds of my 'grand plan' were originally sown.

Building that business was hard work. My chaotic decade during the 1970s was behind me, and I put everything, mostly time, into this business with focus and energy. Because I thought I was good at everything, and had the audaciousness, conceit perhaps, to believe I was infallible, but as I said above, I may well have been a trailblazer, but the mess I left in that trail took some sorting out. I now had to learn to file and copy stuff, and above all communicate more effectively. Rather than just shout at people. I guess you could say my management style was along the lines of 'Do it like this now, or fuck off.' Some style, eh?

Communication is probably the most neglected of assets in all businesses. Never underestimate the importance of that. The left and right hand need to know what's happening and, more importantly, why. I picked my way through this business minefield, and to my surprise realised finally that I didn't know everything, even though I thought I did. How that business survived in those early days I don't know, but it did. Eventually it went from strength to strength, measured I suppose by the four or five people I'd employed full time.

My life with Val fitted around the business, and we married in Sept 1982. My best men were Zolly, my poaching/fishing mate from years back, and Ian Gibson, an English teacher whom I'd met through Meg at her school. Ian was a compulsive traveller, loved curries and cooking, had divorced his first wife, and now had a new wife. We had a lot in common. He also loved cars, and a few years earlier, around 1978, we had a small business working out of a barn doing up Morris Minors. Since I was usually twiddling my thumbs at night up in Leeds, I'd scan the classifieds, and pick these MOT failures up for about £30. Then, leaving my company car behind, I'd take my life in my hands and bring these rot boxes down the M6 to the barn. Ian and I bodged them up mechanically, and bodily, and flogged them locally for £200 ish. It was fun, but we never really made a go of it. During his best man speech he referred to me as a slave driver. I think I must have been, as those paragraphs above allude to. I was certainly driven and determined to make it a success. That was why I was useless with employees. I had the vision, and a short temper to go with it. Not an ideal mix.

I wish I could say that I got on well with my new in-laws, but I didn't. I thought my own family was dysfunctional, but hers wasn't much better. Val's brother was, I learned, beaten by his father so disappeared off to Norfolk where he lived in a caravan, made bongos, ate brown rice, changed his name to Swami, and became indoctrinated with Indian mysticism. Something I could identify with. Val herself seemed to have been treated by her parents as more of a skivvy. Her father was a dominating bully to all of them, especially her mother, but she in turn could be an acerbic, sarcastic, shallow, two-faced snob. She evidently disliked me intensely. In fact they both did when they realised I wasn't born with a silver spoon in my mouth. They misjudged me completely. In reality I was a penniless, debt ridden, but nevertheless an aspiring entrepreneur. And a son-in-law to them I'm sure they wished they'd never had.

Why is it that this older generation from the 1920s and 30s never seem to embrace and support spirit and talent, but actively seek to suppress and crush it? Are the WW2 years responsible? Does that generation see us post-war baby boomers as a privileged, spoiled generation? Maybe we are. We've never had to fight a war. Interestingly I have no recollection either of my own father praising or encouraging me, in fact quite the opposite. They all seemed to want to knock us down. I've never understood it. Years and years later I met one of my dad's friends when he and a few others were walking the Offa's Dyke trail. This guy, whom I'd never met before, seemed to know more about my life than I did. Astonishingly he went on to tell me how proud my dad was of everything I'd done. It was all news to me.

So the company progressed bit by bit, and began to morph into a catering equipment distributor, but in the middle of 1983 Val told me she was pregnant. It delighted and troubled me for many deep reasons, but frightened me too. It was unexpected. I had to adjust to a new situation. Val had a job on which we depended, and I was barely making a living. A huge slice of our overall income was about to disappear.

My son Oliver was born on 10th March 1984, about 8 am on a Saturday. I'd been to a shoot party the night before and was still seriously pissed when I took her into Cheltenham Hospital at 5 am. When he arrived in a slurping mess, he was yellow, and for a split second looked Chinese. There was some consternation from the medics, who had difficulty getting him to breathe, but in my rather inebriated state the seriousness of it was lost on me. He finally burst into life, Val cried, and I stood there slightly shattered. I drove back to Tewkesbury, stopped the car along the way, got out, leaned on the roof and without any evident warning just burst into tears. I was a father. I had a proper family.

1984

As I said before, Oliver James Ralphs Craddock arrived on 10th March 1984. Aka: Olliebeans.

I wrote a poem for him a few months after his arrival based on the fact that he could fart explosively. The name originated from a friend of mine in the 1960s who lived up in North Wales. His name was Willy, and he was particularly flatulent. We all called him Willybeans, although Heinz might have been more appropriate. Here it is.

> Olliebeans is here now
> And he's nearly six months old
> He weighs 18 lb 4oz
> And he's worth his weight in gold
> His cries are irritating though,
> They drive me round the bend
> Yet the smiles are so endearing
> That's it's worth it in the end.
> Our lives have changed
> For good and bad,
> For better or for worse
> The ups and downs

For Mum and Dad
Are a blessing, and a curse
Of all the kids I've ever seen,
Not many, but a few,
There's nowt compares with Olliebeans
We love him through and through.

His arrival sparked in me a new set of contradictory feelings. A future playmate, son and heir, but this was only one train of my thoughts. Someone to take fishing, shooting, play guitar with, and generally inherit whatever I might end up with. Probably large debts, so I thought at the time. He now runs the property company, but even back then, and he's thirty-six now, I was already planning what we would do together, and how we'd do it.

His arrival though was also a bit scary. Val had given up her job, and devoted her time to him virtually twenty-four hours a day, and somehow I had to make up the serious hole his arrival had put in our finances. I couldn't simply double my meagre takings from this business, which was largely still in its infancy. I was worried. The delight of his arrival was tinged with more than a measure of concern. In fact it bordered on fear, and a dose of resentment.

You might think I would have planned this better, but I didn't. Maybe there are always good reasons to delay starting a family, but either way we were where we were.

Of all the mixed-up emotions though, what I didn't see coming was a complete change in the relationship with my wife. With me, that is. No doubt if she was asked she would perhaps deny it, but I'm sensitive to change, and even before his arrival I felt a shift in our relationship. She became absorbed, obsessed, and wholly preoccupied with the forthcoming birth. Quite simply I felt neglected. I was working my balls off, for little or no reward. When I got home there was no empathy, in fact no connection whatsoever. I'd talk business gossip, she'd talk obstetrics. We began to grow poles apart, to the point where I began to feel as though I didn't exist except to fund a roof over our heads.

Mini side story

I needed looking after, I needed attention, I needed input, but it disappeared almost immediately, and once again I found myself 'alone'. I soon reverted to type, the result of which of course was a fairly intense affair, albeit part-time and arm's-length. The woman came to work for me part-time to help build an offshoot coffee services business I'd set up as a sideline to the main catering equipment business. For anonymity's sake I'll call her Trudy, for she will reappear later in the 1990s.

She ultimately became a great friend and confidante, was intelligent, physically inventive, but in a bad marriage. Her husband was in the military and worked away quite a bit. It suited me perfectly, and her too, though once or twice I had visions of him turning up unexpectedly with a grenade for me and a machine gun for her.

Here I go again, I thought. Once more I had two women on the go. I justified it to myself this time as deserving of it. Perhaps the lessons of Meg and Janet had all but faded, though I was still a practised liar when I needed to be. This affair, or alternative relationship, suited us both, eventually morphing into more of a friendship over three or four years. In many ways she became more of a mate and got to know my family well. She subsequently divorced her husband, moved away from Glos, married a farmer in Staffordshire, and got away from the area with a sales job in Derby.

The problem with having an affair is it's easy to justify. Easy to point the finger of blame at the other party and never blame yourself. It's always the other person's fault. If you hadn't done such and such and been so and so I wouldn't have done what I did. That kind of stuff. The longer an affair goes on the more inventive you find you become to rationalise your behaviour. In the end you become almost blameless. For most men, myself included, there's a world of difference between falling in love and just fancying the occasional shag. There is the added thrill of the chase too, and the sheer buzz which comes from the illicitness of it all. For the women though, in my experience anyway, they don't usually see it quite like that.

I remember a friend of mine who was involved in just such an affair, and when he'd finished would look at his watch and think, 'Hmmmm ... time I got going.' All he wanted was to just get back home for his tea and see the kids before they went to bed.

It's a triangle, and for a very good reason. You put yourself in one corner, and then make the other two corners responsible for the situation you yourself have created. Sometimes it's difficult to separate right from wrong. Not like right or wrong in terms of stealing or not stealing. The difference between right and wrong there is self-evident. It's the moral aspect which is tricky. Falling in love with a woman who isn't your wife, is already married with children, and other baggage, is both wonderful and dreadful, and God help you if you're found out. But while it lasts it literally causes you to take leave of your senses. In my case I came up with all kinds of justifications for my infidelities. It's this area where the difficulty arises, to think clearly to separate right from wrong. I guess it just depends which side of the moral fence you're on.

Religion has much to answer for. This idea of putting one man and one woman together for all eternity is nonsense. Males are genetically programmed to sow seeds. Females by nature seek security and stability to nurture their children. That's a bit of an oversimplification, but the reality, if I put it another way, is that males are genetically programmed to wander off. Religion seeks to reverse that biological fact by forcing, or encouraging through fear of damnation, two people to remain together. It's inevitably bound to create strain over time. People grow apart. The institution of marriage tends to suit the woman initially, but even they become bored as the gorgeous husband they married turns into a fat, beer-swilling slob.

Since I'm something of a cynic I think it works equally in reverse too. Women, or so I think, relax after they marry. They've got the man, the breadwinner to provide the income, got the kids they were biologically programmed to have, job done. Then they go to seed, and just don't make an effort.

For someone like me who rejects religious dogma outright, my own personal moral compass was always likely to be dis-orientated, so given my nature it was inevitable that I believed I was biologically programmed to wander. And with no moral check in place to stop me, it was very easy for me to justify my behaviour, even though it caused damage to the other party. At times I was so convinced I was right, that I never ever considered the possibility I might be wrong. It was certainly selfish. But what's wrong with that? That's another morality question. I just get bored easily.

1986

On 24th June 1986 my daughter arrived. Joanna Lucy Ralphs Craddock. I remember remarking to Val when Ollie arrived that 'through this child thy shalt know me' stuff. Even now and all these years later they call him Mini Me. Well up to a point that's true, and sometimes we can clash, but he has a remarkable ability to think in the same way as I.

Joanna was the opposite. She became my conscience. She has a direct honesty which can border on rudeness, is incredibly independent, and loves the countryside. One of the extraordinary aspects of children is how diametrically opposite they can turn out to be. This despite the identical input from both parents. I find it incredible that children can be so personality-opposed within the same family. Joanna is business-minded, but not driven in the same way as Oliver. In many ways they are complete opposites, but I love both of them dearly for their level headedness, and their ability to keep their feet firmly on the ground despite, at times, having the opportunity to live a luxurious lifestyle. Neither of them are snobs, and can mix easily at any social level. If that's success on mine and Val's part then I'll settle for that.

So now we were the Fab Four, but despite the arrival of an additional child, I still felt that my wife and I were poles apart. The children, as so often is the case, held us together in many ways.

As for the business, well it progressed and morphed during the 80s away from domestic microwaves and further and further into catering equipment distribution. This was more my home turf. I sold off the office coffee services offshoot to my partner/director, and then by pure chance in 1987 saw a marketing opportunity to develop a unique product which I felt would put the skids under a major manufacturer. My marketing background, combined with my knowledge of the catering equipment industry, provided that opportunity, of which more later.

During these times holidays for Val and I were virtually out of the question. Very few and far between, primarily because in 1986 I was skint. I'd taken a huge bank loan and bought a four-bedroom detached house. Socially a move upwards, but financially very much downwards. It seemed that every penny I earned went on mortgage repayments, so package holidays in the sun were just a dream. The best we could manage were road trips, and before Joanna was born, we would set off for France in whatever car I could afford, with Ollie in his kiddies' seat, camping gear packed around him. His very first word was 'car'. He was obsessed with them, and still is today. He would shriek 'Car!' every time he saw one.

One summer, mid '85 I think, we were heading down through the Cherbourg peninsula to see Meg's daughter (yes we'd stayed in touch) who was married to a French army guy and lived in the Clermont Ferrand area. From there we went to the Bordeaux region to meet up with friends who were heading north from Morocco. Ollie was in his usual place in the centre of the back seat. I put a Dire Straits tape on and 'Money for Nothing' was the recently released single following their performance at the Live Aid concert. I suddenly noticed he'd started to nod his head in time to the song. He was just eighteen months old. I resolved to get him a guitar at some point. In 2019, when he was aged thirty-five, I found him practising the lead intro to 'Money for Nothing'. That song has stuck with him down the years, and he's now quite an accomplished guita r player.

Around 1987 my father's limited company, run by my brother Martin who reshaped it financially, was to be launched on the AIM market. My dad saw fit for my sister Julia and I to have a few shares before the launch. This meant that we would both get a lump sum out when the business went public. It was an absolute godsend to me. Wholly unexpected but a hell of a relief to me, especially with only myself providing an income. It also relieved a great deal of borrowing pressure and came at exactly the right time. I split the sum up, some to reduce our mortgage, some for a deposit on another Cheltenham property, which I borrowed on yet again to lease to a Mexican restaurant, and the rest I banked. I now had a cushion, and could set up the new company to bring to fruition my plan to take on a new venture.

Masterchef I formed as a separate company in September 1987. The entire idea came to me whilst fishing. In essence I did a deal with the German manufacturer Bosch, to give me a three-year exclusive contract to convert their domestic microwave oven for commercial use. The oven was a combination of three things. 'An oven, a grill, a microwave, Amazing!' That was the strap line I dreamed up for the literature. I went into a 50/50 partnership with a guy in Wigan, a mistake, I eventually discovered, but you live and learn. Wigan, bloody miles from Cheltenham, was a wreck of a town, having lost its pits to Mrs Thatcher's swingeing cuts, Unemployment was rife, but property was cheap, and the area was deemed an 'enterprise' zone. This meant grants were available to encourage new business, and property was cheap. I bought a small 1,700 sq ft factory unit with some of the money left over, and began to market these ovens.

We converted these domestic microwaves to commercial ones, clothed them in stainless steel, beefed up the dials and knobs, increased the power of them from 600 watts to 1,000 watts using a bigger capacitor, and then set up a nationwide advertising campaign, together with smart literature, which was designed and written by me. I appointed eight dealers across the UK and Scotland with exclusive territories, all of whom were effectively one-man bands, and sold these versatile machines to the commercial caterer by demonstration. I was firmly back in the catering equipment business but this time dancing to my own tune. We also made a lot of money. It was never going to last of course, once the big boys came in and prised the market wide open.

At its peak in 1989, Masterchef was employing upwards of twenty to thirty people, including office staff. To reduce the burden of my nationwide travel I re-employed (a now happily married) Trudy once again (remember her?), who took over the Sales Manager role, thus relieving me from the torment of the M6. It became extraordinarily successful, but as I said above, I never believed it would last, and it didn't.

It also took its toll on me. I was running Cheltenham Microwave Centre, with six to eight people based there, then legging it up the M6 to supervise Masterchef, which as it grew needed more and more of my time. I was all over the place, working myself half to death. I was by now forty-one.

Just to add more fuel to the fire and because I never like to miss an opportunity, I had also bought into a sexy underwear business in Gloucester. We called it 'Stocking Tops', an early version of the Ann Summers retail chain, with my ex-partner Lorraine, from the Coffee Service business. We decided to move the business to Cheltenham and take over what was once a chocolate shop. As it turned out we didn't bother, and sold the stock off, but out of the blue I hit on an idea. Among the stock of this underwear business were penis-shaped soaps. I decided to have them made from chocolate.

After some expense to make the moulds, we started a small business which became The Rude Chocolate Company. These chocolate willys … willies? … were produced in milk, plain and white, packaged with a dickie bow, and advertised for sale mail order (male order?) in *The Observer on Sunday* classified section. They wouldn't let us use the word 'Willy' (dear oh dear), we had to describe it as a 'Thingy'. The orders however rolled in and I had to divert some of my Cheltenham Microwave staff to sending out dozens, and occasionally hundreds, of these things. It was good fun, but not much in the way of profit, and also another diversion I frankly didn't need. Anyway my main claim to fame was the distinction of being the first in the UK to sell chocolate willies, and maybe, just maybe, we should have stuck with the underwear business. Ann Summers got it right.

Just to add further complication, in 1988 the Mexican restaurant I helped set up went bust, and the tenants took root in the property I'd acquired. This carried a big mortgage which I simply couldn't fund without rent. Despite my best and costly legal efforts to evict these people, the money I was making with Masterchef effectively paid the legal fees. The law never helped me in the slightest to get these squatters out. It was thrown out twice on 'technicalities' over the lease. In all it took about ten months to effect a solution. I used rather unorthodox means in the end, rather than face more legal costs. I threw them out. I sent the 'boys' round and boarded the place up. The squatters were gone in a week. We'd accidentally cut their water and electricity off. Dear oh dear, and it was February, and quite cold and snowy too. This for me was survival, protection I guess for my family. Had I not done this I would almost certainly have been bankrupted. I feel disinclined to rake up this episode of stress, so I'll leave it there. It's a story all its own, and not a pleasant side story either.

The only thing I really learned from this was that the law and justice seldom collide. From my point of view I'd simply taken on too much. Like those performers who balance spinning plates on sticks. I was running from one wobbling plate to another. More ominously, I believe it was at this point where my marriage began to unravel.

Looking back I can see where I went wrong, hindsight being the exact science it is. An old Sales Manager once said to me, 'Try to catch two mice and you'll end up with none.' I had simply spread myself too thinly. I was effectively ineffective.

By 1988/89 I was understandably knackered, but had at least re-rented the restaurant. Mohammed set up a very successful Indian restaurant business, and he, all of thirty-two years later, is still a trusted friend. Oh, and just to serve as a reminder of those times, we still own the building. In late 1989 to make matters worse, interest rates hit 15% and the UK economy, following a huge freefall in share values two years earlier, then followed suit and the economy slumped into recession. My plans and schemes to make a fortune over ten years and then retire went up in smoke.

By the end of 1989 I'd had enough. I vacated the original property, rented that, and moved the microwave business to another location, again using the company as my tenant, then subsequently 'sold' off this business for a song. The new owner became my tenant. So far, so good. The three properties I owned on mortgages in Cheltenham were now all successfully leased out. I was intent on freeing myself up. The Rude Chocolate Company had run its course too so I put it into dormancy as a limited company. On the side I'd also had a number of flings, usually one-night stands as a diversion from business. I guess it was some kind of light relief, but none of them was serious, so I put those into dormancy too. As always with me it was a diversion. I needed to focus.

Yep, I needed to concentrate, to prioritise. I was forty-one. I suddenly realised my main priority was my children, so decided to give more of my time to them. There were times they hardly recognised me I was away so much. I could almost see them thinking, 'Who is this guy who turns up now and again?'

Perhaps one of the best things to come out of this period in the late 1980s was giving up smoking. Didn't matter what it was, if I could set fire to it and inhale the stuff I would. I'd been out of control with it for years and my secretary fixed up for me to go to a hypnotist.

I've always had something of an obsessive personality (there's a

231

surprise, eh?) and nicotine was no exception. This hypnotist guy helped me to stop. The downside however, as every ex-smoker knows, was weight. Lots of it, and I went up by a stone and a half. Ironic really, save your lungs, and then increase strain on the heart with flab. Trousers didn't fit, shirts too tight, so I went into overdrive and trained in the gym three early mornings a week. It took months to shed the flab and gain some muscle tone, and I'd taken up road-running too, three miles around the lanes three times a week. This running, or fast jogging, had taken off as a serious hobby with me, largely inspired by my dad, who ran half marathons regularly.

My father inspired me for many reasons over the years, and despite his autocratic bullying attitude, as I grew older I began to gain a greater understanding of this. I think having my own children helped me see him in a different, perhaps better, light. I'd worked my balls off for ten years with fuck-all in the way of praise or credit coming my way from him, but my mum told me he was very proud of my entrepreneurial streak. He never said a word about it. On the other hand he was a fitness fanatic and ran, walked, swam, and played badminton (as did I). Even when my brother and I were kids he would always have bags of mixed nuts and raisins in the car for snacks. Never sweets, chocolate or crisps. In that respect he was way ahead of his time.

I remember him saying the heart is a muscle, which obviously it is, and needs exercise to keep it strong. His exact words to emphasise this were 'get breathless for twenty minutes several times a week'. My running and gym work, as well as regular badminton, did the trick, and I became physically much fitter. Unlike my brother I'd always had a sporty attitude, and always felt I needed to exercise even from childhood. My dad was entirely responsible for this. I'm reminded of a Mark Twain quote, who said of his parents, 'When I was sixteen my parents knew nothing, but by the time I got to twenty-one I was surprised how much they'd picked up in five years.'

Ageing brings understanding.

My fitness regime also relieved the stress of business. Bit by bit I was able to focus on Masterchef, where most of the money was coming from. The M6 took it out of me, and still does, but travelling to Wigan, sleeping in the office on a folding camp bed, and then dicing with death on the return journey became tortuous. I got more and more tired as my head filled with the week's events, so I learned to power nap. I'd invariably pull off the M6 at Keele services, and drift off into semi-consciousness for twenty mins. When I awoke I found I was refreshed and ready for anything.

It's a strange technique, one which has to be learned, and worth practising. Having experienced hypnotism to help me quit smoking, I became intrigued in the power of the subconscious, which is always the trigger for lighting up a fag. The subconscious is the thin bit between fully awake and fully asleep. If you can hold yourself there in that tiny space, all the senses become pin-sharp. You can often hear a dog bark, or a car door slam even though it's half a mile away. Although conscious and aware of your surroundings, jumbled thoughts fly through the head. The brain seems somehow to rearrange itself. Almost like tidying up and putting the thoughts away in a filing cabinet. Clearing the decks as it were. Doing this re-energised me, and enabled me to somehow get two days out of one. I always knew immediately when the time came for me to pull the car over, recline the seat, put my hands behind my head, and take a break.

In 1988/9 I'd used some of my money to buy a place in France. £5k deposit and a £30k French mortgage. I'd always harboured a desire to own a lake, and this place had one. Three acres of beautiful carp lake, with an old sixteenth-century mill thrown in (not literally), an acre of garden behind the mill, and two acres of orchard and woodland by the side of the lake. Having visited friends who had moved over there to Normandy, they found this place for me in the Mayenne region, and I fell in love with it immediately. I realised quite quickly that unless I lived there it would require more and more money to develop. The old mill was a money pit, but having made a decision to concentrate on Masterchef, I left it to neglect.

The Moulin du la Tour was a place of refuge for me, but I simply hadn't the means to renovate it. However I began to make plans to extricate myself from the business, and do something to recover the time I'd lost in not having an input with my kids' upbringing. Val was a great Mum, overindulgent in my view, and didn't really have a job, or anything to provide support financially, but I was doing OK with Masterchef, and despite the UK economy faltering and stuttering, the business in Cheltenham was also doing well. Furthermore the properties were rented on leases, and though I didn't make any money from them, they at least covered the fairly substantial loans.

Despite the weekly jaunts to Wigan, my office in Cheltenham, and the looming recession, I had things tied down quite nicely. The businesses were lean, and certainly in Masterchef's case immensely profitable.

Sometimes it's useful to find something entirely different and interesting as a diversion to business. I had met through friends some people who were on the international fly-fishing competition scene. When I'm not pike-fishing through the winter, and during the coarse fishing close season, March–June, some of the best weather and countryside is to be seen in April and May, and fly-fishing for trout, whether lake, reservoir, or stream is a wonderful release from the day-to-day grind of business.

One of these guys was a radio presenter for a fishing programme on local radio, and he asked me to do a few guest slots. The programme was *Tight Lines*, on Severn Sound radio in Gloucester. I became his outside broadcast partner. He was getting on and a bit unsteady on his feet, so I was tasked with interviewing various notable anglers at different venues. I was equipped with tape recorder and microphone of radio quality, and each week I would go to some place, meet up, do the interviews, then deliver the tape to the studio. I loved it. I became moderately famous on the Sunday morning broadcast, and it was odd to sit at home and hear my ten-minute broadcast coming over the radio. This small degree of notoriety led to me being asked to go to Ireland, courtesy of, and paid for by the Irish tourist board, to join in with a group of twenty to thirty famous angling journalists, who wrote regularly for the angling press. This was September 1989.

I was, for the first time, beginning to relax. In fact I was beginning to enjoy myself.

Now I know you're probably bored by now with all this self-indulgent twaddle. In fact I suspect you may well have nodded off. So it's time once again for a little side story, dontcha think?

Irish side story

We started the fishing trip/competition in Killybegs, Donegal, having driven across Ireland from Holyhead. Just three of us, in my old Subaru, stacked with gear. There were loads of angling journalists assembled, some I'd heard of, most I hadn't, from all the various sea, coarse, and trout magazines. Some, in fact most, like me, were just hangers-on, who knew someone who knew someone else and so on. I was hardly an Internationally famous broadcaster, but at least I was world-famous in Gloucestershire. Just about.

As I said earlier, the Irish tourist board picked up the whole tab for this extravagant jolly. There were maybe twenty or thirty of us in all, split into teams of three. The week was divided into three two-day competition sections. The first leg was a sea-fishing one. First day was practice, the second the competition day. We were out on a boat in the mini Atlantic. Well I think it was, since I don't think there's anything much landwise between there and America. I loved it. The sea and the scenery were wonderful. Much to my surprise I won the competition on the second day by sheer luck. I'd like to think it was skill, but was it hell. I just happened to catch the most species of fish. No idea what they were now, and didn't even know there was a prize for that. Anyway that's what I did. Killybegs was a lovely little town, but the harbour was dominated by a big Japanese boat, which I learned was there to take most of the fish from the local trawlers and ship it back to Japan. I presume the Japs had eaten all their own fish so were now over here to hoover up the Irish fish stocks.

The second leg was a lough somewhere. This was the fly-fishing one, which i didn't win. In fact I caught fuck-all. Well maybe a couple of small brown trout over the two days. Wonderful big lough though, with lots of these little brownies. I think the winner might have had all of three or four on competition day. I reckon they must have been all of about four or five ounces. No idea what that is in grams, but basically bugger-all. The weather was foul, strong winds and rain. I was just glad to get off the bloody boat and back into the hotel. The third one was the coarse fishing leg, based at Carrick-on-Shannon.

The day before we got to Carrick had been my forty-first birthday, so by clever maths it must have been September 1989. In the evening I got pissed with everyone. I was boasting about my road-running fitness regime, when suddenly someone bet me I couldn't run three miles in wellingtons. Like a prat I said no problem. They then sealed this stupid boast by sending a pint mug round the room, and filled it with money. This to sponsor the Angling Conservation Association (ACA). I was well and truly trussed up and stuffed. No backing out now. The bet was on.

First thing the following morning, groggy and hungover, I started out from the hotel. Following behind in my Subaru were my two so-called friends, to ensure I completed the task, clocking me along the way. The bastards, I discovered later, added on an extra third of a mile for good measure. I was absolutely knackered when I finished, and despite thick socks my feet felt raw. Nevertheless I raised £150+ for the ACA, the Chairman of which was a guest on this trip. They were delighted. I ignored the applause and hobbled into the hotel to get a shower.

We got to Carrick, drew pegs and fished the Shannon for bream and roach. It was an immense river, and though I caught a few, lost interest. I was still in recovery mode. It was won by a guy who evidently had a big shoal of bream in front of him, and he must've caught all of them. Five hours later we weighed them in at about 120 lb. Two keepnets full of them.

That evening I received a lifetime membership of the ACA. The money was handed over at a ceremony, hosted by the Chair of the Carrick Tourist Association. Surprisingly it was a woman, and a nice looking one at that. She had an enigmatic Enya kind of way about her. Mairead was Irish, about forty, dark hair, green eyes, and seemed to want to occupy me with conversation for most of the evening. I learned she was married, with a couple of young children. Nevertheless she slipped me her phone number before we broke up for the evening and gave me a hug and kiss which was, shall we say, unmistakeable. We were all leaving the following morning for the ferry back to the UK, and I'd told her during the evening I was planning to come over to Ireland on business in the next couple of weeks. She asked me to give her a call. Which I did.

Here we go again, I thought.

I took the ferry from Fishguard over to Ireland and drove up to Dublin about three weeks later. I stayed in some modest hotel, having arranged beforehand to meet the dealer the next day. I'd also rung her ahead of this trip, gave her the hotel details and sure enough she showed up at the hotel in the early evening. The excuse to her husband was a visit to her sister in Dublin. She seemed very pleased to see me, and initially didn't recognise me. I'd grown my beard back, from the clean-shaven runner in wellies a few weeks earlier.

Off we went for a meal and drink, and suddenly we were back to my room in no time at all. The speed we got down to business took me a bit by surprise. I hate this expression, and for all you women who may shudder at this, she really was gagging for it. After two hours or so I shooed her out of my bed around 11.30 pm. Off she went, hot and very flushed, and away to her sister's to maintain the alibi. She was energetic, to put it mildly, with the most perfect tits, and huge stand-out nipples. Nipples which could easily poke you in the eye. It had taken no time at all from the chance encounter in Carrick, to her lying there in a writhing, moaning heap. It also didn't take me long to conclude that she didn't get this kind of attention as a rule, and I was right. As she lay back between occasional gasps, she made it clear she didn't like her husband. I almost began to feel I was some kind of excuse to get back at him. Her dislike seemed to border on hatred. I had no idea who he was, apart from some bigwig in Carrick, and just hoped he never found out. This was still the height of the Troubles, remember. The last thing I needed was to be caught shagging an IRA commander's wife.

The next day I was a bit knackered to say the least. I didn't sleep much either, my imagination working overtime, with dreams about bombs and booby traps. Besides she really had worn me out physically. Nevertheless I kept my appointment and went to see the Dublin dealer, who was utterly charming, and I began to relax. My next stop though was Belfast to meet a dealer there, and I'd already decided to drive the route, primarily to facilitate my meet-up with Mairead. The last stage of my journey was to leave Belfast by ferry to Holyhead. I'd then drive back home from Anglesey, completing the circle as it were.

The IRA Troubles were evident. If anyone tells you there isn't an inherent sympathy in Ireland, a tacit approval if you like, for the cause of the IRA, well I for one don't believe it. Those Irish people I've met down the years are generally funny, charming, irreverent and welcoming. Get 'em tanked up in the pub though, and they'll sing their heads off about Thompson machine guns, and Dublin in the green, in the green. It's almost as though they can't help themselves. These songs they learned on their grandfather's knee, and whatever the British did with Ireland generations ago these sins of the fathers are visited on the sons all right. Memory is long, and regenerated and refreshed through these songs. My own view is that most of my contemporaries in England found the extent of these Troubles bewildering.

As I did when I drove north out of Dublin.

A few weeks earlier the SAS had shot dead three IRA terrorists in Gibraltar. Their bodies however had been flown to Dublin. I assume this was an entirely deliberate act, designed to extract maximum publicity for the cause. These three hearses were driven slowly up to Belfast, even though they could easily have been flown there instead. I'd seen the footage on TV showing the crowds lining the route. As I drove out of Dublin my fears about Irish sympathy were confirmed. The entire length of this road to Belfast had small black flags tied to trees, lamp posts, bus shelters, in fact all along the entire 60-70 mile route to the Irish border. Bear in mind this was weeks after the event. They were still in place. It was unnerving,

I drove out of Dublin and eventually into Dundalk, blissfully unaware that this was a town with serious IRA sympathisers. Everything just seemed normal to me. On to Newry, and that's when I began to comprehend. Naively I got out to take photographs of the telephone exchange just outside Newry. It was festooned with barbed wire. I'd never seen anything like it. Photos done, I then crossed the border into Northern Ireland. All that was there was a signal box with a couple of British soldiers sitting on a bench smoking. They just waved me through. Immediately I noticed how much better the roads and signs were. It felt almost like home. The money spent on maintenance was evident, unlike Ireland, with its potholes and lack of signage.

Onwards to Lisburn and into the outskirts of South Belfast. Everything seemed abnormally normal. People bustling about, shopping, smiling, and suddenly I saw a sign for West Belfast. Since I had time to spare I thought I'd go and see the IRA graves in Andersonstown. I stopped to take yet more photographs of a police station, also covered with metal spikes and barbed wire. I really was struggling to get my head round it all. I was driving my Subaru, which was green, in fact an army-green colour, and as I climbed back into it I heard a racket coming from above. I looked up through the sunroof, and to my astonishment there was an

239

army helicopter clattering away about 100 feet above me. I photographed that too. Even then it never occurred to me that I was being monitored.

As realisation dawned I suddenly got cold feet. I decided I didn't want to go to the cemetery after all. This place had a veneer of normality, but clearly it wasn't. The helicopter drifted away over the rooftops, and I went back into the high street. I was suddenly hungry. I parked the car, and walked to a bakery and bought a pasty. I also needed a Belfast street map, so went into a nearby newsagent to get one. There was a blind man with a guide dog and white stick and sunglasses hanging around outside. I'd noticed him outside the bakery shop minutes before and now here he was again. I was puzzled. I walked slowly back to my car and he appeared to follow me. I was a bit shaken. I got in the car and noticed the blind man had gone. I tried to shake off this feeling of paranoia and studied the street map.

It turned out that my Belfast dealer wasn't that far from where I was, in fact North Belfast (the Protestant side). Following the map it took me to a small industrial estate. I had no trouble finding his premises and parked at the front. Gathering my sales brochures and briefcase I walked into the reception to be greeted by a charming young girl who announced my arrival to my intended customer, who was sitting in his office. I sat down in reception to wait when three burly fit-looking men seemed to crash through the door. I was startled but she didn't appear flustered. They eyed me first, then turned to her and asked for, of all things, a drink of water. She obliged, whilst looking at them oddly, then gave all three cups of water. I simply sat there in poorly disguised amazement. They looked sideways at me from time to time, drank their water, then abruptly left. She shrugged her shoulders, and with a puzzled look in her eyes, ushered me into his office.

My customer asked what kind of trip I'd had from Dublin. When I told him where I'd been, what I'd seen, and what I'd done with a camera he was aghast. He told me I was lucky and that those three guys were on the 'right side'. When I left him to drive to the Belfast ferry he told me not to stop or talk to anyone whatsoever. He was certain I would be followed right up until the time I got on that boat. They were out to make sure I left. I had two hours to kill before I drove on to that ferry. By now I was convinced I was being watched on every street corner, and in the ferry car park. I rang home from a callbox, nervously watching everything around me. I told Val I was on my way back, but she seemed unperturbed when I told her about all this. I could hear the kids yelling in the background. Everything back at home was normal, and here was I surrounded by apparent normality, but it was anything but. As I drove on to the ferry I felt an utter and overwhelming sense of absolute relief.

I've never been back.

Another side story to this side story: A kind of Part 2

Some weeks following this episode, I went back to Ireland with a friend of mine, who'd asked me to accompany him on a salmon-fishing trip. I nervously agreed given my earlier, dare I say harrowing, experience. Mairead wanted to see me again. I only gave her my office number for obvious reasons, and she'd been phoning my office in Cheltenham almost weekly. In the end I told my secretary to blank her. But then I thought why not fit her in on the salmon-fishing trip? One last fling and all that.

We were away for a week, fishing a river whose name I've forgotten, but it was somewhere near Ballymena. So I contacted Mairead in advance, who was delighted to hear from me and more than keen to meet up. I told her my plans and agreed a meeting point and time. It was a small town somewhere halfway between Carrick-on-Shannon and wherever the hell it was we were staying. Wherever the intended rendezvous town was, and I can't recall its name, all I knew, according to my map anyway, was it was right in the middle of Ireland. I just hoped it wasn't bandit territory.

The fishing, as so often with salmon-fishing, was crap, and so was the weather. By now it was late October, cold, rainy, and generally dreadful. My mate and I stayed in a B&B out in the middle of nowhere. The owner, a genial Irishman, plied us on the first night with poteen. If you're ever offered it, turn the invite down. Awful stuff, like liquid fire, and tasteless. More or less pure alcohol. You could burn a factory down with an eggcupful. As well as your throat and lungs. I accepted a glass from our host, sniffed it, sipped it, and threw it into a plant pot in the guy's living room. I doubt the plant survived.

We'd hired a car for this fishing trip, and I confided in my mate of my plan to rendezvous with Mairead on the Wednesday night. He clucked disapprovingly like some kind of mother hen, but wished me luck. We'd fished during the day, pointlessly, so he stayed in the digs to watch TV, and I took the car. I checked the map and embarked on a long drive to find the town. I remember it was dark. One of the blackest nights in fact I can recall. The weather worsened as I drove, and it rained relentlessly.

By the time I found this small town nearly an hour later, I had no idea how far I'd driven or where I was. All I could see was a main street with orange sodium lights, which were amplified in the rain-soaked street, and the whole place glowed orange. I tried to get my bearings, and finally found the bar where we were to meet. I got out of the car and ran into it, as the rain continued to lash down. I was soaked. The bar was brightly lit inside, with just three or four die-hard drinkers sitting at the bar. Other than that it was deserted. I ordered a drink and waited. And there I sat. The clock ticked by. I ordered another drink and began to get nervous. My Belfast paranoia now returned. I was convinced I was being watched once again.

Apart from the barman no one spoke to me, no 'top o' the morning' jollity here, and the few drinkers just eyed me suspiciously. I waited an hour. It was now 9 pm. She was late and I decided she wasn't coming. By now I believed it was a set-up, and some IRA unit would burst through the door and machine-gun me.

What was just as bad was my concern that I was damned if I could even find my way out of this place, and manage the 30 or 40 miles back through twisting country lanes to the B&B in the dark. In the end I called it a day, and went back into the street. The rain continued to clatter down, and I began to run to the car parked just up the road. Suddenly I heard tooting and a flashing of headlights. I turned and there she was, in an old Renault. She apologised profusely for being late. Her husband it seems had got back later than expected. Mentally I thought he'd been to an IRA planning meeting, but no, he'd been to some social business function. She'd then commandeered his car and here she was.

She insisted I get in, slid across to the passenger seat and asked me to drive. Leaving the hire car where it was, I obliged, and off we went in the pouring rain, out of this one-horse town to God knows where. She'd brought a bottle of wine which she opened as we drove, and two glasses. I have no idea where we went, but only a few miles out of the town. We ended up in some muddy cart track in the middle of nowhere.

With the top off the wine bottle we sat there with our glasses in complete darkness. (almost like a re-run of Meg in the stubble field all those years before). She was so pleased to see me again, and didn't stop talking and stroking me. Before I knew it we were on the back seat. She wore no knickers, just stockings, and shrieked and screamed just as she had at the hotel in Dublin. It drowned out the noise of the rain totally, but there was no one around to hear. We must have been on that back seat for well over an hour. It was frantic stuff to put it very mildly, and oddly, it crossed my mind that the car might well sink into the mud as this old Renault rocked and rolled in the incessant rain. There was no danger of any peeping Tom either. Always a possibility, but not in this weather.

In the end I managed to get the bastard out, reversed it up the track almost blind, and back onto the road in the pitch dark. She meanwhile straightened herself up, tidied her hair and readjusted her make-up in the mirror.

All I will finally say about this, is that when I eventually drove back to that town I saw in the street lights the back seat of that car. It was soaked, and not with wine either. With relief I fished out my car keys, kissed her once more, and as the rain still continued to pour down I took off in the hire car. I promised her faithfully I'd stay in touch, but I never did.

How I found my way back through that storm on this darkest of nights to make it back to the B&B I'll never know. For the best part of an hour I expected to be ambushed by a hit squad round every corner. That's how highly strung I was.

My mate had waited up for me. It was midnight when I told him the whole story. He was incredulous.

Chapter 16

In 1990 I'd come to the conclusion that my co-director in Masterchef was something of a liability. He was a live wire in terms of action, but as a strategist was hopeless. The new machine we'd designed and invested huge sums in (to justify his existence as a Director) was a bigger version of our original Bosch derivative, and launched to great fanfare. The development and research costs alone over twelve months were well in excess of £35k. Must be double that today. It was a colossal amount of money, all generated from profit, and paid primarily to a specialist design company.

We priced it at £1,990 to coincide with the year, but the guy we'd appointed to test them to destruction before launch was an incompetent prick, and failed totally to do his job properly. His appointment was one of my co-directors ideas, and unfortunately I went along with it. The machines were an immense marketing success, until, one by one, they began to fail. Frankly they were an unmitigated disaster. My co-director ducked responsibility, and when it came down to it, I was the one who sacked him. This poor guy had moved to Wigan from Essex lock, stock and barrel and brought his wife and kids with him. It was a total shock to him. In fact after I left having given him the bullet, his wife, who we'd employed in the office as a temp, attacked my co-director with a pair of scissors.

This so-called expert, who was responsible for its unreliability, had only been telling me what I wanted to hear rather than the truth. I've always been wary of experts, especially those you pay. Politicians are a case in point, as are teachers in the public school system. They only say what they think you want to hear. We gave all our customers, and our suppliers, their money back, tripling our overdraft facility to do it. We went back to basics and started again. In essence the entire exercise cost us upwards of £70–80k. As I said, probably more than double or treble that these days.

Oh well. Here's another little tale for you.

Side story

Just before this commercial disaster, I'd been to Paris to a catering exhibition with one of our sales guys. I'd found a dealer based in Marseilles who wanted to do a deal for distribution as sole distributor for France. He had a small, dark-haired and very petite secretary, who I learned had a French mother and Morrocan father. This gave her skin a permanent golden tan. Her name was Mireille, she was about thirty-two, single with an exquisite figure. We got on well, and her sense of humour as well as her spoken English was excellent.

I also discovered she was a Buddhist. I knew a bit about that from my jaunt years before in Kathmandu and Thailand, and as I related some of my stories about that trip (obviously not the debauchery in Bangkok), she became more and more fascinated. I took her out one evening for a meal. I began to think … hmm.

A couple of weeks after the exhibition I drove to Marseilles, to check out his business, amongst other things of course. It's a long way down there, but I'd since spoken to Mireille and told her of my plans. As it turned out she happened to be in their Paris office, so I picked her up. Paris is a nightmare for traffic, so I detoured via Cherbourg to meet at some rendezvous outside of that crazy metropolis. She made a cosy companion on the drive down to Marseilles and never stopped chatting, but reeked of garlic. We stopped at one point in some Aire de France picnic area to eat. The weather was hot, so I sat on the grass and munched a baguette, when suddenly, taking me completely by surprise, she threw herself on top of me. The garlic was then all too evident, but I gritted my teeth a bit and fondled her for a while. Continuing the drive in my Toyota Supra, a fantastic car for long journeys, we carried on down to Marseilles, where she had a flat. We stopped several times more along the way, but by the time we got there she insisted I stay at her place. I had it in mind to do this trip over three or four days. It's a good nine-hour trip to Marseilles from Cherbourg, and apart from my business appointment with her boss, and he knew nothing of this sudden liaison, she arranged to take a day off and take me sightseeing.

When we got into Marseilles I realised what a rundown dump some areas of it were. Her bedsit/flat was tiny, located in a crowded, litter-strewn back street, and three flights of stairs to ascend to get to it. I worried about leaving the car parked in the street, the place had such an air of malevolence. Nevertheless I staggered up the stairs with my case, opened the door and was amazed. It was a miniature Buddhist temple. The front room was decked out with Buddhist statues, scented orange and pink paper flowers, and the little fireplace she'd made into a small temple with a huge fat Buddha staring out of it, surrounded by joss sticks galore. She immediately lit one and went down on her knees in front of the Buddha and began mumbling some kind of prayer, or so I assumed. When I say front room, I looked around I realised there weren't any others, apart from the shower and toilet. The bed was a single one, in one corner, and a kitchenette of sorts in another. However, we managed, and I spent the first night with hardly any sleep. I love garlic, but when it's second-hand it's a bit nauseating. I had two days and three nights of this, and there I stayed.

She was one hell of a live wire. I had always thought there was a beatific serenity to Buddhism, and when she prayed there was, but once that little service was done, she lost no time coming down from that surreal platform to engage with me. I really did enjoy her company, and apart from visiting her boss for a morning appointment, I spent all my time with her. She took me to a remote beach somewhere near Cassis, I only remember that name because I believe it's French for blackcurrant. It was deserted, and blackcurrant beach had some sand dunes, so we hid ourselves in there. Taking her bikini bottoms off was easy, and we rolled around in these deserted dunes for most of the day, naked and undisturbed. Sex is easy when there are hardly any clothes on to start with.

I left Marseilles on the Saturday, and since she was keen to visit relatives in Paris I gave her a lift back there, dropping her off at a station on the outskirts. I drove to Cherbourg, and had the windows down most of the way to get rid of the garlic. This was another one I never saw again.

I arrived in Cherbourg, with very little cash, and went to a restaurant, ordered oysters and a small bottle of wine. I'd calculated that the fourteen francs I had in my tracksuit pocket would just about cover the cost with some small change for a tip. The ferry was leaving in an hour so I checked my watch to make sure I didn't overrun.

The oysters and wine arrived, and finishing them quickly I got up to pay the bill. It was twenty francs. I tried to explain that I only had enough money for what the menu had indicated, but the waiter pointed out that I'd ordered the big oysters, not the small cheaper ones. I hadn't of course. After that nine-hour drive I was, to put it delicately, a bit tired and emotional. I resolved this by losing my temper. He tried to push me against a pillar to stop me leaving, threatening me with the Gendarmerie. I don't like people invading my space like that so I hit him, and as he called for help I smacked him again, and over he went. Everyone in the place went quiet. I grabbed the door, and left, hurling the fourteen francs on the counter as I went out. I half expected the police to show up, but they didn't. I was seething, and with a backward glance as I left, saw two of the waiters helping him up off the floor.

I made the ferry with minutes to spare. I was last on, and even as I went up the ramp into the boat I half expected a blue flashing light coming on behind me. This virtually non-stop drive from Marseilles to Paris to Cherbourg had taken it out of me, and I was stressed by the finale to say the least. I slept the whole way back to Portsmouth.

*

One by one these flagship machines we'd launched to great fanfare began to fail. I just knew then I had to get out. I'd done as much with this business in Wigan as I'd wished. I always felt that the life of it was limited, and besides I'd had enough of Wiganites in general, with their staple diet of chips, pies and gravy, and my co-director in particular, who had now got himself into quite a bit of domestic trouble by shagging one of the staff. His wife found out, divorce was on the way, and he went to pieces. In fact he was worse than fucking useless.

As for the business, well I knew I'd stolen a lead on my competitors so it was only a matter of time before the big boys caught us up and blew us out of the water with their bigger budgets, and nationwide distributor networks. Since my role was that of Managing Director who owned 50% of the business, and the (so-called) marketing whizz-kid who had spotted the opportunity in the first place, I felt I'd done as much as I feasibly could. Besides I was sick of the travelling. All the properties I owned (with bank loans) were tidy and covering their loans. I thus resolved in late 1990 to make myself redundant after I'd re-financed the business and paid out a huge amount of money to placate our disgruntled customers, as well as our main suppliers, who had been left holding unwanted parts stock.

Leaving the company meant I would need to replace myself with a UK sales boss who could take over my role across the UK whilst continuing with the existing product range. Fundamentally the business was still immensely profitable. My plan was to use this profit to turn the business around, and get back in the black. The bank was on board, and we cut costs where we could. Me included. I was effectively firefighting to save the business, and nothing more could be done.

What the company needed was a new revitalised face, and I found one in the shape of a smooth, svelte, well-heeled individual, well known in the catering equipment industry, who held an agency for a range of products which complemented ours. He, after some negotiation, took over responsibility for the entire UK sales function. This turned out to be a huge mistake as you will see, but at the time I didn't see. Perhaps I was too keen to get a deal done and escape. This guy proved to be all style and no financial substance, and possibly one of the most plausible liars I've ever encountered. Nevertheless by the end of 1990, deal done, I was able to slip quietly off the scene.

I was sick of business. I'd also complicated my life once again with an ill-judged liaison I'd had a couple of years before with a woman employee at the Cheltenham business. I sacked her in the end when I discovered she and another female colleague were fiddling the books, but have to say was worried for a time that she might try to blackmail me and spill the beans. I got away with that one. Then a year or so later, when I was stuck in Wigan for several nights, I ended up, through boredom as much as anything, having a fling with my secretary. That most certainly compromised my working relationship to a large degree, and as she saw herself the boss's moll she assumed an air of superiority over the other office staff, which they clearly resented. It wasn't good management on my part. The lesson here is never shag your staff. As my co-director had also discovered to his considerable cost.

By early 1991 though I was free of it all. The company in Wigan was set up with a new sales face, still very profitable, and I figured it would take about twelve to eighteen months to recoup the losses, to get back into the black again. Provided of course there were no slip ups. My properties in Cheltenham were being managed effectively. All this took a few months to organise, but I'd cleared the decks. I began to feel almost as though I'd escaped from jail.

January 1991

As I said above, I was sick of it all. The stress, particularly over the past two years had taken its toll, mentally and physically. Now things appeared to be on an even keel. I had a few quid in the bank, a marriage which was comfortable, despite my occasional philandering, and two children, my daughter now aged nearly five and son aged seven.

The economy was in recession and interest rates, which had at one stage hit 15%, were beginning to fall in an effort to bounce the economy back into life. I kept myself fit, continued with the gym three times a week, jogged round the lanes, and even embarked on a Bronze Medallion life-saving course. This involved some serious swimming twice a week over several months, and on a whim I decided to engage in some self-defence skills too. It was some-thing of a kung fu street-fighting course. This gave me some ideas about how I could kill people, well not really kill, but seriously disable people in the event of trouble. Yet here I was also learning how to save lives. The irony wasn't lost on me.

The most important thing of all though, was that I carved out time. Believe me, finding time is harder than finding money. Now, however, I had the time to think. It was just what I needed, and I realised I needed to invest some of this time in my young family.

My impetus for starting in business was never about how much money I could make. The motivation was more to do with my desire to be unaccountable and comfortably off. I like to be in control, to make my own decisions. If I fuck up then I only have myself to blame. I'd certainly learned some life lessons along the way, made some big mistakes, but could never see me going back to work as an employee, nor could I see any opportunities for doing something different on my own, particularly in the current economic climate.

And here's another lesson. Ten years of hard work to build an asset base and retire went up in smoke. With the UK in a deep recession, I couldn't have found a buyer to cash in my chips even if I'd wanted to. So much for clever plans and schemes. The market always dictates, and frankly I don't see how you can beat it. It's like weather. Uncontrollable. All you can do is take some measure of protection.

I'd also realised that time was catching up. I was forty-three, and no matter how hard I tried could never, and quite frankly never have, shaken off that feeling of restlessness. That permanent desire to see what's round the corner. I frequently and often looked back, sometimes wistfully, to the overland trip I made to India and beyond fifteen years earlier. The influence that had on me was immense. It affected so many areas of my life, not least the sheer freedom of travel.

The more I thought about it, the more sense it made to do something like it again, but this time take the family. But how and when?

Fortunately Saddam Hussain, the autocratic dictator of Iraq, had invaded Kuwait, the USA had gone to war, and Saddam had issued threats to all Americans about the 'mother of all battles'. The Americans abruptly stopped travelling, frightened no doubt about terrorist bombs on planes, even though I doubt 90% of them had the faintest idea where Iraq was. They seem to scare very easily.

The price of flights worldwide plunged. Here was an opportunity to capitalise. Furthermore my children were in school, but not involved in any long term or influential exams, and yet were bright, alert, healthy, and aware. I reasoned that some of my clearest memories were from my childhood. I also reasoned that some costs, food for example, would continue whether we were home or away, but if I shut the house down the costs associated with running the place, like electricity, water, gas, heating oil and so on, would also disappear.

My wife was in a comfort zone all her own, having taken root in the local community. Maybe now was as good a time as any to shake things up, so that's what I did. It was time to repeat my travelling desires, but this time share them with my family in an altogether different way.

I told the schools they went to that I was taking them out for six months from April. It didn't go down well with the hierarchy, and today I'd probably be fined for it. Besides I saw travel as a far more useful education, as it had been for me. I went to London, found Trailfinders once again, transformed now into a thriving and extended business, and after a discussion with one of their excellent advisers, bought a package of eleven flights around the world for all four of us, all to be taken within twelve months. This gave us departure flexibility. I stuck to English-speaking nations where possible. I also felt that leaving in April would only lose the children a spring term of formal education, which they could easily make up later, the rest would be the school summer holidays. We sent our half a dozen chickens to my gamekeeper friend, one dog to a shooting friend, and Lulu, my beloved Clumber cross spaniel, went to another friend. My old terrier Dylan had died a couple of years before in 1989, drowning in the pond in the garden. That broke my heart. He was seventeen.

I organised all this in the space of a couple of months, and by the beginning of April 1991 we were ready. I reckoned I could get them back to school in time for the September start.

I had the house boarded up, gave my Visa card details to my brother, with a sum of money for him to pay the monthly expenses on my behalf from wherever we were in the world. The last thing were the jabs we required in case of illness. I didn't want a repeat for any of them like the illness I suffered in Afghanistan (not that it was on our planned route). That digestive problem I'd had in 1976 turned out to be some form of amoebic dysentery. It took three years to clear my system, and I really wouldn't wish it on anybody, especially my kids.

Both of them were immensely excited at the prospect of this forthcoming adventure, and became caught up in my enthusiasm, especially the fact there would be no school for six months. My wife, it has to be said, took a more measured view, and seemed to follow on with the plan rather than actively participate.

I'd kept in touch with my business colleagues, but mostly left them to it.

Suddenly we were free. In early April 1991 with four cases of stuff, and my daughter clutching her constant companion Teddy Ruxpin, we flew from Heathrow to Amsterdam to connect to a flight for Florida. I'd decided the USA would be our first stop. One side to the other. Then Hawaii, New Zealand, Australia, and round and up from there.

In short this world trip took more or less exactly six months. I don't propose to go into every bit of it as much as I did with the 1976 trip, but I'll aim to write a brief résumé of the whole thing. My kids can fill out any of the detail if they feel so inclined, especially my daughter Joanna, whose memory is of elephantine proportions. She can recall the smallest of detail. In many ways this trip would be better written by both of them.

Chapter 17

USA

Arriving in Orlando, after a nine-hour flight from Amsterdam's Schiphol airport, was a relief. Having rented a car, we loaded all our clutter and drove to Clearwater. The time difference was such that I was knackered, and found it tricky initially driving in heavy traffic on the wrong side of the road.

We got there early evening US time. By now it was about midnight back home. My brother Martin had fixed some hotel for us, since his company had a subsidiary based there. Fortunately for us he was over there in Florida anyway. He called me about 6 pm to say he wanted to show me around and have a beer. Reluctantly I agreed. It was still light and warm, and I was lightheaded and knackered. Val was settling the kids down, but off we went in his rented Cadillac, or some other American monster car, despite me being hardly able to stay awake. By now it was long past my bedtime and about 3 am back home. He insisted we went to Melons bar. I didn't protest. Under any other circumstances, apart from extreme fatigue and jetlag, I'd have stayed there for a very long time. All the barmaids were stacked like ... well ... er ... melons, and wore very short skirts. Welcome to America.

My impression of Clearwater was of a lovely coastal town, and I learned much later that the Rolling Stones had stayed here on their first visit to the States. Keith Richards had come up with the riff for 'Satisfaction' whilst here. Evidently he'd dreamt it up one night, played it into a tape machine, and then crashed out, rediscovering it the following morning. Had he not done so the world would never have known.

We stayed in Clearwater for a week to organise. Our next flight out on my package of flights was San Francisco. We had something like eight weeks before we needed to take that, so now we had to decide how best to get across America.

I originally toyed with the idea of buying a big estate car, like a Chevy or something. I had a kind of romantic notion to travel the States as some kind of hobo, but my constant reminder were the two children, which made me realise I was no longer the lonesome traveller heading out west. My idea was to use this old car and sell it when we left, but that was fraught with risk. I could imagine the thing overheating in the Texas desert at some unearthly hour and no help for 200 miles. I suddenly surprised myself. I discovered I'd become more risk averse. Kids do that to you. I was now a responsible adult, not some Easy Rider on a Harley.

In the end it made sense to rent a motorhome, or RV (recreational vehicle) as the Americans call them. Cruise America were a nationwide outfit, so when we finished the trip we could drop it at their base in San Francisco. That's what we did. We hired a Winnebago 'Warrior'. It seemed appropriately named to go west. Except it had no similarity whatsoever to a frontiersman's covered wagon. This vehicle was positively luxurious, slept four of us, air con, velvet-lined seats, kitchenette, and swivel chairs, with a tape deck to play all the music we'd brought with us, from the Beatles to Snoopy Doodle Puppy and other nursery rhymes. It was petrol, it was thirsty, but at $1 a gallon so what?

Once we'd agreed a deal, we were then directed to the AAA (American Automobile Association) offices in downtown Clearwater. We needed some direction or guidance and this lot were brilliant. We spent almost an entire day in their offices, and they were so patient with us. Gently nudging us in certain directions, until in the end they compiled something called a Trip Tick. This document gave us routes and campsites right across the States. All we had to do was follow it, having first hand-picked the places and states we wanted to visit. They expressed some surprise at the ambitiousness of our plans. Most people who rented RVs didn't go far. Maybe a few hundred miles. We were taking on a 6–7000 mile jaunt, across, up and down a bit, and then from one side of the good ol' USA to the other. After a week in Clearwater we were more or less ready to roll.

First off though we had a three-day ticket for Disneyland, which was more or less mandatory and had to be done. If only for the children. The sheer size of this place is hard to describe. The car park alone was a square mile, or so it seemed to me. We lasted two days. Even the kids had had enough of the naffness of it. I gave our remaining tickets away. Frankly I couldn't stand the place. Novel to begin with, but overwhelming. Everything was here, from Donald Duck and Mickey Mouse to Raiders of the Lost Ark, and spaceship rides. Food stalls everywhere, hot turkey drumsticks the size of your arm, and burgers the size of your head. I can see why Americans are so fat. An all-you-can-eat mentality. Sheer greed. I'd had enough of Zip a Dee Doo Dah after two days of this and was relieved to not go back.

What alarmed as much, if not more, was to learn from a fat American woman I sat next to on a bench, while the kids went off to queue for some ride or other, was to be warned by her to keep a close eye on the children. This place is a haunt for predominantly Mexican child-stealing gangs who target small children. Never crossed my mind, but what a perfect place to nick a two- or three-year-old. They were evidently abducted to sell on to rich, childless Californians. I suddenly became extremely wary to the point of paranoia. To emphasise this warning all the police, wherever and whenever I saw them, were heavily armed. We were learning a lot about America fast.

For perhaps the very first time I suddenly realised the enormity of the task I'd embarked on. Travelling alone with just a rucksack is one thing. Taking two young children round the world was something else. America was huge, extremely risky it seemed, and this was only the start.

This for me was my first real dip into America. Although I'd left home with my life-saving medal, and karate/kung fu lessons for self-defence, I was constantly on edge with the amount of guns and gun stores I saw. Karate techniques wouldn't be of much use should I end up facing a mugger with a five-shot automatic.

The Winnebago however proved ideal for the four of us, and having already loaded it with our provisions and clothing, we realised we'd brought too much so decided to jettison some of our surplus luggage and clothing. I sent a suitcase full of stuff back with my brother. I realised we could virtually live for several days in just tee shirt and shorts. So on the seventh day, having put Disneyland firmly behind us, we took off and headed to Cape Kennedy Space Centre (Center!! Grrrrr!!) on the Florida coast. For me the Space Shuttle was by far the most interesting aspect of this, and we had a look around the inside of one of them, as well as the flow of films about the NASA space programme, and of course the Apollo missions. The moon mission of 1969 I especially remembered, all of twenty-two years before. The kids loved it.

I could probably write a separate book just on the USA leg alone, but you'll be relieved to hear I won't. I'll just highlight some of the more memorable aspects of our journey across the States. The people we met were always hospitable, but I couldn't shake off this feeling of insincerity. Maybe it was just the usual cynical me. 'Have a nice day, y'all' became a mantra, which signified an almost robotic response to buying the simplest of things, whether chewing gum, burgers, or fags. I found it irritating.

From Florida we legged it up through Alabama and into Carolina to Charleston, an elegant place. Val was very much in *Gone with the Wind* mode by now, but still seemed to fret about mundane things, and hadn't settled into the rhythm of the trip. One of the great advantages of this Winnebago, however, was the opportunity for Val to cook homemade meals for us all. It would have been so easy to munch on burgers or chicken, or TGI Fridays, these eateries were everywhere, but the comfort of, say, cauliflower cheese or beans on toast was a welcome contrast.

I'd never considered a motorhome as something I'd ever particularly lusted after, but the sheer practicality of moving us all in one go, like a giant family snail, was just so practical. It was thirsty, but petrol at $1 a gallon made it very economic. In fact I calculated later that the motorhome, covering the 7,000 miles or so across America, cost about £600 in fuel. The rental of it was about the same, so for the thick end of £1,200 we were able to transport all of ourselves across the States. Yet there was the added delight of moving our back yard at the same time to a different place, a new scene, where we'd wake in the morning to gaze at a forest, lake, or desert, but retaining the same untidy comfortable mess within. It was just like home.

Into Carolina we went, Charlottesville, Charleston, then headed down to the Smoky Mountains to stay a night or two there. I did some trout fishing, but in a small lake fed by a stream. It wasn't fly-fishing as I usually did, but float fishing for these things with sweetcorn. The trout were small, had been stocked by the campsite owners, and the 'hillbilly, rootin', tootin', catch your own dinner in the creek' lifestyle was false. I caught two and put them back.

Onwards to Nashville. My first real taste of music and TGI Fridays. We didn't stay long, just a night, but I took in some of the billboards and recording studios where Johnny Cash et al had made their names. I think it was the birthplace of Country and Western too, and then on down to Memphis. By and large the roads were in great condition, and some of the scenery quite spectacular.

I've never been an Elvis fan especially, he was marginally before my time, though 'Jailhouse Rock' was possibly the first song I ever heard as an eleven-year-old and realised there was other music apart from Henry Mancini and Humphrey Lyttelton. So it was a given that we had to see Graceland. It wasn't difficult to find on the edge of Memphis, but what a bloody awful disappointment.

I'm not sure what I expected, but the giveaway was the Boeing 737 or whatever it was with 'Lisa Marie' painted on its nose, sitting dejectedly in the car park. The house and grounds were opposite. I was surprised by just how small it all was. Unseen from the car park, the house had been artificially extended to house his collection of gold discs, cars, and shiny rhinestone suits, presumably from his resident stint in Las Vegas before he died. As we walked through the wrought iron gates and up the drive 'All Shook Up', 'Hound Dog', 'Heartbreak Hotel' and so on was piped invisibly from the trees. My abiding impression, as I think I'd always had of Elvis, was of an over-indulged individual. Nice bloke, but not very bright, and severely lacking in strength of character. Inside, the rooms were vulgar. Quite honestly it reminded me of an Essex council house, complete with gold taps and avocado-green bathrooms. All of the rooms were individually decorated to indulge his whims. Great voice, great rock n roll, but what a shame. Too much money, and a severe lack of taste.

After this we went into Memphis itself. In places it was seedy, but Beale Street, the birth of blues music, had a black guy outside a café with Fender Strat and an amp, and sang some amazing blues stuff. This was more like it. However, I felt nervous around Memphis, I don't know why, just a sixth sense. While I was listening to this guy Val went for a walk with Joanna. I watched her walk back to the square with her handbag swinging from her arm. A perfect target for a hit-and-run mugger, all on view, and not a care in the world. People in the UK get mugged for less. I gave her a serious bollocking.

In Beale Street, Ma Rainey had had a plaque erected to her. I didn't know who she was, and still don't, but clearly she was famous for something. One day I'll check her out on Wikipedia or something, but I assume she was a well-known blues singer. I'd only ever heard of her when listening to Bob Dylan's 'Tombstone Blues', where she gets a mention. 'Ma Rainey and Beethoven once unwrapped a bed roll.' Beethoven was nowhere to be seen. Neither was Dylan.

The Peabody Hotel in Memphis had a unique daily ritual so we went along, and made it just in time to see some ducks coming down in a lift. These were pampered ducks, and on Mr Peabody's instruction lived in splendour in the penthouse suite on the top floor. They were mallards actually, and each day they would be chaperoned down the lift by a smartly dressed concierge, and shepherded into the fountain in reception. They would paddle about all day, before being taken in the evening back to their luxurious duck quarters. A novel event which the rich Mr Peabody had thought up. Elvis had one way of wasting money, I guess this was another.

Then I got done for speeding. The ring road around Memphis was probably about 5–10 miles in circumference, and the speed limit had a habit of changing often, but unnoticed by me. 60 to 50 at varying intervals. I was just about to pull off it, and head to the campsite indicated on our Trip Tick, when I saw blue and red flashing lights in the rear view mirror. I pulled over on to the hard shoulder.

Since I was wearing my usual shorts, bare-chested with no tee shirt (it was humid), I thought I'd better smarten myself up a bit. I climbed behind the driver's seat into the back of the vehicle to change. I could see a black and white highway patrol car, lights still flashing, behind me. I heard one of the policemen speak to Val to ask where the driver was, and she told him I was in the back. I opened the centre door to find myself confronted by two black-uniformed, heavily armed policemen. Both wore mirror sun-glasses and their radios crackled on their shoulders. As I descended the steps they took a momentary step backwards. I thought they were going for their guns for a second, then they moved forwards, and effectively frogmarched me to their car. They noticed my pocketknife sheath attached to my belt, and told me to place it on the 'hood'. I corrected them and said 'bonnet', but they took no notice. Humourless lot. Opening the back door of their car, curtly they asked me to step inside. Then slammed the door. I looked around inside. It was nothing more than a mobile cage. I noticed immediately that the door handles and window winders had been removed to prevent escape. They asked for my papers so I handed them my passport and driving licence under a metal grid which separated the front from the back.

Ominously, attached to this metal grid on their side was a pump-action 12 bore shotgun. They pointed out my crime. I'd infringed a 50mph limit by doing 60. Since I'd set the cruise control on the Winnebago at 60 I explained my unawareness. They leafed through my passport, driving licence and rental vehicle papers. It seemed to take an age for them to realise I was English. Then suddenly they caught on, their stern, aggressive attitude vanished, just evaporated, and they turned round and smiled. The 'Hey! Welcome to Memphis' stuff. I suspect they failed to make the grade at the charm school for highway patrollers.

When I informed them about our plan to travel across the States, especially with two small children, they were incredulous. The big logo on the back of the Winnebago emblazoned with 'Cruise America Rental RVs' might have been something of a clue. That was wasted on these two, who were perhaps no more than twenty-five to thirty years of age. These guys probably hadn't been out of the county, never mind the state of Tennessee. I began to realise, and not for the first time, that most of the people I'd met so far in America were entirely ignorant of both geography, and history. For some unaccountable reason, of those we met and spoke to in the entire trip, we were always taken to be Australians. Not that they seemed to have the slightest clue as to whereabouts exactly that country sat on the planet.

The elder of these two cops took a look at my Trip Tick map, and indicated how far the camp site we were heading for was. He handed me a slip of paper with their phone number on, and, all smiles, told me that if we encountered any problems whilst in Memphis to give 'em a call. He'd also noticed that my son Ollie was really upset, seeing his dad hauled off like that. He offered him, 'Gimme a high five, boy.' To his eternal credit, Ollie glowered at him and shouted, 'You leave my daddy alone!' The cop turned, smiled, and with monotonous predictably said, 'Y'all have a good day now, y'hear.' When I got back into my seat, I noticed they'd stopped me about 100 yards short of a resumed 60mph sign. It all seemed petulant, pedantic and overzealous to me. I retrieved my knife from the hood, by the way, and away we went.

New Orleans, Louisiana, has a reputation for music, French influence, and Creole music in particular. It's also famed for being below sea level, which is why they have huge turbine pumps dotted around the city, to pump the filthy drain water, after monsoon-style rainstorms, out of the streets and dump it into the nearby bayous. As we approached New Orleans the bayous, lakes and inlets screamed fishing to me. Miles of them, with small shanty-style shacks along the edges, half hidden among the trees and scrub which bordered them.

J J Cale was a guitar/song-writing hero of mine, a brilliant guitarist, who taught Clapton and Knopfler a fingerpicking style of play. I'm not sure he actually taught them, but they copied JJ's style, notably on songs like 'Cocaine', which Cale wrote. JJ Cale could play the five string banjo too, an instrument I resolved to learn on my return, but it was his guitar and writing technique which made him almost 'famous'. In reality he shunned the limelight, was shy and retiring and rarely interviewed. In fact very few photos of him exist on his albums. In one of his songs there's a line 'well I wrote you a letter, you must've read it wrong'. Miscommunication between lovers, eh? So common, and so brilliantly put.

We were now in Louisiana and this was JJ Cale country. I could quite easily imagine him on the porch of his shack, swaying back and forth in his old rocking chair, guitar in hand, smoking, drinking Jack Daniels, and watching the moon rise over this swampland as he composed new songs. He died of a heart attack a few years ago, aged seventy-four. Here's a perfect example of how a brilliant talent has just ... gone. Wasted. One day perhaps, humans may well be able to suck the essence out of an ageing body and transplant it into a new one, but I also think that creativity and originality fade with age. So maybe it was gone anyway.

I can't remember how many nights we stayed in New Orleans,

two I think, but we went to the aquarium and I saw, for the very first time, the alligator gar fish. It looked like a pike, with an alligator's snout. The evolutionary similarities were obvious. We strolled around the French Quarter, where the essential history of this city is centred, and did most of the usual touristy things. It was the mudbug season, that's American for the signal crayfish, where literally millions and millions of these 'critters' cross the roads at night to make it to other bayous to mate. They're collected by opportunist caterers, and boiled in water laced with chilli and cayenne pepper. They're then served hot, in brown paper sacks, with chunks of fresh lemon and boiled potato quarters thrown in. Miniature lobsters, bright and dark red, fiddly, but delicious. We took a stack of them back to our site, and sat outside for about two hours eating them on a wooden table alongside our truck. We were in bed, and well past midnight, when I heard a rattling sound on the roof, and the patter of paws. A couple of raccoons had evidently ransacked our leftovers and scattered bits of shell and claws all over the top of the vehicle.

The day before we left we took an organised swamp cruise. I saw the alligators first hand, and they would be tempted by half a raw chicken dangled on a piece of string from a stick over the bow of the boat. The guide would tease them into action, and the alligator would hurl itself out of the water and seize the chicken, breaking the stick or string in the process. I asked him about the alligator garfish, which can grow to in excess of 300 lbs, and suggested I bring a rod over and catch one. He gave me a patronising look, but then told me a story about how his 'grandpappy' caught one once way back. It's a story worth relating.

Here you go. Little side story for you

By all accounts this old guy parked his pickup truck down on the edge of a swamp following a huge storm. The pumps had gone into action and junked tons of debris, including stale food, into the swamp. He tied a stout length of rope to the bumper, and attached a small length of chain, on the end of which he put 'a big goddamn hook', which was baited with a whole chicken – head, feathers the lot – then threw this as far as he could manage into the bayou. He went back to the truck and sat in the cab to await events. Eventually the rope began to uncoil silently off the bonnet, oops … I meant hood, and as the line straightened out he started the truck, reversing it backwards, and struck. The truck won, and a huge alligator garfish was dragged, flapping ponderously, on to the beach. It was then shot in the head. I assume they cut it up and filleted it with an axe or whatever. Maybe it's true, maybe it isn't, but judging by the size of these things, it's definitely plausible.

We took off from New Orleans through the Baton Rouge area (which reminded me of Kris Kristofferson's legendary song 'Me and Bobby McGee'). Baton Rouge, I believe, was the epicentre of French Creole, and though I don't understand quite the meaning of Creole, and I should really, the food was always spicy and earthy and well, just honest. Anything with the word Creole on the menu was perfect for me, especially clam or shrimp chowder. We headed west in the direction of Dallas (President Kennedy's assassination, 22nd November 1963) and Houston (the HQ of the NASA space programme).

I don't recall us finding any campsite here, but it was around this time we encountered some very wet weather. It came down in monsoon torrents, making driving almost impossible, so we abandoned the idea of finding the campsite, parking up overnight in a lay-by of sorts, next to a truck stop.

It was here I learned from a truck driver that occasionally young attractive girls would tap on a driver's cab window, to entice these long-distance truckers into parting with money for sex. More often than not, as they opened their door to speak to the scantily-clad girls, who were usually black, a similarly coloured 6 ft muscle man would be hiding to one side with a baseball bat, and the driver would be severely beaten, mugged, or some of his cargo robbed. It was unnerving.

I was pleased we survived the night OK, and found in the morning we ended up parked in a huge overnight lake up to the hubcaps. The rain had beaten down all night. We left for Houston, arriving in the early evening. This city was huge, and as we drove around the ring road we made a decision to not stay, but to head right across Texas to San Antonio on an all-night drive. I fuelled up the vehicle, and with Val nursing a terrible headache as I recall, she got into bed to rest, cuddling my daughter. Ollie and I sat up front and I drove, mostly on cruise control, for ten hours. This was on top of the day's drive to Houston. His job, I told him sternly, was to keep me awake. And he did. We sang along with as many of the music tapes as I had. I have some film of him somewhere singing The Beatles' 'I Should Have Known Better'. So should I. To have embarked on a 600-mile journey across Texas at night, having driven all day too. That was a 'Hard Day's Night' drive, I can tell you, and from what I saw of Texas in the dark it was mostly desert and scrub.

I never realised just how big Texas is. I'm told it's the size of France, but when you look at the overall map of the States, it doesn't seem it. It was a bloody long way, but Ollie did his job well. He kept me alert. In between singing our heads off we occasionally stopped in the middle of nowhere to make a cup of tea. Val and Joanna slept for more all less the entire journey.

We arrived at sun-up, as they say. In fact a beautiful misty dawn greeted us. Something of a relief, having driven mostly in darkness the entire way. We made it into a lovely gladed campsite, beautifully laid out with trees, shrubs, complete with swimming pool and hot tub. All this just on the outskirts of San Antonio. After a swim and coffee, I climbed wearily into the hot tub. It was bliss after that drive. I was knackered and all I wanted to do was sleep. Which I did, and awoke refreshed in the afternoon. I've often found that I need physical exercise, irrespective of how tired I feel, to somehow compensate for a sedentary period of doing nothing, apart from concentrating.

I think we stayed on this site for two or three days, and met up with another couple, who were a bit younger than us, but were also travelling the USA. Like ourselves they had their young daughter along. His RV wasn't like ours. It was some kind of souped-up Ford transit van, emblazoned with Harley Davison artwork, and Daytona race cars. At least that's what I remember. They were from Canada, and we all got on well. Like us they too had developed an antipathy towards America. We stayed in touch for a while on our return, but as with most of life's friends, the contact eventually slipped.

San Antonio is the home of Davy Crockett, at least his last stand at the Alamo, and you'll recall my fascination and escapism with cowboys and Indians from the age of five or six. I can't remember who played the part of Davy Crockett in the film, probably John Wayne, but for weeks I went round as a kid wearing my Davy Crockett hat. His original hat was made from 'coon' skin. The same critters with hooped tails that had demolished the remains of our crayfish meal a few nights before in New Orleans.

The Alamo was in the centre of town. I'd imagined it on the edge of the desert, since that's where it was when Davy was fighting the Mexicans in 1956, or whenever the film was shot, but no. The fabled Alamo wasn't surrounded by Indians, but shops, bars, and restaurants, with the ubiquitous skyscrapers towering over it all. There were a few bullet holes in the stone walls around the Alamo, just to prove it really did happen. Another childhood fantasy dashed.

There was a bar in San Antonio, Durty Nellie's, yes 'dirty' was spelt like that, with huge bags of monkey nuts positioned freely around the place. When you'd eaten a handful you were then obliged to throw the discarded shells onto the floor, and stamp them into bits. The floor was covered in them. It was good fun. A novel concept to encourage drinkers, but still not enough to assuage my disappointment in finding the Alamo in the centre of this glitzy town.

I can't remember how long we stayed around here, but I was in no rush to get behind the wheel once more. The site was an oasis. I remember sitting in the cab one morning with a rod loaded with a reel and line, and tying a peanut on the end. Ollie sat alongside me. I ran the line out through the window and placed the peanut on a picnic table 20 yards away. A squirrel came down from a tree, picked up the nut and made off with it. I'd jerk the rod and the peanut flew out of its mouth. Puzzled, he would come back and chase after it. This game went on for ages and Ollie squealed with delight each time I mugged the squirrel. We let him have it in the end.

Eventually back into the desert we went, this time in the direction of El Paso, before turning north into New Mexico.

The roads in the USA are by and large smooth and wide, and compared to the UK comparatively deserted. To each side desert, scrub, cacti and ranches, then abruptly small towns out of nowhere, and then more of the same on the other side. This was my abiding memory of Texas. I think I may have seen an oil well derrick at some point, but otherwise it was a bit of a wilderness. The New Mexico scenery remained more or less the same.

The Earth doesn't recognise boundaries, only humans do that, with imaginary territorial lines drawn through the desert and mountain. Geologically the planet couldn't give a toss who has responsibility for one side of a piece of rock, or the other. However, the boundary approaching El Paso was all too evident. On the left (south) side we had Mexico, and the opposite side (north) the USA. The shanty town I could see in Mexico was a shambles, rather like a Soweto-style township in South Africa. Trailers, sheds, shacks and rubbish. The other side was glass, concrete and wealth. The boundary between them was thin, but the gulf was enormous.

I can't recall when exactly we turned north, but I put James Taylor on and played 'Mexico'. There's a line in it: 'Never really been, so I don't really know.' It looked very third world.

We headed in the direction of the Grand Canyon and the Painted Desert. Straight out of a Wild West film. But first we encountered the petrified forest. Strewn around the desert and into the distance were what looked like tree stumps, but on closer examination we found these were petrified trees made almost entirely (as I recall) of agate. Agate is a beautiful stone, and can be polished to reveal swirling colours of blues and reds and greens. These trees were solid agate. I have never seen anything quite like them before or since. Just tree trunks of solid rock. Upwards and into Arizona, where we came to the town of Winslow. It rang a bell with me, I couldn't quite remember why, but after searching in my head I found it, and put the Eagles on.

'Take it Easy': 'Well I'm standing on the corner in Winslow, Arizona, and such a fine sight to see.' Well yes it was, but as a town? Nothing out of the ordinary. I found the song on the tape and we played that whilst driving through Winslow. Another one for the memory file.

It may seem as though we raced through all these places, but we didn't. We would pick a destination, usually following our Trip Tick, and if we liked the area we'd stick around for a day or two, or occasionally stay out somewhere, as we did in the painted desert, in a car park or lay-by, though I was always slightly nervy doing that in case of trouble. It was probably this road trip more than anything which instilled in me the sheer independence of not having to rely on other people for transport. Road trips have become a central part of my life ever since, as they have with Oliver, who was equally influenced.

Eventually we came to a campsite in the Grand Canyon National Park.

The Grand Canyon is impossible to describe. The Colorado River is just a silver ribbon at the bottom, and the cliffs are shot through in layers of differing coloured rock. Three miles wide in places, it feels like another world, almost a different planet.

I'd been careful with money, and budgeted more or less every step of the way, but dug into our reserves and booked a flight through the Canyon for the four of us. I doubted I would ever pass this way again (and thirty years later I haven't), so it was an opportunity we couldn't afford to miss. It was wonderful. I love flying, but taking off and landing are the best bits, and to fly low down this valley, which is an inadequate word for this place, and look up at these towering cliffs was an experience never to be forgotten. There are glimpses of it on the film I took, especially the landing and taking off.

Again, I can't remember how long we stayed around here, but we aimed to go to Las Vegas next. The glow from this city in the middle of the darkness of the Nevada desert could be seen from 50 miles out.

Las Vegas struck me as the quintessential essence of America. Casinos, bars, glass, concrete, a chapel you could get married in with about five minutes' notice, and all-you-can-eat lobster for $5. Consumption and glitz on a truly cosmic scale. And all the hotels were gambling joints, notably Circus Circus. My only claim to fame here is I won $15 at a blackjack table. I'm no gambler, but I actually came away from Las Vegas in profit. I felt I'd somehow got one over on them. Last of the high rollers, eh? My daughter Joanna, who had been glued to her teddy since we left home, got another one. Sailor Bear, dressed appropriately in a sailor outfit. We rescued him from the crowds of Circus Circus as we were leaving. He was being kicked around the floor, and subsequently became a lifelong pal for her best friend Teddy Ruxpin.

The campsite in Las Vegas I don't really recall, but I do remember spending a whole day in a water park, with terrifying slides through long tubes. All in all, Las Vegas was the equivalent of a mega Blackpool, but instead of fat chip-eating Northerners, it had fat lobster-chewing Americans. I was glad to get out of it.

Two days in this place was more than enough for me, so onwards we went west in the direction of California and the Hoover Dam. It occurs to me as I'm writing this that I may have messed up these various stop-off points or events, kind of mixed them up, but I'm fairly sure the Hoover Dam came first and Death Valley second. One thing however of which I am sure, is that after circling the Hoover Dam, built originally to block the Colorado River and supply water to California, we were heading directly for Death Valley. What a place that was. It certainly earned its name.

Want another little side story? Here you go then

The more I drove this Winnebago, the more impressed I became. The heat outside began to intensify as we headed across the scrub plain, and mirages appeared on the tarmac in the distance, which shimmered in the heat haze miles ahead. I don't recall much if any traffic either coming or going, and as I checked the temperature outside, I began to wonder why the tarmac didn't melt. The temperature rose to 35°C but the air con in the vehicle kept us in a state of oblivion. What I didn't know then, but do now, is that Death Valley is below sea level by about 300-400 feet, and as we drove down towards it I just recall a glittering lake which stretched away to the pale grey hills in the far distance. Those I supposed were the Rocky Mountains, and as we descended on to the plain with warning signs not to stop, or wander off, the temperature just kept on rising until it passed 40°C outside. As I recall, the temperature in the vehicle was registered in Fahrenheit, so we had to work it out in centigrade.

This flat plain valley was possibly 50 miles wide. I have no idea how long it was north to south or where it began or ended. It was unequivocally the most hostile place I've ever encountered. The sun beat down relentlessly and the temperature just continued upwards. The glittering surface, I discovered, was a mixture of sand and borax, and half way across this valley I saw a small oasis of trees away to my right. I was truly astounded that any plant could survive down here, so we decided to have some lunch, and I decided to walk across this baking surface and find out what type of trees they might be. It was a stupid thing to do, but these trees didn't look far, perhaps a few hundred yards, so we pulled over into a lay-by. Surprisingly there was a car parked there with an older man sitting in the driver's seat. I say I was surprised, because I'd seen very few cars at all. Nevertheless I put on a pair of trainers, opened the door and stepped outside. A wall of heat hit me as if I'd stepped into a furnace, and the hot air entering my lungs made me gasp.

I began to walk towards the little oasis, while Val and the children stayed inside and she prepared some food. I said I'd be back in a few minutes, or so I thought. And that's genuinely how long I thought I'd be, but this little knot of trees seemed to get further and further away. It was odd, I consider myself a good judge of distance, but this oasis seemed to almost be sliding away from me. The ground was hard, rock-strewn; it crackled as I stepped across it, and I began to sweat. It took me possibly twenty to thirty minutes to get there, and frankly when I did make it, I didn't bother to take account of what type of trees they might have been, all I wanted to do was get back to the Winnebago. I saw a small lizard, which slid off a rock and disappeared, and remember thinking what on earth could it ever find to eat. As I looked back towards the road, I could fully appreciate the distance. It was easily three quarters of a mile, possibly more. I started back, and could now understand how easy it was to die in this heat. As I neared the Winnebago I shouted to Val to open the door. I was drenched in sweat, demanded a drink, and immediately downed two pints of orange juice and water. As I recovered in the cool of the air conditioning, with the engine running, she told me the man in the car had come over to ask for help. I looked across and sure enough, he was still sitting in the car.

By all accounts she told me he couldn't get his car started. Wearily I went back out into this blast furnace and knocked on his window. He was huddled in the driver's seat and somewhat reluctantly opened the door. I guess he was about 60-70 years old, overweight, and sweating profusely. Evidently he'd been there for well over an hour. I introduced myself, and summoned him out of the car. Such was the heat, I told him to go and sit in the Winnebago and get a drink. I checked the ignition, it lit up, so I turned the key. All I got was a click. It was an automatic Chevrolet of some gas-guzzling type, so I couldn't bump-start it, and would've needed a tow rope anyway to get it out of there.

The sweat was stinging my eyes when I went across to get him back out of the Winnebago. I had no idea where the 'hood' catch was, so asked him to open it, since I'm no mechanic and couldn't find it. He pulled some hidden lever and it popped open. The engine compartment was filthy, I doubt he'd looked inside for a very long time, and immediately I saw battery terminals that were completely corroded. I guessed they weren't making any decent connection. I got our kettle going and poured boiling water on the terminals, which immediately dissolved the crystallised chemical on them, then tried again. The click was repeated. In desperation I asked him to sit in the car and turn the key on my instruction. I used a screwdriver handle to hammer on the terminals, then physically pressed down hard on each of them with my hands and shouted to him to turn the key. There was another click, before the engine turned over and fired. I don't know what the relief was like on my face, but he just crumpled up and sagged, his head on the steering wheel. I honestly thought he was about to cry. I then told him forcefully that under no circumstances whatsoever was he to turn the engine off, not to stop under any circumstances, and head for the first garage he found, presumably 100 miles from this place, and get the battery replaced immediately. I wasn't sure if he'd either heard me or understood, so I put it more succinctly. Just get the hell outta here!

To my surprise he then got out of the car, engine still running, felt and fumbled in his jacket pocket, found a fat wallet, and pulled out of it what I guessed was about five or more one-hundred-dollar bills. He thrust them towards me with a shaking hand for 'saving his life'. I flatly refused, but he insisted, sweating and mumbling in a demented way. In the end I agreed to take two $20 bills, and told him I'd put them in the children's piggy bank for pocket money. I shepherded him back into his car and he drove away, still sweating and shaking, having thanked me again and again.

It transpired that he had been terrified of flagging down any passing motorist in case he was shot or mugged. I was dumb-founded. This was America at its worst. As for me, I was exhausted, and virtually fell into the RV. I downed another two pints of water, and away we went. An hour later we climbed up and up and into the Rocky Mountains, where the temperature fell to close to zero, and I was now looking for a pullover to get warm. A truly astonishing place indeed.

We headed for the Californian coast, and went to the north of San Francisco for 100 miles or so to see the giant redwoods. These trees were huge, and some had gaps under them which could park a family sized car. The campsite lodge we stayed in for a couple of days had a swimming pool. In the pool I bumped into a girl of about fourteen. Predictably came the usual 'Where y'all from? Australia?' Here we go again. 'England,' I replied. 'Where's that?' she asked as she chewed gum and swam away.

Geography and History most definitely are not the Americans strongest suit. In fact as we progressed over this six to seven week journey across the States, I realised with increasing concern just how ignorant they are of anything which goes on outside of their country. The planet outside of Planet America doesn't exist, it seems.

We were coming to the end of the American leg of our trip, and, after a detour for a few days down to Carmel, decided not to bother with Los Angeles, heading instead to San Francisco. There was a friend of mine back home whose mate ran a bar in SF, known as 'The Mad Dog in the Fog'. Nice guy, West Bromwich Albion supporter. The bar was full of flags, football shirts and WBA memorabilia. In fact it surprised me how comforting it was to hear a West Midland Brummie accent. We stayed with him for a few days, and I gave the Winnebago back to the Cruise America rental company branch in downtown San Francisco, and walked back through some ghetto or other, much to the Mad Dog's consternation. It was renowned for violence, muggings and shootings, not that I knew that. I then rented a car temporarily.

Apart from a visit to Alcatraz, a fascinating but mean place, watching the sea lions sunbathing in the marina, the French

Quarter, and remembering some car chase or other (*Bullit* with Steve McQueen I think) through this city of hills, I don't recall much else, apart from Scott MacKenzie singing, 'San Francisco, be sure to wear some flowers in your hair'. In the late 1960s this city had been a hippy Mecca. There was of course the San Francisco Bay Bridge, the ubiquitous fog, and Saucelito, which lay on the other side of the bay.

After a few days here we left for Hawaii, our next destination on the second leg of this six-month trip.

The reason I wrote more than I intended about the USA is primarily because (in many ways) it was the most memorable. For better or worse. It also gave me an opportunity to see the country and try to understand the mentality of the people.

Having covered six or seven states, the thick end of 7,000 miles, and met dozens of people along the way, I think I'm allowing myself to comment with a degree of qualification.

My conclusion is one of concern for the world and its inhabitants. This country is entirely self-centred, the majority of the people are quite ignorant, have complete faith in God and freedom, both of which are illusory, but nevertheless are proud, patriotic, and gun toting. Home of the Brave and the Land of the Free? I don't think so. A country of conspicuous consumption. It's a worry.

I've never been back, nor do I intend to.

The rest of this trip is a hop, skip and jump, since both Oliver and Joanna can fill in the gaps. I can imagine them both saying, 'No, Dad, it wasn't like that.' Remember, this is my take on it all, and the memories are mine alone. Theirs may be, in fact almost certainly will be, quite different.

Hawaii

Hawaii of course is another state of the USA, and apart from Pearl Harbour, ukuleles, and garlands of flowers round the necks of smiley people, I didn't know much about it. We flew into

Honolulu, but opted to get another flight to the island of Kauai, about twenty minutes away. Kauai seemed, on the face of it anyway, to be less commercialised, more authentic, more Hawaii … ish. I think it had a rumbling smoky volcano in the middle too. All the Hawaiian islands were originally the lip or the remains of a giant volcano, which presumably exploded. We stayed for a couple of weeks in a beachfront shack for $30 a night, which Val found more or less by accident. One room for all four of us, with a couple of big ceiling fans for company. A great opportunity to rest and relax after all that driving.

The surf crashed on to the beach just below, and the kids discovered blueberry muffins, served by way of an instant breakfast. They made a beeline for them each morning.

I got a bit bored after a while, and dipped into our reserves to take a tuna-fishing trip. The weather was hot but incredibly windy, and no sooner had the boat left the sanctuary of the marina than it was immediately knocked about by huge waves. There were six of us on board this sport-fishing boat, but only four rods, two of which were on outriggers. We were each given letters drawn by the two-man crew for our rod designation, which we drew from a tin, A, B, C and so on. I drew F. Each of the rods was marked A–D and whoever had that letter was in charge of it for thirty mins. If one rod got a take, then whoever had the appropriate letter earmarked to that rod took on the fish. Since I came last I had to sit it out for half an hour or so until my turn came. I decided to go up top and chat to the crew. The boat rolled and swayed around in the heaving swell like some fairground waltzer. As we progressed out to sea, one by one my fellow anglers began to drop out, and turn green. Just like dominoes they all took it in turns to vomit, each clinging to the sides of this heaving boat to project their breakfast into the sea. Not me though. It seems I have good sea legs. Within forty-five minutes all five of them were incapacitated, all sitting hunched in a very sorry, sick-streaked state in the cockpit. The downside was the smell. The upside though was I had all four rods to myself.

We dragged, or trolled, big rubber squids about for a further half an hour or so, and eventually I got a hit. The power of a 20 lb tuna is something to behold. In fact I had two. The speed they took line off the reel was such that I couldn't touch it without burning my hands. Once the fish slowed though, it became manageable, and I was by now belted to avoid joining them in the water. The weather progressively worsened, so back to harbour we went. The other five were by now rolling around in the well of the boat, which was swamped with puke. The stench was overpowering. I was glad to get off the thing.

I had my photograph taken with these fish, and thought I'd take a chunk back with me, but wasn't even offered a slice. Before I knew it, I was back at the hotel.

We developed a taste for freshly cut coconuts, which were served under the coconut palm trees on makeshift wooden tables erected on the beach. I went with my daughter Jo one morning to buy a couple. When I felt for my $20 note it had gone. I had no idea how or where. We trudged back along the beach empty-handed, Jo running ahead under the trees. She suddenly exclaimed that she'd found our note blowing around in the wind, except that it was a $50 note. A 150% profit on my earlier loss. Such is my daughter's luck. She regularly wins raffle prizes, even today at thirty-three.

We went to view the Pearl Harbour wrecks on our last day, which were clearly visible in the clear water, these ships of course having gone down in the harbour when the Japs attacked. This attack killed 3,000 or more American sailors and servicemen. The only positive thing to come out of it which I could see was that it at least (and at last) got the Yanks off their arses to join the fray, subsequently entering World War II two years after it started. Better late than never.

We at last made our way to the airport. New Zealand was next. A nine-hour flight.

New Zealand

We crossed the Date Line over the Pacific, and lost a day, or gained a day, I can't remember which, but landed in Auckland, on the North Island. Once again, I was faced with a dilemma. We'd opted to stay in NZ for about three weeks, and the change in weather from the sunshine and blue skies of Hawaii was a shock. It was now late May. Spring in the UK, but heading for winter here, with chilly evenings, combined with damp and drizzle at times. But how best to get around the country?

We stayed in some kind of B&B. Val had a migraine or very bad headache, so I went for a walk in the evening with the children, and noted the cleanliness of the city. It was spotless and neat. Very English-looking houses.

The following day we took a drive to the harbour. The Greenpeace boat *Rainbow Warrior* was moored up here. This was the base they used for harassing Japan's whaling fleet. Good for them. Some weeks after we left NZ it was mysteriously sabotaged, and sunk.

We watched bungee jumping from a crane over the quayside. They wanted me to pay $50 for the privilege. I would have needed them to pay me ten times that to indulge in this insane exercise. Following this we took off in a boat to see killer whales in the harbour. We were lucky, it was killer whale season. I threatened to drop Ollie over as bait to the pod of whales circling the boat. All in all my impression of Auckland is of a lovely clean city.

In the end I opted to rent another motorhome. We'd had such success with the Winnebago it made sense. Having spent some time with the NZ Yellow Pages, I found a company willing to let us have one. Most were being prepared to go into winter storage, since it was now out of season. They un-mothballed it for me, tempted with payment in cash (£300), and off we went. It wasn't a patch on the Winnebago but did the job. and once again we spent the next 2-3 weeks driving round the North Island.

There are some similarities with England geographically,

especially areas of the Lake District, and I was intrigued to see a large number of Triumph Heralds and Morris Minors on the roads. I often wondered where they'd all gone.

The first night was disconcerting. We'd parked near a reservoir on a grassy lay-by. I planned to put a spinner through the lake in the morning to see what trout if any I could catch. At midnight we were treated to two cars which came to do wheelies, skimming the RV by yards, sliding in the mud and grass around us. It was alarming. We were entirely alone out here. Basically pissed-up kids in souped-up Ford Escorts. They left after an hour of this mayhem, but I didn't sleep well. At one point I crawled out in the dark and hid under the steps with a metal bar, just in case of trouble. There wasn't, and these joy-riders pissed off eventually. And no, I didn't catch anything in the lake either.

Down to Tarpo and to an area of volcanic activity. We stayed for a couple of days on a site which had wooden cubicles marked with degrees of hotness. The hot sulphur springs had been diverted through these sheds. Shed number 1 was the hottest, since it was closest to the source. Shed number 10 was therefore cooler further down the row. Lovely place, with a hot swimming pool. The mornings were frosty, and barefoot through the frost we all went to climb into a huge swimming-pool-sized bath, which once in, none of us wanted to leave. There were geysers which shot plumes of steam into the air, and some incredible waterfall we visited nearby, where swallows flew below us through the spray, presumably feeding on hatching insects from the torrent below.

The weather was unpredictable, the ferries weren't running to the South Island, so back north we went in the direction of Rotorua. It's an odd feeling, heading north to a warmer climate.

I fished Lake Rotorua, having spent more or less all day trolling it with lures and fast-sinking fly lines, and despite electronic fish finders, was unsuccessful. I wasn't having much luck with New Zealand's legendary trout. I'd discovered that the streams and lakes of New Zealand held some of the best rainbow trout fishing anywhere in the world. What I hadn't realised was that these fish had been brought over 200 years before from Canada (as ova) and introduced into the catchments as fry. I had assumed they were an indigenous species, but it must have been a hell of an ambitious task to bring these fish all this way on a sailing vessel.

All the streams and lakes were full of them, and en route north to the Coromandel Peninsula we stopped around lunchtime by the Green Lake (there was a blue one too nearby, according to the map). I spent ten minutes casting a spinner in it, and hooked almost immediately a decent rainbow which fought like hell. I think it was in excess of 7 or 8 lb. I was just in the process of putting it back when a car screeched to a halt on the road by the motorhome. I looked up at a very angry and irate individual, who lambasted me for illegal fishing. He informed me in between shouts and gesticulations, that this was a Maori lake. By all accounts it was their preserve, or reserve I suppose, and told me in no uncertain terms we were likely to be beaten up if the Maoris caught us. He didn't appear to be of Maori extraction, nor was he police, so I don't know what his credentials were for this apparent authority, but I took him seriously. I put the rod away, forgot the lunch Val had prepared, and we legged it. This was the second event in a matter of days which made me mildly uncomfortable.

Virtually all the animals which live wild in NZ are non-indigenous, introduced by human beings after Captain Cook discovered it 300 or more years before. Stoats and mink have done immense damage to some of the original wildlife. Particularly ground-nesting birds. And there were pigs living in this wilderness. The original pigs released by Cook when he left have now multiplied. They call them Captain Cookers, and these feral pigs live in the forests and are hunted in the same way as wild boar, though nowadays there may be some protection in place for them.

The Coromandel Peninsula reminded me of North Wales. We parked up alongside a near-deserted beach. Val took the kids for a walk on it while I took a rest. She came back shaken and flustered.

Some stranger had accosted her on this deserted beach and flashed himself to her. We left immediately. Another cause for concern. Then, just as it does in Wales, it began to rain, and heavily.

Now almost dark, in this lashing rain we found by map a campsite which was in the process of closing down for the winter. The owners welcomed us, despite the place being deserted. Val and I had stopped at one point to buy a stone of green-lipped mussels from a guy at the roadside, and the owners of this place offered us a chalet for the night while the kids stayed on board the motorhome, which we parked outside the chalet door. We now had the means to cook the mussels in a giant pot on an electric stove in the chalet. Never have I been so sick and tired of the sight of mussels, but between the two of us we ate the lot, accompanied by a big jug of warm brown ale kindly supplied by the owner's husband, who brewed his own beer. It was an extraordinarily memorable night. We were damned lucky to find this place in the middle of nowhere.

Back to Auckland uneventfully, except for a bank cashier I met, who in turn introduced me to his father-in-law, an accountant. I'd expressed interest in potential property opportunities, and he by all accounts was the man to speak to. Months later, when I was back in the UK, he sent me a colossal bill for keeping a 'watching brief' on my behalf, and threatened to sue me in the High Court. Needless to say it got nowhere, but the experience of these unnerving events decided me once and for all that New Zealand wasn't a place I was ever likely to go back to in a hurry.

I subsequently learned years later that 90% of the serious crime in New Zealand is perpetrated by 10% of the population, or 'trailer trash' as they're known. This is a well-kept secret by the authorities to avoid deterring tourists. Well at least it's no secret any more. You now know!

Australia

We left Auckland sometime around the end of May / early June and landed in Sydney, staying with my old friends Mike and Helen, with whom I'd stayed in touch over the intervening 15 years. It was hard to believe I was last there so long ago, so much had happened to me. They put up with us for about two weeks in their splendid house in Queenscliff. They'd moved since I was there last, but only round the corner, now overlooking the magnificent Pacific from their clifftop residence. The kids loved it, and we went back over the sights in Sydney I'd seen all those years before.

Australia had changed, and not for the better. The opera house hadn't moved of course, but Manly Beach was now heaving with people, far more than I recalled. There just seemed to be more people and more officiousness. Something I'd never noticed before. Don't do this, don't do that, park wrongly and you'll be fined. Speed limits on virtually empty motorways were rigidly enforced by cameras, and heavy fines imposed. It really bothered me. It seemed all wrong in a country with such magnificent wide-open spaces, and the lure of freedom. I was genuinely surprised at the more restrictive feel which had apparently developed over those fifteen years.

After two weeks of having half of their house to ourselves we were ready to go north, and no doubt they in turn were pleased to see the back of us. We planned a route to Cairns, with Mike's help. We also celebrated Joanna's fifth birthday. 24th June 1991. I have a video clip of her dancing in a grass skirt to the Travelling Wilburys. That album certainly resonates with this leg of our trip, as does this poem. Jo was a livewire, and sometimes couldn't sleep, but given we were on the road day and night it wasn't altogether surprising. I wrote this for her to help her drift off.

For Joanna (aged 7), who couldn't close her eyes

Empty your head
Of all horrid thoughts
And drift away on the breeze
There's a town down below
With a cuckoo-clock church
And parks full of people and trees

There are fields to the left
And deep woods to the right
One river, two lakes, and three farms
On the bridge by the mill
Where the race rushes by
There's a boy
With a girl in his arms

She smiles into his face
And he gazes at her
Smoothes her hair, holds her face
In his hands
You can see they're in love
For the world's passed them by
And all's quiet and still as time stands

A trout gurgles and splashes
In the current below
Then slides lazily downstream to hide
It's time we were going ... quick
Catch up with the breeze
And look for a dream whilst we ride

We could swoop out to sea
Soar up to the sky, or take off
To hot faraway places
Lie on beaches of sand
Or quite simply hold hands
And play marbles
With all our friends' faces

There are places we haven't yet started to find
You can go where you choose
Look and peep
And when you've discovered a suitable dream
You can use it to help you
To sleep

A couple of days later I rented an estate car and we left, rolling the kids up in sleeping bags in the back if we were in for a long drive.

Over a three-week period we went up through Newcastle, the Gold Coast, Brisbane, Gympie, Fraser Island, but fell just short of Cairns. Joanna left her ever faithful Teddy Ruxpin behind in Gympie where we'd stayed with some friends. She was heart-broken, but we collected him after his weeks holiday there on our way back. So all was right in her world once more.

We found Airlie Beach and the Whitsunday Islands, a beautiful area, and there we took root for the week in a lovely chalet. I was desperate to visit the Great Barrier Reef, and we took a boat for the thirty-minute, fifteen-mile run out there. It was truly magnificent. The tide rushed over the coral. I dived, met with a giant grouper, and the scenery below was indescribable. This trip was more memorable for me because Joanna learned to snorkel for the first time, with the help of her Polyotter buoyancy aid. I'd tried so many times to show her how it was possible to see under water with goggles, but she always tore them off in anger. Yet when someone else persuaded her to try it, she was delighted. 'I can see fish, Daddy!' I dunno, kids, eh?

Whilst at Airlie, I dived Manta Ray Bay, and watched in wonder as these huge aquatic stealth bombers glided effortlessly over the sand and coral. We took our final day on the *Whitsunday Dreamer*. A rather unorthodox skipper did a 'health and safety' talk as we took off from the quayside, telling us to mind the steps up and down the boat, or we'd likely 'break our bloody necks'. This was the Australia I'd originally fallen in love with.

Back down the Pacific Highway we came over two or three days, collecting Teddy on the way in Gympie, and driving much of it at night with the kids asleep in the back. Doesn't look much on a map, maybe a few inches, but it was a bloody long way. Probably a thousand miles or more. The length of the UK at least.

I said earlier I felt Australia had become more officious and more careless. Just to underline this feeling for what I perceived as negative change, in fact an almost urgent desire to embrace Americanism, I was done for speeding. A re-run of Memphis perhaps? Except this was 11 o'clock at night in the middle of nowhere on straight and empty road. Apart from the road trains of course, which we occasionally encountered as they roared along in clouds of dust. I was waved down by two zealous cops with torches, who had hidden in the gum trees alongside the road looking for an easy target. That was us. They fined me on the spot and told me to pay up at some police station or other. I can't remember the amount, but it was enough to piss me off.

We were about to leave Oz a day or so later. I didn't bother paying.

Australia was the first country on this trip to which I'd been before. Change at home is gradual. You adapt to it, hardly notice it. It just becomes the norm. The gap here was fifteen years. You notice that, and why I was shocked. I wanted it to be the same but it wasn't. You could probably argue that as a footloose twenty-eight-year-old, my perceptions were quite different to those of a forty-three-year-old with a wife and two young children, and you'd be right. They didn't notice, but I did. I could see and feel the difference. That's the problem with memory and ageing.

Sometimes it's best not to revisit, and to just leave the memories in a box. Another lesson learned.

'There are places I remember, all my life, though some have changed, some forever not for better, some have gone, and some remain. All these places had their moments ... and these memories lose their meaning ...' (The Beatles, 'In My Life')

Bali

I don't recall the length of the flight to Bali. What I do recall is landing, Val examining hotel options on the information board, hiring a Suzuki jeep, loading our luggage into the thing, and weaving out of the place and into the countryside, following the coast. The roads were tricky, pot-holed in places, and mopeds, scooters and rickety cars needed avoiding. Some of these were overloaded with people, animals, and vegetables. Pigs, chickens, donkeys, cattle, and the occasional backpacker wandered around and through some of the little shanty-town villages. The weather was gloriously hot, and humid.

We found a hotel by accident. There were several along the coast, and the one which was available did us a deal. It was a collection of small thatched round cottages, with a central reception, swimming pool, and close to the beach. In fact it was all palm-fringed and lovely. We planned to stay for the week.

Of all the things we did, perhaps the most memorable was a visit to the bat caves, with subterranean caverns covered in bat shit, floor to ceiling, and the screeching hordes hanging up there in the gloom. I don't know the species, but fruit bats of some sort. Oliver got bat shit on his tee shirt and freaked out. Not the bold Batman he used to be when he was four.

More interesting for me was the village square outside, where cockfighting cages were stacked in preparation for contests. They weren't 'proper' contests but set up to show the tourists. In the event, I met a taxi driver who agreed to take me to a proper cockfight.

Overdue a side story? Here's one.

The taxi driver picked me up from the hotel late one afternoon, and we drove several miles past rice paddy fields to a remote village, a collection of grass huts amid the scrub, dirt, and litter piled everywhere. Woodsmoke from the cooking fires hung in the air.

As the sun began to sink, the atmosphere was filled with excitement, the villagers gathering round to place bets. I remember a pig roast nearby, which made a further contribution to the smoke filled, heavy air, which hung like fog in this little valley. The pig was being hacked up and sold. I got myself a beer, and the serious business of betting began, with fistfuls of dirty notes being waved and thrust towards the competitors, the shouting and arguing becoming ever more intense. I didn't understand a word, but got the gist. My foreign presence didn't seem to bother any of them. The whole village seemed to be there in this circle of dirt among the huts. Sipping my beer and staying close to my taxi driver host, I looked around and noticed there wasn't another tourist 'type' to be seen. This was in many respects the real Bali.

The cockerels themselves were scrawny, long-legged, and fit. There were possibly twenty of them in baskets. Two were hauled from their wicker cage, and a hush descended. The owners held a bird each and then pushed them forward towards each other. The idea was to goad them into battle. Both birds I noticed, had affixed to one spur only a sliver of shiny steel. The normal spurs looked deadly enough, but extending them with a dagger made them into lethal weapons. The blade itself was a thin, very sharp, deadly-looking blade about 4 inches long. Somehow they tied this onto the right spur with string. By the time the birds had been wound up, they were then released in the dirt, and these two angry birds flew at each other in a rage. The quietened crowd erupted into roars and screams, and the fight began.

The birds leapt into the air and hurled themselves in fury at each other feet first, in a flurry of feathers and screeching. The crowd were manic and became almost hysterical. I worry about mass hysteria, it seems to develop a momentum all of its own. I stood back. There was no skill employed on the part of the birds. It was pure luck as to which one plunged the thin stiletto in by accident. Or bad luck for the recipient. I watched horrified and fascinated.

Inevitably, after only a matter of minutes, one bird landed a lucky thrust, and the wounded bird collapsed and crumpled immediately with blood frothing from its beak. The crowd by now were screaming in a goggle-eyed state of blood lust. The other bird continued to jump on it, in such a rage it was oblivious to the mortal wound inflicted. The dying bird was declared the loser, but just to make sure and settle the matter, the referee took the injured bird, put it in a large cage and the other bird, the evident winner, leapt up and down on it, thrusting the blade into the creature's back. This was now officially declared the winner. No surprise there, then.

Once the result was agreed, some of the crowd surged forward to collect their winnings. The still alive but seriously injured bird, covered in blood, was swiftly handed to some kid of about ten, who took it round the back of the huts. I followed him to watch. He took a knife and cut the leg off the bird to retrieve the stiletto, which he delivered to the next combatant. Then he returned round the back of the hut and proceeded to pluck this still-alive, one-legged bird, as it gasped and jerked its last breath. I was appalled by the evident cruelty.

I returned to the ring, and a repeat performance followed. Suddenly I became more and more angry and annoyed with the total lack of humanity and respect shown to these dying birds. On the third occasion I intervened, took the bird off this kid, much to his astonishment, and promptly knocked it on the head with my empty beer bottle. When I was sure it was dead I handed the corpse back, for him to resume the plucking of this bloody mess of feathers. A silence suddenly descended, and as I looked around fifty villagers stared at me. The hostility was tangible.

My taxi driver found me, took me by the arm, and making some quick explanation to the crowd, ushered me to the car hurriedly, and we left.

In the nicest possible way he explained on the way back that it was only with permission I'd been allowed to watch this. Foreigners don't go. These cock fights are their Friday-night entertainment, like bingo or horse racing are for us in the West, I suppose. It's a big deal to gather for this show, and I'd interfered. I felt truculent, justified in what I'd done, smug almost. Perhaps I'd given them just the briefest pause for thought about the way they treat any creature, but it became clear that, with total politeness, the taxi driver was seriously pissed off with me. He was no doubt pleased to dump me back at the hotel, and I suspect he'd think twice before fixing another tourist visit.

It's only now I realise that this was their affair, and my instincts to do the right thing very nearly got me into serious trouble.

We left Bali the following day, but just before we did I got Oliver and Joanna to throw their accumulation of unwanted plastic toys out of our hire car. Mostly rubbishy McDonalds freebies, given away with Big Macs, and other junk food. The Balinese are subsistence-poor, and the children chased down the road after the car, grabbing and fighting over these Western treasures in the dust trail we left behind. We threw out unwanted biscuits and bread also, since we didn't need to travel with this stuff. They scrabbled and fought in the dust for that too. It reminded me of the Afghan children all those years before, who crawled around behind the bus picking up the cigarettes, biscuits and sweets we'd thrown out for them. This was a lesson for my own kids.

Singapore

Singapore is a gleaming glass and concrete city, spacious and clean. Wholly different from Bali. No graffiti, no litter and, like Australia, it had changed massively in the fifteen years since I was there. Singapore had become ever more fastidious and obsessive over any transgression, however small. It felt well-ordered and antiseptic, in a police state kind of way. Drop chewing gum, spit or piss in a public place, and if you're caught, off to jail you go. it still had the 'No Durians' around the public transport system. I concurred with that.

We stayed in a splendid hotel in the middle. I've no idea what it was called, but the young Singaporean staff loved Ollie's long sun-bleached hair, and would stroke it at the slightest opportunity. Two of the staff, girls of no more than perhaps twenty, babysat for us. Val and I went out for a meal. First time I'd been free of the kids for months. Seemed odd without them actually.

Perhaps the most interesting aspect of Singapore was our visit to the notorious Changi jail.

One of my teachers from my school, Humphrey Perkins in the 1960s, had been imprisoned there by the Japs during the war. He hated the Japanese race totally and unconditionally. When I got to Changi I could see and understand why.

As fourteen-year-old schoolkids we couldn't either understand or appreciate what he'd been through, what he'd endured, and the magnitude of the scars it must have left. This teacher, Beaky we called him on account of his large nose, was always in an irascible state. He despaired of my class, and shouted and threw things at us. His fuse was permanently lit. I reckon today it would be put down to post-traumatic stress disorder, but we had no idea at the time. He was a target for our jibes, the goal was to wind him up into an incandescent rage. It was easy. He was always on the edge of losing his cool. Changi jail, it turned out, was the prime reason for his state of mind, and I now feel thoroughly ashamed for being party to this baiting.

Changi jail is now a tourist attraction. It lies between the city and what I guess originally was the jungle. I don't know the entire history of how it was captured by the Japs, but my dad told me this fortified place was held by the British, who were expecting the attack to come from the sea. While they were busy scanning the horizon, the Japanese overwhelmed them by riding in behind through the jungle on – get this – bicycles. I don't know how many British troops were captured, but 50,000 or something like that. If they weren't sent to labour camps, many of them ended up in Changi.

There was some kind of shrine by the entrance to this jail, where the families of long-dead prisoners, as well as former inmates, had placed flowers, drawings, poems and letters. I read most of them, and they were truly heartrending. The torture these people had endured, mostly captured British troops, was inhumane, to say the very least. What bothered as much, if not more, was the inventiveness of some Japanese brain who had devised and designed these in monstrous actions.

In fact it was hard to believe that only a matter of days before, I had been teaching the Balinese a lesson about respect, consideration, and endeavouring to stop their barbaric inhumanity over the life of a bloody chicken. The scale of brutality by one human being towards another was unfathomable to me, and it still is. The sheer and absolute hatred one side had shown towards the other was utterly appalling. However do minds and mindsets become twisted in this way? There are times when the human race horrifies me. The tortures were unbearable. Starvation, beatings, water tortures, impalement, fingernail and tooth removal, pregnant women cut open, with bets on the sex of the unborn child. It was both pitiful and indescribable. If Beaky was witness to these horrors, it was hardly surprising he saw us as a bunch of spoiled twats.

We left Singapore after a few days, having stayed in this smart hotel, and took the train up the Malaysian peninsula to Penang. It was largely boring with not much to see apart from oceans of rubber and banana plantations. This was the only leg of our journey we didn't fly. We stayed overnight in Penang, and caught the train to Bangkok the following day. This was our destination before our penultimate flight, to Honk Kong, and then home.

Bangkok

Both our train journeys seemed to take forever but we watched as the rubber plantations gave way to open countryside, eventually arriving at Bangkok central station. It was mid-afternoon and total chaos. Just as I remembered it. If anything, the chaos in this city was worse.

Hauling our luggage off and gathering ourselves together we made our way down this crowded dirty platform, and out into the sunlight. The Bangkok fumes hit me with force. Taxi drivers were everywhere, and all vying for our business. Again it was hot, humid, and sweat dripped off us, but we picked a taxi which looked like it had air conditioning, an old Merc. It did, and we sank into the thing with some relief. We now needed a hotel.

As ever with Bangkok it takes an age to get anywhere, and after about half an hour of solid traffic, which stop/start crawled, he found us a 'nice' place, or so he said. Before we disgorged our possessions, I went in to check accommodation availability. The reception was full of middle-aged men with eighteen-year-old Thai tarts on their laps. Under any other circumstance I might have been tempted. The Thai girls were gorgeous, though for the first time I realised what a ridiculous sight it was to see these sad old gits with them. Yes maybe I was becoming one of them, and it might have suited me, but didn't think the kids would approve, or Val either, so back into the taxi I went. We continued our battle with the traffic, and thirty minutes later found a better hotel. This was much more upmarket. Our budget was by now getting thin, but to hell with it. We decided to stay. It had a pool on the roof, ten storeys up, and we could at least try to escape the fumes up there above the streets. We had one room for the four of us, which was spacious and agreeable, and on the ninth floor was a massage parlour. Right up my street.

You'll perhaps recall the last time was in Bangkok. Fifteen years on, the hotels are now cashing in on sex tourism. There was more naivety back then in 1976 when most of the girls had been sent by their families to Bangkok to earn money. And they did in the only way they knew how. The hostels they were sent to were run by a mama-san, matrons who kept an eye on the to-ing and fro-ing of their girls, As I mentioned before, the influx of young women from the countryside were there to service the American troops who used Thailand as a base for R&R whilst taking a break from their insane war in Vietnam. When the USA eventually beat a hasty retreat from Vietnam in 1974, the forces went home in ignominy and humiliation. This then left a huge surplus of women behind, all desperate for the dollars, and all targeting gullible Western men. It was a playground, and now an industry. Not wanting to miss out, the hotels were now cashing in on it.

The ninth floor of this hotel was devoid of accommodation and given up almost entirely to the 'parlour'. We checked into a room on the fifth floor, but I went up to the 'parlour' for a sneak preview.

The big rooms were sectioned into cubicles, and it was full of lovely-looking Thai women, most wearing doctor/nurse-type white coats. This was a massage parlour on a grand scale. I've always booked a massage, especially when I've been travelling, but this was unlike anything I'd seen before. These small curtained cubicles had occupants, and I could hear moans and groans emanating here and there. I promptly booked a massage for later that day.

The Thai girl assigned to me was gorgeous. She wore killer high heels. Under her white coat were stockings, and not much else. Probably about twenty-five, and very pretty. Thai girls have the most beautiful olive velvet skin and lustrous black hair. I definitely have a weakness for the breed (if you see what I mean!).

It was a good massage, and came with extras, needless to add. She asked if I would like her to come down to my room for the evening, so she could spend more time with me. She had in mind several hours. It was tempting, but I declined her offer. I didn't think it would go down too well with my wife and two small children.

Bangkok hadn't really changed much. Still choked with fumes and traffic, still had street food vendors, and still had the usual bars, and strip joints. I think the children sort of enjoyed it, and saw sights I wouldn't especially have wanted them to see, but it's all part of an education. Their teachers back home would have been horrified.

Hong Kong

On 1st September 1991 we flew out of Bangkok and onwards to Hong Kong. Our last destination before home.

I don't usually remember the names of hotels, but Val had developed a knack of going to the notice boards to check accommodation availability, and found the Omni Prince Hotel. It was just about affordable for us, and going through some major renovations. With bowed apologies for the mess, the receptionist promptly upgraded us to a presidential suite at no additional charge. This room was colossal, like a two-bed flat. A huge double bed, and two singles in a side room. Slippers, dressing gowns, exotic shampoos and body lotions, it had the lot. Including a well-stocked mini bar, with exotic prices to match. We were now seriously tight for cash, and literally down to our last few quid. I removed the entire mini bar contents, including chocolate and nuts, put them to one side threatening the kids not to touch any of it. Down to the street we went, to an 8-till-late shop. In two carrier bags we stocked up with soft drinks and wine for a fraction of the mini bar price, and took this lot back to our room. By the time I got back Oliver had discovered room service, and was on the point of ordering something. I soon put a stop to that. We took the phone away from his bedside. This was by now a shoestring budget.

Like Bangkok, Hong Kong hadn't changed much. We saw and did the usual things, wandering round, and going down to the Kowloon ferry, and I can't quite recall, but possibly the Tiger Balm Gardens too (I'm still a big fan of the stuff today). Now virtually out of money, my Visa card had taken a battering over six months. When I tried to explain that there was no point in us trying to draw money down from a cashpoint, Ollie just couldn't understand it. Why didn't I just use my 'Craddock' card like I always did?

I recall speaking to someone about the runway at the airport, which was allegedly the shortest international runway in the world. I had noticed, as we flew in at night, and as I had years before en route from Australia, all the skyscrapers, with apartments lit up, were above us as we descended. I discovered also that if a 747 didn't get the lift-off exactly right, weighed down with fuel and people, it would simply tip over the edge of the runway into the sea. Not for the faint-hearted, and certainly a white-knuckle ride. I wished I'd never asked whichever smartarse it was. A little bit of knowledge is definitely a dangerous thing.

I believe nowadays the airport has now been modified and the runway extended into the sea to make it much safer. Might be worth wearing a mask and snorkel on board. Just in case.

The journey home from Hong Kong took fourteen hours. The kids embraced it and were brilliant. By now both Oliver and Jo were experienced travellers, who were able to hold their own in adult conversation, both colourblind, and accepting of any race or religion. If I'm proud of one thing in my life, especially as a father, it's this trip. The added bonus of course is that I got to spend more or less twenty-four hours a day for six months with two children, who were of an age where their character formation is perhaps most important.

Home

In September 1991 we returned home to find, depressingly, that the recession was still very much on. I half thought we might have escaped the worst of it. Not so.

We unlocked and un-boarded the house, all still intact. We retrieved Lulu, my wonderful Clumber cross Springer spaniel, and Dinah, her black and white daughter, and eventually the chickens, which we'd farmed out to my gamekeeper friend. The dogs, having gone to different 'homes', were delighted to see each other again as much as we were delighted to have them back. Within a matter of days everything was back to 'normal'. The children put on their school uniforms, and by my forty-third birthday on the 8th of September returned to the classroom. They were the same kids, they looked the part, but fundamentally they had experienced an adventure which by definition made them very different from their classmates.

As for me, I had no idea what I was heading into in 1992. As it turned out, it wasn't good.

Chapter 18

As I said, I rather naively assumed the recession of 1990/91 would be over when we got back. I still had the properties, albeit mortgaged up to the hilt, and my 50% stake in the business in Wigan, which was, as far as I was aware, running smoothly. The new UK-wide dealer I'd appointed was running the sales team. Frankly I was no longer needed, and now in need of a fresh challenge, especially after six months abroad. The kids settled back at school, Val resumed her mumsy duties, and took on childminding as a 'career'.

The general economic outlook was bleak, the banks were, as they do, clamping down on excess borrowing, having encouraged massive borrowing in the 80s. The expression that the banks lend you an umbrella when the weather is fine, and want it back when it starts raining was never more apt.

A boat sales business in Tewkesbury, run by a couple of friends of ours, had gone bust. No one wanted boats, they were a luxury. All were too busy battening down their hatches at home. These friends were fairly desperate to find another source of income and in some serious financial shit. They suggested to me a joint river trip business as a collaborative project. Tea and scone trips up and down the River Avon from Tewkesbury. It would generate cash, which is what we all needed. You can't eat bricks and mortar. Then I thought why not evening 'carnivore' cruises too, steaks and salad trips in the evening, as I'd experienced by our trip on the *Whitsunday Dreamer* months before in Australia. I saw myself as that irreverent skipper who couldn't give a shit about health and safety. Primarily it would be a summer business, but an instant source of cash.

I still had a little bit of capital left over, which was 'urgent' money, and never earmarked to be spent on our trip. I've always liked to keep some of my powder dry just in case. This attitude has stood me in good stead over the years and is probably a legacy from my Grandma Craddock, who would always tell me to put some of my pocket money away for the proverbial 'rainy day'. This was now a rainy few months.

We got through the remaining few months of 1991, and in spring 1992 we went into business with the *Pride of Avon*. A 65 ft, 66-seater, 20-ton river trip boat, designed by the owner in Bristol, and built along the lines of an Amsterdam water bus. It cost £47K, and he was struggling to sell it, so I put £10k in as a deposit, and arranged a private mortgage with the owner. This would be paid annually from the income. The banks wouldn't even look at the possibility of lending against it.

Deal done, we brought it up the Sharpness Canal, parking it on moorings in the centre of Tewkesbury. I then had to learn to drive what was ostensibly a super-long barge, having passed my test with a miserable jobsworth from the Marine and Coastal Agency. The business took off just in time for summer. I handled the sales, marketing, and promotion, Val oversaw the catering, and the other two had control of the operational side of the business. Except that suddenly our two partners were facing criminal charges for fraud in the original boat business.

This cast a shadow over the entire thing. I decided there and then to remove their involvement from the limited company and the equal partnership we had. I quickly discovered that the adverse publicity from his messy affairs made the success of the venture much harder and more difficult to promote. He was well known in Tewkesbury, and mutterings about how he had managed to afford this new venture were rife.

The long story short is that we didn't get on. Their mentality wasn't mine, and ultimately we fell out. In the end I walked away from it. I set up a lease for them to run it alone, as long as they paid their rent, and I was able to fulfil my obligations to the owner and repay the mortgage over time. This experience underlines the importance of being in control of your own assets. Partnerships ultimately don't work. As I was about to discover with the business in Wigan.

1993

By the end of 1992, having gone our separate ways with the boat business, the Wigan business ran into trouble.

Although I wasn't actively involved in managing it on a day-to-day basis, the UK dealer I'd originally appointed became ever slower in paying his bills. To add insult to injury, he'd also started an affair with Trudy, the woman I'd appointed as Sales Manager, and with whom I'd also had an affair off my own back in the mid-1980s. Before I left on our world trip, she and I had a clandestine meeting. I had entrusted her to act as my lookout, to keep tabs as it were, whilst I was away. I was now faced with disloyalty on two fronts, three if you include the machinations of the boat people.

This UK dealer, I now discovered, owed us a substantial amount of money, something in the region of £78k, I recollect. We tried for meetings, and threats to stop supplies, but the horse had bolted. In late 1993 this crook declared himself personally bankrupt. It was a massive bad debt. In short we were stuffed. The bank wouldn't extend our overdraft, despite the company's underlying profitability, at least not without substantial guarantees. The Inland Revenue, ever unhelpful, then proceeded to start insolvency proceedings, and took us to court for non-payment of the VAT. This was an action for VAT owed on the debt we couldn't recover. No matter how hard we tried to get through to the Revenue to explain, it was useless. We had a cash flow problem of epic proportions, and this alone forced a perfectly profitable company into liquidation.

Even writing about this in 2020 still stirs a visceral hatred within me, and which I've never truly been able to shed. The stress and pressure on me became intolerable. When I investigated this guy's affairs, which is something frankly I should have done in the first place, I then discovered, through this crook's insolvency administrators, an astonishing trick. He had carefully loaded his pension fund with our money, by paying himself an extraordinary salary. Pensions in those days couldn't be touched for bankruptcy purposes. They can now, I'm pleased say, and this loophole is now closed. This clever and illicit trick enabled him to move our cash to a place where no one could touch it legally. It was theft, pure and simple.

I thought at the time that had I been able to kill him and get away with it, I would have done so. Everything I had worked so hard for over the past thirteen to fourteen years was now threatened.

The bank called in my guarantees of £20k, then carried out a distress valuation on all my assets, including our house, as well as my interest in the boat business. All the valuations were rock-bottom, needless to say. We were still at the bottom of the recessionary trench. I was now faced with ruin. I had built up an asset base over ten to twelve years and was now in serious danger of losing the lot. Neither could I bear the thought of having to start again from scratch.

I needed some time to plan my way out of this mess and turned first to finding another company who could take on what was still very much a profitable and successful product.

I then managed to temporarily rent the unit in Wigan, much against my solicitors wishes, and successfully sold this 1,500 sq foot unit a few months later. One down and a few to go. My negotiations with other companies to take on the product from the ashes of this business were still ongoing. The product was still very much in demand. In the end my dad and brother Martin came up trumps. I sold the whole thing out on a 'knowhow' agreement, and provided the finished product to Lincat, a catering equipment manufacturing business which they ran in Lincoln. They seamlessly put it into their product range and made a success of it. I was paid a commission on each one sold. That source of income enabled me to get the bank off my back, who were clamouring for their £20k guarantee to be paid. I eventually paid them off over three years. I'd managed by this time to negotiate a discount of 50%. They settled for £10k, so in dribs and drabs I managed to pay them off. Eventually I came out of this whole mess clean, with my integrity and credibility intact. I still had no idea though of exactly which direction I was going. I'd saved my house though, and retained my still heavily mortgaged properties.

I'd been through the mill of stress once before of course, back in 1987, when I had to employ unorthodox means to recover my restaurant in Cheltenham. As if to pay me back for taking six months off on a jolly round the world with my family, some shit god or other was now once again kicking me in the bollocks and putting me through it all over again five years later. Frankly I was struggling to survive. I'd like to say my wife Val was right there beside me through all this, but she seemed oblivious to it all. If I was to point to one single thing which put the final nail in my marriage coffin it was this. She had her head in the sand, concerned more by her social standing in the community, and the kids' schooling. Important as those things might have been, they didn't come close to ensuring we kept a roof over our heads. If ever there was a case of fiddling while Rome burned, this was it. We had very nearly lost the house, and now I finally realised that despite my previous marriages (plural, because my life with Meg was a marriage in all but paperwork), this particular marriage was over. I needed a fighter alongside me, someone to roll up their sleeves and get stuck in.

Everything heads back to the ground. It begins to decay from the moment it arrives, however imperceptible that decay is. From the moment a person is born they are ineluctably destined to head back to whence they came. Actually strictly speaking that's not quite true, is it? Ultimately it's back to the soil we go, or rust in the case of a car. Everything attempts to destroy itself and all head back to its original constituent parts. A universal law of nature, I suppose, all to be reabsorbed.

Since the law of decay is undeniable, the same went for my marriage. This though was more of a slow decline into indifference. Which in some ways is worse. Death by a thousand cuts rather than a clean break. Frankly the children were the glue which held us together. This was something I hadn't experienced with either of my (previous) marriages. It was new territory for me. I tried to work harder at it, or so I thought, but our aims and goals were hopelessly out of sync, as was our chemistry, or perhaps communication. There was no instinctiveness, no togetherness, like I'd experienced with Meg. I guess Val didn't match up to her in the way I wanted, and no doubt I didn't match up to her ideal either. I didn't realise this was an unfixable problem, and denied it to myself. Put more simply, I was fighting against this natural law of decline.

I've often wondered to myself why I struggled against the odds. Maybe I felt this was third time lucky, and if I didn't succeed with this I was a hopelessly useless marriage case. Which was probably true. I don't really know, but someone once said to me that I was the most unmarried married man they'd ever met. Maybe they could see the things I couldn't. I did my damnedest to make changes. Eventually I realised I was I, and she was she, and nothing would really change. You can try to make it all work for a while, but eventually, inexorably, things slide back to the way they are. Another universal truth. Once again I found myself becoming over critical. She had no interest in poetry, art, and music. Anything which might give her a sense of purpose. An identity even. The fundamental problem wasn't so much that she didn't share my thoughts, ambitions and interests, I can accept that, but she seemed to have none of her own. She seemed to pin the responsibility for her own happiness and self-esteem entirely on me. It's not an easy responsibility to shoulder either and thus if she wasn't happy, it effectively became my fault. It was a kind of emotional blackmail. Try as I might to encourage some independence, some alternative pursuit, nothing happened. My wife was a great mum, honest and loyal as a person, great qualities, but as a wife? Not really my idea of a great partner for the rest of my life, and I think she probably felt the same about me. I had to bide my time though. I had responsibilities, and old-fashioned though it may be, I'd made a bed in which I now had to lie. For me the most important factor of all was to see my children into adulthood.

From a business point of view, the economy was gradually getting back to something like normal. Interest rates were falling quickly in an effort to stimulate the economy, so the loans and mortgages cost less, the income stream from property rents therefore widened.

I toyed for a while with a pub business locally, and taken it on to turn it into a fish and chip emporium. That was the menu. Fresh fried fish and chips, well mushy peas too, but that was the concept. I employed a friend and his wife to run it. My idea had been to link the coach trips we got for the boat business in Tewkesbury to the pub business, providing fish and chip suppers for their return journey. It took off, and started to become quite successful, but the friend who managed the place was rather dominated by his wife. She hated the place and since she was studying to become a teacher, running a glorified chip shop wasn't her idea of career direction. It simply never gelled. After six months I abandoned the project and gave the tenancy back to the brewery.

Here's a little side story. Haven't had one for a while, eh?

Around this time my brother Martin had moved down to Banbury from Lincoln to run a factory his company had bought as part of its group expansion. He moved primarily to get away from the unblinking scrutiny of our dad, and frankly I didn't blame him. At some point my wife Val, in her role with the local school as head of their parent–teacher association, was asked to stage an American-themed musical evening. I asked my brother Martin if he'd like to get involved, which he did.

303

I said earlier that I resolved to play the banjo, partly inspired by bluegrass music in the USA, and partly because it reminded me of my old metal one I got from a toyshop when I was about eight. I eventually found a good one and bought it. I couldn't even tune it, let alone understand quite how the fifth string was plucked. At the time it was hugely expensive for me (£400). I worked on the basis that if it was expensive it would force me to learn and discipline myself, otherwise the money would be wasted. Thus I began to learn fingerpicking bluegrass style with this thing. Although I played guitar, banjo was an uphill struggle. I found with age that learning a new instrument becomes ever harder, but bit by bit with the help of tutorial books and tapes I began to get the hang of it.

Martin and I were always musically inclined, he more so than I, but nevertheless I persisted with this instrument, having been inspired by the US leg of our trip, and then on my doorstep in Cheltenham I discovered Bill Zorn, who was originally from Arizona. I'd seen him play in Cheltenham with his band, and he was an incredible banjo player. I located him and persuaded him to give me lessons. Nice guy that he is, he agreed and we got to know each other well. After a few months of occasional tuition I asked him if he would help out with the musical event Val was planning. I was honoured when he said he would. This American evening was predominantly country style music. The venue was a barn, the stage the back of a trailer complete with a few hay bales. Very down-home hoedown stuff.

Mart and I hadn't played together in public since our teenage years. To say we were rusty and nervous was an understatement, but the genial Bill gave us encouragement. Val and I, in an effort to do something together, had also become involved with a new social group in Malvern, and we took up ballroom dancing. I was crap at it, but the guy I'd met who had introduced us wasn't a bad drummer. Initially I thought I might ask him to accompany us for the musical event, but one of the women who worked in Mart's office in Banbury had a husband who was mad keen on drums. He'd never played live, but then neither had Mart or I for at least twenty-five years. In the event we asked him to come over with a scaled-down drum kit, and nervously he agreed. We fixed up a couple of practices, just the three of us, and chose a few songs we hoped we could get away with. Mart dug out his old Fender and amp, I had my banjo, and an acoustic guitar, and this guy with his drums.

On the night we did the three or four songs which we'd practised, but Bill Zorn was undoubtedly the star of the show, along with a mate of his. They were quite well established on the pub and folksy circuit. The new drummer, Greavsie, enjoyed the experience, despite sinking three or four pints of lager before he played to control his nerves. I was more concerned with the possibility of him getting so pissed he wouldn't be able to keep time, but he did, and our three- or four-song slot, mostly Beatles stuff, went down well with the audience.

Both Mart and I played guitar, combined joint vocals, and Greavsie did a decent job on his kit. The experienced Bill must have seen something in this little trio of ours, and took me aside later and suggested we form a fully fledged rock band.

As it turned out, Greavsie had a work colleague who was a good lead guitarist in the vein of Chuck Berry and Keith Richards, taciturn, humorous, and pernickety over chord sequences, just like my brother. Russell was keen to get involved, and he in turn brought his old school friend Darren, an exceptional bass player. Suddenly we had a five-piece band.

We practised together for the first time at Mart's house in Ratley with a few of the songs we all liked. I had by now taken on the role of lead vocals, the others having persuaded me we had enough guitarists. It was a nice polite way of saying I was crap. My main problem is remembering to change chords when I'm singing. I can remember the words to thirty rock songs without having to look at them, but damned if I remember to move the chord shape in good time. In effect I'd always be a fraction of a second behind the others. In many ways, for me anyway, it's a bit like rubbing your tummy and patting your head. Mart has the reverse problem. He can remember and find the chords OK but can't remember lyrics. In some ways we complemented each other. Once I stopped hiding behind the guitar I gained more and more confidence in revving up the crowd.

At one of our very early practices, with me busting a gut singing 'Twist and Shout', I suddenly thought to myself, 'Y'know what? This isn't a bad little band.' There was a definite chemistry between us which was hard to define. I suspect it was mostly our sarcastic sense of humour, but it worked, and surprisingly we gelled quite well. In between laughing our socks off. In many ways the practices were more fun than the gigs, but we developed quite a following over the years. So was born the infamous Ratley Snakes.

1994–7

This period of my life is a bit blurred, and I'll tell you why in a minute. I know I've put in a three- to four-year period here, but a lot of it was mixed up with the boat business, which I still worked on occasionally. I did the Saturday-night steak barbecues mostly, and as a business it was doing OK, but still essentially a summer operation. Despite a tricky start, our relationship with the people I'd leased the boat to was cordial. The tenants were paying their rents, and I needed something to do, partly because I was bored.

So I embarked on another affair.

This came about primarily through the music scene. The Ratley Snakes were playing fairly regularly, and I knew some people from Malvern who were also involved with the music scene there. She was amongst this lot.

She was married, and I had enough experience to spot the signs. She was also in a state of boredom. A full-time hairdresser, but loved music, especially teaching ballroom dancing in her spare time. I went along to some of her evening classes a few times for a laff. Small, blonde, perfectly formed and good-looking. Her best friend, it turned out, was also having an affair with some guy in Cheltenham I knew vaguely. Maybe she felt she was missing out.

Both women were in their mid-forties and fitted the profile I alluded to earlier. Both well off with indifferent husbands, time on their hands, children off their hands. Both needed one final throw of the dice, both read *Hello* and *OK* mags, wanted some excitement, some fling, some reassurance that romance wasn't dead, and that perhaps their looks weren't fading. It's a familiar story. I'm not sure if I targeted her, or vice versa, but the inevitable happened, except that this one got her claws into me.

The mobile phone was now becoming the must-have accessory. In the early 90s I'd had one about the size of a brick. I realised how much freedom I'd suddenly got. I didn't need to be stuck in a bloody office any more. By 1994 texting had arrived but was still in its infancy, and it took me a while to learn it. Now though there was no escape from the damn thing. It became addictive. Just witness what's happened in the thirty years since its invention. Conversation has died. These days the kids are glued to the bloody things. In 1994 my new Nokia 6310 was about half a brick. Today they're like a wafer. Ms A, as I shall refer to her from now on, had also discovered texting. She bombarded me with them, all day, and sometimes at night. Flattering to begin with, but then became and irritant.

I must use that crass phrase once more, because Ms A was undoubtedly gagging for it. My belief was she'd been starved of affection, sex, physical intimacy. By all accounts her husband preferred the pub and his mates. This isn't at all uncommon. My experiences in Thailand had stood me in good stead. I was fairly accomplished at finding my way around a woman's body and knew exactly which buttons to press. This may sound like a boast, but it's the truth.

In fact I'd had a number of flings and one-night stands since my original trip to Australia in 1976, many of them with married women, and time after time I was told what unimaginative bores their spouses had become. I've never slept with a man, so don't expect me to confirm any of this, but I've laid back on many a pillow afterwards, having completed my task, fag in hand, and listened to various women criticise their husbands mercilessly. Mostly it seems to be indifference which is to blame. I said earlier, there is a huge difference between men's perceptions of sex as a shag, and women's perceptions of true love. In my case it was the former. However, I cocked this one up. Excuse that expression, no pun intended. Instead of allowing this fling to fizzle out, I found myself saying 'yes' to her instead of 'maybe', and 'maybe' instead of 'no'. She was very manipulative, and I was too weak. I'd put my head in a noose this time, and over three years it tightened on me. I was being led by my dick, not my head. Not for the first time either, I'm sure you'll agree. For my part it was unadulterated lust. She just fell in love and wanted permanency.

The bottom line is that if you intend to leave your wife/ husband it has to be for something better. I certainly didn't view Ms A as that. Besides, I was a relatively old father at forty-six with children of ten and twelve, and I intended to fulfil my responsibilities. As I alluded to earlier, I was very old-fashioned in that respect. A deal is a deal.

The fact that both my wife and Ms A's husband suspected something was going on is almost beside the point. I believe both knew, but in some ways were in denial.

I can't quite remember who said it, but some famous actor declared that getting women isn't a problem. Getting rid of them is. Ms A was a case in point. The whole thing was getting out of control. No it wasn't. It *was* totally out of control.

Ms A hounded me with texts and calls, and became more and more demanding. I took her to France a couple of times, and various other places, and she was lively, informed and generally interesting company, but she constantly pressured me in wanting to know when we were going to take off and live together. I ducked, dived, and lied and lied. It was shameful. Somehow I had to break this circle of which I was the architect. Well that's not strictly true, she was a bit of an architectress too. As always in these situations I needed some form of escape. Quite what and how I wasn't sure.

I'd always harboured something of a desire to get into the fishing tackle business. I put an ad in an angling magazine, and surprisingly got a few replies. One was a small Bedfordshire float manufacturing company, and in 1996, after some meetings and negotiation, I took a small share in it. This turned out to be a huge mistake.

Side story! Well, more of a business lesson really

Image Angling was a small business set-up in a unit just off the M1 Bedford. They predominantly made floats and other stuff for competition fishing. It was a subject I really knew nothing about. Pike-fishing yes, but competition fishing? I couldn't see the point.

Nevertheless, the two guys who started it were essentially well-known match anglers, One was the sales side, the other had manufacturing expertise, and they were not only good mates, but built this little business out of nothing. By the time I got involved they were employing half a dozen people. The problem, as far as I could see, was the guy they'd brought in to manage it. He was a delusional and secretive individual, and one of the most self-important people I had ever met. He was about my age, forty-six, computer-literate, which I wasn't, and repeatedly hid information on the system, denying to us the true state of the business.

The two original backers who had put money in originally to kick-start it had literally backed out. They sat on their shares. 40% of the business was owned by them, and trying to grow it only enriched them. I suspect that's why they wanted to involve me, to try to either buy them out or remove them. This MD spent most of his time trying to outmanoeuvre them. He held big meetings in London with high powered lawyers, who followed up with big fees which the business could ill afford. He was obsessed with their removal and eradicating their involvement. Somewhere down the line, and unsurprisingly, he'd pissed off these two money men, so they'd walked.

My role was to look at the market and try to expand the business, but the machinations of removing the 'cuckoos', as it were, became all too consuming, and this MD's secretiveness was such that he controlled all the passwords for the computer. None of the office staff had a clue about the administration of the business and its true financial state. Me included. I should have been more diligent.

How the bank continued to support the company was a mystery. I should have perhaps forced the issue, but in my haste to geographically distance myself from Ms A, I just seized the opportunity to do something different, away from the area, and in effect was in denial about the state of this business.

I stayed over in Bedford a couple of times a week, but after a few months the two directors asked me to get rid of this MD, since neither of them could stand him and neither could I. They hadn't got the wherewithal to sack him. So that's what I did.

I forced his resignation (in a hotel lobby in Leamington Spa) with the help of a legal business colleague I knew. I'd met him when I planned to go into a retail business with a mate of mine. We didn't in the end, and in fact it was around the time I was planning in 1987 to set up the catering equipment business in Wigan. It's a good idea to stick to what you know. Besides, my good friend's business philosophy wasn't mine. I prefer to grow a business organically from profit, whereas his view was to borrow gargantuan sums of money and open a chain of shops. He borrowed heavily, until interest rates hit 15% in 1990, and predictably it all came crashing down. The cash flow of the business simply couldn't sustain the repayments. It was around this time I met this legal guy. He knew his way around company law, so I introduced him to my big-spending mate, who was by now facing personal bankruptcy. He helped him avoid it.

This is a lesson in not going into business with a mate. You can make a mate out of a business friendship, but it doesn't work the other way round. Partnerships are OK as long as both are in agreement, but time plays its tricks, priorities change, and sooner or later the relationship falters and ends in recrimination. With it of course usually goes the loss of a good friend.

It was now I enlisted Legal Eagle's help to remove this idiot from the fishing tackle business.

It proved to be quite a coup, a sting really. I'd arranged for the two other directors to come over and wait in the hotel car park for exactly ten minutes, then to walk in and join the meeting. Mr Legal Eagle and I then presented the rogue MD with an ultimatum to resign. We just had enough shares between myself and the other two directors to vote him out. Foolishly he believed those two were on his side, until they walked into the hotel lobby after exactly the ten minutes we'd agreed. They never said a word, but nodded with my decision to oust him. He left in an embarrassed rage. We bought him out at share cost, and only then did he give up the passwords to the computer. With the help of one of the staff we accessed it, and I ended up over there in Bedford more or less full time. This proved to be virtually another year out of my life. And still the texts poured in over in Worcestershire from Ms A.

When I got to the bottom of the accounts, I found the business was bust. The valuations which had been put on some of the stock were laughable. On the balance sheet it all looked good. The reality was that most of it was junk and unsaleable. This guy had deliberately inflated the value for the books, and the bank. The business was insolvent. It took me three months to find a buyer for the brand, which was about the only thing of value since the name was well respected. In the end I broke it up and walked away. The Sales Director became a freelance sales agent, the other one went over to live in Denmark, participating in fishing competitions professionally. I somehow wriggled the business out of the terms of its lease, squared things with the bank, and the original two outside shareholders ended up with nothing, as did I. As for the rogue MD, I have no idea. I never saw him again.

As I said above, the primary reason for becoming involved with this business was to attempt to distance myself from a very demanding mistress, who continued constantly to profess her love for me, and demanded more and more of my time (and body). As always with affairs, they are exciting because they are illicit and secretive, but despite disinterest in my own marriage, I found myself being backed more and more into a corner by her. Her husband, with whom she was still living, was clearly suspicious. It's hard to believe now, but this affair lasted for about three years, until she eventually moved out of the marital home. But this was in the future.

The result of my inability to be stronger with her meant that I hadn't been anywhere near firm enough in making my position clear. To this day I don't know how I was manipulated like this. The bottom line was that I wasn't intending to leave or go anywhere. She really believed we would eventually run away together. I didn't, apart from one occasion where I almost deluded myself into thinking we could live in my caravan in France. It was really and truly a ridiculous idea.

The fact was I didn't love her, she was fit and funny, and I liked that, but as always, affairs provide a percentage of whatever was missing from the marriage. I was getting 100% more or less, but from two different women. For me it was fun and a diversion from the more mundane aspects of life. For her I suspect she saw it as a way out of a stale marriage and a new life ahead. As I said earlier, there's a world of difference between the occasional shag and a full-blown relationship.

Side Story. I know I've just done one, but this isn't a business one

Sometime earlier, around 1993 and a year or two before Ms A made her appearance in my life, my pike-fishing mate Zolly was made redundant. Irreverent as ever, he felt he needed a blow out to celebrate. (He subsequently went on the dole and played the system for the rest of his life.)

We booked a couple of rooms at the Marine Hotel in Criccieth. It was summer, it was hot, and we just decided to take off to do a bit of sea-fishing. I knew both the hotel and the town like the back of my hand, and many of the locals too. It was his treat. He knew I'd been through the mill quite a bit sorting out the business in Wigan, so it was a kind gesture. I had assets but very little money spare. Asset-rich, cash-poor. A familiar story.

We travelled up to N Wales, fished from the beach, and discovered the mackerel were in. To get at them properly we needed a boat. That night in the bar we befriended a local who had one and for a small fee offered to take us out the following day. We ate at the hotel, and went back to the bar. By 11 pm I was pissed. I couldn't hold a candle to him when it came to alcohol consumption. We played pool (badly) until eventually about midnight we noticed all the locals had gone. The owner said we could finish our game, and off he went to bed. We carried on playing with as many 20p coins as we could muster. Apart from us, the bar was totally deserted. Halfway through a shot Zolly squinted at me, and remarked that they'd left a whole bar to ourselves. And so they had. It was unlocked.

For an hour afterwards we helped ourselves. I have no idea what or how much we helped ourselves to, but by this time we were legless, and falling around the place. He suddenly went from relative sobriety to slumping over in the corner, completely arseholed. I however was sobering up. It was possibly 1.30 am by now. I smacked him round the face once or twice, and poured a glass of water over him. We needed to get out of there and off to bed. Assuming I could find the way out. If we were fishing later that same morning we needed to be awake and alert. Given our state I counted that as a remote possibility. I dragged him to his feet and somehow got him on to my back. His feet trailed limply behind me as I hauled him towards reception. Somehow I had to get the bastard up the stairs. He was certainly no lightweight. Just as I was about to embark on this Herculean task I heard a tap running in the bar area. I dropped him on the floor, and smacked him again in an effort to rouse him. He sort of came round and I had to keep shushing him. Funny how you shout a lot when you've had a few. We managed to stagger back to the bar, and I had to look several times to take in the scene. The whole lounge area was awash with beer. I must have left a beer tap on, or Zolly had, but recrimination was pointless. How long it had been running I've no idea, but gallons of the stuff was all over the floor, soaking into the carpet, and running in a river under the barstools.

We vainly tried to mop it up with beer towels, crawling around on our hands and knees, but it was way too late for that. Eventually he muttered 'fuck it' and promptly slid into a beer-soaked heap propped up against the bar. Once again I got him on to my back, and dragged him to the foot of the stairway. I have no idea how long it took to make those stairs. Possibly ten minutes with him grunting and groaning. I made it to the top face first where the landing meets the stairs, and saw a pair of slippers with feet in them. As I followed these feet with my eyes up the pyjama-clad legs, there was a dressing gown and the owner of the hotel was wearing it. Despite my inebriation I could tell he was seriously pissed off with us. He made it clear he would 'sort this out in the morning'. How I managed to get Zolly to his room I have no idea. I just dumped him in there. When I made it to mine I didn't bother getting undressed. I just lay down with the room spinning. It must have been about 3 am, I don't know, but I had serious doubts about the fishing trip.

I must have slept, and somehow made it downstairs to breakfast. All the tables round the edges were occupied with guests so I had no choice but to sit in the centre of the room. They stared at me wordlessly, with a few mutterings, and I had nowhere to shrink into. Of Zolly there was no sign, despite me banging on his door.

I gratefully accepted a pot of tea from a flinty-eyed waitress, when suddenly there was a crash, and Zolly appeared still in his beer-soaked clothes. Always short-sighted and without his glasses, the door he'd flung open crashed against the breakfast trolley. All the juices on it in the jugs shook and almost toppled over. He hung on the door frame for a second or two, staring myopically, then recognised me sitting in the centre of the room with my cornflakes. My instinct was to say fuck off, I don't know you, and bury my face in the cereal, but it was too late. He tried to make his way across to my table, sideways like a crab, grabbing tables and chairs to hang on to as he tried to focus on me. There was by now even more tut-tutting from the guests. Eventually he made it, slumped down, and slurring his words asked me if I'd checked out yet. I said I hadn't. On his collision course down the stairs he'd evidently encountered the owner, who'd confronted him in reception. He admitted our crime, owned up to us helping ourselves, as he put it, 'to a few drinks' and offered him compensation. He gave him a fiver. I was gobsmacked, incredulous. We must have drunk our way through ten times that amount. To add insult to injury everyone in the place could smell the river of beer permeating the place. I reckon he'd need a new carpet at least. Besides, stale beer is not the most attractive of smells first thing in the morning. It can put you right off your breakfast.

We left the hotel with our tails very much between our legs and made the fishing trip in the boat, which leaked like mad and we had to bail constantly. By the end of that day we were knackered, and in between bailing slept for most of the time. We caught bugger-all and eventually went home, still semi-drunk, and bright red from sunburn.

I've put that little story in to give you an idea of this old college friend of mine.

Another Zolly side story

Fast forward now to 1995, a couple of years later. Zolly and I were back in Criccieth again, but we steered well clear of the Marine Hotel. We'd booked a small hotel on the seafront, Mor Heli, which was owned by an old friend of mine from the time we were in our teens when we lived up on the hill in tents. However, this time we had our own boat, which I'd parked up on the shingle beach round the corner from the castle. Once again the weather was fine, hot and sunny. We arrived on a Thursday evening, settled in and planned our fishing for the following day. After breakfast Zolly went to the car to sort our fishing gear, and I went up to my room to change.

As I came down the stairs to the hallway, two women appeared, having just arrived. One was blonde and slim, the other plump, attractive, with dark hair. I knew they were foreigners, but couldn't pinpoint their accents, despite their English vocabulary, which was excellent. They asked me if I had any rooms. I explained I wasn't the owner, and I'd get him to see them. They then suddenly asked me what my plans were. I have no idea why. I said we were out fishing all day. It turned out they were from Norway, Oslo to be precise, and worked for Shell Oil. Oslo, you may recall, I knew fairly well, having escaped from the Norwegian madman, and the Icelandic jumper scene. These two women, aged mid-thirties I guess, were on a two-week road trip round the UK. I was fascinated by it. They'd taken a ferry from Oslo to the East Scottish coast, Aberdeen I think, then driven to Edinburgh, Newcastle, and planned to make their way in skips and jumps down to the south coast, diverting to Wales on the way. Their plan was to get another ferry from Dover to Zeebrugge, up through Belgium, Holland, Denmark, Sweden, and back home. I was intrigued. It was a road trip I'd never considered.

They then invited me to bring any fish back to the beach, where they proposed to gut them and would light a fire to cook supper for us. I told Zolly, and he was all for it.

So out we went in our little boat, but struggled to find mackerel at first. Eventually we did, and we took the boat to the beach, delivering about a dozen fish to these two women, who were now sunbathing. The blonde bikini-clad one I noticed had a decent figure, but the chunky one covered herself with a shawl. That's yours Zolly, I thought. He and she had similarly matching figures. Then off we went back out to sea for more, having made arrangements to meet them at 8 pm on the beach.

We probably finished fishing about 6.30 pm and beached the

boat. We caught a few more mackerel, but Zolly wanted a pint or three first since he'd developed a thirst out on the boat, so off we went. Five pints later, we made our way to the rendezvous, and sure enough the girls had a fire going with driftwood, had cooked potatoes and asparagus, gutted the fish in the sea, I was impressed, and were busy grilling them. They also brought two bottles of wine, and we contributed with some of Zolly's gin and bitter lemon. He had a habit of mixing it all in one bottle.

The food was excellent, and by 10 pm it became chilly. Since the hotel was just on the Promenade behind us, we elected to congregate in my room. All three of them smoked roll-ups, with packs of tobacco – but not me. I'd given up – and the room was filled with smoke. My eyes stung so I opened the windows overlooking the sea, and gazed at the full moon, which had just risen. It's fair to say we were all pissed by now, and as it hit midnight, and having had a full day at sea I was knackered.

With difficulty I shooed them out of the room. Zolly's was just across the hall, the girls' room down on the first floor. I stripped, crashed into bed and had just turned off the light when there was a sudden knock at my door. I said come in, and there outlined in the hallway light was the blonde. She claimed she'd left her pack of tobacco behind in my room. Groggily, I got up on one elbow and started to look for it in the bed covers, when suddenly she jumped on me and started kissing me fiercely and frantically. In my state it took some time to realise the tobacco was an excuse. The next minute I was instinctively tugging her jeans down. She wore nothing underneath her tee shirt or jeans. I groaned inwardly and thought, 'think of England'. And that's exactly what I did. How I managed to satisfy this Nordic blonde I don't know, but she was hot and very accomplished. After half an hour she was gone. Whether or not she retrieved her tobacco I have no idea, but I slept dreamlessly.

When I awoke, I thought for a second it had all been a dream, but a few blonde stray pubic hairs served as a reminder. I wondered whether the chunky one had gone to Zolly's room and done the same, but it turned out she hadn't.

He and I were first down to breakfast when they appeared. I'd said nothing to him up to that point about the events the previous night. They sat down at a neighbouring table, and as he cut up his bacon, he stared at the blonde one, who admittedly did look a bit dishevelled, and said 'G'day, hope you don't mind me saying, but you look a bit shagged out.' I kicked him under the table, gave him a look, and no more was said. I filled him in later.

We left them sitting there to go fishing once more, thanked them for their company, and the blonde one winked at me as we left. They moved on that day, never to be seen again.

And that is what I mean about chance encounters and occasional shags.

1996

In the 1990s interest rates dropped like a proverbial stone. Oddly I didn't really take any notice to begin with. The country was still trying to come to terms with the recession, but it was nothing short of an interest rate crash. Even today in 2020 rates on savings accounts are miniscule. It's hard to believe they were hitting 14-15% only a few short years before, but I suddenly found I was able to provide for more or less all our family needs from the property income, so I devoted my time to managing them more effectively. Now I'd sold off the Wigan business, cleared the decks with the fishing tackle business in Bedford, I found I had a steady but fluctuating income. I occasionally worked on the boat to help out with the steak cruises, but wasn't involved day to day any more, despite owning and renting it.

There was always something which needed to be done with the properties though, but by and large I found myself with a huge amount of freedom, and as I said earlier the mobile phone was the key to it. Life had changed dramatically. Who needs an office to be bound to?

I'd seriously underestimated that instrument. At last, I didn't have to be in one place. I could go anywhere, and any property problem which arose could be resolved from wherever I happened to be.

It was usually North Wales, where my parents had by then bought a property on the seafront in Criccieth, the small town on the coast where I'd spent a good deal of my childhood, and of course more latterly my adventures with Zolly. I twiddled my thumbs mostly or went fishing, and ducked and dived from Ms A's clutches.

From an early age I was always interested in trees. There's something ineffably peaceful about them. It's a bit like being out on the sea, nothing but waves and wind. I decided to buy a small wood and do a bit of woodland management, and enhance it where I could for the wildlife. The Forestry Commission was selling off small unmanageable plots, and this one was just down the road in Llanystumdwy. My dad had bought one also not much further away, near Bryncir, so by way of a change I immersed myself in woodland management. My dad had inspired me to some degree, since he'd bought 250 acres of heathland and a decrepit farm in Aberdeenshire. Miles away, and a nine-hour drive. This farmland was rough ground, mainly had sheep on it, and with grants it was planted up for forestry.

I don't know the hows and whys, but eventually the house in Criccieth and the woodlands in Wales and Scotland would be made over to me for inheritance tax purposes. The house in Criccieth needed some serious expense and renovation. In order to achieve this I sold off the timber from the two woods in Wales, mostly Sitka spruce and Douglas fir which had reached their sell-by dates, and used the cash (after agency and harvesting expenses around £30k) to renovate the house, but this was a year or so away, but I enjoyed the organising of it all, and was able to base myself largely on the coast, which I loved.

Ms A was still in my life, she in Worcestershire, me hiding up in Wales. She didn't share my love for the sea or the countryside, but I took her up to the house in Criccieth occasionally.

The band, though, back in Warwickshire, went from strength to strength too. The Ratley Snakes played regularly, sometimes once a fortnight, but often once a month and we developed something of a following locally. I really enjoyed the camaraderie. Musicians tend to develop an affinity with one another. I can understand how The Beatles became such a tight unit sharing so much of their time together in the early days. With the Snakes we almost became a closed shop to others, a kind of family of sorts, but for me the best thing of all was our shared sense of humour. We developed an instinctive communication on stage, where we all shared this humour, not that the audience would notice or be included.

1997

By now I was dodging between my family home in Corse Lawn, my house in North Wales, and my caravans in France, occasionally taking my increasingly demanding mistress to the latter two. It was madness, and I found myself going round in ever decreasing circles. You would have thought by now I'd learned my lesson.

But first: A side story, en Francais!

When I bought the old mill in France some ten years earlier (1987) and then realised the amount of money required to renovate it, I mothballed the project. I was too busy firefighting with business problems at the time.

Originally, I'd bought it on a whim while visiting friends who lived near the southern Normandy town of Gorron. I never had or harboured any intentions of buying a property in France. It simply never crossed my mind. Let's face it, it's full of French people.

However, visiting these friends made me realise what a beautiful country it is. One idyllic afternoon sitting in their garden, my friend's wife asked me why I didn't buy a place over there. Property was extremely cheap by English standards, but then they do have more space. This is what they'd done themselves. Upped sticks and left the busy and parochial Tewkesbury behind and started a new life in France with their two school-age children in a lovely location. They paid something like £10k for this crumbling four-bed cottage in an acre of ground. It would have been twenty times that in the UK. The fact that neither of them spoke French hadn't deterred them. They went for a lifestyle of quality and simplicity.

They'd been there a year, and she by now had a job working for an English/French property agency, and had developed a reasonable grasp of the language. He stoutly refused to learn, but was a skilled builder, which was handy for the English property invaders. In the mid-80s there had been a general exodus of Brits, all of whom wanted a new pace of life. A bit of a property rush by the Brits followed, and they began buying up property wrecks. I was surprised to find that the French seemed to find this obsession with buying up old buildings puzzling. Nevertheless the Brits did. These were usually renovation projects, cottages and farmhouses, situated predominantly in Northern France. It was relatively easy to whizz over from Portsmouth to Le Havre or Cherbourg, and your money for the rabbit hutch in the UK went a very long way in France.

I was somewhat cynical of this property bandwagon back then, but on this particular afternoon in the summer of 1987 I was well into a bottle of Cotes du Rhone and more amenable than usual. I declared that if I ever bought somewhere over here I would want a lake, and since it's almost impossible to buy one in the UK, threw down the gauntlet. To my surprise she picked it up. Within ten minutes she came down from her office and into the garden with three sets of particulars, telling me she'd made viewing arrangements for properties with lakes. Semi-comatose, I said when? She said now.

Frankly I couldn't really be arsed, and wished I'd never said a word, but not wishing to let her down I stumbled into her car and off we went.

The Moulin de la Tour was the last one we viewed and I fell

hopelessly in love with it. It was just into the Mayenne region, and I agreed to buy it on the spot. It cost the French equivalent of £35k.

This sixteenth-century mill was a wreck, it had a huge garden at the back, but across the lane opposite was a quiet reed-fringed 3-acre lake, an orchard and some woodland. I couldn't possibly resist. Not only had I agreed to buy it, my friend's wife fixed me up with a French mortgage of £30k. I put down the £5k deposit. The deal was done and dusted in a couple of weeks.

One of the things about buying property semi-pissed is that it took a while for me to realise the enormity of what I'd done. The building needed a huge amount of money to renovate. I didn't have that kind of dosh. Was I intending to live there long-term? No I wasn't. I hadn't got anything like the funds to even begin to get the place into any kind of habitable order. It was the lake. That was the attraction, that was the compensation. Where on earth could you ever find a secluded carp lake like this back in the UK? I didn't need the mill, the money sponge. I had no choice but to mothball it.

In the early days we went as a family on the ferry from Portsmouth several times, but as the children grew, and I was planning our world trip in 1991, we spent less and less time there as a holiday destination, although it as great to catch up with our friends there. Over time the whole lot became hopelessly overgrown and neglected. The fact is I more or less forgot about it, despite my regular mortgage payments, even though I wasn't sure why I continued.

For a few years, around about the return from our world trip in 1991 to sometime in late 1995, I never went near the place. Then out of the blue a notaire (solicitor) in the nearby town of Laval made contact with me. How he found me I've still no idea, but he did, and said he had someone who was interested in buying the mill. As I said above, it was fun in the beginning, but as with most things in life, everything moves on. The novelty now of bunking down in this dusty, spider-webbed mill had paled, especially for rapidly growing kids then aged twelve and ten, so I pursued the enquiry.

Having by now realised what a monumental task it would be to stay on top of this place, I agreed I'd sell it. But not the lake, just the mill with its acre of jungle garden at the back. I fully intended to keep the fishing for myself. That lake was a Holy Grail for me of carp, roach, and tench fishing forever, something I had hankered for all my life. I loved the place, despite not visiting for a while.

Together with the bit of woodland around the edges I saw it as a secluded bolthole. A little paradise. I wasn't letting that go.

It is quite unusual, almost impossible, in French law anyway, to split property and sell it off separately. I was adamant though. The lake had to be split away from the mill, or no deal. Quite happy to sell the mill, but the lake and ground were not negotiable. Out of bounds.

In the end I prevailed, despite me being desperately keen to get rid of that mortgage. We agreed on a price of £30k, and I wiped the mortgage out. I don't know how the notaire managed all this, but he did. He achieved the legal split on the whole property. Thus I sold off the liability and retained the rest. Basically I owned a lake and woodland which stood me at all of £5k. For me it was a brilliant result. Especially in a foreign land, having to deal with the intractable and obstinate French. To be honest I felt a bit jingoistic, like I'd just won a battle. To hell with Agincourt. Here was another English victory for the books.

Purely by chance and about the same time as I sold the mill, a mate of mine told me he had a static caravan in Brittany which he needed to get rid of. By all accounts it was a knackered old thing, and he'd been given notice to move it from some smart site. Evidently it was letting the side down, spoiling the view it seems. The French are sniffy about things like that. Did I want it? Too right I did. I didn't give a damn about its condition. Besides, it would be well hidden in the trees.

A couple of weeks later we had it shipped down from Brittany on a low loader, and several hours later plonked it down under a huge walnut tree by the edge of the lake. It sat there for a couple of years. This by now was late 1995, and even though I hardly ever went near the place, I had future plans for this caravan, even though back home at the time I was still preoccupied with business stuff.

On a whim, sometime in 1997, I decided to take Ms A down there. We crossed on the ferry from Portsmouth to Cherbourg, and drove down to St Hilaire du Maine to see how it was all doing. It was a jungle. The grass was head-high, and the orchard was full of small walnut trees. The red squirrels which abounded there had planted them for me. I took some of these little walnut trees back home eventually. The lake was the same, and I watched carp in the evening rolling in the shallows. I met my relatively new neighbour, a surly individual from Laval, who'd bought the mill and was renovating it. Good luck to him with that. He didn't speak a word of English, but had done a magnificent job of tidying the back garden. I reckon that alone would have taken a year. Other than the occasional wave, I didn't have much to do with him.

I could hardly call this static van romantic – it was brown, mildewed, and mostly made of woodchip – but once I'd got a gas cylinder on for the cooker, and placed candles everywhere, lit a big fire outside, and stocked up the cupboards it was, with a bit of a leap of imagination, cosy … ish. Ms A and I spent a few days there, cutting the grass and making something of the place. It was quiet, the skies were radiating starlight, and with the fire and a couple of bottles of wine, I fell in love with the place all over again. I realised it was an oasis, a jewel which I needed to improve.

Ms A and I also had a tendency to shag each other senseless, and on one memorable night was so engrossed and half-pissed that I accidentally knocked one of the bedroom candles over. The room was filling with smoke before I realised I'd set fire to the bedspread. I flung the whole flaming lot out of the window. It was hot stuff all right.

When I eventually got back to the UK I contacted an English outfit, Key Camps, who ran various sites in France. They also had a policy of disposing of ageing vans which they sold off at about ten years old. But at least more modern than this glorified shed. I bought two for £3k each, unseen. My mum paid for one of them, she liked the idea of having her own, not that she ever used it, and the other I bought. Deal done, I then arranged to have them taken down there on flatbed lorries.

To cut a long story short I enlisted the help of a local farmer who used his low loader to clear the site and move the old shed of a van across the orchard. I'd use it as a store house. An English guy I'd befriended, Ralph, ran a bar in the local town of Ernée. To his eternal credit, and being the man on the spot, he organised for me a septic tank, and fixed an electric and water supply to the site. I don't speak French, Ralph did, and he was brilliant when it came to dealing with these monopolistic, moribund, bureaucratic outfits. If you think BT need a kick up the arse here in the UK, this lot needed a bomb. So these two gleaming statics were sited, one where the old one had been under the walnut tree, the other down by the side of the lake. Luxurious by comparison with the old one, fridge-freezers, comfortable beds and seats, and even a cd player. I listened to Mozart mostly in the warm evenings. Anything of his can transport me straight back there.

For the finishing touches I went over with a couple of mates, who plumbed the caravans in properly, ran electric cables from the meter, and generally helped me get the site looking like home. We made gravelled paths, some of it nicked from the local churchyard and shovelled into the back of my old Subaru pickup. It was mostly quartz for graves, and these paths sparkled in the moonlight. It looked great. I justified this theft since I've put enough money in church collection boxes down the years, so didn't think God would mind us liberating some of this stuff. Besides the Catholic Church is rich, and they were helping the poor.

The three of us usually went to Ralph's bar in Ernée for a few beers after grafting all day, but most of the time I'd been there on my own. Although I enjoyed their company, I relished the solitude. All in all, getting this place sorted took weeks, most of the time I was on my own, rarely meeting anyone, and sometimes going for days without seeing another human being. I jogged most mornings down the lane under the cool of the sweet chestnut trees, and fished most evenings. Completely self-contained, I wrote, painted, listened to music, played the guitar, talked to the squirrels and wildlife, and I absolutely loved the place.

By the end of 1997 I had resolved to dispense with Ms A once and for all, and make an effort to fix my marriage. I suspected Ms A 's husband knew, and I'm pretty sure my wife did, but despite three years of this affair I still denied it all to everyone.

I decided to make Christmas '97 memorable, some kind of turning point. And so it was, but for all the wrong reasons.

Although I was fairly skint, my income just about keeping pace with my outgoings, I drew down £1,000 in cash. The plan was to shower it over my wife Val on Christmas Day. I think it was all in fivers, which made it seem more. I saw it as something for her to splash out with entirely on herself. I like Christmas Eve, perhaps the only part of the whole thing I do like, and looked forward to it. In my head I had already dispensed with Ms A's services.

Arriving back about 7 pm with my hidden packet of cash, I walked into the house. Val was sitting in a daze. Her face was ashen. I knew immediately it was something serious.

Anonymously in the dark late afternoon a jiffy bag had been dropped through the letterbox addressed to her. In it was a cassette tape. She'd played it. The contents of it were self-evident in her face.

With my mind set upon getting rid of Ms A, fun to begin with but now blighting my life (all self-inflicted of course), I listened in horror to the tape. It was all about me, and her despair at my intransigence, and how she couldn't understand why I wasn't with her. My wife just sat there dumbstruck.

It transpired that her husband had secretly taped a telephone call Ms A had made to one of her friends. He'd suspected it for ages, and now here was the proof. I discovered later that he'd also delivered about fifteen of these tapes to all their friends. He'd humiliated himself to prove a point. Quite a brave thing to do, I suppose. The cat was well and truly out of the bag, it was at last undeniable and completely disfigured the new Christmas start I'd planned. The timing was exquisite, and designed to ruin our Christmas, which it did. I felt anger and upset, especially since I was powerless to do anything, apart from go round and smash his teeth in.

To worsen the situation for me, he threw her out, or at least she left, and found herself a flat. Now the pressure on me to join her was really on. I'd singlehandedly blown myself out of the water with all this, as only I could. It was inevitable of course. I can't bear to listen to Annie Lennox singing 'No More "I Love You"'s'. That song takes me straight back to this nightmare.

I tried to convince my wife that all would be well, but this had thoroughly rubbed her nose in it. At the same time any last shred of trust had gone straight out of the window. Equal and opposite to all of this was a vixen in a flat, demanding to know why I hadn't moved in with her, since it was by now common knowledge.

I began to hate her, but the blame fell squarely on me. I thought I might have been able to control all this, but emotions take over and go in unexpected directions. I had no excuses left. Except one. I was in the process of buying four flats in West Malvern, three leasehold and tenanted, but the top one I thought I may move into myself, and I very nearly did. During all of this, a phrase uttered by my old Law lecturer at college came back to haunt me: 'Where passion enters, reason departs.'

Which is just another version of a more succinct expression by a Cherokee squaw to a young Indian bride-to-be. 'Remember,' she said, 'the harder his cock gets, the softer his brain becomes.'

I gave my wife the money on Christmas Day, and to her credit she made the best of it. The taped revelation overshadowed everything of course, but for the children's sake, always excited by Christmas, we made the best we could of it.

The New Year's Eve party Val and I went to wasn't easy. She

became totally pissed, and I became angry. We still hadn't discussed this development as a couple, and when we got home it turned into a fight. It was almost as if the booze had had an enraging effect. She rounded on me in the kitchen, and I really lost my temper. From memory she picked up a knife or scissors or something, after I'd thrown a whole carton of milk at the kitchen wall. I was so angry I almost lost control, but disarmed her, clipping her on the lip in the process. If I'd punched her properly I honestly don't know what would have happened. Looking back now I believe it was the culmination of years of misunderstanding and frustration between us. I felt wholly unappreciated, and I guess so did she.

All I was after was an open and frank discussion. We clearly had problems, and we needed to iron out the issues, but somehow she seemed to bury it all, like icing over an ugly cake, all for the sake it seems of keeping up appearances. What I needed was to have a completely frank and open discussion to attempt to bridge this immense gulf between us, get it out in the open, try to put it behind us and move forward. The reality, though, was that I had absolutely no idea where to start. You can't have a conversation with someone who doesn't want one.

1998

Bit by bit, I withdrew from Ms A, but my wife and I still didn't discuss the situation. We just jogged along in an uneasy truce. Ms A was now in her flat, and the whole thing was turning into an angry and sour relationship. Hell hath no fury and all that.

1998 turned out to be a pivotal year. The start of any new year is a chance to wipe the slate clean and start again. I know that's bollocks in reality, but psychologically it isn't. Nevertheless, what I was hoping for, looking for, was a way somehow to rebuild, renew and reset. Besides it was also the year I was heading for my fiftieth birthday. Time perhaps to grow up, get a grip, and make some plans.

For the first few months of 1998 I played for time, was non-committal about everything and anything, and felt that over the next few months the dust would settle. And it did up to a point. Still nothing was said or discussed between myself and my wife, but I went ahead and bought these flats anyway. It became a project I could focus on. Meanwhile I continued to wriggle, twist, and play for time with Ms A. She was the personification of tenaciousness.

By April 1998 I'd decided to renovate the flats in West Malvern, particularly the top flat. It was almost an attic studio flat, with spectacular views across Herefordshire to the Black Mountains of Powys. I felt I could live here in splendid isolation, on the basis that if I couldn't mend this marriage, it would provide the perfect bolthole. A situation which looked increasingly likely. Somewhere though, in the back of my head, I was very much aware that I'd messed up two previous marriages. I was determined that this had to be third time lucky. But I was delusional. It proved to be unlucky, as you'll see if you stick with me.

I hope you're managing to keep up. I can't escape the feeling, as I've been slaving away over this laptop, that most of it is self-indulgent rubbish. I have a feeling that you may not have even got this far. Is it boring? Feedback please to: JC@icouldntgiveatoss.com. Anyway, wakey wakey, I'm on the last and most important leg, I'm sure you're pleased to hear.

I'm now about to head to the edge of the cliff.

The self-inflicted turmoil I found myself in with this ridiculous domestic mess, entirely of my own making, reached a turning point in April 1998 (and about time too, I hear you say), so here it comes. Another ...

Side story

Next door to the flats I'd bought in West Malvern lived a clairvoyant, or psychic, as the brass plaque proclaimed. Oooooer, I thought. An astrologer, a soothsayer, maybe a real life witch. It crossed my mind to introduce her to Ms A, a fellow witch. Anyway it all seemed a bit spooky to me. Her name was Angela something-or-other.

I may be an atheist but I do at least recognise a spiritual need in the human race. Unfortunately this need has been highjacked by religion. Spirituality is there in art, poetry, photography, music, or the natural world. I see it as a necessary and reflective human creative force, in fact we seem to be the only species who possess this need to create, and for no particular reason. Whatever it might be, I still don't see why we need to pin this spirituality on superstitious belief and call it God. Astrology, as far as I was concerned, was just another layer of superstitious nonsense.

With that attitude firmly in mind, I knocked on Angela's door. It was a Wednesday at 10 am. My intention, as a good neighbour, was to advise her of the potential mess we might make, since we proposed to do some building work on one of the flats, Inevitably there is always some disruption, so I felt it only right and proper to do the decent thing. I was also curious to meet her.

The door was opened by a large blonde woman in a voluminous lilac dress, her hair held up by pins, and a very bright red lip-sticked mouth. She had the smile of a woman who runs a brothel.

I admit I was suddenly a bit nervous. I don't really know why I should have been, but I opened up with 'Hi, I'm your next-door neighbour, but no doubt you already knew that, ha ha ...! She smiled a welcoming smile, then frowned a bit, then invited me into the kitchen with a wave of her fat arms. She offered me tea, which I accepted.

We made some small talk, then she suggested we went down a flight of stairs to her studio taking our tea with us. I entered a room with a large mahogany desk, two comfortable sofas and dimmer-switched lights, which hung down from the ceiling. Most of the lights were blue or purple. The walls were covered with astrology charts, stars, suns and planets. I perched on one of the sofas and she sat her more-than-ample frame and bosom on the sofa opposite, and just stared at me.

Suddenly she smiled, and sipping her tea must have felt my consternation. 'You don't believe in any of this, do you?' she murmured as I looked around the walls. I laughed as confidently as I could, and shook my head. 'No, I don't, and frankly think it's largely a made-up game to help direct weak-minded people through their lives'. Blimey, I thought. Did I just say that? I half hoped it might just tip her off balance, but it didn't. She gave me a patronising look, and patiently went on to explain to me that everyone is unique. I know that, I thought, but that didn't stop her. Oh no, not a bit. Each individual arrives at birth on this planet at a precise point in time. This in turn gives them a special place in the world, all due to the gravitational pull of the planets in the solar system, and beyond that the cosmos. My cynicism must have showed. I felt an argument coming on.

Maintaining politeness, and rather tongue-in-cheek, I suggested that the astrology charts I read in the paper couldn't possibly apply to one twelfth of the population. At this point she bristled, dismissing these 'so-called' astrologers as frauds and charlatans. Akin to snake oil salesmen, I guess. I now realised I was in the company of a real professional. This stuff was serious. I paid attention.

This meeting turned into something of a revelation for me. It was a bit like going to the doctor or dentist, and I began to feel really nervous. All thoughts of commanding the conversation and talking about building work disappeared. She assumed control, and without warning pointed at me and said, 'What's wrong with your neck?' I replied, 'Nothing at all, why?' She insisted that I had a problem with it. Unknown to her was a chiropractic appointment I'd arranged at 12.30 pm that day. I was suffering with a trapped nerve in my shoulder. I insisted I had no neck problem but eventually admitted to the trapped nerve. She clapped her hands in mock triumph. She then went through more physiological stuff. 'Heart's in good condition, watch your diet, Virgos have a weakness in that area' and so on.

My mouth must've dropped open. She had no idea what my

birth sign was, I hadn't told her, nor any idea of my past digestive ailments. There was no doubt in my mind that my digestive tract was weak. Appendectomy when I was nineteen, dysentery in Afghanistan at twenty-seven, problems I'd had with a peptic ulcer aged twenty-eight, the latter brought on by my lousy diet of madras curries and pints of beer when I was living on my own in 1979. The observations she made shocked me. I'd revealed nothing about myself and yet she seemed to know. This very much reminded me of my encounter in Delhi with the little Indian mystic twenty-odd years before.

If she was out to get my attention, she certainly achieved that. Suddenly I was all ears, almost as though I'd been hypnotised. She seemed to know she'd gained my confidence and I began to believe in her. I don't think of myself as gullible, maybe I am a bit, but I asked how she knew this stuff and she just smiled. I learned that her main office was based in Richmond in Surrey. She also had a few celebrity clients. I was impressed. Her premises in Richmond were her 9-5 base five days a week. West Malvern was her 'spiritual' home where she came back to whenever possible for R& R, and primarily to rid herself of all the accumulated negative energy she'd absorbed from her consultations. Yin and Yang, she explained. I imagined her somehow scattering this lousy energy over the Malvern Hills, and refilling or refuelling herself with positive energy up there. To be honest I began to find this whole Yin/Yang thing intriguing.

Positives and negatives, eh? Up and down, in and out, yes and no, high and low, hot and cold, north and south, wet and dry and so on. I'd never really thought about any of this before. What she was saying in essence was there are negative people and positive people. She put me in the positive energy category, and told me to beware of negative people who are drawn to suck that energy out of you. It made me stop and think for sure.

She then told me I was at my best around water. Why was that? She then proceeded to tell me about the elements of the Zodiac. Earth, air, water, and fire. There are three earth signs in the astrological calendar, each three months apart, one of which was me, a Virgo. The other two earth signs are Capricorn and Taurus. I didn't know any of this.

Partnerships (or marriages), she told me, should ideally be made up of complementary opposites or of the same signs. Why is that then, I asked? A water sign with an earth sign is good. Water nourishes the earth. I got that, unless it's seawater? She frowned at my flippancy. A fire and earth sign is very bad. Fire scorches earth. Ouch! Equally, water and fire signs are bad. Why? Water douses fire. Air and fire? Very good. Fire needs air to go whoosh! You get the gist? Beneficial opposites, all linked to positives and negatives. Took me a while to work it all out, but I began to see where she was coming from. Ms A was a fire sign. No wonder I felt singed! My wife was an air sign. Benign, as far as my earth sign was concerned. True enough. My wife and mistress, however, may well have got on well together. Somehow I doubted that. I did try later to find out the signs of some of the other women I'd known, but I couldn't really remember their birthdays, though I do recall Meg being an earth sign, which was good for me.

This revelation began to give me some belief in the authenticity of the subject. It was true I was best around water. Fishing, swimming, diving, sailing, wading in it with rod in hand, all seemed to have a beneficial effect on my personal well-being. This woman, I thought, knew more about my life than I did.

She then referred to an aura of some colour around my head, evidently a sign of confidence. I can't say I was feeling it right then, but this affinity I have with water made sense. My place in France had a lake, and my house in Wales was on the seafront. This relationship I have with water was the source of my energy, she told me. I felt I had to agree.

In effect what she meant was that some people derived positive energy from their surroundings. In my case it was water. The great outdoors, as it were. I got that. I was therefore deemed positive. Negativity comes from needy people who are for whatever reason unable to provide themselves with positive energy. Make sense?

I've certainly met a few. Negative people therefore are apt to attach themselves to positive people and in effect, as I said above, drain the energy from them. She warned me to 'beware of needy people'. What I also didn't need in my life was a fire sign.

My initial scepticism gradually began to give way to a more basic understanding of these concepts she had provided. However, what she said next floored me.

She stared at me for some time while I was attempting to digest the contents of her philosophy. Then, continuing to bore into me with her eyes, she suddenly asked me how direct I wanted her to be. I was actually on the point of leaving, my head buzzing with all this Yin/Yang stuff when she delivered a missile. Shouldering my masculinity like suit of armour, I looked her in the eye and told her she could be as direct as she liked. I'm a man, see, I can take it. She stared at me for a few seconds as if weighing up her words, then said simply, 'You're involved with two women.'

I remember the floor swaying a bit and I was thunderstruck. There was no way she could have known this. Then she delivered the coup de grace. 'I'm going to tell you something now which you may or may not like. Neither of these two women are any good for you.' I looked for a pit to jump into, but actually I think I just stood there aghast. That was the first and only time anyone had had the guts to tell me that. I'd been see-sawing from one to the other for damn nigh four years, unable to decide where the path lay, and the truth finally dawned on me that there wasn't a path at all. After this lightning bolt hit me, she continued in a very quiet and measured voice. 'One of them I see as a counsellor type, who likes to know everyone's business, is very demanding, and has an answer for everything. The other is a bit of a millstone, a ball and chain if you like, who you try hard to please, but nothing ever seems good enough, no matter what vision you strive for. True?' I just nodded. She said of course she had no idea who they were. I did though. I knew exactly which was which. Or should that be witch was witch? It was time for me to get off the fence.

That, dear reader, was the turning point I referred to. And here was another one. I was shaking quite a bit when I went up the stairs and back through the kitchen to her front door. As I put my hand on the handle to open it, she suddenly said from behind me, 'Who's the third woman?' I turned round and stared at her. 'I don't think you've been totally honest with me, John. I can see a third woman in your life.'

At that point it occurred to me that she was mad. As if I hadn't got enough on my plate as it was, she was now suggesting there was yet another woman. I half-laughed in disbelief. As if I hadn't got enough on my bloody plate. I felt my temper rise just a tad, but then rounded on her and made it quite clear there was no way I could even begin to countenance another complication. I was already washed out mentally, and wading around in a minefield of emotion. To be quite honest I was glad to get out of the place, but as I opened the door to step into the street she said, 'In which case then she must be just around the corner, and that's the one, that's the one for you. I wasn't to know it, of course, but it turned out she was absolutely right.

I never saw Angela again, despite the building work starting next door. She'd confided in me during our meeting that she was on the horns of a dilemma herself. Her dilemma was whether to stay in Malvern with her current partner, or start a new life in Australia. I assumed her psychic skill would have given her pointers to whatever direction she should take, but apparently not. She claimed her powers enabled her to guide others, but not herself. No good asking me, I thought, I wouldn't have a bloody clue. A month or two later I discovered she'd made her decision. She moved to Australia, and the property was sold.

I walked out of her place that morning in something of a daze, and off I went to my chiropractic appointment. I asked him where this trapped nerve was located. It turned out the problem was in the C7 vertebra in my neck. Well, well, well, I thought. She'd been absolutely right about that too.

*

I mulled over this conversation with Angela for a few days. I couldn't figure out if all that she'd said just happened to fit with my mental state at the time, or if I'd suddenly woken up to a philosophy which had been wholly alien to me. Something I knew about vaguely but had dismissed. Effectively I'd put astrology in the same bag as my contempt for belief. In the end the more I thought about it, the more I decided it was perhaps some kind a pointer. I treated it as a reality check. The very idea of suggesting I was involved with yet another woman on the side was laughable. It was a ridiculous and insane thing to say. I decided in the end to set out to prove this psychic wrong.

Over the next week or two I moved fast. I finally pulled the plug on Ms A, amidst much howling, gnashing of teeth and furious phone calls and messages.

Although I had come out of this 'reading' emboldened, I was still disgusted with myself for being weak and dithery. Enough procrastination, it was time for action. I'd made the start with Ms A, but now I was equally bent on putting my dysfunctional marriage back on track, determined to disprove these predictions. Given my catastrophic track record with previous marriages, I was utterly determined this wasn't going to be third time unlucky. I also needed to change myself, and try to alter my behaviour. This marriage had been on a knife-edge anyway for three years, so I resolved to become a better and, in some ways, a good stay-at-home husband. I made plans for us all to travel, go shopping, take up gardening, learn DIY, that kind of stuff, and generally try to be a more domesticated husband. And I did for a while, but fuck me, I was bored.

I like to think I tried hard and was rewarded with a renewed relationship. It wasn't easy to try to rebuild the shattered trust, but so focused was I on making changes and improvements to my behaviour that it took some time to realise these weren't having much effect. I don't know what I expected in return, but there was bugger-all in the way of reciprocation. If anything, I felt I was being punished, and like anyone who feels guilt, I accepted it.

People don't and can't change. I see that now. They may make a few small adjustments, but it's very difficult to change a formed character. It wasn't long before I began to slip back to my old ways. It was now mid-May 1998. I was just a few months away from my fiftieth birthday. If ever I'd been through a midlife crisis this had been it.

The loss of my extra marital relationship with Ms A had left a gap, some kind of vacuum, and I desperately needed to fill it. The by now infamous Ratley Snakes came to my rescue. My other family as it were. The band was doing well, we were playing regularly, and had become a pretty slick outfit, and we played some fantastic gigs, but when I eventually went home everything just seemed flat.

I needed to fill my time, so would escape to France just to change the scene a bit, and usually on my own. I didn't beat myself up especially, but found the isolation gave me a chance to reflect, to perhaps discover the new me. So I ran off over there for a week or two.

I decided to paint, and write. Something I used to do quite a lot when I was younger. Not only was my lakeside retreat a wonderful place to be in late spring, but the light was pure, and clear. Just being on my own with the lake, trees and the wildfowl for company gave me peace. I slept well, and would get up at first light and run the lane each morning, under the cool of the sweet chestnut trees. Shower, breakfast, and set up my pastels and easel.

Over the years I'd been going there I'd also made a few English friends who lived in the area. Ralph ran Jagger's, a bar in Ernée, and unsurprisingly loved the Rolling Stones. He'd also been immensely helpful, especially with the language barrier, when the static vans were installed a couple of years before. In the evenings I would go over there to talk music, and have a few beers after a hard day painting my new masterpiece.

One evening as I was sipping a beer he suddenly asked if I'd bring the band over for a musical festival in June. Ernée was twinned with some town near Portsmouth. There would be a musical knees-up in June, with an exchange visit of different bands. The whole town was taken over by various bands from the UK playing live in the square on the back of trucks and trailers. Jagger's would be hosting a couple of bands too, and he invited us. It was a few weeks away, and a bit short-notice, but was something I could get my teeth into as it were, something to motivate me. On my return I put it to the guys during one of our practices in Ratley. Much to my surprise, they enthusiastically agreed.

Weeks later we were down in Ernée, complete with an entourage of friends, and carloads of equipment. I'd gone ahead to prepare the caravans and get provisions in, notably large tins of cassoulet heated up in big pans on the fire. The band all duly arrived late Friday afternoon, and after spooning down the meal, and a few beers, we did a quick acoustic practice under the walnut tree, playing through the set in preparation for the gig the following night. The weather was about as perfect as we could wish, with hot, cloudless June skies.

We set up in the bar on the Saturday morning. Part of our set included a song by a new band Ralph had 'discovered' by accident when he'd bought a cassette tape in the market in Ernée. Cracker, a Canadian band we'd never heard of before, and he played it often in the bar. I'd copied this tape and took it back with me for the band to hear. They all loved it, so we rehearsed 'Someday', a track from the tape as a nod to Ralph, that was now included in our set.

That song means so much to me now. Not only does it conjure up perhaps one of the most memorable weekends of our lives, but Ralph died a few years later of cancer. At the ridiculously young age of forty-seven.

The gig: June 21st 1998

As lead singer I was nervous. I'm usually keyed up before any gig, but this one brought its own unique pressure. Not only did we have three or four hours to kick our heels, but my biggest fear was my inability to speak French. I had no idea how I would fill in with my usual banter between songs. There's a limit to how many 'bonne nuit's I can utter over two or three hours. I never eat or drink before we go on either. I never have before any gig. I work on the basis that hunger keeps me alert. A lion hunts best on an empty stomach, eh? Avoiding alcohol also helps me remember the lyrics. Singing thirty-odd rock songs and memorising all the words is something I seem to be able to do. Pissed up though, I had my doubts.

The town was buzzing, it was a really warm evening, so to kill time I just wandered off on my own around the town to watch and listen to some of the other bands playing in other venues. The whole thing was clearly a big event here, and street food, mainly fried chicken and c, were being washed down with beer. I'd never seen this town so alive before. Basically Ernée is an agricultural outpost, populated by old men in caps, and fat grey-haired old ladies in thick tights, with severe faces. So it was all something of a surprise to me to see so many young, gorgeous, lightly-clad girls, rocking and rolling in the market square, where the music boomed out from the band on the back of a flatbed truck.

We were billed to go on last at Jagger's, but had no clear idea of what time last would be. My brother Mart, and the rest of the band, Darren, Russ, and drummer Martin buggered off somewhere to a bar, together with a few of the friends who had come over to support us, but we'd agreed earlier to convene back at Jagger's about 11 pm. When we all duly arrived we couldn't get in. The place was heaving. We had no stage as such, more of a raised platform which the five of us would have to squeeze on to, but the band who were on ahead of us were occupying it.

They were a professional outfit from Portsmouth, and apparently fitted in this gig on their way home from a six-week tour in the South of France. Lucky bastards. They were also shit-hot. They even had their own entourage of very gorgeous, adoring groupies in tow. The crowd loved them, and Jagger's was rammed. Eventually we wormed our way through this tightly packed throng to the stage area, and just to compound my increasing apprehension they finished their set to tremendous acclaim. They unplugged their guitars, acknowledging with a hint of arrogance the plaudits they received from the audience, and graciously thanked us for the use of our monitors and amps. As I climbed on to this little stage and stared at the crowd, I thought to myself how the fuck are we ever going to follow that?

The band made its way to the bar, with back-slapping from some of the crowd, but as I stood there I was dismayed to watch most of the crowd leave. We plugged in and started, with a Beatles song, 'You Can't Do That'. Those stragglers who remained, maybe about 20% of the audience, looked at us, drank up, and began to move to the door. We were losing them. This previously jam packed bar was virtually deserted.

Fortunately for us, the next song on our set was 'All Over Now'. I watched intrigued, as some of the crowd in the process of leaving, paused, looked, and came back in. I knew the French had always had a love affair with the Rolling Stones, and this song had caught their attention. So we re-jigged the set slightly and put a couple more Stones songs next on the list. If I have to say one trumpet-blowing thing about the Snakes, we do Stones stuff well.

Within twenty minutes the place was heaving. Most of the stuff we do is Stones related in some way, with quite a bit of Chuck Berry thrown in for good measure. They loved it. By the time it got well past midnight the place was rocking and throbbing. We were so tightly packed on that stage I had no space for Jagger theatrics, and in the end took my radio mic and somehow squeezed through this heaving mass of dancing, drinking people. I climbed the stairs leading from the bar just to get some air and space, and for a while the crowd could hear my voice but had no idea where I'd gone. Eventually they spotted me hanging off a rail on the balcony and turned en masse to cheer. I waved back, and could see the band across this hot smoke-filled room, just grateful to get a bit of elbow room, and they were playing out of their skins, having just let themselves get caught up in this electric atmosphere. It was almost as though the band and crowd performed as one. They sang all the Stones songs word for word. There really was no need for me to have worried about the language barrier. We had a universal language. Music, and bloody good rock music at that. Ralph behind the bar was beaming and rocking with his staff and the beer flowed. From my perch up on the balcony I managed to look out through the steamed-up windows. What I saw outside astonished me. The police (gendarmerie) had closed and cordoned off the road and an even bigger crowd of perhaps 200 people, those who couldn't get in, were literally dancing in the street. I felt almost as though the whole town had heard and made their way to see us.

We finished our set about 2 am, but the crowd wouldn't let us go. We started the entire set all over again. By now I'd resumed my place on the stage, and waved my hands and arms in their direction until they all followed suit. The power I seemed to have over them was incredible. They followed every move, even those outside. I don't know how many there were altogether, perhaps 300 or so in total, but to see them all behaving as one was a dizzying experience. I felt I could have sent the lot of them into battle. And I reckon they'd have gone willingly.

We eventually crawled off about 3 am, having played for three or four hours solid, with Ralph and his crew somehow ferrying drinks over to us. In due course the crowd began to thin, apart from a few pissheads and die-hard rockers, and even the police left. I was absolutely drenched in sweat, and utterly drained as the adrenaline subsided. At 4 am we loaded a crate of Rolling Rock beer into the car and made our way the few miles back to my caravans in the peace of the orchard, where we sat on logs and chairs and drank, as we watched the sun come up on what promised to be a beautiful June morning. We were all in a state of utter euphoria, and for the first time I suddenly realised the power of music. We've played many gigs over the years, but this was the most memorable for us all, ever. The highlight for me personally, though, was that one or two of the members of the professional outfit from Portsmouth had stuck it out, and as we were leaving, he put his arm round my shoulder and told me it was one of the very best live performances he'd ever seen. That was gratifying.

The following night, Sunday, we lit a big fire, organised food and drink, and some of the local women joined us. We had new fans, one of whom told me how the careful insertion of an Alka-Seltzer tablet, combined with a spoonful of creme de menthe can enhance the vaginal experience. I didn't know any of that – did you? Anyway, read into that what you will, but my only thought was ... I bet it doesn't half make your cock sting. During this unlikely conversation, and no I didn't take her up on it, I realised the adoration that rock stars must feel night after night on tour. It's a heady feeling all right, this ability to command, through the music, a huge swaying crowd. The danger of it all going to my head was quickly quashed of course. My brother and bandmates were on hand to prevent me getting too far up myself. We all left the following morning, each of us having felt we'd had a weekend which was special. And by God it was. Even today we still, twenty-two years on, recall that night. We've never come close to repeating it, and I'm not sure I'd want to climb that pinnacle again, with or without creme de menthe.

July 1998

Shortly after this musical triumph, about two or three weeks later, we were asked to play at a fiftieth birthday party locally in Ratley. It was a seemingly impromptu affair one Saturday, and since we'd played the night before in my brother's pub in Avon Dassett, I stayed over at his place. Claire was the birthday girl, and a good friend of my brother's, and we set up on a patio in the grounds of a beautiful well-ordered garden just down the road from his place.

Flushed with our recent success in France, we were by now tinged with a degree of arrogance, at least I was, and I set out to replicate my apparent ability to get the crowd going. I always watch the crowd quite carefully to see who sings along, generally direct my attention on them. As the light began to fade about 9.30 I found myself watching a couple dancing, but suddenly they stopped mid-song, moved away from the dancing and became engaged in an earnest conversation. She wore a red dress, had blonde-red hair, walked slowly off the dance floor and leant against the patio wall. Then put her head in her hands. To this day I have no idea why I was intrigued. I've said this before, but as lead singer I watch the dancers and it gives me a kind of insight into how the gig's progressing. Some are wild and throw themselves about, others are wooden, and unused to making an exhibition of themselves. Usually because they have no interest in music, or perhaps have no sense of rhythm or timing, but not this one. She was an exceptional dancer. I'd already taken in her impressive figure, lovely hair, and in high heels had good legs. We took a break from playing, and the couple resumed their conversation over by the wall. I didn't take much notice of him, in fact I can hardly remember what he looked like.

Now I think about it, I got the feeling there was some kind of drama being played out before my eyes, and being naturally curious I mingled a bit with the other guests before heading casually in their direction, beer in hand. They were in earnest conversation, so on impulse I interrupted them, and turning to the blonde in the red dress told her I had a song for her in the next set to match her dress. Her partner looked at me quizzically. 'Lady in Red'? I smiled, said it was a good guess, but no. Nice song but not exactly rock n roll, eh? The song I had in mind was a straight twelve bar blues rocker 'Hi-Heel Sneakers'. Ominously and prophetically it opens with the line 'Put on your red dress baby, 'cos we're going out tonight'.

This song we have always done, right from the time in the 1960s when we were still at school. It was guaranteed to get people up on their feet. When we resumed the second part of the set, I made some mention of it, and away we went. I saw her dancing to it, though she didn't look in my direction. When I next looked, she'd left.

We finished the set by 11 pm, a disco of sorts ensued, and I danced with one or two women there, but of the Lady in Red there was no sign. Eventually I noticed the band had left, and even though I was enjoying myself it was now about 1 am. I'd had enough. I walked up the road and back to Mart's place. It had been another good gig, not in the same league as the French one, but most had appreciated us playing, especially Claire, whose birthday we'd been celebrating. I left for home the following morning.

Two days later found me on the M40 en route from a meeting in Watford. I'd been interviewed by a firm of management consultants, and for a while toyed with the idea of becoming a management consultant. On impulse I called in to see Mart, who lived not far from the M40 Gaydon junction. Claire, the birthday girl, was in his kitchen, returning some of his borrowed dishes, and she thanked me for a 'splendid' band performance. I hadn't really got to know her on the actual night, but accepted the praise with as much humility as I could muster. Which wasn't much! As we chatted, she said the only cloud on the horizon that night which had marred her birthday party was that one of her best friends had split up that night with her partner, and the relationship had finished. I almost didn't need to ask who it was. I just knew. She told me it was Ailsa, but I didn't really know who she meant until she mentioned the blonde hair and red dress. So that was what the drama was all about. Rather offhandedly I suggested she should give me Ailsa's number, since I was also nursing a broken heart. Well I wasn't really, just that Ms A had left a bit of a gap now that she was history. I suggested to Claire that maybe the Lady in Red and I could empathise with one another? It was a flippant remark tossed casually in her direction, and with that I left.

I was, it has to be said, missing Ms A, for the most obvious of reasons, but I was making a determined effort to stick to the straight and narrow with my wife, primarily to confound the predictions of Angela the Psychic, and felt it was working up to a point. I never gave any more thought about this conversation.

August, September, and October 1998 came and went. My life was adjusting to marriage with no outside physical or emotional interference. No question it had left a gap, or vacuum, and I tried hard to fill it by keeping myself busy. Nevertheless, there was always this constant nagging feeling that something was missing. Which of course there was. Early November came, with the dread of dismal, shortened, drizzle-soaked days. I hate this time of year, impatient for the equinox on 21st December, when the days gradually begin to lengthen. Suddenly out of the blue I got a phone call from my brother. Claire had invited the pair of us to dinner. The Saturday night in question happened to be the day after we were playing another gig down at Avon Dassett in the pub Mart owned, and which we'd played many times trying out new songs. It fitted for me, and I accepted the invite. Anything to alleviate the boredom, and meet new people. Then a light bulb went off in my head, and I thought surely not? Mart asked me if I was bringing my wife, and instantly I said no. He then decided not to take his girlfriend either, so we sat out the after-the-gig day at his place, strumming guitars and generally messing about. Then down to Claire's place we went together.

My assumptions were correct. Ailsa had been invited, but so had about twenty others, and I didn't recognise her immediately. Her blonde hair had been piled up, she was in a short black dress, high heels, and somehow looked different, until she pulled the pins out and her hair tumbled down. And there before me stood the woman I remember in the red dress. Claire seated us together – surprise, surprise – though she seemed to spend most of her time talking to her neighbour on the left. I discovered however she had a Scottish accent. It had been Anglicised a bit, and wasn't the harsh Billy Connolly type, more a soft burr. It took me some time in fact to distinguish her voice, despite the proximity. I usually pick up on regional accents quickly, but not this one.

Bit by bit I learned she had two children who lived with her, another one at Uni, and a couple of cats and a dog. She'd divorced a year or so before, and worked at an estate agency in Stratford.

And that was about it. Ah, shame, I thought. This was a big minus. Baggage, that's what it was. I'd had enough of Ms A's demanding daughter, who was possibly the most indulged only child imaginable, to even contemplate the complications associated with other distractions. Naturally I was evasive about my own circumstances, but mentioned the band, France, my place in North Wales, and that I lived near Cheltenham. She told me she'd loved the band and the music, and remembered clearly my remark about the red dress. As well as music I also discovered she liked fishing. This was the first woman I'd ever met who did. Now that was a big tick. I could see a dilemma opening up.

The meal finished and for some reason Claire's husband decided we'd all play cards. Ailsa stuck by my shoulder as all ten to fifteen of us played blackjack. Claire's pedantic husband insisted on being the banker, and seemingly made up the rules as we went along. I mentioned to Ailsa at this point that we were intending to play a gig on New Year's Eve, a few weeks away, and if confirmed I'd let her know. She had no plans, would love to go, so I asked for her phone number, which she wrote down on a slip of paper.

She must have brought me luck. After arguing with the 'banker', probably better spelt with a W, on the validity of splitting two aces I'd been dealt, I went on to win two five-card tricks. Triumphantly I picked up the dosh from the centre of the table, and retired from the game.

It was about midnight when Mart and I walked slowly back up the lane. He just knew what was going on, and asked me if I got what I wanted. I told him I had her number. He asked what I intended to do. In a split second I thought kids, baggage, trouble, deceit, more broken promises, and my own duplicity would fuck her life up too. From the little she'd told me, all of it had a familiar ring with her previous bloke, some of it resembling my own nefarious activities during the past few years. I made a split-second decision, took the paper from my pocket, rolled it into a ball and threw it into a hedge. These days I was a reformed character, and firmly on the straight and narrow. I was determined to not screw things up again. My determination was to prove the psychic wrong, not that the meeting I'd had in Malvern months before had really crossed my mind. I was on a new track, and that was that. I decided not to make contact with Ailsa, and never expected to see her again. Nor, incidentally, did we play the New Year's Eve gig.

1999

Christmas 1998 came and went, as did New Year's Eve, and life settled down to something like normality. I don't actually hate the winter as such, but these short days restrict my rather itinerant lifestyle, which mostly revolves around travelling or pike-fishing. There was no point visiting my place in France, all locked down, though the house in Criccieth demanded my attention from time to time, but the seaside didn't appeal, since I can't fish or swim. I began to consider what 'project' I might embark on in the coming year, and considered selling the woodland in Aberdeenshire, inherited (gifted) by my dad, and in which I was never likely to be actively involved since it was a ten-hour drive up there and wholly impractical.

I needed cash for any project, and though the properties and boat business were performing well, and my previous dalliances with fishing tackle and pubs were firmly behind me, I felt it was time to look for an investment. With interest rates having plummeted from the dizzy heights of the late 80s when they hit 15%, to around 2%, all in the space of ten years, I felt that now was the time to maybe borrow once more, or cash in on an asset which wasn't doing anything, and turn it into an income-producing one. A 5% return on property was better than cash in the bank. I decided I'd find another property. The woodland in Scotland was a cost. There were management charges. Far better to get rid of it, and use the cash for something which would contribute rather than drain my resources. I deferred to my father, since it had been gifted by him, even though I owned it, and surprisingly he saw my point and agreed with me. I put it up for sale.

In the end it didn't take too long to sell. Despite a gloriously expensive shiny set of particulars, with a mass of wistful photographic scenes of the wood and land, and Scottish heather clad hills in the distance, it turned out that the farmer next door bought the lot. Therein lies the lesson. Land is always of more value to the property owner next door than it is to someone who doesn't live locally. I could have sold this place in a phone call. As it was, the selling agents picked up £5k for their fees and glossy brochure.

By the spring of '99 I had cash in the bank and went on the hunt for a suitable property. My ever-supportive mum sent property particulars to me on a regular basis, especially of those coming up for auction, but I took my time. I did toy with the idea of buying a small riverside property in Tewkesbury as an office for the boat business, since the relationship with our two former friends who ran the boat business was now on a more businesslike footing. In the end I decided not. I was still mistrustful of them. Herein yet another lesson. I've said this before elsewhere, but it's far better to make friends out of a business relationship than to try to turn a friendship into a business relationship. Business partnerships between friends are doomed to fail, and if perchance the business doesn't fail, the friendship almost certainly will.

You'll have gathered by now that I like to be in complete control of my assets. This lesson was learned the hard way. Success or failure is my responsibility and falls to no other but me. I like it that way.

By June 1999 things were ticking along nicely. I found myself financially self-sufficient, managing the properties OK, my relationship with my wife seemed to have stabilised and at best I'd say it was on an even keel, and importantly, although they were perhaps aware of the rocky relationship between myself and their mother, both my children were settled in school. I was beginning to feel smug almost.

Around this time I decided to make plans to get the two remaining woodlands in North Wales harvested. It was something of a sideline project, but I hoped to generate more cash. The trees there were well past their sell-by dates, and with the cash, if I ever got any given the agency and harvesting costs, planned a major redevelopment of the house in Criccieth, which was in desperate need of attention. My plan was to sell the trees, keep the land and regenerate with broad leaf trees. Both woods had been stocked by the Forestry Commission fifty years earlier with Douglas Fir and Sitka spruce, neither of which I particularly like. The ground under them was sterile mass of pine needles. The money I hoped to generate would more than provide the means for a comprehensive renovation of this house. My wife showed little or no interest in my plans, so once again I found myself footloose, spending increasing amounts of time away up in Wales. I seem to revert to type quite easily.

As I spent more and more time up there, I bought an old Land Rover to rattle around the woods in. Wholly impractical but good fun, and my boat, a Norwegian 14 ft crabber painted bright yellow, sat on the sea front. June in Criccieth used to be a good time for the mackerel, but climate change, or overfishing more likely, has seen a gradual decline in the stocks. That also goes for skate, bass, black bream, and other species.

I love boats. I've always had one in my life. The freedom and isolation it provides suits me well. This yellow boat I'd bought for £400, complete with trailer, and for me an early-morning summer dawn, sliding this thing down the beach and into the waves, then heading out to fish on a flat calm sea, is about as perfect as it gets. This place Criccieth, combined with the boat, together with hot days, takes me back immediately to my boyhood. I love that. The memories are so rich, as they were more latterly with Zolly. In my mind's eye I can see my mum and dad, and us three kids lazing at the base of the castle, and swimming in gin-clear water from the shingly pebble-strewn beach. I have an intense affinity with it all. I only wish I could slide back through the years and recreate those times. But here I was, on my own, just revelling in this simple lifestyle.

I had now sold the Scottish woodland and banked the cash. The trees were being felled and I was up there most days watching the proceedings and making plans with local builders to embark on a comprehensive renovation of Adref, my Criccieth house. In between times I did some painting. The light on the middle floor was perfect, and I turned it into a bit of a studio.

Side story

One particular idle thought I'd had whilst whiling away my time in Wales supervising the woodland clearance was that at some point in the future I might try to acquire a stretch of the River Wye in Herefordshire. I had fished this river since the late 1970s, particularly for pike, but just for a second scroll back to my childhood in Cheddleton when I was ten. Those fish have been an obsession for me all my life, and during my hair shirt time in Wychbold, after the final split from Meg, you may recall my only social activity was working on Saturdays in my mate's fishing tackle shop in Bromsgrove. Through this he'd had access to fish the River Wye, but only outside of the salmon season, which at the time was February to October. This gave us a limited opportunity, November to January, to fish this glorious river for pike. The River Wye in the winter months is fickle, and prone to huge spates which make it almost impossible to fish, thus the opportunities were scarce, especially since Geoff had commitments to the shop, and my Sales Manager's job meant I was on the road five days a week. We just had to get lucky with the weather.

The pike-fishing though could be spectacular, given the right conditions. Many of the pike we caught were big double-figure specimens, and the Herefordshire countryside and river were exquisite. Even in the depths of a snowy winter. On one such occasion sometime around 1984/85 I had met the owner of the beat for the first time, who caught me out when I was up there on my own. He had the salmon angler's mindset that all pike were a curse. I asked him if he'd mind me fishing up here, and on the spot gave me his permission to fish for pike whenever I wanted. I was delighted. However, the permit came with a condition. I was to kill every pike I caught. I promptly agreed to that. But I never did.

This owner of the beat lived in Shrewsbury. He struck me as a kindly man, but our paths didn't cross and I never actually met him again. I was immensely grateful to him though for the permission and continued to fish there whenever the opportunity presented itself, all throughout the 80s and 90s, but only during those crucial months. I respected his desire for me to not fish from February onwards and nine times out of ten would be up there on my own. Pike anglers tend by nature to be solitary creatures, which suited me fine, but more often than not I would also be there with my infamous pal Zolly.

In November 1994, with the floodwaters in retreat, I caught my best ever pike there on a wobbled dace deadbait. My preferred method. I remember it swirled lazily up to take the bait, turned over sideways and went back down to deep water under some overhanging willow. I knew it was big, and shouted down the river to Geoff to bring the big landing net. It weighed in at 29 lb 10 oz and was set up in a glass case up for me by Geoff, who was by now free of the fishing tackle shop and working as a ghillie further up the river near Hay-on-Wye, and who had accompanied me for the day. He'd more recently developed an interest in fish taxidermy. Having helped me land this particular fish, he persuaded me to kill it. I very reluctantly agreed to let him have it to try his new skills on. I said earlier I didn't kill pike, and I don't, they are hugely important for the health and ecology of the river. This magnificent fish though was the exception. It now sits in its case just above me as I write this in my little artist's studio twenty-five years on. I've never killed one since.

For twenty years, right up to 1999, I continued to visit this stretch of river, in fact it got under my skin to such a degree that I became possessive of it. If I saw anyone else up there I would challenge their authority. Since I was reasonably flush with cash from the Scottish woodland sale, and looking for a new property project, it dawned on me that I should try to buy it. I decided to track down the owner. Salmon-fishing had declined dramatically, the river was clearly neglected, and I saw an opportunity to perhaps acquire this half-mile beat.

It was ambitious, I had no idea what it might cost, but was worth some investigation. It turned out the kindly owner who had given me permission had died a few years before, which was news to me. The beat had been acquired, without my knowledge, by a guy who owned the upstream beat adjoining this one. I knew nothing about him, but eventually discovered he lived near Chepstow (more of him later). He in turn agreed that I could continue to fish for pike only, please, to kill them all, and only to fish in those particular months. When we spoke he refused to discuss the possibility of selling it. Later in the winter of 1999 I had another go at him.

In the meantime, having dwelt on my obsession with pike-fishing, just to remind you we're now back in June 1999, with me messing around in Criccieth.

Around the end of this month I was returning from North Wales with a friend of mine. I got home to find one of my mum's regular property auction newsletters. She knew I was still actively seeking a property investment, and by now I was busy, with plans to harvest the timber in Wales, and carry out restoration work on the house up there, but I still felt I needed to find an income-roducing property.

I leafed through it, as I did on a monthly basis, wondering why she insisted on sending these things, after all I had my ear to the ground locally. Some of these auction properties she sent were miles away. Usually London or Manchester, and way too far to be managed effectively.

Nevertheless as I read through this thing I picked up on a property, five flats, three of which were leasehold, two freehold in Alcester in Warwickshire. It was a town I knew well. My solicitor had his office there. It caught my eye predominantly because given the guide price it was within range of my budget, and only a thirty-minute drive away. For whatever reason it hadn't sold privately, and was going to auction in Birmingham. I decided to go along. I sat in this crowded bustling hall, with properties coming and going in seconds. When this lot came up its guide price was £90k. It didn't reach the reserve, and I'd pulled out at £60k. The auctioneer then withdrew it from sale, and commented that any interested parties should contact the agent direct. This was an outfit called Bigwood in Stratford-upon-Avon. I decided to pursue it.

I got home and made the call, which, as it turned out, changed my life.

The lady who's dealing with the viewings for six Church Street isn't in at the moment, I was told by the receptionist, but would be back shortly. I explained I'd been to the auction and was following up. I left my name and number, and was told that multiple viewings were being arranged for interested parties the following week, July 9th. I pencilled in 10 am, and asked who the lady in question was. 'Ailsa' came the reply. I put the phone down and thought shit, surely that can't be the same one I met at Claire's dinner party nine months before. Or can it? That's some weird coincidence if so. It's not a common name, and I recall her telling me she worked for an estate agent. It just had to be the Lady in Red. I'd thrown her number in the bushes all those months before, and by sheer chance, thanks to my mum's newsletter and an abortive visit to the auction, fate had somehow contrived to reintroduce us. If indeed it was the same woman.

I went back up to Wales later that day and mulled over the chances of fate throwing us together again after all this time. I dismissed it as fanciful.

I had spoken to my solicitor in the meantime, whose offices were in Alcester, and he knew the town and this particular property well. He then asked if he could accompany me. I agreed but lied and told him the appointment was 10.15. If it turned out to be *that* particular Ailsa then I needed to get my excuses in fast, and didn't want him in the way. So much time had elapsed since that fateful dinner party, and I'd promised to call her about the New Year's Eve gig (which we didn't do). I was firmly on the straight and narrow now, and had been free from emotional entanglements for more or less a year. I have to admit there had been the occasional meet-up with Ms A, but mercifully by now it had fizzled out entirely, and I was finally free of it.

The following day I arrived at the property. I was a bit nervous. It was also the first time I'd actually seen the place but I walked into the Victorian walled garden on the dot of 10 am, and there she was. Her face showed no real trace of surprise, her hair was cut shorter and curly, but she still possessed a lovely figure in a pale green dress. For a moment I was speechless, but I was prepared, and apologised immediately for not calling her. She brushed off the apology. I went on to say I had been through the emotional mill a bit, and didn't want complications. This was absolutely the truth. She admitted the same, saying her on/off relationship with the guy I saw her with a year ago at the dance had finally finished.

At that point my solicitor appeared, and after a brief introduction, we spent half an hour viewing the property before the next clients arrived to take over. Ailsa greeted her new arrivals, at which point my solicitor and I walked back down the alley and got into my car for me to take him back to his office. And then a very strange and unusual thing happened. Something quite frankly which has mystified me to this day. My solicitor, whilst buckling his seatbelt, asked me if I had said goodbye to the agent. It was an odd question with no evident relevance. The fact was I hadn't really, I'd just walked away. My solicitor and I had been friends for many years, and suddenly, without any warning, he gave me a bollocking for my evident rudeness, and basically instructed me to go back across the road and say goodbye to her. Dutifully I got out of the car and went back across the road. By this time Ailsa was engrossed in conversation with the new people. I signalled to her from the alley entrance that I would call, not wishing to interrupt, and turned away. Immediately and suddenly she broke off from the group, walked across the grass, and asked me point-blank what I was doing for lunch. I was taken aback completely. This had never happened to me before. I stammered a bit, and said something like no especial plans. She told me she finished at 12.30, and could we go for lunch? Without thinking any of this through I agreed. When I got back to the car I was shaking, but didn't mention a word to my solicitor about this peculiar and extraordinary development. Having dropped him at his office I drove off, then sat in the gateway of a cart track for an hour or so to kill time. I read the paper but couldn't concentrate. I kept thinking to myself, what the fuck am I doing?

In some ways this is the beginning of a new story, and the end of the old one. I was nearly fifty-one, and although I've never felt age as such, wondered how on earth life can begin again. But that's exactly what happened. Angela the Psychic had been right all along. This turned out to be the woman who was round the corner. The one for me. The only thing which bothers me still is that this woman had been right in front of me twelve months before, from the moment I'd seen her at the gig. For my part I'd done my damnedest to avoid complication. I'd been utterly determined to prove the psychic wrong, yet through all these twists and turns of fate, somehow life had conspired to prove me wrong. Who or what marks out these invisible paths of collision? Ailsa has a simple explanation. It was just meant to be.

Chapter 19

Idon't think it's really worthwhile noting every detail of this last chapter as such, even though I bet you want me to. Where I am now some twenty-one years later can easily be recounted by others. And I know it's been a self-indulgent reminiscence, and that's the way I intended it. In other words if you don't like the story so far, well tough, but it's my attempt to put down my thoughts and feelings over what I perceived as a short lifespan. This is my opportunity to look back at a life liberally interspersed with wives, other women, business, music, travel, art, writing, and generally making a nuisance of myself. Complete of course with all the stress, anxiety, and worry, wholly self-inflicted of course, that a life well lived brings. The truth is that having written all this, I've only quite recently woken up to the fact that it's been a much longer life than I originally thought.

It's only when you reach later life that you find time really does appear to fly. Some events don't seem too long ago, but actually are, and writing all this has made me realise the truth of my father's line he sent to me all those years before when I was hippy and halfway across India. 'Life is a long time in some ways, but now mostly yesterdays.' And so it is. I didn't quite get that remark when I was twenty-seven, but heading to seventy-two (a nice reversal of numbers) I do now. I am genuinely and honestly surprised, having written this biography, at the life I've led, and the events I seem to have packed into it. I really mean that. I've tried not to moralise, but have at least tried to maintain some kind of integrity. I know I'd never make a priest, or vicar, or professional moraliser, and I hope I haven't tried to justify my own morality, or lack of, but I think it best if I leave that for you to decide.

Anyway, I imagine you're dying to know the next bit. No? Well if you aren't you should be! Here goes, and guess what? Yep, we'll make it into a ...

Side story

I went for the lunch appointment, yet I felt a weird tension between us as we walked through the streets of Stratford. This was a woman I barely knew. It somehow seemed as if we should be holding hands. As we sat at the table, I couldn't stand it any longer, and on impulse I put my hand across the table and took hers. The tension vapourised.

A few days later we met again. This is a bit cheesy I know, but as we sat outside chatting, I suddenly felt I'd known her forever. The conversation flowed, and she began to finish off my sentences, as I did hers. I was puzzled, and as only I can, spent ages on the drive back analysing all this. Two weeks later we met again, but this time at her house. You can get an idea of someone's life by just looking round the place. Her two children Alice and Jennifer were living there, but it was their away day/evening at their father's. Their presence was evident with toys and books and the usual clutter, but the place felt homely, lived-in, and decorated with family knick-knacks, including a dog and two cats. There might even have been a pet rabbit. It felt comfortable.

I was heading for the Cambridge Folk Festival that evening to meet up with my mate who was pitching my tent for me in advance. After a glass or two of champagne in the garden, I rang him and said I wasn't coming. It was a difficult call to make, but I assured him I'd be there in the morning. And surprise, surprise, Ailsa and I ended up in bed. Even today neither of us can recall the exact lead-up to all this, but that's what happened. In fact one of the strangest things about this particular evening, once I decided to stay, was that I went to change my clothes. The evening was getting cold, so I dug out some warmer clothes from my bag in the car. Ailsa went upstairs to do the same. When she came back down we were dressed identically. Me blue top, black trousers, her blue top and black skirt. We both immediately laughed at this coincidence. In fact we've more or less done this unintentionally ever since. You may not think it weird, but I do.

My mate was severely pissed off with me for not turning up on the Thursday night, but frankly by now Ailsa was far more important. I left her house early on the Friday morning heading for Cambridge, having asked my irritated friend if he could manage to get a spare ticket. This festival is usually sold out months in advance, but she was more than happy to join me on the Saturday if she could, primarily because James Taylor was headlining on the Sunday evening. To my immense surprise and gratitude my disgruntled mate miraculously secured a spare ticket. He'd nailed a request on a tree, and eventually forgave me when I explained what had happened. I called to tell her, she was delighted, and drove over on the Saturday morning. The weather, music, and atmosphere of this festival was just perfect. By the time the weekend was over we were hopelessly in love. It scared me to death. This was different to anything I'd ever experienced before. Love really is a bewildering state to be in. She also happened to be an earth sign, but one way or another this was likely to be a long, tortuous slog.

Oddly I never thought about Angela the Psychic at the time. My meeting in Malvern had taken place fifteen months earlier. Almost a year and a half. Twice fate had put Ailsa in my path, only for me to ignore her 'woman round the corner' prediction. Despite that throwaway remark, fate had somehow conspired well over a year since I'd first seen her at the gig, and some ten months after that dinner party, to give me a third chance, in the most bizarre combination of circumstances. I reflected on this.

Had it not been for my mother sending me property stuff, I wouldn't have gone to the auction, had I not done that it wouldn't have led to the appointment, and even then it fell to my solicitor to scold me back out of the car and so on. Very weird. Fate most certainly intervened, and I almost thought it might have been

God. Some hidden hand or something. To this day I simply don't know.

I think we both knew immediately that this was IT. Somehow meant to be. An old Law lecturer once said to me, 'Where passion enters, reason departs.' I wondered briefly if this might be one of those. It wasn't. This was much, much bigger than that, and there were a multitude of hurdles we both had to navigate in our personal lives. The moral here is follow your heart's desire, but use your head to guide the way.

From the outset I said to Ailsa the path would be steep, narrow and rock-strewn, and, as I said above, tortuous. And by God it was. Several times over the next few years we felt it best to part, but we just couldn't. We embarked on a love affair of such intensity that each of us wrote down our thoughts in a series of school exercise books when we weren't together, and then swapped them over to each write the next instalment when we met, however briefly that might have been. And that's where I'll leave that side story. At the end of the beginning.

Perhaps one of the most important aspects of our rapidly developing relationship, and which I briefly mentioned before, and which quite frankly I hadn't considered until recently, was the fact that Ailsa liked fishing. She used to go with her dad as a young girl. Imagine that! A woman (no less) who loved fishing! To me it was unheard of, but what a bonus. She soon became familiar with my pike-fishing obsession and joined me on the river whenever the opportunity arose. I have a picture of her some-where with her first pike, 12 lb, holding it in her arms and wearing a scruffy boiler suit (not the fish, her). The scene is wholly at odds with her brightly painted red nail varnish.

And speaking of the river, here comes the sequel. I had bought the Alcester flats in September 1999, and began to make plans for 2000 to renovate some of them. I also had some money left over from the purchase, so resumed my contact with the owner of that stretch of the River Wye, the section I knew by heart and had fished for twenty-odd years. With an enthusiastic woman angler now in my life I felt quite emboldened to try once again to buy it. I went down to Chepstow for a face-to-face meeting with the owner. He wasn't the easiest of guys to deal with, pleasant, charming, but very tough and firm on his position.

Eventually and to my utter surprise he agreed to sell me the two-thirds of a mile I wanted. It was a slog of a negotiation, and he clearly didn't need the money, judging by the size of the house he lived in, but we finally agreed on a price. £18k. Seems cheap now. When my solicitor (yes, him again, the one who had shoved me out of the car on that fateful day to say goodbye) received the contract from the owner's solicitors, I never realised that for this sum I'd also acquired the opposite bank. It was a shock and complete surprise to me. I'd have paid £18k just for the single bank alone! It was a hell of a result. Suddenly I had complete access and exclusivity. I uttered up a silent prayer to the original owner, who had granted permission to me to fish in the first place. Without that chance meeting I would never have achieved this. Neither would I have afforded it without my dad's gift via the Scottish woodland sale. I was elated, which frankly is something of an understatement. I rang Ailsa immediately with the news. She was equally delighted for me, and incredibly supportive. I just knew right there and then that this was the woman for me.

Midnight on New Year's Eve 1999 was unbearable. Millenium Eve. Here we were on the brink of a new century, and yet not together.

I also didn't know that this situation would continue for the next five years

Chapter 20

Procrastination is a curse, and complacency a virus. I don't know which is the worse. Success in either a relationship or business can lead to smugness. That's the danger. I now know it's really important to not sit back, but continuously quest for new ideas and new directions.

Towards the end of 1999 I was facing a major decision with Ailsa and where we should go from here. Decisions can be easy to make, but difficult to execute, and though I didn't think I was procrastinating, in our case I was, with a hint of complacency bordering on arrogance thrown in. I knew I wanted to be with her, that much was obvious to me, but there were simply too many other considerations in my life, and though I can be selfish and single-minded (can't we all?) I do have something of a conscience. My children are incredibly important to me (as they are to my wife), but I felt a duty, a sense of responsibility, to stick by them and at least see them into further education. Ailsa had a similar duty to her own children.

Domestic upheaval was always going to be inevitable, I could see that, it was just a question of when. It may be old-fashioned in some ways, but the way I saw it was that it was I helped bring them into this world, and it's a responsibility I felt impelled to shoulder. They were the innocent parties in all this. Equally the same applied to my wife. We'd married in 1982, and I like to think I tried my hardest, against the odds in some ways, to make it work, despite my philandering nature. It's quite a difficult one to argue. Was my philandering a cause, or was it a symptom of a failing relationship? I've no idea. You decide.

Meeting Ailsa made me realise once and for all that no matter what I did, and how hard I tried, some things are just impossible.

The words of the psychic continued to haunt me, but a bit of me thought she was just plain wrong with her predictions. I'd sought to prove her wrong, and failed miserably. How all this came to be mystifies me to this day. The other side of this double headed coin of course was Ailsa's circumstances. Likewise she needed to work as well as rear and educate her two girls who still shared the house. I knew it would be messy and it was. My overriding concern, however, was financial. If Ailsa and I were to be together the last thing I wanted was for her to have to work. We both needed to be free.

Equally, and despite my shameless ducking and diving, there was no way I would ever leave my wife penniless. I needed to split my assets for the benefit of us both, with enough left over for me, and above all I wanted to at least ensure she had some security and continued to live in the house unencumbered by mortgage repayments.

It was a difficult almost impossible circle to square, and many, many times I almost gave up.

The decision in the end was made for me. It was one of those unintended consequence things. Just as the dam was about to break, suddenly and unexpectedly the river got diverted.

My mother-in-law died. She had been ill for some time, and towards the end my wife had, as only she could, been utterly selfless and spent the last three months caring for her. I had always had an uneasy relationship with Val's parents, especially her bullying and selfish father, and it was only now I realised just what a bastard he'd been.

Just before she died, her father had begun to lose the plot mentally. In my view this had been a deteriorating process for several years, and culminated in him becoming violent, at times beating his sick wife. He was carted off eventually to some psychiatric sanatorium by the men in white coats, never to come out. What was a shock though was to discover his will in the safe, before he was taken away. It was just one page. We found he'd left his entire estate to charity. Nothing there for his wife, my wife or

362

her brother. Nothing whatsoever for his grandchildren either. In his twisted mind, he'd decided to ensure the Revenue didn't get their hands on any of it. Charity, in his mind anyway, definitely didn't begin at home. What really threw me, though, was his wife had also signed it. That was the measure of bullying power he'd had over her.

I'd seen through him some years before all this, and had begun to despise him. I despised him even more for this shitty trick. My wife was heartbroken. It was bad enough watching her mother decline, but this was the final kick in the guts.

To her credit she persuaded her mother, who now had power of attorney over his affairs, to revoke the will, which she did. Thus, it was altered in favour of my wife, her brother, someone I'd had virtually no contact with over twenty years, and a portion left over for her grandchildren. All in the nick of time. She died shortly after.

For the first time in her life, she was now able to anticipate complete financial freedom, and promptly issued me with divorce proceedings. I suspect she knew what assets were coming her way, and wanted to ensure I had no part in it. I didn't blame her in the slightest. What did surprise me, though, was there had been no discussion or conferring about this development whatsoever. I just walked into the kitchen one day to find a letter on the kitchen table from her solicitor, advising me of intended proceedings, even though she was all of three feet away from me preparing supper. My wife was never one for confrontation and I should have realised that. Nevertheless she must have been feeling nervous as I opened it in front of her. When I read the contents my feeling was one of utter relief. We'd been living separate lives within the house, and skirting round the subject for a very long time. Now I had my marching orders in writing.

It was early 2005 now, and four years of trying to keep the lid on my relationship with Ailsa. We'd had our ups and downs, and many times of despair. We'd split up on one or two occasions only to be tearfully reunited. I'd said at the outset that this would be a long, hard, narrow, rock-strewn road, and believed at times we would never make it. There were circumstances and events which were always outside of our control. But we stuck it out. Love is stronger than Araldite.

Meanwhile, on the other side of this bent coin, Ailsa had seen her eldest daughter Jennifer off to uni in London. Her eldest child, Jamie, was based at his father's house but studying for a degree in engineering in Newcastle. Alice, the youngest, was still at school in Chipping Campden. Things were gradually coming together through circumstance.

I'd bought the Alcester properties in 2000, renovated the two shorthold tenancy flats during the following couple of years, and rented them out. Ailsa meanwhile had sold her house and bought one of the three leasehold flats in the block of five in Alcester. It was almost a spiritual homecoming. A constant reminder of the day we met on the lawn there.

Then her dad, who lived in Ayrshire, died suddenly. She subsequently sold the Alcester flat, using the money to buy her father's house in Scotland, paying off her brother Stewart for his share of that asset. The house up there was then rented, keeping her capital intact. Having done all this she then moved herself and Alice to a rented cottage, which was local enough to enable Alice to complete her education at Chipping Camden. The income from the Scottish house of course went some way to offsetting the cost of the rented cottage in Honeybourne.

Things were now beginning to move fast, all through circumstance rather than design, and my impending divorce was finalised in December 2005.

I tried at all times to ensure the divorce was amicable, or as amicable as possible given the shenanigans. During this time I sacked my own solicitor, having been down the route of divorce before, knowing how lawyers seek to foster friction between divorcing couples to justify their exorbitant costs. That left my wife's solicitor no choice but to deal directly with me. My wife and I sat in the garden one sunny morning, and over a pot of coffee agreed how we should deal with all this. And that's what we did. We agreed everything, asset split, finance, children's well-being, the lot. My wife retained the house, and I took on the personal responsibility of a loan to clear the mortgage. She now had the security of knowing she wouldn't have to move.

Our deal was presented to the judge, who evidently expressed surprise at this jointly signed statement from two supposedly warring people, who weren't, and in December 2005 it was done and dusted.

I was a free man again. Except of course I wasn't. I was in love with Ailsa.

2006

Now, the reason I put this chapter in as a complete decade was to avoid you having to plough laboriously through every last detail of this year-by-year stuff. It's basically the last chapter, I'm sure you'll be relieved to hear, and besides, the people around me today (December 2020) can fill in any detail over the past fourteen years, should you have the energy, time and patience to be bothered to enquire. Nevertheless, 2006 is a year which stands out on its own. It was a pivotal year for me for all the wrong reasons, and is deserving of a special place in this 200,000-word monologue. Here goes.

Five years earlier I had been on the horns of a major dilemma, and five years later things, yep it was a long five years, were beginning to resolve themselves.

In fact in 2000, so taken was I with the two refurbished flats, 2 and 4 at 6 Church Street, Alcester, that I decided not to rent Flat 4 but make it into a kind of temporary base for myself. A kind of halfway house just in case I was caught out with my ducking and diving. It was a lovely cosy flat, with a beautiful outlook onto the long Victorian walled garden.

I remember years ago reading about an author who couldn't write unless he had the right conditions. I find my desire to paint needs that same vibe, and my desire for writing too, for that matter. This flat was just right. It proved an ideal art studio. The light was excellent, and poured in from a huge bay window. I returned to doing pastel artwork, which I love as a medium. In a way it was also a kind of office too, with a big double bed. This was occupied by Ailsa and I from time to time despite the fact that she had her own place in the adjacent building. In fact I was painting one morning on 11th September 2001 when Ailsa came up the outside staircase, made some coffee for us both, and told me two planes had flown into the Twin Towers in New York, killing 3,000 people. This was the start of a decade of Islamic fundamentalism.

Remember back some time ago when I warned you to 'beware of zealots'? Never more true than with this lot, who would happily kill themselves to eliminate people who weren't of their same twisted mindset.

But we're now in 2006, I was newly divorced, and decided that moving into the cottage in Honeybourne, where Ailsa and Alice now lived, wasn't the best of ideas. I needed time for the dust to settle and for everyone, my children especially, to adjust to the new situation. I'd rented out Flat 4 in the intervening years, so I moved into Flat 2. This was directly below Flat 4, which was now occupied by a Ghanaian princess (allegedly). She was a black African woman of about fifty, who had married my original tenant. He was a likeable enough bloke but a bit of a bumbling old soak who, it turned out, had a liking for the bottle. Lots of them. I felt, or at least hoped, this newly married couple perhaps would prove good neighbours in the flat above mine.

In some ways my move to Flat 2 was a PR exercise. I needed that breathing space not just for myself, but to send a signal to everyone that I didn't intend to just disappear from their lives. Settling immediately with Ailsa would have been seen as moving from a perceived frying pan to a wok. It also served as a place where family could visit, since none of them had met Ailsa or Alice, particularly the latter. I felt they may have thought I'd just acquired a new readymade family and decided to abandon them. That was never going to happen. But it was a future hurdle I had to contemplate, and why I made a stepping-stone move.

So I settled in to Flat 2 in January, and found I quite enjoyed it. In the February Ollie and I took a week's holiday on Lake Nasser in Egypt with my longstanding mate Geoff Franks and his son Andy to fish for Nile perch, something I'd done a few years before. It gave Ollie and I some much-needed time together.

Sometime in the 1990s, I can't remember which year, the Queen described it as an annus horribilis. Her spoiled, feted, privileged children were facing divorces and press scandals and Windsor Castle had partly burned down. Something like that anyway.

Though the year started out OK, 2006 became my own personal annus horribilis, as I alluded to above.

The woman tenant who occupied Flat 4, just after she married the old soak, had expressed an interest in buying out the whole of the premises. I thought about it for a while, and thought yeah, why not. I didn't intend to stay there forever, and of the five flats in the building the three leasehold ones were a pain in the arse, with tenants arguing all the time about who had responsibility for what. As their landlord, I felt like some bloody schoolteacher having to intervene in their petty squabbles. The 'princess' in Flat 4 told me her substantial wealth was hidden away in a Swiss bank, and that getting the money out might take some time. Nevertheless we agreed on a deal to buy out the whole lot, including Flat 4 and 2, the rental ones. I believed her, it was plausible, and I set up the necessary arrangements with my solicitor (him again). She agreed to pay a deposit of £5K, since she had expressed interest before this but it had come to nothing. That's why I insisted on a deposit, a goodwill gesture if you like, to get the deal moving. She gave me the £5,000 on a banker's draft, and all was well. Or so I thought.

Having returned from my Egypt jaunt with Ollie, I settled back into Flat 2, to await events with the exchange and completion on the property. In the meantime I had transferred the ownership of the tenancy to her as an individual and the Old Soak was removed. She then, unbeknownst to me, stopped paying rent. Bear in mind these were the days before internet banking, so it was a month or two before I found out. My bank statements usually turned up monthly, and were delivered to the communal postbox in the hall of the building. Except I never got them. I first thought this was a bank cock-up and they'd been sent to my previous address, and just like today, getting hold of anyone with a brain at the bank was a pain in the arse.

My solicitor never believed for one moment the princess had the means or the funds. I should have listened to him. Her tenancy finished at the end of April. Exasperated with the months of delay to buy the place outright, I gave her notice to quit. It wasn't 'fuck off'. More politely it was 'piss off and stop wasting my time'. I began, slowly I have to admit, to realise this woman was a fantasist

I finally got my hands on the copy bank statements: no rent for three months, and no the bank hadn't cocked up. Not only had she not paid the rent, she'd stolen my bank statements. She denied it of course, but there was no other explanation. Angry with her platitudes, apologies and bullshit, I couldn't wait for the tenancy to finish in April and get shot of her and this alcoholic twat of a husband. The end of her tenancy arrived at the end of April, and she and her alcoholic husband bolted and barricaded themselves in Flat 4. This was now 'tenant from hell' territory. The law is weak when it comes to protecting landlords' rights, and still is to this day. It meant a court order for eviction. This was shades of the restaurant in Cheltenham in 1987, when the courts very nearly bled me dry with costs. I'd been here before. I reacted to this blatant piss-take in the way I did before. I called in the heavies.

I had acted legally with appropriate notice, but there was no way I was going to allow these squatters to stay there and use the long-winded arm of the law to make decisions for me. I employed a couple of guys who were anonymous, then took off to Thailand to direct the mission from there. They were my 'builders', who went in and effectively threw them out, making the place uninhabitable in the process, basically cutting off the water and dismantling the outside stairs with a chainsaw. We took out a couple of windows for good measure. She couldn't say she wasn't warned. I'd been careful to ensure that part of her notice was to send in builders for refurbishment. The police got involved, but I was nowhere to be seen, and besides it was a civil matter. They metaphorically shrugged their shoulders. They had more important things to do, speeding fines, stuff like that.

When I got back from Thailand there was uproar from the local community, and accusations of false imprisonment. A criminal offence. Who? Not me for sure, and besides I'd lost the contact details for these builders. Ultimately I was interviewed by the police on a Sunday afternoon on these charges, including illegal eviction. The upshot was there was no case to answer. When they learned of the duplicitous and devious nature of this woman, they let me go. So had the princess, and the old soak. Later I received anonymous Haitian death threats which were texted to my phone. Then out of the blue a week or so later along came a letter from solicitors in Stratford. They had somehow tracked me down to Ailsa's house. The contents of that five-page letter accused me of illegal eviction. The last page threatened me with damages in excess of £50K. It was a worry.

As it turned out none of these threats, including the police interview I was compelled to attend, came to anything. That was a relief. The stress on me however was intense. After a couple of weeks the dust settled. I never saw the princess or the old soak again.

There is, though, a sting in the tail to the story. Not only was Flat 4 an uninhabitable hovel, I then discovered she had borrowed the original £5K deposit she'd paid me from someone she hardly knew. This generous woman benefactor had lent her the money out of kindness. It was money earmarked for her daughter's wedding. She never did get it back.

After her eviction, where it was assumed by everyone locally that I was the evil, greedy landlord, the light dawned. Bit by bit it transpired she owed money all over the town. She was not only an archetypal con artist, she also gambled heavily and was well known at the bookies. She evidently took the old soak for a sizeable sum too. I didn't see this situation because in all honesty I didn't want to see it. I had been too focused on doing a deal with her on the property. She never ever had the money or the means to buy the place. In fact, it was later suggested to me that she may have been a plant for slush money, which corrupt military and political despots in Ghana or Nigeria wanted to launder. This illegal money is siphoned off from aid money given by the West. By all accounts there are millions if not billions sloshing around in Swiss banks. It's plausible, but I'll never know. All I can say is that she was one of the most accomplished liars and cheats I've ever met. A dedicated and clever crook. Eventually my reputation in the town, assuming I ever had one, was restored to at least one of understanding. I rid that town of a liar and a thief.

Much later though I discovered she's split from the old soak. It was a marriage of convenience, it seems, and the poor bastard was fleeced by her in the process. Some £30K plus. I could have done with some of that. It cost well in excess of £10K to put this trashed and filthy flat back to its former splendour. I was truly astounded at the state of it. Inside reminded me of one of those shacks in Soweto. It was a disgusting mess.

To add insult to injury in this sorry tale, I was compelled by law to return some of the deposit I held, having deducted the rent and an amount for wear and tear. It was ludicrous. I gagged at the very thought, like having to swallow some foul-tasting medicine, but I'd already trodden a knife-edge with the law, so I complied. Then in one of those light bulb moments I had an idea. I had to return £1,700 to this witch by cheque, so I sent it to the solicitor who had threatened me with those colossal damages. I'd guessed correctly. She'd never paid their bill, so they didn't give her the cheque. Neither could they cash it. It never was.

By May or early June 2006 I was exhausted of it all, but despite the cost and the physical and mental toll this woman had caused me, we finally put Flat 4 back to something like it was, and relet it.

Barely a week had elapsed after all this hassle, when I saw on the telly news right before my eyes, that the police had raided a flat in Cheltenham, and bugger me, it was one of mine.

This ground-floor flat in Cheltenham had been rented to a Chinese couple courtesy of my property manager, who had a lettings agency. They'd paid cash into my account every month, on time, and seemed model tenants. I hardly had cause to go near the place. The human trafficking operation was big news nationally, and in short this Chinese couple were running a brothel. The fact it was on the TV news made me suspicious. This is evidence of collaboration between police and the media. They tip off the TV network, giving them time to set up their cameras and crew in advance of a raid. It's sensationalising crime. It's also a trend I disapprove of. Here's proof of the police doing a good job, all to titillate a bored public. They didn't, however, bother to let me know. Something they could have easily done by checking the ownership through the Land Registry. I was outraged.

I immediately went down the following day, and contacted the police to tell them they'd just broken into my property. When I got into there, I met a couple of police officers from Special Branch, who were 'guarding the place'. I asserted my authority to be there and surveyed the scene. I have never seen a condom factory, but this was their warehouse, or whorehouse. Boxes and boxes of them piled high to the ceiling. Sex toys and dildos of varying sizes, red light bulbs, skimpy underwear strewn around. It was a sex dump, that much was evident, but of the girls not a sign. The police explained to me the girls had been taken into custody. The place was a shambles. As for the Chinese tenant and his wife? They'd scarpered, just ahead of the raid. It was those two the police wanted.

As luck would have it I was able to give them details of the woman who had originally applied for the tenancy, and the passport number and car reg of the Chinese guy who had done a runner. The police were really pleased with me, which made a change. Suddenly I was a do-gooder. A month or two later while he was still on the run, the man was picked up by automatic number plate recognition in London. Arrested, he was subsequently imprisoned for three years in Gloucester jail, before being deported back to China.

Special Branch asked me to help, since I had the Chinese woman's telephone number, and suggested I should try to lure her to Cheltenham. I complied, spoke to her, and she caught a train up from Cardiff. The police believed she was the ringleader or mastermind, and they lay in wait until she got to the property to meet me. As she walked in through the door the police pounced and she was immediately arrested. She began screaming hysterically. Frankly so would I. I'd never met her before, but she was all of a tiny 5 ft, and to be suddenly surrounded by four scowling 6 ft plus burly men would have been enough to terrify anyone. Still howling and wailing in that high-pitched fashion which seems peculiar to the Chinese, she was unceremoniously frogmarched to the police vehicle. I just stood there like the proverbial spare prick. If she could have killed me with a look as she was handcuffed, I'd have been vaporised on the spot. I don't think I've ever seen so much hatred in a pair of eyes.

As for the working girls, well they were held without charge for twenty-four hours, subsequently released, and I assume drifted back to their Chinese masters. The woman ringleader was deported.

Funny how life has a way of throwing spanners in unexpectedly. In the space of six weeks I had gone from being the bad-guy landlord, who had ruthlessly thrown out the poor tenant from her cosy flat, and arrested by Warwickshire police for charges of false imprisonment and illegal eviction, to now being the good guy who was helping Special Branch in Gloucester track down and bust this Chinese sex trafficking operation. It's an upside down inside out world all right.

Later I discovered it this sex trafficking business was a nationwide racket. The Triads, the Chinese crime bosses, moved these passportless girls from town to town across the UK. The variety and change in scenery was designed to keep the regular paying customers stimulated. Sex sure is a powerful motive for making money, eh?

So here was another mess to clear up. In mid-July 2006 I sent the painters and decorators in to sort it out and renovate the place. I can't remember what we did with all the condoms and sex toys. I guess they ended up somewhere?

This next bit needs ... you've guessed it.

Side story

Somewhere in all this diatribe is the story of the boat. I'd been in Criccieth, had a wonderful day on the Saturday with beautiful weather, moored the boat off the beach and swum in. Then the weather turned overnight, and I was faced on the Sunday with swimming out in heavy seas to rescue it. (I made it the subject of another **side story** all of its own further on.)

Weather, I've learned, can often change on a full moon and often in the blink of an eye. I'm no scientist, but somehow big tides and weather patterns seem to have something to do with the gravitational pull of the moon. This was the case here. I never once stopped to think I could lose my life doing that swim.

Boat now rescued and moored up safely, we parted company with our friends, and Ailsa and I left North Wales on the Sunday night for home. It had been a memorable weekend as it turned out, but for all the wrong reasons. Weather isn't the only factor dictated by a full moon. Suicide rates are known to rise dramatically too.

I was busy with stuff generally on the Monday, but on the Tuesday morning I went down to the whorehouse to see how the guys were getting on with the repairs. All was going according to plan it seemed, then I heard my mobile ringing out in my car parked across the road.

By the time I retrieved it I saw a missed call from my mum. I rang her back immediately. Her voice was breaking, and she told me my dad was dead. I went into complete shock. He'd shot himself on this brightest and sunniest of days. It was July 27th 2006.

I headed for Lincolnshire, calling Ailsa en route to pick her up. Like me she was in total shock, and we broke every speed limit to get there. I rang my brother Martin too. He was in Majorca. The disbelief in his voice was evident even at that distance.

The scene which greeted me was exactly as I expected. My sister Julia and her husband were already there, Mum was sitting quietly with a cup of tea, and there were several policemen there. They quizzed me about my dad's mental health. I could barely suppress my anger, and told them that this man was possibly one of the most lucid and rational men I'd ever known. I walked into the garden holding my sister's hand to find my father still sitting in a white plastic chair, under a willow bower he'd made. It was adjacent to the pond, and the scene was at odds with the goldfish swimming lazily around without a care. My father was slumped in this chair, with a neat bullet hole in his forehead, and blood trickling from his right ear. He looked incredibly peaceful, as though the years had dropped away from him. Almost as though he was sleeping. I felt an impulse to shake him awake. His cap, and cup of undrunk tea still remained there in the grass beside him. I kept those.

My Dad had always been rational, to the point where he rarely let emotion sway his thoughts. I always knew he'd kept (illegally) a .22 automatic pistol, circa 1950s, in his attic. and referred to it as his 'pea-shooter' or 'exit pack'. He was vehemently opposed to keeping people alive for the sake of it, believing that religious belief gets in the way of medical fact. He would argue that keeping people alive beyond their 'sell-by date' was wholly irrational. Life and death are and always will be intertwined, and to try to deny that was a ridiculous human failing. He believed in controlling his death, and became vexatious with the medical profession, whom he viewed with disdain. He saw it as a conspiracy, a body of self-appointed judges, who denied a patient the opportunity to end one's own life at a point of their choosing. He was way ahead of his time in his euthanasian attitude.

Two months before this tragedy, in May 2006 while the shit was still raining down on me with these rogue tenants, Ailsa and I had gone to the house in Criccieth for some much-needed respite.

Mum, Dad, and one of Mum's friends joined us, but stayed locally in a hotel. This family of mine had such an affinity with this town it was almost like old times. Just my brother and sister missing. The weather was glorious, like the old days we remembered so vividly as kids. 26th May 2006 was their sixtieth wedding anniversary. I had completed the renovation of the Criccieth house, much to my mum's approval, and despite their hotel facilities, we cooked for them at the house. Well Ailsa did. I'd caught lobster, so we served that cold, and roast duck. It was, frankly, a wonderful meal.

It's only when you haven't seen someone for a while you notice changes. I noticed my dad would doze off without warning, and then suddenly wake. This wasn't like him at all, and he told me he'd been having some problems with mini strokes, or small bleeds known as TIAs, and had lost some feeling on his right side. This had made him angry and impatient, and was causing him some annoyance because his body was less capable. Quite simply it prevented him from doing what he wanted. That lack of ability really irritated him. It's something I understand completely. I expect of my body and it needs to do what I want. Quality of life is so very important. Then without much in the way of warning he just cleared off on his own. I noticed he took a walking stick. I offered to join him, but he wanted to be alone.

He was a long time gone, and Mum became worried. I went to search for him and walked the beach. I eventually found him slowly making his way back. I noticed he had definitely lost some vital something. It was wholly unlike him and it disturbed me. I know it now, but didn't fully realise then. This was his way of saying goodbye to a place we all loved.

When eventually he returned, I could tell he wasn't himself. He fell asleep almost immediately. This was definitely uncharacteristic, and I learned that he'd been under medical surveillance for these TIAs. Some time before this he'd confided to me, in his usual irritated and bad-tempered manner, that he was finding it harder and harder to engage usefully with his love of walking, especially long-distance walking. I could now see where this was leading. He knew his time was up. His body's abilities were in terminal decline, and perhaps for the first time I finally recognised that. My dad was a hero to me, an icon. He was always the ultimate father figure. Unique in many ways, and unlike anyone's father I'd ever met. I say that despite my criticism of his authoritarian behaviour elsewhere in these pages. He was eighty-three. I never took account of his age; he was simply a force of nature. He'd always been there for us. How could this be happening? It upset me a great deal to witness this decline, and I was suddenly aware of this mighty wake-up call. Change is constant, and old age is a bastard.

We left him to sleep for a while. My mum and her mate hardly noticed, so busy were they with their gossip and chatter. When he awoke, after maybe ten minutes or so, he asked me to step outside to his car parked opposite. Wrapped in a plastic Debenhams bag, hidden in the boot, was his pea-shooter. This was a seven-shot .22 automatic pistol, circa World War II. I was shocked and a bit surprised, I knew he'd had it for years and years, but it was a long time since I'd last seen it. He explained that he couldn't remember quite how to load the thing. It was rusty, needed cleaning and oiling, and since I had twelve-bore shotguns, and a .22 rifle, all legally held, he handed it to me and asked me if I could clean it for him. His hands had become increasingly feeble, and he couldn't release the clip. I managed to remove it. It was unloaded thankfully. I examined it, and though I know nothing about pistols, told him if he was ever caught with it he'd get six years in jail. He just looked at me scornfully.

I took the gun and agreed to clean it for him. After a couple of ice creams from the famous Cadwalladers, they left and went back to their hotel. The following morning the three of them left Criccieth. When I think back now to my mum's attitude and behaviour, there was a nonchalance about her. Not that she didn't care for him, she absolutely adored him, it was more of a disconnect from what I could clearly see. He was deteriorating health wise, and although he was sharp in mind, I think he was finding it unbearable to face the loss of physicality. I can understand this. My mum didn't seem to, or was in some kind of denial. Either way I think in sixty years they had both gone in very different directions. They were together because they just were.

Two weeks later he called me to ask if I'd cleaned his 'pea-shooter'. I lied and told him I'd forgotten to bring it back and left it up in Wales. He was pissed off with me for that and just told me to get it back. Two weeks later he called again. He was coming to Warwick to see a consultant about his various tests, and asked me again about it. I said I'd got it back, and with that he brusquely told me to meet him the following day over there. I told him I was busy and didn't need to justify that. I was in the process of detective work for the police regarding the whorehouse. Again he was seriously pissed off with me, but I made it clear I needed more notice.

I knew the way his mind worked, and by now knew the way he was thinking. I did my best to stall him. Another two weeks went and another appointment with his consultant loomed. Again he called, but at least it was in advance. Rather than me go to Warwick with an illegal weapon, I persuaded him to come for lunch with Ailsa and I in Honeybourne to collect it.

So over he came for lunch. Ailsa cooked and nattered in the kitchen to Mum while I went upstairs to get it. I'd cleaned and oiled the thing and hidden it in an old video case. It was obvious he didn't want my mum to see it, and threw dark looks at me. She hardly looked at it in between drawing breath, but I deliberately put it out on the table. There was no doubt now he'd got it back. He'd forgotten how 'to work it', as he put it, so outside we went, and I explained how to release the clip and load the thing. He then told me he couldn't find the bullets for it back at home. This was a seven-shot automatic .22, and since I was licensed for a .22 5 shot bolt action rifle he asked if I could 'lend' him some ammo. With an increasingly depressed feeling I went upstairs to my gun cabinet, took five bullets, and with a heavy heart and a feeling of dread gave them to him. 'Here's five,' I said. He looked at me with a half-smile. 'I'll only need one.'

Two weeks later he was dead. When I saw him slumped in that chair there was no gun. The police had already taken it. Apart from the shock and infinite sadness of looking at my dead father, the second wave of shock hit me. My fingerprints would be all over that weapon, and the bullets too, and furthermore, were those legally held bullets traceable to me? I suddenly felt a degree of panic that he had potentially incriminated me without any apparent thought for the consequences. Ultimately it was his decision, and too late now. This gun was the 'exit pack' to which he'd so often referred.

His body was lifted gently from the seat, the police having taken numerous photographs, then they took him away in a big white van to the mortuary for a post-mortem. Frankly I didn't think it was necessary. It was bloody obvious what the cause of death was.

Back in the house after they'd gone, I searched the most likely places for the remaining ammunition. An air of calm had descended inside, and my mum seemed curiously detached. I, however, was anything but calm. My mindset was one of cold, rational logic. I needed to find those bullets. I half expected the police to come back with a search warrant. Apart from a twelve-bore shotgun, rusty as hell, loaded, and standing behind the curtains in their bedroom, I eventually found the .22 ammo. It was in a little tin on his bench in the garage. I opened the tin. There were just three. My best guess is he'd used one to run a test, probably at the bottom of the fields where no one would hear. The other he used on himself.

My mum believed he would have written a long, heartfelt letter to her before he died. I hoped for her sake he had, but that wasn't his way. I suspect he had risen that morning, and made a spur-of-the-moment decision. This was a good day to die. He was in complete control of his life, as he was his death.

I'd spoken to him only the night before as I was on my way to badminton. He'd sounded croaky, his voice wasn't quite right, and he was angry about that, but it never entered my head, despite knowing his intentions, that he'd execute himself the following day. Significantly there was a full moon that night.

The only consideration he left to anyone, apart from two envelopes with cash in them to pay the cleaner and the gardener, which he'd stuffed in one of the top pockets of his shirt, was a simple note to my mum in the other top pocket of his shirt. 'Sorry for the distress, but whichever way, there was bound to be some. Just had Enough. All Love as Ever. Jack. x'.

It was interesting to me his use of capital letters in this note. I've pondered the significance of that ever since, but try as I may, I can't find any. There never was any long explanation or any other letters to us, as we'd all hoped. He must've got up that morning and thought, 'Fuck it, today's the day.'

For myself, initially I was angry with him. That state of mind remained with me for about two years as I digested and thought about how selfish it was of him to leave us like that. But that was me thinking only of me. Of how I couldn't refer to him any more, how much I valued his opinion on certain matters. He'd taken that certainty, that reference point away from me. I never ever, at that time anyway, thought about it from his perspective. I do now. It was an immensely brave and courageous thing to do. My feelings since have turned from anger to admiration.

There was the inevitable autopsy, as if they needed one, and a coroner enquiry, which was merely a formality. My mum's primary concern was more to do with bad press. How it might reflect on her if his death was blamed on his balance of mind being disturbed. For me that wasn't an issue. Never would they ever know what a lucid and rational human being he was, wholly unperturbed by superstitious belief.

My dad's funeral was minimal, just as he would have liked. Despite his devout atheism we sang a few hymns we knew he'd liked. He used to say he didn't see why God should have all the best tunes. And that was it. All over and done with, except for my mum. She'd had too much to drink, fell down the stairs on the evening of the funeral, broke her arm and ended up in hospital. Having returned to Worcestershire, I now found myself back in Newark the following day to take her home. I was by now worn out.

We were just about halfway through this momentous year. It was by now August 2006 and by the end of that month I realised how physically and mentally shattered I was. Surely there must be some light at the end of this dark 2006 tunnel. Things surely couldn't get any worse, could they? They most certainly could.

By September 2006 I desperately needed a break, so Ailsa and I took off on a road trip to France. I was driving my Porsche 993 at the time, and it was a huge relief to just get away from everything. The Porsche was eminently well suited to the superb tarmac in France. We drove over two days to Toulouse where our Australian friends had a Dutch barge moored on the Canal du Midi. Having spent a couple of days with them, and some light relief, we then left for Andorra, over the Pyrenees and into Spain. Two or three days in, Ailsa hurt her back. She could barely walk such was the pain and just climbing in and out of the car was agony. We aborted the trip and headed back to the UK via Santander to see a specialist.

This was the start of the next part of the 2006 nightmare. Eventually her back recovered and things went back to normal after a week or so, but then it was my turn. After a visit to the toilet I noticed blood. Two weeks went by and it happened again. I mentioned it to Ailsa, and vowed that if it happened three days in a row I would go to the docs. It did and I went.

The (female) doctor was fairly dismissive, suggesting I put more fibre in my diet. This was utter bollocks. My diet was excellent, and I told her I wanted a second opinion. Slightly miffed at my suggestion, she agreed. I called the number immediately, and by sheer good fortune was able to get a cancellation. Two weeks later I went along with some misgivings. The blood in the bowl was now a regular occurrence. Shortly before my appointment I'd met a retired radiologist. Without actually mentioning symptoms, I asked him if an all-over body health scan might be a good idea for a man of my age. I was fifty-eight. He scoffed at this, saying it was a waste of time and money. The best thing, he went on, for a man in his fifties is a colonoscopy. I didn't know what that was, but in effect it's a camera up the arse.

I saw the specialist a few days later. I'd had a blood test, was generally fit and well, and he examined me, predominantly with rubber gloves. As I got off his couch and pulled my trousers on he declared that for a man of my age (fifty-eight), I was as fit as the proverbial fiddle. There was no mention of anything untoward whatsoever. He went to bid me farewell, but I turned back to him and suggested I had a colonoscopy. There was the briefest of a surprised look from him that I even knew the word, but then he looked again at my notes and generally agreed it wasn't a bad idea. So worried was I about all this that I told him I'd pay for it, but he fixed it for me on the NHS.

Colonoscopies aren't much fun. There are the three litres of foul-tasting clean-out fluid to be taken the day before, then the waiting around in the hospital in what amounts to a flowery apron, with your arse sticking out the back where it's been loosely tied. You then enter a brightly lit room, with scary machinery and TV monitors, and given a sedative. Your arse is then smeared with KY Jelly, laid on a couch, and a man in a mask then approaches with a long black pipe which hisses with what I assume is water. There is a spotlight inserted on the end. This thing is then stuck up your arse. You can watch all this on the monitor, and up it goes, round the numerous bends in the bowel and colon until it gets to the small intestine. There it stops, and it feels like the worst stitch imaginable, despite the relaxing sedative. Bit by bit it's pulled back until the operator spots a polyp. Out the end of this pipe a circular wire pops out, lassos the polyp and, once grabbed, the wire is heated and the little pink polyp is burnt off. Four polyps were found and removed. However, there was a big one lower down which couldn't be lassoed by the cauterising wire. I would need to go to the recovery room and speak to someone about this. Despite being slightly dazed from the sedative, I took it all in.

And there I was, in November 2006, sitting in bed with tea and biscuits, with Ailsa by my side. Then a rather abrupt individual arrived in his green theatre gown. He picked up my notes from the end of the bed, frowned, then looked at me and said, 'Now, about this tumour.'

Polyp to tumour in seconds. I was completely numb. He asked if I was fully cognisant of the words he was using. I nodded. This was a big deal he told me, on a par with heart bypass surgery. By now I was fully alert and in shock. I would need an anterior resection. I asked him to convert this into English. Essentially, abdominal surgery to take out a section of the colon containing the tumour and then reconnecting the colon. The burning question was whether this tumour was malignant. He just shrugged, told me the odds were 50/50, threw the notes back on to the bed and walked away.

I was dazed and numbed by this news. The vacuum I entered for two weeks while they got the results of the biopsy were possibly the worst of days. We ran to Criccieth, (where else would I go??) and bolted ourselves in. The news finally came back that this tumour was indeed malignant. I had colon cancer. I was shattered. My next concern was whether the thing had spread.

I now know there are five stages of colon cancer. The first is the polyp turns bad, second it travels through the colon wall, third the lymphatic system, fourth liver, fifth lungs and there is no sixth stage. Basically, that's it.

The day after Boxing Day 2006 I was in the hands of a top-rated surgeon, who since has become a very good friend. I was operated on and ended up with fifteen stitches in my abdomen. I spent the next six days in hospital and contemplated the previous twelve months. It was a shit end to a shit year, and having spent New Year's Eve in the hospital, with Ailsa in a camp bed by my side, resolved once and for all that 2007 was a clean-out year if I survived. For the very first time in my life, I recognised my mortality.

I got out on 2nd January 2007, and went back a week later for a consultation. It turned out I was extremely lucky. The polyp had indeed gone bad, but not to the second stage. I needed no chemo or radiotherapy, and was free to go and get on with the rest of my life. I also resolved never to trust the local GP's advice ever again. Time here is absolutely of the essence. Had I not acted decisively, knowing my body well enough to make a judgement, I wouldn't be here today, writing this.

2007–2009

2006 wasn't quite done with me yet. The final kick in the bollocks was halfway through January, when the wound in my gut didn't heal. It leaked and was infected. Frankly an unsightly mess. The medical men didn't seem overly perturbed but I bloody well was. I get really pissed off with some of these dismissive 'nothing to worry about' people and their platitudes. I've learned my lesson here. I don't trust them. And why should you? When you stop and think about it, in the scheme of things you're just another number passing through the cattle market of the hospital business. I can sort of see why. Under financed, understaffed, bureaucratic, and faced with an avalanche of increased population. It's a neve ending supply of people, most of whom, to me anyway, take little in the way of responsibility for their own health. This state of affairs I think has led to the entire medical profession becoming an army of box tickers. Compassionate people by nature, of that I'm sure, but so many pass through their hands it just becomes a routine.

I went to my local GP in the end. I'd run out of dressings and was using sanitary pads to mop up the infection. In between all this I also had some serious pain. The GP was the opposite of what I described above. An exception to the rule. He showed extreme concern for me. He sent away a sample for analysis, and back it came three days later. It was MRSA.

Now I think about it, I feel the hospital staff were in some kind of denial. Targets for performance include cases of infection developed in the hospital. A black mark on their record. MRSA is a common bug which happily lives in the nostrils and sinuses. By and large it's completely harmless – until, that is, it enters cut skin and flesh. Then it becomes an absolute bastard. It literally began to eat me away. I think the medics call it a granulation of the flesh. Either way it was serious, and most antibiotics don't touch it. It wears a hard hat. It needed an application of heavy-duty antibiotics. My generally healthy immune system was no match. I lost a stone in weight in four weeks. The scar it left isn't pretty. (Is any scar?) Fortunately I'm covered in fur, and my hairy belly obscures it quite well. The colon also decided to play silly buggers too. It took more or less two years for my colon and bowel habits to settle. My scatalogical record was fourteen visits to the bog in one day. The softest of toilet tissue felt like barbed wire. Is this what they mean by gut reaction? The overall lesson here is to avoid invasive surgery wherever possible. I had no choice, but it was a small price to pay for life, so I mustn't whinge.

By March 2007 I was more or less in the clear, and I moved fast with my plans. I was now on a mission. I sold the flats in Alcester and put the memory of that hideous episode with the Ghanaian princess firmly behind me. The property in France went on the market too. Both were sold quite quickly, and I banked the cash.

During my time with the medicine men, I was also dealing with my father's estate as his appointed executor. His will was a straightforward affair, and not especially complicated. My sister was a joint executor but if anyone can complicate a simple situation she can. She delegated the task to her husband, whom my dad had previously dismissed as an executor. It was clearly an attempt to smooth ruffled feathers, though why on earth my dad had put him on in it the first place was beyond me. This became another unnecessary link in the communication chain. I wanted to move fast with all this but was hobbled by her intransigence, and her pedantic husband. It took far longer to sort than needed, and probate could have been handled by any local provincial solicitor. But no. My sister and her husband wished to use possibly the most expensive accountancy firm in the land, who dealt with probate for wealthy people. It was a ridiculously and unnecessarily long-winded process. Despite my frustration, I abided by my mum's plea to just 'go with the flow'.

Most of my father's wealth was tied up in shares in his company, of which he and my brother Martin were the majority shareholders. The will specified that his own shares were split 40% to my mother and the remaining 60% shared equally between myself and my sister. In due course I inherited 30% of his estate and the dividends they produced gave me the benefit of a secondary income. With some of this windfall I decided to buy another boat. A bigger one. The reasons for this follow below in another little ...

Side story: July 2006
Just another kick in the 2006 bollocks which I'd almost forgotten about.

I'd acquired a Channel Island 22 fishing boat in 2004. Two years before my dad died. I'd moored it in Porthmadog, a town adjacent to Criccieth. I named it *Calico Jack*. I'd always had a fascination with pirates ever since I can remember. *Treasure Island* is one of my all-time favourite books. *Calico Jack* the pirate was a flamboyant character, who had two women on the go. Something I could easily identify with. (I need a smiley face emoji in here.) Eventually caught by the Royal Navy, arrested, tried, and found guilty of piracy in the Caribbean, he was hung on a gibbet in Kingston, Jamaica, and left to rot. A dire warning to the nefarious band of seafarers raiding Spanish ships in that part of the world in the 1700s. The story of Calico Jack is worth reading. But that's not the real side story.

A few pages back I described briefly my attempt to rescue this boat in the teeth of a howling gale on the Sunday morning. This was the fateful weekend of the full moon, when the weather changed abruptly, and two days later my father was dead. I sometimes wonder if had I drowned might anything have changed. My death might, just might, have changed his mind. Somehow I doubt it.

This is now the story of that so-called seafaring adventure, or very nearly seafaring calamity.

We'd all arrived in Criccieth on the Friday night, and planned to take *Calico Jack* out early the following morning to fish. My closest friend Brom, and his wife Pat, had joined Ailsa and I for the weekend. The weather early that Saturday morning was still, with the promise of a gloriously sunny day in prospect. The sea was clear blue and flat calm. We caught mackerel, then I moored the boat at low tide on a remote beach. We lit a driftwood fire, and cooked the fish. It was the most perfect of days, and we spent most of the afternoon lazing around until the tide returned. I eventually brought the boat back to Criccieth beach, and given the calm, fine, hot conditions, made a decision to anchor overnight opposite the house, rather than make the hour's trip back to Porthmadog. Having dropped them off in the inflatable dinghy near the beach, I took the boat some 300 yards out to sea, dropped anchor, and swam back. It was 9 pm as the red sun sank over the horizon. As I got out of the water I noticed a stiff breeze had suddenly developed, and shivered. I turned and glanced back at the boat, then noticed the flat sea had begun to chop. It was a fine clear sky, not a cloud, and the sharp glinting stars began to appear, but the boat sat out there quite happily. To my eternal regret, I didn't check the forecast.

I cannot ever recall a time when the weather, as my Granny would say, 'turned on a sixpence'. At 11 pm, having eaten, I went back outside. I could see the boat silhouetted against the sky, but saw a dark line on the horizon making its way slowly from the west. It was a black blanket coming in to cover the sky. We went to bed, but I couldn't sleep, By 2 am Sunday morning it was pitch dark and a raging gale, the wind tearing at the open window, and waves crashing on to the shingle below. This weather had come out of nowhere in the space of a few hours. I spent the entire night peering out through the rain-soaked bedroom window to get a glimpse of the boat. And I could, just occasionally. The waves by now were foaming and smashing on to the beach and Castle rock. Just now and then I got a glimpse of the boat wallowing offshore, then it would disappear behind a trough. How that anchor held is still a mystery, but incredibly it did. At first light we all went down to the beach, dragging the inflatable with us.

The waves hitting the beach were 3-4 ft high, and no let-up with the wind. My guess was storm force seven. It was relatively calm beyond the breakers, and after many panicked attempts to get the dinghy into the water, I found I just couldn't get it beyond the surf. The waves simply tossed it back on the beach, flinging it contemptuously like a leaf. In panic and despair I knew I'd have no choice but to swim out, but suddenly and by extreme good fortune I managed to find a ten-second break and launched the dinghy beyond the breakers. I then plunged into this foaming weed and debris and began to swim out, pushing the dinghy in front of me. It wasn't at all an easy task.

It probably took me ten minutes or so to get within range of the boat. *Calico Jack*'s stern was bucking and twisting and hurled 6-10 ft up into thin air, exposing the prop. Then back down it would crash. This boat weighed a couple of tons and only now do I realise what an incredibly dangerous thing I was attempting. Hanging on to the dinghy for support I waited for my chance, and as the stern came down somehow I got the dinghy rope attached to the ladder at the back, then waited for the next opportunity to grab it, when it plunged back down into the trough. After two or three attempts, I grabbed the ladder rail and was jolted and lifted out of the water, like a plug out of a sink. I clambered up in stages like some fallen horse rider attempting to get back in the saddle, and over the gunwhale I went falling face forward on to the deck. The cockpit of the boat was chaos. All our carefully stored fishing gear, bait, pots, pans, cups and saucers were strewn everywhere. Staggering into the wheelhouse I hoped there was a god, and prayed the engine would start. Prayers answered, it coughed into life immediately (obviously then there is a God, and he loves me!).

I know most boats, especially motorboats, can broach easily on the turn, be knocked sideways and over they go. I inched the boat full ahead into the storm. Once I gauged it to be over the anchor chain, I pressed the button to retrieve it, taking the pressure off the chain. Clanking and rattling, up it came out of the sand 30 ft below. The waves smashed on to the bow, and spray made visibility almost impossible, but I spotted a flattish area behind one wave. At full throttle I turned the boat as quickly as I could on this flat bit before the waves had a chance to gather themselves and crash into the side. Miraculously I got away with it. With a following sea surging behind and threatening to swamp the cockpit I made for Castle rock, where I thought there was at least relative calm from the force of this south-westerly. I dropped anchor in the shelter of Castle rock, even though it was still pretty rough, got into my bucking bronco of a dinghy, and finally paddled to the shore where the other three were waiting, Ailsa holding a towel for me. I was cold and knackered.

There was no let-up all day with the wind, though the rain had eased off. Eventually I had to make a decision at some point to get it back to the berth in Porthmadog, seven miles and a couple of hours away. The tide was the crucial decision-maker. I needed to make a run for it to enable me to get over the sandbar at the mouth of the river. The water at low tide barely covered it, and an outgoing tide with an incoming wind are ill-suited bedfellows, especially crossing a sandbar which was barely covered at low tide in the best of weather, and the narrowest of channels to get through.

Given this unwanted timetable Brom, Pat and I took the inflatable back out into the bay around 3 pm and hauled it on board *Calico Jack*. I placed it on the roof of the wheelhouse and we started up the engine. As I moved off, the protection of Castle rock was suddenly lost and the wind hit us full force. The inflatable, like some malicious kite, lifted off the roof and crashed down into the cockpit. Pat had been holding on while I was manoeuvring the boat and the inflatable hit her in the face. She was clearly injured, with blood trickling from a head wound, so I immediately dropped anchor once more. This whole exercise was proving to be a disaster. We heaved the inflatable over the side, and somehow got her into it. She was shaken and pale, and obviously in shock. I stayed on board and Brom rowed her back to the shore 100 yards away. He had some difficulty but once there Ailsa took care of her. He eventually managed to row the thing back to me, and we tried again. We'd lost thirty minutes as a result of this, with a fast-running outgoing tide. This would make the sandbar even more hazardous.

An hour or so later we got to the mouth of the estuary, and as I'd expected the sea was boiling over the sandbar. We could see the white surf crashing over it some two miles out. With more than a hint of trepidation we put on lifejackets and made a run for it. As we hit it, the boat was thrown in all directions, the sand scraping the hull as we crossed over. Eventually we made it through, and mercifully into the relative calm of the river mouth.

I have never felt such relief. If I was to continue to engage my fishing exploits off the Welsh coast, I realised, this boat was too small for my requirements. I needed a heavier, bigger, more robust one which could deal with big seas like this, and not be tossed about like corks to the degree we'd been when dealing with this kind of unexpected weather. I put it up for sale.

This was the last Sunday in July 2006, before that fateful

Tuesday forty-eight hours later when my father died. I said 2006 was a bastard, and this was yet another example. We left for home unscathed, and very lucky.

Given the tumultuous events of 2006, of which this boat business was just another, and culminating in my abdominal surgery in December, I embraced 2007 with a fervent and optimistic hope.

I'd sold my tricky Channel Island 22, and bought a Mitchell 31. I named it *Calico Jack* too. This was much bigger and 10 ft longer. Altogether more robust. Never did I intend, ever, to be caught out like that again in such appalling and treacherous conditions.

By mid-2007 I had wings on my feet. I wasn't hanging around for anything or anyone. I sold the flats in Alcester, sold my bolthole in France, and sold the boat business off, having split the proceeds with my ex. I'd also managed to bank a reasonable amount of cash from all this. Furthermore, although still suffering haphazard bowel habits, I felt I was finally on the mend from my colon cancer operation. We moved my mum in the meantime down from Lincolnshire, to a more manageable property for her near Henley-in-Arden, and as it turned out just in time before the market collapsed.

The financial affairs left behind by my dad were gradually sorting themselves out too, with probate, a nauseating and messy business, finally granted by the Inland Revenue. I had a sizeable income stream from the dividends produced by my share of Dad's shares. Combined with the income from my remaining properties, after I'd divided the assets with my ex-wife following my divorce in 2005, it seemed I was sitting pretty. My house in Wales had been refurbished too, using the proceeds from the sale of timber from the woodlands. It had crossed my mind on more than one occasion to live up in Criccieth, but the ties of Worcestershire, particularly with Ailsa's daughter Alice still at school, made my desire to live by the sea somewhat impractical, so we continued to live happily in the rented cottage in Honeybourne. Besides there was always the pull of the River Wye for my pike-fishing, which had in many ways supplanted the lake in France, now sold. Towards the end of 2007 I was well on the road to finally sorting myself out. Clearing the decks as it were. I almost felt smug.

I look back at that shit year 2006 in some kind of bewildered astonishment. It reminded me a bit of the weather. There's snow, and rain, and sun, and averages of all of them in any given year. If you get prolonged doses of any one of those, there's always the comforting thought that sooner or later it will change for the better. Life is like that. Sometimes you have to take the rough, knowing or hoping there'll be a smooth at some point. This is a fact of life. It seemed to me, however, that 2006 had put a lifetime's rough on me in the space of twelve months. Where the fuck was there ever going to be a smooth? Frankly I was more astonished that I'd survived it. If I were a religious type, I'd swear the gods had had it in for me. It comes back to that old adage, it's not the size of the dog in the fight, but the fight in the dog. But believe me, there were times when I nearly succumbed to it. So 2007 was a turning point for the better. I made the most of it.

Then out of the blue, at the end of 2007 there was a financial crash. They called it the credit crunch. The banking industry had lent to people who simply couldn't afford to repay. Greed as usual drove it, and the resulting mess meant many big banks were bailed out by the taxpayer. In the ensuing mess in early 2008 the entire UK economy slid into recession.

My luck however had changed for the good. Here was some smooth arriving at last from eighteen months of rough. Not only did I discover I had sold out some of my assets at the top of the market, my brother Martin had also concluded the sale of one of the company's factory premises, and just in the nick of time it seems. It was decided by the directors to apportion the windfall from this sale among the shareholders. As a result I picked up a huge and wholly unexpected dividend. It was incredible to think that two or three years before I'd gone through my own financial crisis. My divorce was the main factor at the end of 2005, culminating in my illness at the end of 2006. Suddenly I was completely financially independent. I already had a substantial amount of cash in the bank and the economy was in recession. It provided me with the ideal opportunity to find a bargain of a house and move into it with Ailsa and Alice, who had by now left school and got a job. For the very first time in my life, I didn't need to borrow. Not that the banks were lending anyway.

2008

By early 2008, and still in recovery from my operation twelve months before, with 2007 gone and 2006 a distant bad dream, I decided it was time we did some travelling. Any idea of looking for any type of business deal or actively seeking to expand my property collection went out of the window. I'd survived a serious warning which had threatened my life, and not for the first time I now reflected on a factual realisation, something I'd ignored for most of my life. I was actually mortal. I could have died. Death is real. I have to tell you that this obvious fact, known to most but not to me, hit with some force. No more of this 'in five years time I'm going to do this that or the other'. The time was now.

So travel we did, and we took off in February 2008 to South Africa, driving across the Garden Route for two weeks, then onwards, eventually, from Johannesburg to Perth, rented a four-wheel drive and continued our elongated road trip up the west coast, finally returning to Perth, where we flew to Sydney, stayed with old friends and did the same again with a rental car. It was reminiscent of the trip I'd done all those years before in 1991, but this time no motorhome, no kids, just my soulmate to share the experience with. We had a wonderful time and on return decided to finish with the rental cottage in Honeybourne. Alice had by now left her job and intended to take a sabbatical, or gap six months. I encouraged her in this and off she went, ending up in, of all places, Australia.

We found our bargain house, and completed on it in July 2008. It's where we live today. This is now May 2020. Given the recession still manifest in the country, we got a good deal and I bought it outright. For the very first time in my life, I needed no mortgage, no lender to go cap-in-hand to. The freedom and sheer exuberance I felt from my new-found wealth was indescribable. Cash, as they say, especially in a recession, is most definitely king. This novelty struck me in a peculiar way. Despite the freedom to pretty well do what I liked, I didn't. My working-class cautiousness still kept me in check, but not having to account to a lender or bank was particularly liberating.

I suppose that's the way I am, but I do love unaccountability. Like the house in Wales this one needed some renovation and refurbishment. It was, however, spacious. Small enough for the two of us, but big enough to accommodate visitors, with an acre of orchard, and a river running along the boundary, with wonderful views of Worcestershire, and a half-an-hour drive to my beloved River Wye. Ideal for me. But like most of my property interests, I had an eye for future redevelopment, to thus enhance its value. But that's me just being me – much to Ailsa's annoyance. This was a proper home, not a business deal, she reiterated ad nauseum. Nevertheless, she was right. It was she who made it a real home for me, because she was there for me to come home to. I always wanted that, and now I had it.

Ailsa and I had our first proper Christmas together in our own house in 2008, and given this new-found freedom and wealth, I began to think through the next stage.

2009

By the time 2009 arrived I was suddenly aware and in control of my destiny. It was a heady feeling. I knew, though, that my brother Martin's longer-term plan was to get out of the business which had so dominated our dad's life. He wanted to live life on his terms and, like me, be free to control his own destiny, without the spectre of our dad hanging over him. He was faced daily with the constant reminder that he was somehow solely responsible for this 'family' legacy. He told me confidentially that he was in discussion with an unknown potential buyer, with a view to lining up the sale of the whole group. He could then take his substantial stake out, and freely move on with his life. Frankly I couldn't and didn't blame him. He had been hugely influential in enriching this family.

As for me, I knew that if this sale happened I would pick up a substantial share of the proceeds. Even though he wasn't in a position to tell me the details, I knew that if this deal came off I would suddenly be faced with an avalanche of cash. I went along to my accountant and asked his advice. On paper I was already substantially wealthy by most standards, but this sale was of Croesus proportions. I needed to know where I stood with potential inheritance tax liability. Having already been made aware of my mortality, and a cancer diagnosis, is a great way to concentrate the mind, I was also single and divorced. The implications for a serious inheritance tax hit by the Inland Revenue were very real. The accountant simply looked at me and said, 'Stage one, get married.'

Inheritance tax is a bastard. It's something which most people don't either want to talk about or deal with when they're alive. It doesn't affect you personally of course since you're 6 ft under, but I learned a lot when I was dealing with my dad's affairs. My sister and I were advised to vary his will, eschew the shareholding we'd been left, and put it into our Mum's name since she can inherit free of inheritance tax. She would then gift it back six months later. This was a wheeze to save tax, and it worked. It was possibly the only really useful advice we got from KPMG, the very expensive tax experts who dealt with his estate, but at least it stopped the Revenue diving in.

I swore that after I'd divorced Val, and settled our finances mutually by agreement, that I'd never marry again. I was still completely in love with Ailsa (and still am), but was fed up of living with a woman who went by the name of Mrs Chorley. It particularly irked me that our cases, when we travelled, were in different names, as were our tickets. That alone seemed a good enough reason, but I'm sure she did it on purpose to piss me off.

On 19th September 2009 we married, and it was without doubt the best wedding I'd ever been to. Both my children had accepted, embraced, and taken to Ailsa, and likewise her three children had with me. That fact alone was one of delight. I took a large Georgian house, rented the cottages in the grounds and invited all our family, and close friends. My son Oliver was my best man, delivering one of the best speeches I'd ever heard. I chose not to speak, there was nothing to add. Besides, the band did the talking for me. I played at this wonderful party, then fell into bed about 3 am. We had a whale of a time. I still to this day refer to her as my tax-dodge wife. She's a natural Craddock and we're a perfect fit. Just like finding that essential piece of jigsaw.

2010–2020

By the end of 2009 I knew my brother Martin was on the brink of selling the business, and in early 2010 the deal was done. Under the circumstances it was a brilliant deal, done in the depths of a recession, against the odds really, and the credit is entirely his. As a minority shareholder my shares were compulsorily sold.

When I think back now to my earlier years, receiving this windfall aged sixty-two was almost too late, but I wasn't finished yet. Not a bit of it. I was fit, energetic, certainly not as ambitious perhaps, but in the back of my mind I began to hatch a few plans. Money doesn't bring happiness, but can be used to make life happier through choice. That's what money brings, above all else. Choice.

Back at the accountants I was now faced with a major problem. I wasn't just a millionaire, which I was before this. I was now a multi-millionaire. Did it change me? Did I feel any different? No, I don't think it changed me one bit. Sure, it provided even greater choice, but it also brought responsibility. I could never shake off the thrifty attitude which had been drummed into me with my pocket money all those years before, as a scruffy kid growing up in North Staffordshire. My share of the sale was substantial. I opened an account with Coutts, and put on deposit enough money to pay off the other bastard, Capital Gains Tax. This was due eighteen months hence. Since I'd inherited the shares free of charge, I was faced with a maximum hit, at the time 28%. But what now to do with the rest?

My inheritance tax liability had also increased substantially, given that all my assets were now held by me personally despite being married. Sure, the assets can be passed to my spouse free of inheritance tax, but what would happen if say we both died together? The Revenue would rub their collective hands together and put their shovel in for 40%. I began to think this through very carefully. I was well off before, but I was even more so now.

Having substantial wealth brings its own unique set of problems. I hadn't earned most of this, I'd had it gifted. I needed to protect it for the benefit of all the family. This wealth had to all intents and purposes just fallen from the sky, and I never looked at it as mine to spend freely. In fact I didn't actually need it. I was already comfortably off. It wasn't there to be squandered, but if I could use it to enhance my personal wealth and provide an income for future generations I'd need to invest it carefully. But where and how? Fundamentally I didn't trust, and never have, financial advisers, or the stock market. I needed to achieve an income, an investment, and set up something which was more or less inheritance-tax-proof.

The answer was before my eyes. I knew about property. I could invest as little or as much into it as I wished, and retain control, rather than leaving it in the hands of some smart alec financial whizz-kid.

I set up JRC Property Holdings Ltd. Since JRC are both my initials and my dad's, it was a nice touch. That was stage 1.

Stage 2 was an offshore trust. Sounds a bit highfalutin, pretentious even. It wasn't, it was only in the Isle of Man. The purpose of this was to place funds outside the UK and grow them (hopefully) in a light-touch tax environment just in case I snuffed it prematurely. I just needed to survive for seven years, i.e. 2019. I did, and have! The whole trust is then exempt, and can be used to pay whatever my inheritance tax liabilities might be. It was a smart move, but it still irks me to think that money has to be put aside just to get shot of the Revenue. I mean it's not like I'd be about to remonstrate with them, is it?

Stage 3 was interesting. In order to then start to build the limited company with property acquisitions I needed to transfer the bulk of my tax-free cash into it, in the form of a director's loan. So I sat down with my (trusted) financial adviser and made plans. My property experiences in the 1980s and 90s had stood me in good stead. We were still in the depths of a recession, and it proved to be good timing. Property prices were more or less on the floor and cash was now king. The initial idea was for the company to acquire four £500,000 properties, preferably commercial, to produce a steady income stream, then over time move the existing properties I owned personally into it. It was also handy being married too, since I was able to transfer the ownership jointly into Ailsa's name before moving them into the company. Thus I was to save on Capital Gains Tax. It was handy being married to a tax-dodge.

I didn't intend the above to sound like a financial lesson. Not a bit, but faced with this new set of circumstances, and a desire to protect my dad's legacy, I had to think long-term. In the long run we're dead, and for a very long time, never, as far as I know, to return.

It was around this time that I remembered someone writing about the twin demons of life. The first half you borrow, invest, survive and have no choice but to kowtow to demon number one, the bank. Having accumulated your assets, you then have the second one on your back, the taxman. I never in a million years expected a scenario quite like this, but this was now my dilemma.

With my new-found appreciation of mortality, my sole aim was to provide a secure income for future generations of my family. In my head I had my infamous ten-year plan.

The first property I bought in the company name in late 2010 was 15 Regent Street, Cheltenham. I then went looking for the others.

In the meantime. I looked to acquire personal property. Personal investments like watches, cars, and paintings. In short things which I really liked personally and had never had the opportunity to buy, but whenever I did I always had an eye on appreciation. I bought things which I hoped would at least hold their value and not lose me a shed load of money, and yet, if necessary could easily be converted back to cash if the need arose. Liquidity is very important. Asset-rich, cash-poor is a common problem. You can't exactly break off a chimney pot and go shopping in Tesco with it.

Another big consideration was staying alive ... oh yes ... and keeping fit, in order to see this new project through. Just as important, I needed to keep the taxman at bay for at least seven years! So what did I do? I bought a swimming pool. A hydro-therapy pool in fact, which included a real luxury for us: a hot tub. Each day since I had this pool installed I've swum every day. To hell with the additional and fairly substantial cost of the electricity it used, for me I had no problem justifying it. My days of road-running were gone. Arthritis beckoned, and despite badminton once a week, this exercise was far more beneficial on my joints and lungs. Besides, I never liked public swimming pools. It wasn't so much the chlorine but the people who got in my way, as well as on my nerves! Health clubs are all very well, but I tire of the routine, and the sheer motivation of going diminishes after a time. In the end the desire just fizzles out.

Eventually I also built my own gym, but the pool I've used daily ever since. I reckon I swim 2 miles a week and I'm still going strong eleven years later as I write this.

One of the main lessons I've learned from all this, as I alluded to above, is that being rich on paper with sizeable assets isn't good enough. There is always a need for liquidity, in other words hard cash, in case of unexpected emergencies. Life can be immensely unpredictable. This is a lecture now. Always bear the piggy bank stash in mind; you never quite know when you'll need to break into it.

Fortunately, I've been brought up in a family which has its feet firmly on the ground. From the days where I watched my dad cycle off to work in Stoke-on-Trent on dark drizzly mornings in the 1950s on his old bike, with nothing more than a pack of cheese sandwiches in his knapsack to sustain him, to him eventually living in relative splendour in Lincolnshire. Both he and my mother never let wealth go to their heads. Well maybe my mum did once she got into shopping mode … but I can also say the same for myself, brother Martin and sister Julia. Both my children Oliver and Joanna have inherited the same attitude. It's true of Ailsa and her family too. Humble beginnings set a standard for thrift. By most measures we're extremely well off nowadays, but never once can I recall any of the above adopting an attitude of pretentiousness. That pleases me no end.

Chapter 21

Following my newly hatched grand plan, and with the first property in the bag, I found the other three by chance, which happened to be owned by one family, all brothers whom I knew well. The properties were splendid Regency buildings in the Promenade in Cheltenham. Two of the brothers, Michael and Roger, I knew well enough, having shot with them on many occasions over the years. In short the properties were jointly owned by all the brothers, but as so often happens, each wanted his share out to be free to go his separate way. The three properties had been largely neglected, with broken leases, and a lack of investment in their maintenance. I suspect the brothers had occasionally squabbled over how to manage them and who would pay. I sought the advice of an expert in commercial property. His advice was to leave well alone. It was a mess of broken leases and poor management, and besides I was nervous doing business with friends. Maybe, I just thought, it wasn't meant to be, so having listened to this advice I walked away.

But something niggled me. Had I just missed a golden opportunity? In the end I decided I had. I couldn't shake off the thought that these three properties would have fitted with my grand plan perfectly. My annoyance and irritation were compounded in January 2011 when I caught up with Michael at a shooting party in Anglesey. He told me, with delight, that all three properties had now been sold to an individual who intended to put them into a pension scheme.

I was livid. I was so angry with myself for not being brave enough to take them on and kicked myself all the way back from Anglesey. I may have just missed the bargain of a lifetime. Why was I so indecisive? What had happened to me? Why was I so lacking in bravery to go for it? Maybe it was me being over-cautious, overprotective of my dad's legacy perhaps. I don't know, but I really beat myself up over it. I'd had a deal in my grasp and let it slip through my fingers. I'd been in business in Cheltenham for years, knew the place like the back of my hand, and knew that the Promenade was possibly one of the most high-profile and desirable areas to be. In thirty years of working there all the properties in that row were rarely ever unoccupied. Most of them were upmarket estate agents or legal and accounting practices. A perfect profile for me. I had deliberately avoided looking at retail premises, simply because the internet and online shopping had put a hole in most town centres. That wasn't the way to go, and I was proved right. What I wanted were good quality, safe and secure tenancies. These were that, and dickhead me had let them go.

I calmed down after a while, since the UK economy was still reeling from the banking crisis and JRC Ltd, courtesy of me, was loaded with cash. I knew that sooner or later I would find property number two.

To help me in this quest, in February 2011 I brought Oliver in to the business. He was already working with the love of his life, BMW, but had already had some property experience with his own house redevelopment. BMW were paying him well, but in terms of lifestyle it was a harsh environment. He worked as a business manager for them, knew his way around percentages, and at twenty-five had been with them for six or seven years. I'd already made it clear to him awhile back that my future plans were entirely family orientated, and having explained my grand plan to him, we drew up a profile of the type of properties we would seek to acquire. I envisioned him running the business eventually, with me holding the reins. I wrote out a simple ten-point plan. He had the aptitude, and thought very much in the same way as I did. He also had acquired considerable business skills at the University of BMW.

We resumed our search, but this time jointly, drawing up a

geographical and manageable area to search and investigate potential properties to acquire.

And then, without warning, serendipity kicked in.

In May 2011 I heard that my friend Michael, the elder brother of the Promenade clan, had been admitted to hospital. It was a Saturday, and by chance I was on my way to look at a shotgun in Witney, not a million miles from Oxford, where he was recovering in a private nursing home. On impulse I called his wife to enquire as to his progress, and asked her if he was up for unexpected visitors. She was delighted to hear from me, and said my visit with Ailsa would cheer him up no end. Off we went to see him. He was grumpy. He'd been banned from smoking and drinking. His room was strewn with newspapers and books, and he declared he was bored rigid with this enforced incarceration, and somewhat depressed.

To make matters worse, he told me the individual buying the three properties in the Promenade had pulled out, with no reason given. I was absolutely delighted, though I tried hard not to show it. This was my chance. Maybe it was meant to be after all. I told him I would go for all three properties and, in order to keep our friendship intact, would deal independently with his agent in Cheltenham first thing Monday morning. And that's exactly what Oliver and I did.

By the end of 2011 JRC Property Holdings had acquired all three, and we had money to spare, since they came in under my original budget of £500k each. That they needed work was an understatement, but my advice is to never buy any property without the means to refurbish it, as well as ensure you enhance the value. For us, additional value came from sorting out the mess.

It took several months to complete on the acquisition of these properties, and there were various complications financially with the younger brother, who had previously borrowed on the equity in them. Since he had neglected to repay any of the loans, there was a charge on them. In order to sell them the charge had to be lifted, and was probably the main reason the original buyer pulled out. In the event, the other three brothers stumped up to bail him out, and eventually the charges were removed. It was a hassle at times, but nevertheless by the end of 2011, and in one fell swoop, we now had the four properties I'd planned for originally, and three of them had come in one deal. The income stream was such that they all needed managing on an almost day-to-day basis, as well as us planning a major refurbishment in 2012. This really is where Oliver came into his own.

He took charge of the day-to-day relationship with the tenants and contractors, and together we planned an ambitious restoration of these beautiful Grade-II listed buildings.

2012

Well, we're heading to the end of the journey now. I can hear the sighs of relief all round from you. But I'm not quite done with you yet! I can't wave you all farewell without yet another little ...

Side story: The last one, I promise!

Michael, the guy who was hospitalised, and then informed me about the deal falling through with the Promenade property, thus paving the way for us to acquire it, was also influential in another capacity too.

Whilst on that shoot in Anglesey in January 2011, and gnashing my teeth over the missed Promenade opportunity, another opportunity had presented itself to me at around the same time. I was generally in a bad mood on this shoot. This arose primarily because I'd recently met up with the owner of the upper beat adjacent to the one I bought back in 1999. Remember him? Mr Mott. I discovered that he had it in mind to sell this beat which adjoined mine. Just as before, we couldn't agree on a price. I wanted it, that much was true. I was sick of him letting everyone and his dog fish there and, as wayward anglers tend to do, gradually start to encroach on my hallowed bit (in other words poach). However, I just dug my heels in and refused on principle to pay the full price. It was just me being bloody-minded, even though in my new financial state I could afford it.

Michael, who was there with the usual team, queried my mood. He's very kind like that. When I told him about this business on the river his advice was simple. Buy it, and buy it now. It was a wise remark, and the fact was the chance may never present itself again.

Despite the fact I could afford it, I had it in my head that I just couldn't justify it. I needed a deal, but Mott clearly wasn't going to budge. Michael's view was that sooner or later Mott will die. The consequences of this probably meant that this beautiful stretch of river may well pass out of his estate, go to auction, some wealthy hedge fund manager would spot it, and simply write out a cheque. The essence of Michael's advice was that the opportunity would be gone, never perhaps to reappear.

It was sound advice, and even though I squealed a bit in my head, I bought it. This entire beat of 1.3 miles is now my exclusive preserve, including about 5 acres of woodland and scrub alongside the bank. I cannot tell you the pleasure this part of the river has consistently provided to me over the past eight or so years. It is emotionally impossible for me to place a value on it, such is the sanctuary and peace it confers on me. This property was subsequently transferred to my company, JRC Property Holdings Ltd, to keep it out of my personal estate, and provides me with all the justification I need for fishing, and enhancing the place with tree and wildflower planting. In short I acquired an untainted piece of countryside paradise.

I'd always missed my place in France when I sold it in 2007 – the lake, the trees, the log fire – and now here it was on my doorstep in Herefordshire.

This side story is in honour of Michael Lear, a man to whom I shall forever be grateful.

*

2012 was more or less consumed by work on the Promenade, and whilst Oliver dealt daily with the inevitable problems over the Prom's renovation and refurbishment, he also soothed ruffled tenant feathers, when they fell over bags of plaster or cement. As for me, apart from interfering occasionally and monitoring cash flow for the entire project, I diverted my attention to taking on personally, together with Ailsa, a redevelopment of our house. This to include a new four-car garage, workshop and gym below. In the process, we gutted the kitchen, and bedrooms to give the whole house a greater feeling of space. Both Ailsa and I like light and space, and that was our focus. She also had a dedicated plot at the back of the garage to develop her own vegetable garden, which she, to this day, guards like an Alsatian dog.

2013

By spring 2013 the properties in Cheltenham were finished, let, and in sparkling condition, Despite the considerable cost, some £130k, we'd enhanced the value dramatically and secured all our tenants on new leases.

In all it took about six months to restore them to their former Regency splendour. These days, in 2020, they're fully let, and Regent Street, the first property I bought in 2010, was restored in 2017. Oliver runs the company on a daily basis and the grand plan has been pretty much achieved. It's his job now to take the business forward, and as of March 2020 Joanna is now a Director, with responsibility for continuing my river legacy. She shares my love of this place, and it's where I hope my final remains will be placed. On the bank preferably. That water can be bloody cold!

By now Ailsa and I had freed ourselves up to make the most of whatever time we have left, and this wonderful wife of mine, constant companion, and soulmate, have had some wonderful times together. We've travelled extensively to far-flung destinations, and indulged perhaps our favourite hobby, road trips to Europe in a Porsche 911.

I've said this somewhere before, but what I've realised is that nothing stays the same forever. Change to one's life is constant, and to sit back and rest on one's laurels is dangerous. It leads to complacency, and that can be fatal. But human nature is about endeavour, experience, taking chances, continuous education, and improvement. Sometimes for the better, but not always.

I'm now finishing this book finally, yes, once and for all, in the year of 2013. It's the best year to leave it. My mum died of a stroke on 20th September 2013. It was the end of an era for me, and has left a huge hole in my life, but as I referred to above, change is constant. I can hardly believe that six years, now seven as I edit this, have elapsed, but they have.

I think of her most days, in fact as I come over to my writing shed across the orchard I have a picture of her pinned to the wall, with a rueful, almost scolding, look on her face. I always say hello to her before I sit down at this keyboard. She's with me a lot. She never answers back. She doesn't need to.

Strangely I think of my father less, despite him originally providing the crucible for this unique wealth opportunity, which resulted in my ability to build a business for the benefit of all my family, stepchildren included. The reality of course was that it was my brother who actually grasped the opportunity to realise this locked-in wealth. It was a smart move, and enriched us all in the process. I hope as a result that in the past ten years I've built on this. Actually I know I have. It's a pity my dad isn't around to see it; I think he would have been quite proud. He'd never have told me, of course.

Perhaps one of the oddest things in all of this is my perception that both my parents got together during World War II out of necessity, and they stuck it out because that was what you did. I think I inherited that attitude in some ways. Both of them were so diametrically opposed to one another in personality. It sometimes makes me wonder if their conflict has manifested itself with both my brother and sister, as well as myself. A kind of weird schizophrenia. It sometimes makes decision-making hard, like we all have two different personalities, with one of each parent on our shoulders. Irrespective of this they both proved to be a tremendous influence on us. For good and bad.

Dad died in 2006 by his own hand, as I've described. Mum followed him seven years later in 2013. In some ways she was more of a mystery than he was. Highly intelligent, but incredibly naïve in very many ways. Almost unworldly. She was the dreamer, he the realist. She had a stroke on Tuesday 17th September. It was a big one, and she was rushed to hospital in Warwick. She lasted in an unconscious state for four days and died on the 20th, the day after our fourth wedding anniversary.

It was pitiful to see the oxygen and saline drips, but the stroke had taken hold and she was unconscious. I couldn't reach out to her and felt utterly helpless. I recalled though when she had been hospitalised before with pneumonia how she complained they never gave her anything to drink. It was the same here. A big sign above her bed: 'Nil by mouth'.

Before Ailsa and I went over to see her the evening of the 19th, I went to the river in the afternoon. I needed to be alone and to think, and besides I couldn't think of anywhere else to go. I stood on the bank watching the leaves floating downstream and thought here goes another leaf off the tree floating to oblivion. I wept and wept for the first time in a very long time, then sat down and wracked my brains to think of some comfort I could give to this unconscious woman. Suddenly I hit on an idea. When I got home I mixed a gin and tonic for her in a little bottle. I smuggled it to her bedside, and once I'd ensured the coast was clear of nurses and experts, I fed it to her by means of a linen napkin between her parched lips. She drank the lot.

The last I saw of her was the following day, Friday 20th, but it wasn't really her any more. Despite the tubes in her arms, overnight the oxygen supply had been removed. I just knew then there was no way back for her. But at least she'd had one last drink, her last ever. She died that night at 7 pm on Friday 20th September, just three weeks short of her ninetieth birthday.

And that leads nicely to the next most likely candidate to fall off the perch. Me, and as the eldest of this peculiar Craddock family, that's why I've written this. I begged both my mother and father to write of their life's experiences, how they met, their time in the forces during the course of that hideous war in 1939–5, but neither of them ever did, and there's now nothing to show for their existence on this planet apart from faded photos in dusty old albums. Frankly most people don't really give a shit about that.

So just to prove that I exist, this is my attempt to at least leave something behind. It's hardly world-shattering prose. It might be a good read, it might bore the pants off you, I don't know, and frankly don't care. Yawn, yawn … zzzzz. It's here and it's done! Hopefully someone, anyone, will read it in years to come and make up their own minds about what kind of life I've led through the latter part of the twentieth century and the early years of the twenty-first.

Such is life, and death.

The Prostate Cancer Bugle

I've just thrown this in for a laff, even though it wasn't funny!

Episode 1
22/02/20

In order to save time pissing about individually updating those who are/might be interested, I thought I'd bring you all up to speed.

A few months ago I didn't know whether to opt for invasive surgery, or radiotherapy. Since I had abdominal surgery thirteen years ago, scar tissue within may have caused complications potentially the surgeon having to remove quite a bit of tissue around the prostate, so radiotherapy was deemed the best solution. In order to shrink the tumour/s I was put on testosterone blockers. I've been on this shit now for about six months and I hate them. Imagine having flu which persists and drains you, and from which you never seem to recover. That's what these things are like. I could've opted for oestrogen jabs, which are marginally more effective, but debilitating to the point where I would've been a regular visitor to Dorothy Perkins to check out the latest cup sizes. The guy I saw yesterday in Newport told me I'd made the right decision. Lesser of the two evils, as it were.

In the event I've stuck with these pills, which at least gives me a measure of control over my medication. Control?? Moi???

The oncologist allotted to me in Cheltenham back in August proved to be a complete wanker. (He looks like a cross between Mr Bean and Dracula.) No doubt brilliant at oncology, but his communication skills are zero. My last discussion with him was November, he suggested private radiotherapy in Bristol, or NHS in Cheltenham. Not only didn't he tell me he'd booked me in at Bristol – four weeks, five days a week – to begin at the end of Jan, he failed to book a slot for identical treatment with the NHS. My intention was to weigh both options as we'd agreed. So now I've opted for Cheltenham it's put me back three or four weeks.

What decided it for me, apart from the hour each way to Bristol and back, was that this outfit were a bloody shambles. Genesis Care they're called, except that they don't, apart (presumably) from getting their hands on the dosh. Just so's you know, twenty days of daily radiotherapy is £35K. This outfit was bloody hopeless, and given Mr Bean's non-communication, I had no idea they even existed until they contacted me unexpectedly by phone mid-Jan. (I put the phone down on them thinking it was a scam.) No contact, no reference, nothing. They also started booking taxis for me to get there, so I was getting a series of texts advising me that a blue Citroen would pick me up at 1 pm. I deleted them, since I thought that was a scam too, then the penny dropped. Whichever poor bugger the texts were destined for never got them. In the event, I decided on the NHS, except that it's now back a month. So Mr Bean screwed up my cleared Feb diary.

My PSA, which is the marker for this (now very common) disease, has been rising over four years and hit 20. Hence my biopsy in June which detected it. I have two small tumours, apparently organ-confined. One is aggressive (I've called it Jack, after my dad), the other less so (Jill, though it should be Joan, after my mum). These hormone pills have however had the advantage of knocking my PSA down from 20 in July, to 11 in Sept, to 5.4 in December, so there's a pay-off of sorts. The last one I only found out about a couple of weeks ago, some five weeks(!!!) after my blood test. When I went to see Mr Bean, he hadn't been informed by his secretary, so it was down to me to tell him what the result was. Turns out the local medical practice here in Pershore sent the December result to

Worcester, not Cheltenham, another communication fuck-up. Sorting out this shambolic miscommunication I really could have done without.

Then serendipity kicked in.

A guy I occasionally shoot with rang me two weeks ago. Not heard from him for ages. His son had prostate cancer diagnosed some years ago when he was about fifty-five (he's now sixty-plus) and having investigated his options at that time, decided on proton beam therapy, in the US. It was a new technology and not available in the UK at that time. Protons (as I'm sure you all know) are little pieces of fried bread you sprinkle on soup, as opposed to photons, which are something to do with cameras.

Anyway I spoke to his son last weekend. I don't know him well, but knew he'd had this treatment and we had a good chat. He spent six weeks in the US in Santiago, had proton therapy and is now clear. No requirement for further drugs to suppress testosterone, which is what I'm after. I need to ditch them. It sounded ideal to me. Unsurprisingly, apart from being quite well off (he used to have a significant interest in Southampton Football Club) he's now put money into the Rutherford Group, and they have four cancer centres open in the UK, one of which is Newport, where we went yesterday.

Proton beam is only good for brain tumours and prostate apparently. (Remember that little boy the NHS refused to treat? Now cured.) Mr Chairman fixed it for me to talk to the medical director, who in turn put me in touch with a brilliant oncologist, a world away from Mr Bean, and we had a good discussion yesterday morning. Things then moved fast. I like that. At his suggestion I had another blood test last week, and my PSA is now down to 3.8 (a good thing!), and a further MRI scan after my chat in Newport. That took over an hour. If you've never had an MRI scan, it's akin to a pneumatic drill at full speed in a disco. I had a headache afterwards that you could have photographed. Then they fixed it for us to go down the M4 for a further 30 miles to Bridgend hospital, to see a Urologist at who was great. I learned,

Brom

Zolly

following a finger and ultrasound scan (glad I'm not gay) that the lining between the rectum and the prostate is 2 mm. Both radiotherapy and proton beam therapy don't just blast the prostate, but can cause damage to the rectal area. Doesn't happen in women. Aren't they lucky? He plans to insert a small saline-filled balloon between the prostate and the rectal area to eliminate any chance of damage from these croutons. And that's where I'm at. Pre-med in the Nuffield next Monday, 'Operation Balloon' on Valentine's Day (good timing?) and ten days later proton beam stuff, so if I'm covered in breadcrumbs after, you'll know why. The other thing about the proton beam treatment is I only need seven sessions, (as opposed to twenty) it's way more accurate, no collateral damage, (fingers crossed) and I can give up these effing pills. Oh, and no more Mr Bean.

Finally, there's an 85% chance that Jack and Joan haven't escaped and gone elsewhere. I consider those good odds. So I'll take that.

Episode 2
16/02/2020

The story so far: I had the balloon implant as described, and I can't say it was much fun, but the oncologist, Mr Lester, tells me it's a 'game changer'. I'll say. I walked like John Wayne for a few days, but without the horse. I'm not allowed to ride a bike or go weight-lifting either, neither of which will bother me. Oddly enough, and by an amazing coincidence, I got a call from the endoscopy unit in Cheltenham to attend my two-yearly colonoscopy. I turned it down. They were pissed off about that, but I can't have them dislodging my balloon with their camera, can I? The balloon is apparently degradable within the body within six months, so that puts paid to me doing a Phileas Fogg and going round the world in eighty days.

As an alternative we are planning not so much a balloon flight, but a road trip to Europe in April. All being well of course. (This time Germany is in our sights – and this time, Sam, I mean it!)

Tomorrow I start radiotherapy in Newport, South Wales, and for those who aren't any good at geography, don't be concerned. At the moment even Coronavirus doesn't know where Newport is. Well not yet anyway. This is an unprepossessing town, which I believe is twinned with Idlib, or possibly Beirut. One of those anyway. It's a bloody mad world already, so arguing over territory while the planet falls to pieces seems a bit pointless.

Apparently radiotherapy isn't a BBC channel like Radio 4. Radiotherapy is designed to destroy DNA in the prostate, and hopefully not much else. Evidently normal cells take six hours to regenerate, but the cancer cells simply can't. So after all this, that should be that. Well, that's the plan anyway. Maybe in 100 years' time (if we aren't all wiped out) we'll go to the docs, be told we have cancer, prescribed a pill, and – hey presto! – cured. Unfortunately I haven't got that much time to wait for them to develop it.

I have twenty days of this radiotherapy stuff, every day, weekends off, but 10 am each day Monday to Friday. I'm trying to imagine it as a long drive to the office, and am advised that I will be feeling the effects by day ten. Not the drive on the M50, the treatment!

I also have to listen to my body, I'm told, and take it easy (as usual). So given this advice I've decided to buy a new car. Well not new, but a Jag, a posh one, though I haven't actually got it yet, and my intention is to be chauffeured down on day eleven, or before. I can then do sudoku puzzles (the easy ones) and stuff like that while relaxing in the back.

The treatment finishes on 7th April, so I'm reversing the countdown – 20, 19, etc – and ticking each day off as it comes. Then I'll take it even more easy than normal when I've finished, and (hopefully) we'll take off for France after that.

Cue jaunty music. 'Tune in next time for Radio Therapy. The nation's favourite cancer station.'

Jeeeeeezzzz! . . . Now where's that bottle gone???

Episode 3
Captain's Log. Stardate 14:03:2020

Lift-off was Weds, and my first close encounter with the space station. The machine is called Elekta, (not 'Alexa', Patsy) and it doesn't respond to requests for The Beatles either. It whirrs about over the body silently, and occasionally emits whines and pinging sounds, like some giant space telescope. Neither have I seen any photons or protons. They're invisible, so proving difficult to catch.

In an adjacent darkened room are banks of flickering computer screens, all designed to match my prostate and bladder with the original map they made, and once lined up, Elekta is then set to work to fire these invisible bullets into me. Surprisingly it doesn't hurt. I can see it's only a matter of time before I become vapourised, and instead of walking back to reception, they'll beam me back, and suddenly and unexpectedly I'll materialise in front of The Wife. (She started it by calling me The Husband on her cooking blog), who is usually to be found sitting patiently drinking coffee and reading *The Times*.

The controllers of this multi-million-pound computerised gadget are ... get this ... three women! I know this is sexist, but it's unnerving. Like a woman pilot. Or a truck driver. When have you ever seen a woman in charge of an Eddie Stobart monster? Anyway, not one of them dresses like Captain Kirk, or Spock, though one of them has suspiciously pointy ears. It's the Welsh (Newport) accent I can't stand. Bring back Scotty, even though that accent grates a bit. (The Wife being the exception, obviously.)

And as for Newport (thanks Tammy for that link, and you too Russ), Coronavirus still hasn't ventured down there. It doesn't dare!

I met one of the Newport residents when we stayed locally on Thursday. Surly hoodie bastard, who didn't seem terribly welcoming. Pic attached.

I also got the Jag. Picked that up yesterday. It didn't have a Jaguar cat on the bonnet like in the olden days, so we put our own on (pic also attached). I shall call it 'Enterprise' since it's like a starship inside. Not the cat, dickheads . . . the car!

Nothing much else to report. Three stardates down and seventeen to go. I may need a chauffeur, and am out to get a one-size-fits-all uniform, probably a tracksuit and woolly hat, for whoever is prepared to take on Newport, and of course the galaxies of the M4 and M50. So far I'm doing OK, but it is early days, so I may need someone with a clean spaceship licence. I don't qualify. I just got done again.

Keep you posted. Over and out.

Dr Who

Episode 4
Captain's Log. Stardate 21:03:2020

Joanna bought me a *Star Trek* mug, and a Captain Kirk logbook (which I'm writing up daily), and the Jaguar 'Enterprise' is proving a good buy. I've used it a couple of times to swish up and down the M50, but Ollie had to give it a try on the M4 and M5 last Monday, convinced it was a quicker route. And I have to tell you it is, but he did have it on warp 3 or 4. He doesn't hang about. I've now had it specially polished, and a special glaze applied, and it's gleaming. So much so that I don't want to get it wet, so I'm using the Freelander, or what I like to think of as a spacetractor. One or two people asked me what this Jag looks like since the cat got in the way of the last one, so pics attached.

Covid-19 has now taken hold. That name sounds like a gang of anarchists, don't you think? Whereas Coronavirus sounds more like the drink. And those of us who are old enough remember Corona as a pop, not a beer.

My abhorrence of closely confined, intensively reared species isn't just based on cruelty and welfare, but the prevalence and speed with which disease can spread. Whether chickens, salmon, pigs (or humans), all are far more vulnerable, and those who live cheek by jowl in big cities are most likely to get the worst I reckon.

And so it seems. At the risk of being ever so slightly controversial (moi? … non!) this disease seems on the whole to be quite selective (but so is flu which is what this is … sort of) and taking out the older, infirm, and unwell. People who are kept alive perhaps well beyond their 'sell-by' dates. (I'm not including myself … obviously). Maybe God has intervened? So that's all right 'cos he can stop it if we pray hard enough. Oh! Not allowed to pray together so an online church might be handy?

Nevertheless in my reduced state of immunity The Wife and I are self-isolating. Something I've been doing anyway for most of my life. And don't worry girls (and Jamie) about the missed opportunity for not visiting on Mother's Day, I'm perfectly capable of filling that gap.

During this radiotherapy I'm still on these testosterone blockers, Bicalutamide they're called, and have produced some odd and weird side effects, which have revealed themselves in different ways over the past nine months. It started with my beard and chest hair not growing, yet strangely the hair on my head began to thicken. Sore nipples too, and cold hands and feet. More so than usual at this time of the year. Evidently they reduce efficient heart function, which in turn reduces circulation. So it's somewhat ironic to think that I'm in the process of being cured for prostate cancer, only to find I'll probably drop down dead of a heart attack. Another strange side effect I discovered a few months ago was a phase I went through of demanding special foodstuffs. Salted peanuts and cashews were top of the list for a while. It got to the point where I began to wonder if I was pregnant.

The latest thing is scratching. This has only just begun to manifest itself in the last few weeks, and I'm reminded of *The Jungle Book* (great film!!!), where Baloo the bear relieves his itches by rubbing himself up and down on a tree. I'm like that, but use the doorframe instead. Or The Wife's fingernails. I may even apply for admission to the monkey house at Dudley Zoo if they're not all in self-isolation. Just a thought. Can chimps get it?

The Rutherford, my private cancer centre (note how I've spelt 'centre', Linda!! … No Americanisms or Canadaisms here!), have offered me pills to stop this. Anti Histomines. I've never taken them, so don't know how to spell them, but I turned them down. I have a theory about drugs anyway. At school I was crap at Chemistry. I would mix sulphur and oxygen and ammonia nitrate and magnesium and stuff like that in a test tube, and watch in wonder when it blew up on the Bunsen burner. And that's why I hate pills, because I visualise my stomach as a test tube, so I have no idea what is happening when all these various chemicals are mixed up. I've opted for E bah gum forty-five cream instead, which I can at least apply myself. So far it's worked.

I'm coming to terms with Elekta, and the radiotherapy I have to say is beginning to knock me about. For fifteen mins each day, which isn't much, I come out feeling like I've done five three-minute rounds with Mike Tyson. I had a review on Wednesday, asking me personal questions about poo and stuff like that, but apart from crashing out at 9.30 each night, and sleeping like a log, I've had no especial problems. I have another review lined up next week, but this time with the Good Doctor.

I have added a few new readers, scroll from the bottom if you can be bothered! Sian & Paul, Ade and Kate (not Kate Adie) I've added to the list, but if any of you don't want to receive this missive, text STOP to maninselfisolation.com and I will. I won't be offended and promise not to cough on you.

A young, but very old, friend of mine is in a similar boat to me, but she has had a pipe fitted permanently into a vein in her arm, and every two weeks has shitty chemicals pumped into her. And this goes of for six months. No doubt about it, it's lousy timing to be ill with other stuff. I've got it easy by comparison. Eight down and twelve to go with Elekta, as well as ducking and diving from the Covids of course. I can't help thinking this is a big wake-up call, and not just economically. Those of a certain generation who've grown used to their pizza deliveries at the click of a button, or that voting on *Love Island* or *Strictly* was of world-shattering importance, may have just had a dose of what we . . . ahem . . . older generation call reality. And it ain't reality TV either.

Live long and prosper (if we can). Now beam me up Scotty!

Yours in self-isolation and self-destruction,

Cap'n Jim Church

(The Scottish contingent will get that)

PS. The Wife has come up with an ingenious solution to stop the hoarders. Ban the bloody trolleys. Baskets only. Eeeek! Simple!

Episode 5
Stardate 27:03:2020

Space, the final frontier. Something that I have, but the rest of the world hasn't right now because everyone's in solitary confinement. I have been given a special pass which I can wave at any overzealous Space Copper, enabling me to roam the universe.

The world is an upside down place just now, and this report seems somewhat trivial, given the fact that the end, for a number of people, is most definitely nigh. And it does make me feel slightly ashamed. The desire or motivation for the medical men to keep people alive (like me) for as long as possible has been ruthlessly laid bare by this disease sweeping the planet. Clearly those who perhaps should have shuffled off long ago are being singled out and despatched.

Whether something like this will wake up the human race to the reality of death is another matter. I hope it does, and that we can look dispassionately and rationally at helping terminally ill people out of this life at a time of their choosing. For me it comes down to quality of life, and keeping as physically fit as possible has made the difference. I have my dad to thank for that. I can tell you all this though, that had I been severely physically disabled and/or mentally retarded (who sniggered????), I most definitely wouldn't have embarked on this journey, and wasted everyone's time. Including you lot having to read this shite.

The end of this treatment is now in sight, and I have to say, apart from getting irresistible urges to relieve myself only to find I end up peeing in weak spurts, I haven't felt any especial side effects. I still have a week to go however (thirteen down, seven left), so it may all change. I've still managed to maintain my daily swimming, and been lucky enough to have this pass as an excuse to go to the river and piss about up there (as the spurts allow me of course), and have been chain sawing some of the trees washed down in the recent floods. So I've got it easy. Especially in this weather.

The very best thing about this week, however, is that the Good Doctor has signalled an end to these effing testosterone-blocking pills, which were turning me into a girl. Soon I will be back to my nauseating, aggressive, bad-tempered self. Can't wait! So I won't be shopping at Ann Summers or Dorothy Perkins any time soon. (Not that I could anyway). I'm still itching like mad though. I reckon I'd fit in well with a flea circus.

This will be the penultimate missive (was that clapping I heard?), then I'll be bringing the good ship Enterprise back to base. Just as well really since Newport, I discovered today, has

Two enemas left to go, no more pills, and probably no more Bugles. Well maybe one for the road, and a not-so-grand finale. Aintcha lucky?

Dr Basil Cheesegrater-Brush

PS: Ffion's recipe for Welsh rarebit. Here goes: Grated strong cheddar, dollop of dijon mustard, splodge of cider (yes ... cider, Ffion likes strong, cloudy stuff ... and no I don't know if it's sweet or dry, Patsy), squirt or two of Lea & Perrins. Mix it into a paste. I didn't and it was too runny (and now I know why. She told me this morning she forgot to tell me that she heats it in a pan first). This is a worry, she puts me under the grill every day! Spread the mixture on toast, and stick it under the grill.

Given this new-found culinary skill, I now intend to set up a cooking blog to rival The Wife's and call it 'Johnny Gets Cooked' (no F in cooked). Which is true. I now know what toast feels like.

Episode 6: Over and Out
Stardate 07:04:2020

Well over, but maybe not so much out, as banished to another time zone. For good I hope. Follow-up in July. I'll be relieved not to go under the grill any more, and pleased to have annihilated my deadly enemas. Nevertheless I'm going to sort of miss the drive down (even though it was Newport). Anyway, I bet you lot are relieved more, not having to put up with this weekly crap.

What has surprised me most is the sheer weight of weaponry which has been brought to bear over the past nine months in order to destroy these microscopic little bastards. CTs MRIs, blood tests galore (eek!), biopsies (ouch!), balloon spacer (ouch ouch!), pills, grills, the bloody lot. As well as the amount of time it's all taken. If anything similar shows up in the future, then it's palliative care and a case of whisky I reckon. I'm not sure I can be arsed to do it all again.

One or two have asked about libido (nosy bastards) since I don't seem (on the face of it) to have suffered much in the way of physical side effects. All I can say is I've ditched the mistresses, but not the top-shelf mags, and burned the Dorothy Perkins spring collection. And I've also become rather preoccupied with perfecting Welsh rarebit recipes. As The Wife will testify.

The care I've received down there at the Rutherford has been quite brilliant, and the team (predominantly spacegirls) have been incredibly kind and attentive. Sorry you've all had to put up with the incoherent ramblings of a time traveller, but it's been a bit of a diversion for me, even if not for you, so hope you enjoyed the ride.

Thanks for all your support, much appreciated, and I'll see you in the next Galaxy, or Milky Way, or Mars Bar, along with THE Supernova Super Star wife. (That's enough grovelling. Ed.)

Dr Willy Wonka (and all of us here at Radio Therapy)

xxx

Postscript

A man is a success if he gets up in the morning, gets to bed at night, and in between he does what he wants to do.

BOB DYLAN

Phew! I've finished! Haven't I??

Well, I thought so. I've no doubt mentioned this before, but editing was a pain in the arse, and now I've had to do it yet again. It's tiresome and time-consuming, but this time round the whole thing was easier because I had a 'professional' editor to hold my hand. She had the unenviable task of going through it and tidying up after me. I cringed at the thought of her reading it.

Having now re-read the whole thing again, I began to think I should have called it *The Diary of a Lecher*. It wasn't meant to be like that. I just wrote stuff as it came into my head, hoping to put in a few pearls of wisdom and maybe a life lesson or two along the way, but ultimately, and weirdly, the whole thing took on a shape of its own. There was no form, no structure, it almost wrote itself and at times it was a beast with which I battled. My editress ... is that a word? ... knocked it into some sort of shape.

There were many, many more experiences (female and otherwise) which aren't in here, and occasionally I'll think of something or someone and wonder if it went in. Maybe I'll do another one called *The Missing Bits*. I'm not trying, and have never tried, in any way whatsoever, to justify myself nor ask others for their judgement or opinion. It is what it is and entirely from my own perspective. My brother Martin and sister Julia may well

423

have a different take since they were around in the early days, but to me it's largely an irrelevance. The clue is in the title.

Almost subconsciously I tried to thread or weave these experiences into my own learning of the life I've led, and if that sounds a touch arrogant, well it probably is! Whichever way, it's been an experience, both to write and re-live and in many ways, whether with success or failure, all of it has been the price of an education. None of this is of world-shattering importance. Except to me of course.

I began to write pre-Covid, and the pandemic was a bonus. It forced me to become more disciplined. Like doing homework, polishing my shoes, or getting my satchel packed for school in the morning.

Turning seventy was the key, or the kick up the arse I needed, and the sudden realisation that I'd always meant to do something but never quite got round to it.

As I've said elsewhere, age brings awareness, and if you're lucky a measure of wisdom. It's because of this that my view of the world has become jaded. These days all I seem to see is a generation of cosseted and indulged individuals who rely entirely on social media, look for offence in the slightest remark and want to make an issue of it. Kind of like it's really, really, important. (I also hate people who 'kind of like' put in two 'really's.) A generation whose priorities revolve around Love Island, Deliveroo, and who are aided and abetted in their fragile state by indulgent parents. Moi? Non!

I also perceive a generation of robotic box-tickers, who seem to have little in the way of initiative, innovation or adventurousness. They stay on script, shirk decisiveness, shift blame, and believe the State has a responsibility to take care of them forever. How has this happened?? No idea. Maybe they should go online and buy a sense of humour from Amazon. They're on special offer just now. Buy one get one free.

But this is me talking, my perception, and I can almost hear my own granddad reiterating a similar diatribe about my generation never 'having had it so good'. And he was right. I have nothing to complain about. My generation has lived through the best of times. We've never had to fight any war and had, without a shadow of doubt, the best music. The fact is we've arrived at this place and time in our lives relatively unscathed.

Perhaps in this recent awakening I'm more alert to the human obsession for growth, GDP being the politicians' guiding light. Infinite growth is impossible with a finite planet. Growth comes at environmental cost. We need to think about shrink. I'm as guilty as the next (says he with four cars and five guitars), but as a species we do need to stop. I wish we could remove the consumer gene within us. I realise now that the Industrial Revolution is entirely responsible for the mess we've made of this planet. Up until then we largely worked in harmony with nature. Unfortunately we can't uninvent it. We are, as they say, where we are, so let's learn from the past, hope for the future, and try to do something in the now.

When you get ill, and end up spending too much time at the medical centre, that's when you know you're getting old. Two cancer diagnoses , now both cured, don't banish the big black cloud which always lurks over the horizon. It never goes away fully, and I try to ignore it. I'm fed up of being on the radar, prodded, scanned, and blood-tested every so often. It's like a revolving door. No sooner do you get out than you're back in again, with pills, potions etc designed to keep you alive. Well, the way I feel is that I'll continue to do as much as I can to hold all this off and keep going for as long as my body will allow. Just keep in mind that death is nature's way of telling you to slow down.

Over and not yet out.

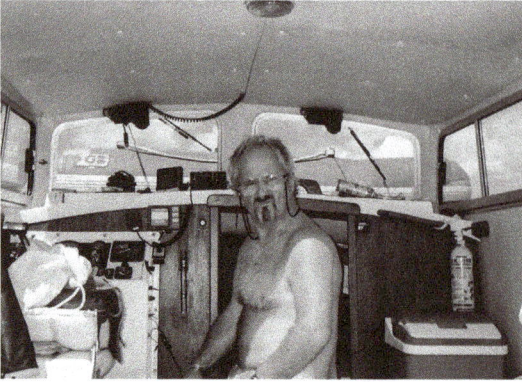

www.ingramcontent.com/pod-product-compliance
Lightning Source LLC
Chambersburg PA
CBHW040412110426

42812CB00033B/3358/J